DOGMATIC THEOLOGY

Volume III

The Sources of Revelation

★ ★ ★ ★ ★

Divine Faith

by Monsignor G. Van Noort, S.T.D.

Translated and Revised by
JOHN J. CASTELOT, S.S., S.T.D., S.S.L.
WILLIAM R. MURPHY, S.S., S.T.D.

THE NEWMAN PRESS · WESTMINSTER, MARYLAND
1961

The present volume is a translation of the 5th edition of Msgr. Van Noort's *Tractatus De Fontibus Revelationis* and *De Fide Divina*, edited by J. P. Verhaar. Because of the extensive revision made by the translators, the English translation may be called the 6th edition of Msgr. Van Noort's dogmatic treatise.

Nihil Obstat: C. HARRY DUKEHART, S.S.
Censor Deputatus

Imprimatur: JOHN F. DEARDEN, D.D.
Archbishop of Detroit

December 21, 1960

The *nihil obstat* and *imprimatur* are official declarations that a book or pamphlet is free of doctrinal and moral error. No implication is contained therein that those who have granted the *nihil obstat* and *imprimatur* agree with the opinions expressed.

Copyright© 1961 by THE NEWMAN PRESS

Library of Congress Catalog Card Number: 60-14816

Printed in the United States of America

Preface

The term "dialogue" crops up today more and more frequently. It emerges before the reading public in publications as diverse as *Theological Studies, Time, Harper's,* or the *New Yorker.* While this book was never intended by its author as a contribution to the dialogue between estranged Christians, it does deal with matters that lie at the heart of that estrangement. It deals with Scripture, Tradition, Faith. While it is doubtless fruitful for divergent Christian sects to exchange viewpoints on specific topics such as "Church and State," or "birth-control," or "Ecumenism," it is obviously more important to understand the broad, fundamental principles which ultimately control the specific answers divergent Christian sects offer for specific problems.

Scripture, Tradition, Faith—these three topics form the subject matter of the present volume, and conclude the section of theology called Fundamental. Because fundamental theology pours the concrete foundations on which the whole vast edifice of theology will be erected, the topics herein treated are discussed, not for their own sake, but with an eye always on what is to come, the final building with all its specialized corridors.

Because of this aim, fundamental theology treats Scripture, Tradition, and the act of faith from a strictly *theological* viewpoint and with a theological methodology. It would be a mistake, therefore, to look for a treatment of specialized questions of Scripture or, at least, to look for them in any great detail. Biblical science is a vast field of its own, with its own methodology. Here the reader is given a general treatment of the entire field of Scripture from a theological point of view. Similarly, it would be a mistake to look, in the section on Tradition, for questions that find their proper place in specialized fields like Patrology, or Christian Archaeology. Finally, it would be a mistake to look in the section on Faith to find answers about specific doctrines of faith which are taken up in various branches of dogmatic theology. This book discusses, instead, broad principles covering a proper theological orientation toward Scripture, Tradition, and Faith. The treatment is theolog-

PREFACE

ical. It seeks to find out what revelation, the Church's teaching, and sound theological reasoning have to disclose to us about the sources of revelation, looked at precisely as *sources*, and the act of faith looked at precisely as the act by which we personally lay hold of the truths contained in the sources of revelation. The present treatise, besides being theological in its methodology, is also primarily theological in its aim. It not only appeals to the Church's magisterium and the data of Scripture and Tradition as proofs of its theses; it is also geared to building a theological outlook in the mind of beginning students of divinity. It is not uncommon to find theological students in their second or third years still using a purely philosophical, or purely apologetic, or purely biblical approach to specific branches of theology. If such students have never learned in fundamental theology the place of the Church's teaching authority, the force of tradition, the meaning of the analogy of faith, etc., they may remain frankly skeptical of some theological theses simply because they cannot demonstrate the point exclusively by the use of their reasoning, or find it limpidly expressed in equivalent terms in their own copy of the New Testament.

As in previous volumes we have supplied an outline for each article in the text, new bibliographies, and a Scriptural, author, and general index. Apart from these purely mechanical aids, we have written one entire new chapter: *Faith and Reason*. We have pruned the remainder of the original text of some points that seemed no longer useful, rearranged and enlarged some sections, and incorporated both in the text and in the notes much new matter that was totally absent from the original. In so doing we have tried to alter as little as possible the author's original framework and substance because it still seemed to us to be basically sound. The places where emendations have been made are too numerous to be specifically singled out, but a more than casual glance at the text and notes on the treatment of "inerrancy" or "theological notes," for example, will suffice to indicate the general tenor of revisions made in other places.

What we have deliberately omitted in our work of revision has cost us as much thought as what we have included. In the field of Scripture, for example, developments during the last forty years have been so extensive that one could not possibly hope to incorporate matters which are best treated in the field of Scripture itself. But we do hope we have given sufficient indication in notes

PREFACE

and references of where such specific treatment may be found. Again, for example, in the treatise on Faith while we are quite aware of how much speculation and writing has taken place about the role of grace in the act of faith and new insights provided by modern psychology, we have not deemed it necessary to devote a special chapter to this subject. This for two reasons. In Van Noort's treatment of theology, all that pertains to faith as a grace is discussed in its proper place in the treatise on *Grace and the Infused Virtues*. Here the act of faith is viewed in isolation the better to examine its rational justification, its peculiar properties, and its function as the means by which we lay hold of revealed truth. Consequently, and rightly, faith is here studied from the viewpoint of its intelligibility as a human act rather than as the product of God's grace, or as a part of practical apologetics on how to attract men to faith. Similarly, we have resisted the temptation to deal with the mystical side of faith because such a treatment belongs not to dogmatic, but to ascetical and mystical theology.

For the rest, we do not believe that everything new in theological speculation should be introduced into a textbook merely because it is new. There are plenty of periodicals in which the latest conjectures of the latest theologians can always find publication. In taking such a viewpoint we do not feel we are being unduly conservative; we have tried throughout to keep in mind the needs of beginning theologians who should, we feel, have served up to them only such theology as is solidly established and clearly articulated. Their teachers can always direct them to do research into new approaches to ancient problems.

We should like to express our gratitude to the staff of the Newman Press for painstaking and important work on the manuscript.

JOHN J. CASTELOT, S.S.
WILLIAM R. MURPHY, S.S.

October 7, 1960
Feast of the Holy Rosary

List of Abbreviations

AAS	*Acta Apostolicae Sedis*
ACW	*Ancient Christian Writers*
AER	*American Ecclesiastical Review*
Bibl	*Biblica*
CBQ	*Catholic Biblical Quarterly*
CCHS	*A Catholic Commentary on Holy Scripture*
Coll. Lac.	*Collectio Lacensis*
CTSA	*Catholic Theological Society of America—Proceedings*
DAFC	*Dictionnaire apologétique de la foi catholique*
DB	Denziger-Bannwart-Umberg, *Enchiridion Symbolorum*
DBS	*Dictionnaire de la Bible. Supplément* (Pirot-Robert)
DBV	*Dictionnaire de la Bible* (Vigouroux) and *Supplément* (Pirot-Robert)
DTC	*Dictionnaire de théologie catholique*
EO	*Echos d'Orient*
HE	Eusebius, *Historia ecclesiastica*
KL	Kleist-Lilly, *The New Testament*
LZ	Lebreton-Zeiller, *The History of the Primitive Church*
NRT	*Nouvelle revue théologique*
RBibl	*Revue Biblique*
RSS	*Rome and the Study of Sacred Scripture*
S.Th.	St. Thomas, *Summa theologica*
TCT	*The Church Teaches*
TD	*Theology Digest*
TS	*Theological Studies*
VD	*Verbum Domini*
ZfKTh	*Zeitschrift für Katholische Theologie*

Contents*

	Page
Preface	v
List of Abbreviations	ix
General Bibliography	xiii

The Sources of Revelation

Introduction	1
I. Sacred Scripture	11
Article I. The Canon of Sacred Scripture	15
Article II. The Existence of Inspiration	28
Article III. The Nature and Effects of Inspiration	53
Article IV. The Use of Sacred Scripture	98
II. Sacred Tradition	135
Article I. The Existence of Sacred Tradition	145
Article II. The Preservation of Sacred Tradition	157
Article III. Some Specific Documents of Tradition	167

Divine Faith

Introduction: The Notion and Division of Faith	181
I. The Object of Divine Faith	193
Article I. The Formal Object of Divine Faith	196
Article II. The Material Object of Divine Faith	203
Article III. The Subject Matter of Divine-Catholic Faith	219

* A detailed outline is found at the beginning of each article.

CONTENTS

Article IV. *Increase of the Subject Matter of Catholic Faith or "Dogmatic Progress"* 231
Article V. *Theological Truths* 260
Article VI. *Theological Censures* 280

II. THE ACT OF DIVINE FAITH 293
Article I. *The Subjective Principles which Produce the Act of Faith* 296
Article II. *Preparation for the Act of Faith* 310
Article III. *The Analysis of the Act of Faith* 335
Article IV. *The Properties of Faith* 350
Article V. *Who Has Faith? and Is Faith Necessary?* . . 369

APPENDIX: FAITH AND REASON 385

SCRIPTURAL INDEX 403

INDEX OF PROPER NAMES 406

GENERAL INDEX 413

General Bibliography

Scripture

Arbez, E. P.-Weisengoff, J. P. Unpublished notes. Catholic University of America, 1953.
Auzou, G. *La Parole de Dieu*. Paris, 1956.
Bainvel, J. *De Scriptura Sacra*. Paris, 1910.
Balestri, J. *Biblicae introductionis generalis elementa*. Rome, 1932.
Barton, J. M. T. "The Holy Ghost," *The Teaching of the Catholic Church*, New York, 1949.
Bea, A. *De inspiratione et inerrantia Sacrae Scripturae*. Rome, 1947.
———. "Inspiration et inerrance," DBS, IV, Paris, 1949.
Benedict XV. *Spiritus Paraclitus*, Rome, 1920.
Benoit, P. "Note complementaire sur l'inspiration," RBibl, 63 (1956), 416.
Billot, L. *De inspiratione*. Rome, 1903.
Brown, R. E. *The Sensus Plenior of Sacred Scripture*. Baltimore, 1955.
Chauvin, A. *L'inspiration*, Paris, 1897.
Coppens, J. *Les harmonies des deux testaments*. Tournai-Paris, 1949.
Crehan, J. J. "The Inspiration and Inerrancy of Holy Scripture," CCHS, 34 ff.
Crets, G. J. *De divina bibliae inspiratione*. Louvain, 1886.
Dausch, P. *Die Schriftsinspiration, eine biblisch-geschichtliche Studie*. Freiburg, 1891.
Fel. *De evangelii inspiratione*. Paris, 1906.
Forestell, J. T. "The Limitation of Inerrancy," CBQ, 20 (1958), 1–8.
Fuller, R. C. "The Interpretation of Holy Scripture," CCHS, 39b ff.
Holzhey, K. *Die Inspiration in die Anschaüung des Mittelalters*. Munchen, 1895.
Hopfl-Gut. *Introductionis in sacros utriusque testamenti libros compendium*. Rome, 1940.
Hugon, E. *La causalite instrumentale dans l'ordre surnaturel*. Paris, 1924.

GENERAL BIBLIOGRAPHY

JOHNSTON, L. "Old Testament Morality," CBQ, 20 (1958), 9–18.
LEO XIII. *Providentissimus Deus*. Rome, 1893.
LUSSEAU-COLLOMB, *Manuel d'études bibliques*, vol. I. Paris, 1936.
MACKENZIE, R. A. F. "Some Problems in the Field of Inspiration," CBQ, 20 (1958).
MCKENZIE, J. L. *The Two Edged Sword*. Milwaukee, 1956.
MERK, A. *Institutiones biblicae*. Rome, 1937.
MURPHY, R. "The Teachings of Providentissimus Deus," CBQ, 5 (1943), 125.
NICOLAU, M. *Sacrae theologiae summa*. Vol. I. Madrid, 1952.
PESCH, CHR. *Zur neusten Geschichte der katolischen Inspirationslehre*. ("Theologische Zeitfragen," 3ᵉ Folge), 1902.
———. *De inspiratione Sacrae Scripturae*. Freiburg i. Br., 1906.
PIUS XII. *Divino afflante Spiritu*. Rome, 1943.
POPE, H. *The Catholic Student's "Aids" to the Study of the Bible*. New York, 1926.
RAHNER, K. "Über die Schriftsinspiration," ZkTh, 78 (1956), 137.
ROBERT-TRICOT, *Guide to the Bible*. 2 vols. Translated under direction of E. P. Arbez and M. McGuire. Tournai, 1951.
———*Initiation biblique*. 3rd ed. Paris, 1954.
RUWET, J. *Institutiones biblicae*. Vol. I. Rome, 1937.
SCHMID, FR. *De inspirationis bibliorum vi et ratione*. Brixen, 1885.
SCHROEDER, F. *Père Lagrange and Biblical Inspiration*. Washington, 1954.
SIMON-PRADO, *Praelectiones biblicae*. Vol. I. Torino-Madrid, 1938.
TROMP, S. *De Sacrae Scripturae inspiratione*. Rome, 1945.
VAWTER, B. *A Path Through Genesis*. New York, 1956.
VOSTE, J. M. *De divina inspiratione et veritate Sacrae Scripturae*. Rome, 1932.
WIKENHAUSER, A. *Einleitung in das neue Testament*. Freiburg i. Br., 1953.
ZANECCHIA, D. *Divina inspiratio ad mentem sancti Thomae*. Rome, 1889.
———. "Scriptor sacer sub divina inspiratione, responsio ad p. Van Kasteren," *Studien*, 34, 581.
ZARB, S. M. *De historia canonis utriusque testamenti*. Rome, 1934.

Tradition

BAINVEL, J. V. *De magisterio vivo et traditione*. Paris, 1905.
BELLARMINE. *De Verbo Dei*.

GENERAL BIBLIOGRAPHY

BILLOT, L. *De sacra traditione contra novam haeresim evolutionismi.* Rome, 1904.

BOUYER, L. *The Spirit and Forms of Protestantism.* Westminster, Md., 1956.

BURKE, E. "The Scientific Teaching of Theology in the Seminary," *CTSA Proceedings*, New York, 1949.

CANO, M. *De Locis theologicis.* —

DANIELOU, J. "Ecriture et Tradition dans la dialogue entre les chrétiens séparés," *La documentation catholique*, LIV (1957), 283 ff.

DEJAIFVE, G. "Bible, Tradition, Magistere dans la theologie catholique," NRT, 78 (1956), 135–151; see TD, 6 (1958), 67 ff.

DE SAN, L. *Tractatus de divina Traditione et Scriptura.* Bruges, 1903.

DI BARTOLO, S. *Nuova esposizione dei criteri teologici.* 2nd ed. Rome, 1904.

DIECKMANN, H. *De ecclesia.* Freiburg i. Br., 1925.

DIEKAMP, F. *Theologiae dogmaticae manuale.* Tournai, 1949.

FRANZELIN, J. B. *Tractatus de divina Traditione et Scriptura.* 3rd ed., Rome, 1882.

GEISELMANN, J. "Das Missverständnis über das Verhaltnis von Scrift und Tradition und seine Überwindung in der katholischen Theologie," *Una Sancta*, 2 (1956), 131–150; see TD, 6 (1958), 73 ff.

LERCHER, L. *Institutiones theologiae dogmaticae.* Innsbruck, 1951.

PARENTE, P. *Theologia fundamentalis.* Rome, 1950.

SALAVERRI, I. *Sacrae theologiae summa.* vol. I. Madrid, 1952.

SCHRADER, C. *De theologico testium fonte deque edito fidei testimonio seu traditione commentarius.* Paris, 1878.

SMITH, G. (ed.) *The Teaching of the Catholic Church.* New York, 1949.

TANQUEREY, A. *Synopsis theologiae dogmaticae.* Paris, 1949–1950.

WINKLER, M. *Der Traditionsbegriff bis Tertullian.* Munich, 1897.

Faith

ADAM, K. "Glaube und Glaubenswissenschaft im Katholizmus," TQS, 150 (1920), 131–135

ALDAMA, J. *De virtutibus infusis*, Vol. 3 of *Sacrae Theologiae Summa.* Madrid, 1953.

GENERAL BIBLIOGRAPHY

ANTOINE, P. "Foi," in *Dict. Bibl. Supplement.*
APPEL, E. *Der Göttliche Glaube.* Bamberg, 1890.
AQUINAS. "De fide," in *Summa Theologica,* IIa-IIa, q. 1–16.
AUBERT, R. *Le Problème de l'acte de foi,* 2nd ed. Louvain, 1950.
BAINVEL, J. *La foi et l'acte de foi.* Paris, 1898.
BERAZA, S. *De virtutibus infusis.* Bilbao, 1929.
BILLOT, L. *De virtutibus infusis.* Rome, 1901.
BROUWER. *De fide divina.* Louvain, 1880.
CARTECHINI. *De valore notarum theologicarum.* Rome, 1951.
CATHREIN, V. *Glauben und Wissen.* Freiburg, 1903.
CHENU, M. D. *Is Theology a Science?*, Vol. 2, *Twentieth Century Encyclopedia of Catholicism.* New York, 1959.
COVENTRY, J. *Faith Seeks Understanding.* New York, 1951.
CRISTIANI, L. *Why We Believe,* Vol. 107, *Twentieth Century Encyclopedia of Catholicism.* New York, 1951.
D'ARCY, M. *The Nature of Belief.* New York, 1951.
FRIEDRICH, G. "Pistis," in *Theologisches Wörterbuch zum Neuen Testament.* Fasciele VI. Stuttgart, 1955.
GARDEIL, A. *Le donné révélé et la théologie.* Paris, 1910.
———. *La Crédibilité et l'Apologétique.* Paris, 1928.
GELIN, A. et al., "Qu'est-ce que la foi?" in *Lumière et Vie,* 22 (July, 1955).
GRAIL, A. et al., "Qu'est-ce que la foi?" in *Lumière et Vie,* 23 (November, 1955).
GUARDINI, R. *Faith and Modern Man.* New York, 1952.
HARENT, P. "Foi," in DTC, vol. 6, col. 55–514.
HEALY. "Theological Qualifications and the Assent of Faith," in *CTSA Proceedings.* New York, 1951.
JOLY, E. *What Is Faith?*, Vol. 6, *The Twentieth Century Encyclopedia of Catholicism.* New York, 1958.
KAISER, E. *Sacred Doctrine.* Westminster, Md., 1958.
LUGO. *De virtute fidei divinae.* Paris, 1868.
MERIT. *La foi, sa nature.* Paris, 1886.
NEWMAN, J. H. *Essay on the Development of Christian Doctrine.* 2nd ed. London, 1878.
PARENTE, P. *Anthropologia Supernaturalis.* Rome, 1943.
———. "S. Tommaso e la recente psicologia della Fede," in *Doctor Communis,* I (1948).
PESCH, C. *De virtutibus theologicis.* Friburg, 1922.
QUILLIET. "Censures Doctrinales," in DTC, Vol. 2, cols. 2101–2113.

GENERAL BIBLIOGRAPHY

Rousselot, P. "Les yeux de la foi," in RSR, 1 (1910), 241–259, 444–475.
Salmanticenses. *Cursus theologicus.* Paris, 1870.
Schiffini, S. *De virtutibus infusis.* Friburg, 1904.
Suárez, F. *De fide, spe et caritate.* Vol. 12, Vivès ed. Paris, 1858.
Tixeront. *Histoire des dogmes,* Vol. 3. Paris, 1905.
Trethowan, I. *Certainty.* London, 1948.
Turinazz, Msgr. *La Foi catholique.* Paris, 1905.
Wilmers, G. *De fide divina.* Ratisbon, 1902.

Introduction

The Sources of Revelation

I. *Our Lord Designed the Church's Teaching in Each Generation as a Norm of Faith for the People of That Generation*

II. *The Doctrine of Christ Comes to the Church of Each Generation from Preceding Generations by Way of Tradition*

III. *The Term Tradition May Be Understood:*
   1. As the doctrine transmitted;
   2. As the transmission of the doctrine;
   3. In both senses.

IV. *Active Tradition Is Divided Into:*
   1. Constitutive tradition;
   2. Preservative tradition.

V. *Two Views on the Rule of Faith:*
   1. Protestants look to Scripture as the unique rule of faith for all.
   2. Catholics acknowledge two rules of faith:
      a. Proximate: the teaching of the Church;
      b. Remote: Scripture and tradition.

VI. *Division of the Treatise*

Introduction

I. Christ Made the Church's Teaching the Norm of Faith

The two preceding treatises, *The True Religion* and *Christ's Church*, established this general conclusion: Christ, the Ambassador of God, brought the truth from heaven to earth and established the Catholic Church as an indestructible and infallible institution which would preserve and teach His doctrine until the end of time. It follows from this that the teaching of the Church in each generation was designed by Christ Himself as the norm of faith for the people of that generation. Note the qualification, *in each generation*. Christ had no intention—indeed, it is physically impossible—that people of the twentieth century should receive instruction in the faith directly from the preaching of the Church of, say, the second or tenth century. Just as our forefathers learned what they were to believe from the Church of their own day, so we are obliged by the law of Christ to turn to the Church as it now exists. By the Church, of course, we mean the teaching Church, that is, the Roman Catholic episcopate, which is a continuation of the Petro-apostolic College and shares by rightful title both the command and the promise of our Lord:

> "Go, therefore, and initiate all nations in discipleship: baptize them in the name of the Father and of the Son and of the Holy Spirit, and teach them to observe all the commandments I have given you. And mark: I am with you at all times as long as the world will last."—Matt. 28:19-20.

II. Where Does the Church Get Its Doctrine?

Now since no one can give what he does not himself possess, the question arises: where do the supreme pontiff and the bishops *of today* get the doctrine of Christ which they are to preach to us and to all the peoples of the earth? Since it is obvious on the one hand that they never personally heard Christ Himself or the apostles teaching through the Holy Spirit, and equally obvious on the other hand that they do not get the doctrine of Christ by way of fresh, direct revelation, then the only possible answer is that this doctrine comes to them from preceding generations by way of *tradition*.

III. Various Meanings of the Term Tradition

The term *tradition* may be understood in a variety of ways. *Objectively* it signifies the doctrine which has come down to us from antiquity. *Actively*, it indicates the act or series of acts by which that doctrine has been handed on. Used in its *full connotation*, it can mean both the doctrine which has been handed down and also the process of handing down that doctrine.

When we say that the teaching Church of today possesses the doctrine of Christ as a result of tradition, we use the latter term in the active sense, to indicate the process by which the original deposit of faith has come down to the present age from the ones who first revealed it, Christ and the apostles.

IV. Constitutive Tradition vs. Preservative Tradition

It is moreover necessary to distinguish between two sets of acts in this process. There are the acts by which the body of doctrine is definitively formed. These make up what is called (*active*) *constitutive tradition*. And there are also the acts by which this body of doctrine, once definitively established, is handed on to later generations by those who first receive it. This is called (*active*) *preservative tradition*.

Constitutive tradition could be conceived, at least theoretically, in three different ways. It could be conceived as being consigned to writing in its totality under God's special influence and care. Or one could take the view that the sum total of God's teaching came to us without any of it having been consigned to writing under divine influence. Finally, it could be considered as having been promulgated partly by the direct *viva voce* preaching of the heralds of revelation and partly written down under divine inspiration.

Preservative tradition is theoretically susceptible of a similarly diverse interpretation. This latter, however, need not necessarily parallel that of constitutive tradition. For even if one grants the fact that a body of doctrine was established either wholly or in

INTRODUCTION

part by oral preaching alone, it does not necessarily follow that those who heard it, directly or indirectly, did not put it into writing. Surely it is not antecedently impossible that a doctrine, preached orally by the heralds of revelation, be subsequently given written form by men on their own initiative, or even that many men do this at different times, in different localities, and in different styles.

Tradition, then, in the broad sense in which it has been used up to this point, embraces both written and unwritten, or oral, tradition.

V. Protestant vs. Catholic View of Constitutive Tradition 3

With this as background, we can proceed to examine the Protestant view of the origin of constitutive tradition. They assume that the whole of Christ's teaching, insofar as it was to be preserved for posterity, was written down under divine inspiration, and so they revere Sacred Scripture as the only source of revelation. It is for them the unique storehouse to which one must go to get the heavenly doctrine or the message of God. The Catholic Church, on the contrary, contends that the doctrine of salvation was not given to the Church in Scripture exclusively, and that it was not all written down under divine inspiration. And so it recognizes, in addition to written tradition, oral tradition also; and this latter it has come to call simply Tradition, in a *restricted sense*. As the Vatican Council put it: "According to the belief of the universal Church, supernatural revelation is contained in books written [under divine inspiration] and in unwritten [uninspired] traditions."[1] It acknowledges, then, two sources of revelation: the inspired Scriptures and divine-apostolic Tradition. Tradition is to be understood here in its full connotation as that doctrine originally placed in the deposit of faith by way of oral preaching and faithfully preserved for us (prescinding from the question of how that preservation was effected).*

---

* We must not, however, imagine Scripture and Tradition to be like two distinct reservoirs receiving the waters of divine truth from distinct and separate springs. There is in a sense but one source of revealed truth, *viz.* divine Tradition, by which is meant the body of revealed truth handed down from the Apostles through the ages and contained in the doctrine, teaching and practice of the Catholic Church. Yet since a large and important part of that revelation was committed to writing both before and after the time of Christ the Church is accustomed to speak of two sources of revelation, oral Tradition and Scripture. The peculiar character and importance of Scripture

INTRODUCTION

4   The above remarks bring to mind another, no less basic, error of Protestants concerning the rule of faith. Since they do not recognize the age-old teaching office of the Church as having been divinely established and endowed with divine authority, they hold that Sacred Scripture, as the sole source of revelation, is at the same time the *unique rule of faith*, the only authentic norm in accordance with which the faith of Christians is regulated, and in accordance with which every single Christian, as directly as possible, is to define the material object of his faith. Note the qualification: *authentic* rule or norm. They do not deny that people generally get their faith from the instructions of their parents or from their ministers' sermons. In fact, they even draw up formulae or "confessions" of faith; but they insist that neither the preaching of their ministers, no matter how solemn and unanimous, nor the confessions of the "church" suffice all by themselves to give full certitude. Everyone has the right and even the duty to determine, to the best of his ability, whether and to what extent the confession of the church corresponds to the data of Scripture. This, of course, leaves the individual free to reject the confession of the "church"; indeed he must, once he has decided that this confession does not reflect the real meaning of Scripture. Obviously, in the Protestant view, public preaching and the Church's solemn confession are not worth much more than parental or private catechetical instruction are in the Catholic view. Generally speaking, in the case of children and uneducated people, the presumption will be that the confession of their sect is true to Scripture. As long as this presumption holds good, and the opportunity for personal research is wanting, they are safe in following it—but that is all. A confession can bind in this provisory fashion *because and to the extent that it is presumed* to agree with the written word of God. It has, however, no intrinsic and absolute authority because there exists no divine guarantee that it *does* so agree.

—the written part of this divine Tradition—derives solely from the fact that it is the inspired word of God, . . .

The two streams of oral Tradition and Scripture happily mix, for in the living magisterium of the Church these are living waters springing together unto life everlasting. It is the Church, the holder of Tradition, that gives life to the dead letter of Scripture. Experience shows that it is only in the life of the Church, the Bride of Christ, that Scripture, divinely inspired as it is, becomes 'living and effectual, and more piercing than any two-edged sword' (Heb. 4:12).—CCHS, le.

INTRODUCTION

Different by far is the teaching of the Catholic Church. It holds, of course, that our faith must of necessity correspond to the word of God as found in the sources of revelation. It holds, furthermore, that Scripture (together with Tradition) is a true and infallible rule of faith. But at the same time it insists that there exists yet another rule of faith which is equally infallible, namely, the preaching of the Church's teaching office or *magisterium*. Because this teaching office, by reason of the aid given it by the Holy Spirit, enjoys infallibility when proclaiming Christian doctrine, it carries with it its own guarantee and binds everyone absolutely, all by itself. Consequently no one can have an objectively valid reason for departing from its teaching, any more than one can reasonably depart from the true teaching of Scripture.

Moreover, if Christ willed that there be *two rules of faith*, there must exist some order between them. The divinely established order is as follows. The Church's preaching is for the faithful the proximate, direct rule of faith, while Scripture and Tradition, on which the Church's preaching is based, constitute the remote or indirect rule of faith.

The Church's preaching is the *proximate* rule of faith because all the faithful as such, be they uneducated or learned, can safely and directly determine the material object of their belief on the basis of that preaching and indeed they must. For precisely as believers, i.e., as far as regulating their belief is concerned, they can never be obliged to do research in Scripture and Tradition. For by granting the Church the gift of infallibility, God has seen to it that its preaching will never waver from the data of Scripture and Tradition in even the slightest detail.

Scripture and Tradition make up the *remote* rule of faith because they regulate directly, not the belief of the faithful, but the preaching of their teachers. Although the reading of Sacred Scripture and the study of Tradition can be very useful for others than those who fulfill an authoritative teaching office, and even though these pursuits may be even necessary for other purposes (besides that of regulating faith), it was not God's intention in inspiring the Scriptures that each individual should seek his faith therein. No, but He did establish the teaching office of the Church to safeguard and explain them faithfully under the guidance of the Holy Spirit. Consequently, any Christian who studies Scripture and Tradition and thinks he has found therein a doctrine really and

INTRODUCTION

truly contrary to the teaching of the Church, must unhesitatingly give the latter the nod over his own personal opinion. This is not to say that the Church's word carries more weight than the word of God. What it does mean is this, that God Himself has assured us that if any meaning given to a passage of Scripture disagrees with Catholic dogma, it cannot be the true meaning of that passage, cannot be the word of God.

These observations on the preaching of the infallible Church as the rule of our faith are a mere summary of all that could be said, and deliberately so, for most of this matter has already been covered in the treatise on *Christ's Church*.[2] They will become clearer shortly, when we take up the question of understanding and explaining Scripture and Tradition. They have been mentioned here only in the interests of a fuller understanding of Catholic truth and Protestant error.

8 Attention can now be focused on the subject of the *sources of revelation*. We acknowledge on the authority of the Church the existence of two sources and the principal points which must be held with regard to their nature and use. Where could one possibly go with more confidence for information about the vessels containing the treasure of divine revelation than to her to whom God has entrusted the preservation and stewardship of that treasure? There is no room for doubt that the Church's infallibility, which has been proven elsewhere, extends in a special way to questions concerning the sources from which Christian teaching is drawn. It will be our task to explain the teaching of the Church on this matter, to give an orderly presentation thereof, and to set forth the various arguments which prove it.

9 **VI. Various Titles Used to Describe This Treatise**

The present treatise, which, as said above, is divided into two chapters, one on Sacred Scripture and the other on Sacred Tradition, is entitled by some authors: "The Word of God." The difference amounts to little more than this: they indicate by their title merely what is contained in the sources of revelation, and we indicate both what is contained in those sources and the sources themselves. Still others use the title, "The Rule of Faith," and this is quite acceptable if the treatise considers, in addition to Scripture and Tradition, the preaching of the Church. Otherwise it would be a bit inexact. For although Scripture and Tradition, inasmuch

(8)

INTRODUCTION

as they remotely regulate our belief, can be called the rule of faith, still it seems more advisable to restrict that term to the Church's preaching. The fact is that we apply the term "rule" or "norm" to the instrument which is used to regulate or measure something directly. We meet, finally, the title, *Theological Sources* (*Loci Theologici*). The storehouses or deposits whence any science draws its arguments have been called since Aristotle's day the *loci* (*topoi*, lit., places) of that science. Now since theology must take its arguments ultimately from Scripture and Tradition, those two storehouses, which are sources of revelation and of belief for the Church and for each of its members, can quite properly be styled the *loci* of the science of Theology.

It is true that several theologians, following the lead of Melchior Cano, list ten *loci* or sources. But they get this number by adding to the strictly basic sources those called *derived*,[3] and by adding to the strictly theological sources those called *common*.[4]

Notes

1. DB 1787. See I. Salaverri, *op. cit.*, pp. 730 ff; A. Tanquerey, *op cit.*, I, 710 ff.; George D. Smith, *op. cit.*, I, 27 ff.

2. See the articles on the institution of the hierarchy (chap. II, art. 1 and 2) and especially on infallibility (chap. III, art. 1), with its sequel on the rule of faith (no. 100).

3. Sources which are *proper* (i.e., used in the science of theology alone) but *derived* are: the agreement of the universal Church, councils, supreme pontiffs, the fathers, and theologians. They are called derived, not because the authority of the Church and of its *magisterium* is borrowed from Scripture, but because the doctrine which they set forth is derived from Scripture and Tradition.

4. *Common* sources (used also by sciences other than theology) are: the light of reason, philosophers, historians—all of which are really only one: the power of natural reason.

Special Bibliography

BERTHIER, J. J. *De locis theologicis.* Turin, 1888.

BOUYER, L. *The Spirit and Forms of Protestantism.* Translated by A. V. Littledale. Westminster, 1956.

CANO, M. *De locis theologicis.*

COTTER, A. C. *Theologia fundamentalis.* Weston, 1947.

DE SAN, L. *Tractatus de divina Traditione et Scriptura.* Bruges, 1903.

INTRODUCTION

Di Bartolo, S. *Nuova esposizione dei criteri teologici.* Rome, 1904.
Dieckmann, H. *De ecclesia.* Freiburg i. Br., 1925.
Diekamp, F. *Theologiae dogmaticae manuale.* Tournai, 1949.
Franzelin, J. B. *Tractatus de divina Traditione et Scriptura.* Rome, 1882.
Lambrecht, H. *De locis theologicis.* Ghent, 1890.
Lercher, L. *Institutiones theologiae dogmaticae.* Innsbruck, 1951.
Parente, P. *Theologia fundamentalis.* Rome, 1950.
St. Robert Bellarmine. *De verbo Dei.*
Salaverri, I. *Sacrae theologiae summa.* I, Madrid, 1952.
Smith, G. (ed.). *The Teaching of the Catholic Church.* New York, 1949.
Tanquerey, A. *Synopsis theologiae dogmaticae.* Paris, 1949–1950.

CHAPTER I

Sacred Scripture

I. *Definition*
II. *Inspiration and Canonicity*
III. *Division of the Chapter*

Article I
THE CANON OF SACRED SCRIPTURE

I. *Definition: Etymological and Real*
II. *Distinction between Proto- and Deuterocanonical Books*
III. *The Alexandrian, Palestinian, and Tridentine Canons*
IV. PROPOSITION. *The Canon of Trent Is a Faithful Expression of the Mind of the Early Church*
    Proof: 1. For the books of the Old Testament:
        a. Unanimity of fathers in first three centuries;
        b. Appearance of scattered doubts in middle of fourth century;
        c. Constant unanimity of common doctrine of universal Church.
    2. For the books of the New Testament:
        a. Obscure beginnings and reasons for same;
        b. Testimony of earliest documents.
V. *Insufficiency of Historical Arguments. Only the Authority of the Infallible Church Fully Guarantees the Complete Catalogue of Sacred Books*

CHAPTER I

Sacred Scripture

I. Brief Definitions of "Sacred Scripture," "Inspiration," "Canonicity"   10

Sacred Scripture (the Holy Bible) can be defined in the words of the Vatican Council as the *collection of books which, "written by the inspiration of the Holy Spirit, have God as their Author and, as such, have been handed down to the Church itself"* (DB 1787).

If a book is to be considered part of Sacred Scripture, it must fulfill two simultaneous conditions, inspiration and canonicity. First it must have been written under the inspiration of the Holy Spirit, it must be *inspired;* and it must have been handed down to the Church precisely as an inspired writing. Since the testimony of the Church regarding the books which she receives as inspired rests chiefly on the fact that she has acknowledged such books and has listed them in her official catalogue or canon, the second requisite condition is, quite briefly, that a book be *canonical,* i.e., listed in the Church's official canon.

It goes without saying that the Church's acceptance of a book does not affect the nature of that book. It contributes nothing to its intrinsic worth and dignity.[1] One might wonder, for instance, whether an inspired book which has not been entrusted to the Church—should any such book exist—would be considered Sacred Scripture. To answer this, a distinction must be made. If "Sacred Scripture" be understood simply as a book of divine origin and so in itself of divine authority, and nothing else, such a book would of course be Sacred Scripture. But if the term be taken to indicate a book of divine origin *which is in addition a source of Christian revelation,* on which are based the Church's preaching and the Catholic faith, then one would have to give a negative answer. As it is, the Church and Catholic theology use the term "Sacred Scripture" exclusively in this latter sense. And this is only right, for they treat Sacred Scripture and use it precisely as a source of revelation. Obviously the Church could not base its preaching on a book as inspired unless it had learned of its inspiration from Christ or the apostles.

Since factually there exists no inspired book which is not at the same time canonical, the terms "inspired" and "canonical" are often used interchangeably. Still, the ideas behind the two terms are really distinct, though there is a certain overlapping, for canonicity supposes and includes inspiration.

11 II. Why Canonicity Is Discussed Prior to Inspiration

Since inspiration ontologically comes before canonicity, many theologians take up first the question of inspiration, and then that of canonicity. The opposite order is preferable. The term "canonicity" primarily and *expressly* tells us that such and such a book is accepted by the Church as sacred, as an authentic source of revelation, but does not state distinctly the basic reason for this acceptance, i.e., inspiration. Inasmuch as acceptance by the Church is an external and public act, it is more easily discernible and demonstrable than inspiration. Moreover, once one has established the fact of the Church's acceptance, he has a very valid, even if indirect, proof for inspiration.

III. Division of this Chapter

We shall consequently proceed in the following fashion. In Article I we shall speak of the canon of Sacred Scripture and seek to determine whether the Church has always accepted the books which it now puts forth as Scripture. If she has, then it is quite credible that Christ and the apostles took the same view of them. In Article II we shall see whether these books are rightly called inspired. In Article III we shall take up the nature of inspiration and its effects; finally, in Article IV, we shall summarize the factors involved in the use of Sacred Scripture.

Article I

THE CANON OF SACRED SCRIPTURE

I. Meaning of Canon and Canonical

Canon, from the Greek, *kanon* (*kane, kanna:* reed), was for the Greeks an instrument used by artisans to bring stones or planks into alignment, either to cut them or to put them together. The Latin equivalent is *mensura*, measure, norm. It was used metaphorically to indicate anything which served as a norm of belief or of action: *ho kanòn 'tes āletȟeıas, 'tes 'pısteōs* (the canon of truth, of belief; the Creed); ecclesiastical canons or rules. We speak today of the canons of good taste, of literary criticism, etc. It is in this sense that the fathers, especially the Latins, quite frequently referred to the books of Sacred Scripture as canonical, because they serve as a rule or norm of faith and morality. And in this sense, too, they sometimes called the actual collection of sacred books the Canon.

The Greeks used the word *kanón* also with the meaning of list or catalogue, and it is especially in this sense that the word was applied, from about the fourth century on, to the matter under present consideration. The *canon of Scripture,* then, was *the list of those books which the Church received as divine* and read publicly as such in its assemblies. Canonical books were books which had been put on the Church's official list. This meaning continued to predominate as time went on, but not to the exclusion of the other one mentioned above, for by the very fact that certain books appeared in the Church's list, they were acknowledged as the rule of faith.

The opposite of the canonical books were the *apocrypha* (*apokruphos:* hidden), i.e., those books which could not be read in the Church's public assemblies because the Church excluded them from its list of sacred books. This is without doubt the original and universal meaning of the term, for in many cases it is used practically as a synonym for pseudepigraphical, and even for heretical.[2]

(15)

14 II. Distinction Between Proto- and Deuterocanonical Books

The canonical books are usually divided into protocanonical and deuterocanonical. *Protocanonical* books are those about whose divine origin the Church of God never entertained the slightest doubt, about whose inspiration all were always in agreement: *homologoúmenoi:* agreed upon. *Deuterocanonical* is the term applied to those books about whose inspiration some individual fathers or churches sometimes felt some hesitation, books whose authority was sometimes denied: *antilegómenoi:* spoken against, opposed; *amphiballómenoi,* tossed around.

A word of caution is in order here. The terms proto- and deuterocanonical,[3] invented by Sixtus of Sienna, must not be taken to mean that the Church at one time drew up a *definitive* list of all the sacred books (protocanonical) to the *positive exclusion* of any and all others, and then later did an about-face and took others (deuterocanonical) into an expanded and revised canon. It was never the Church as such that had doubts about these latter books, but only some individuals or groups at different times and in different places.

The deuterocanonical books of the Old Testament are: Tobias, Judith, Wisdom, Ecclesiasticus, Baruch, 1 and 2 Maccabees; to these must be added the following parts of protocanonical books: Esther 10:4–16:24; Daniel 3:24–90; 13 and 14.

The deuterocanonical books of the New Testament are: Hebrews, James, 2 Peter, 2 and 3 John, Jude, Apocalypse; to these must be added the following parts of protocanonical books: Mark 16:9–20; Luke 22:43–44; John 7:53–8:11.

15 III. The Alexandrian, Palestinian, and Tridentine Canons

There are three canons of Sacred Scripture deserving of special mention: the Alexandrian, the Palestinian, and the Tridentine.

a. **The Alexandrian Canon** indicates that collection of all the books of the Old Testament contained in the Greek translation called the Septuagint, which appeared in Alexandria during the III century B.C. This collection was completed in the first century before Christ, and included all the deuterocanonical books and passages, and not as an appendix at the end of the volume, but intermingled with the protocanonical books. We may conclude from this that the Jews of that era, at least those in the Diaspora—

and Alexandria was perhaps their chief center—acknowledged as divine not only the proto- but the deuterocanonical books as well. There is, however, no way of knowing what criteria they used to determine the inspiration of these books.

b. **The Palestinian Canon.** This term indicates a collection of the protocanonical books of the Old Testament, divided into the Law, the Prophets, and the Writings, a division retained in modern Hebrew Bibles. There is one thing certain about this collection, and that is that the Palestinian rabbis, towards the end of the first or the beginning of the second century, looked upon it as containing completely all the divine Scriptures. However, we are altogether in the dark as to who made the collection, when it was made, and the criteria which governed its compilation. There is, above all, room for doubt that the Palestinian Jews, even at the time of Christ and before, rejected the deuterocanonical books. Quite a few scholars, among them van Kasteren,[4] positively deny that they did, and think it more probable that even the Palestinians at one time considered as sacred at least several of the deuterocanonical books. In their view, the so-called Palestinian canon is later than that of Alexandria and is the spawn of Pharisaic particularism.

In the light of all the facts bearing on this matter, it cannot be maintained that there was a time when there were two rival canons in Judaism, i.e., two different canons clearly settled by authority or tradition, and that later the narrower Palestinian canon prevailed and crowded out the broader Alexandrian canon. From this it follows also that the *expression* "Alexandrian canon," although employed quite widely, is not correct. There can be no question here of a canon in the proper sense, i.e., of a collection with definite contents clearly settled by a recognized authority or tradition. What we have is the fact of more or less definite differences between the contents of the Hebrew Bible and those of the Septuagint. For convenience sake we may use the expression to call attention to the fact of these differences, but not to imply the existence of a real canon different from the Palestinian.

But what may we infer from that difference? Or rather, how can we account for that difference without supposing two rival, different canons of Scripture in Judaism? We may legitimately take as our starting point that the precise limits of the "Writings" had not as yet been definitely fixed before the Christian era. That being so, the Palestinian Jews will not have had any firm conviction on the point. If the limits of the canon are to be conceived as fluid, it should occasion no surprise if some books would be more or less tentatively received by some and not received by others. It appears that in Egypt several books (varying in number) may have been taken more or less definitely into the Bible without arousing the opposition of Palestinian Judaism. Palestinian Jews, narrower and more conservative in the matter of Scripture as in other matters than were the Alexandrian Jews, had their faces to the past and saw in the closed past the norm and rule of their religious life. They gradually came to hold that prophecy and, with it, the writing of Sacred Books had ceased some time after the exile. The Greek-speaking Jews, on the other hand, were more willing to admit the possibility of new manifestations of the Divine Spirit. Hence for them the canon of Scripture would not be something settled and closed once for all, and they could admit the possibility of some additional books being given a place in the canon. They could even receive some such books more or less definitely, but without any final, formal judgment which would close the question of the canon irrevocably. Then, later on, when Palestinian Judaism, which served as the norm for the Diaspora in essential matters, fixed the Jewish canon, this Palestinian canon could be accepted without any feeling that it meant a reversal of judgment with regard to the deuterocanonical books on the part of the Jews who had entertained more liberal views on the subject.

The Jews of succeeding ages, including those of our own day, follow the Palestinian canon, which they usually attribute to Esdras. This attribution, historically untenable, is behind the term, "Canon of Esdras."

17   The *Reformers* were by no means unanimous on the question of what sacred books were to be accepted. All modern Protestants (Lutherans, Calvinists, Anglicans) agree at least in considering the *deuterocanonical books of the Old Testament* as "apocryphal." Lutherans usually append them to their bibles as "useful," but not so the others, at least not as a general practice.

As for the *deuterocanonical books of the New Testament*, Calvinists and Anglicans accept all of them. Lutherans relegate *Hebrews, James, Jude,* and the *Apocalypse* to an appendix in their New Testaments, accepting the rest as canonical.[5]

c. **The Tridentine Canon** is that published by the Council of Trent and confirmed by the Vatican Council. It contains *all the* *books of both Testaments.* We must therefore show that the Council of Trent was justified in drawing up its canon, i.e., that it accepted only those books which the Church had revered as Scripture from earliest times. However, this matter is rather the province of *Biblical Introduction,* and we shall accordingly give just a broad outline of the proof, leaving a full treatment to the science to which it belongs.[6]

IV. PROPOSITION. *The Canon of Trent Is a Faithful Expression of the Mind of the Early Church*

After having listed the individual books of both Testaments, the Council of Trent continues:

> If anyone, however, should not accept the said books, entire with all their parts, as they were wont to be read in the Catholic Church, and as they are contained in the old Latin Vulgate edition . . . let him be anathema.—DB 784.

It was the Council's intention to safeguard the authority of Scripture in the Church, i.e., in the form in which it had customarily been read for so long a time in the universal Church and especially in the Latin Church. The meaning of the phrase "with all its parts" will be discussed later together with the question of the authority of the Vulgate.

Proof:

1. For the *books of the Old Testament.*
   a. It can be definitely established from the writings of the fathers—and Protestants themselves admit this—that the universal *Church in the first three centuries* used as Sacred Scripture, both in public and in private, all the books of the Old Testament listed by Trent,[7] and without making any distinction between the books now called proto- and deuterocanonical.

   If one looks in the writings of the fathers themselves for the reason behind their accepting these books indiscriminately as sacred and divine, he will find one constant answer. It is the fact that they are "in every day use, public, common, received" in the Church, that this is the public tradition of the Church, that "the churches of God in each succeeding age have so handed them down to us."[8] It was, then, their firm conviction that the Church had received all those books from its founders, Christ and the apostles.[9]

Even though we cannot demonstrate that our Lord or the apostles canonized all the books of the Old Testament by a solemn and specific pronouncement, the conviction of the primitive Church is proved by its very universality and finds strong support in the books of the New Testament. For the New Testament authors quote the Old Testament most frequently according to the Septuagint, and they cite deuterocanonical books in the same fashion as protocanonical.

20 b. We must admit that *around the middle of the fourth century* a certain hesitancy about the deuterocanonical books began to appear in the writings of some of the fathers. This was true at first of some Eastern fathers and later of some Western fathers who had contact with the East. St. Athanasius,[10] St. Cyril of Jerusalem,[11] and a few others take a more or less unfavorable view of them and assign them a position somewhere between canonical and apocryphal. In the West, SS. Hilary and Rufinus adopt this same attitude. St. Jerome goes even further. He sometimes calls them simply "apocryphal" and seems at times to deny them any authority at all.[12]

But all this wavering was unable to shake the age-old conviction or to weaken its force. For (1) the churches went right on almost universally using the deuterocanonical books just as they had always done. (2) Many lists of sacred books were drawn up which contained deuterocanonical books along with the others: the Roman Canon of 382 during the pontificate of Damasus; that of St. Augustine;[13] those of the Councils of Hippo in 393, of Carthage in 397 and 416; that of Innocent I in 405, and that of St. Gelasius in 495. (3) The very fathers named above—and not even Jerome can be completely excluded—quite frequently use the deuterocanonical books as Scripture, or as sacred. By so doing they show that the distinction between "second place" (*anagignōskómenoi*, ecclesiastical) and "canonical" books did not have in their minds that absolute sense which at first blush it seems to have. Or it shows at least that for all practical purposes they subordinated their own private hesitations to the public practice of the Church.[14]

21 It is hardly necessary to remark that the hesitancy or disagreement of the aforementioned fathers influenced the opinions of many later writers. However, all doubt vanished in the East in the twelfth

century. And if in the West some few medieval scholars embraced the view of Jerome in somewhat mitigated form, the far more common doctrine, corroborated by the universal practice of the Church, always stood firm for the ancient tradition. This latter the Council of Florence openly espoused in the Decree for the Jacobites, and finally the Council of Trent made it official by solemn definition.

2. For the *books of the New Testament*. 22

a. The beginnings of the New Testament are fairly obscure, but this is not surprising in the light of the following considerations. When the first churches were founded by the apostles and their aides, no New Testament book was yet in existence, and the religion of Christ had already spread far and wide throughout the various districts of the world when the books came out one by one during the years 50 to 100. They were written in different places and as occasion demanded. They were not addressed by their authors directly to the universal Church, but rather to a particular church or, at most to just a few; often enough, in fact, to some one person. In this way the several books came to individual churches together with a guarantee of their authenticity, without the other churches being immediately aware of what had happened. And there is no need to suppose that the receipt of the missive was reported to all the churches; at least there is no need to suppose that this was done in any hurry. For although the churches, as circumstances permitted, had contact with each other, it is not hard to understand how, in those early days when the voices of the apostles were still ringing in everyone's ears, not too much attention would be paid to writings. This would be true especially of those writings which in scope and content were of relatively minor importance, or were concerned primarily with strictly local affairs.

On the supposition, then, that none of the apostles gave explicit approval to all the books of the New Testament *in globo*—something not at all necessary, and not in fact demonstrable—the situation could have shaped up somewhat as follows. After the apostles had died, authentic guarantee of individual sacred books would be available here and there in the Church before those books had as yet been gathered into one corpus, in fact, before any particular church was aware of the complete list of all the books. It is historically certain that a complete[15] collection did not yet exist at that time, and it may be assumed as a probable hypothesis that no complete list was anywhere to be found. If this really is the true picture, then we can easily understand *(1)* that in the ensuing years the canon of the New Testament could be determined only by carefully collecting and studying the traditions of individual churches. History witnesses to the fact that the fathers actually did employ this method. *(2)* That this research was not always easy, especially in view of conditions obtaining at that time, and so could have given rise to legitimate doubts and even to erroneous notions regarding at least some of the writings. *(3)* Finally, that a sound and definitive judgment about all the books together came to rather slow maturity and took deep root in all the churches still more slowly.

b. Testimony of the earliest documents.[16]

23   *(1)* Towards the end of the first century (80–100) there were in existence two collections, one of the Four Gospels, the other of thirteen Pauline Epistles (i.e., all except Hebrews). These were read publicly in almost all the churches together with the writings of the Old Testament. To these were added everywhere *certain other books,* now more, now less, about which the churches were not in such general accord.

24   *(2)* From various documents dealing especially with the history of the Gnostics we gather that about 140 and thereafter *all* the Greek and Latin churches[17] agreed on accepting on an equal footing all the books later listed by Trent, except for Hebrews, James, and 2 Peter. Opinion was divided on the latter just as it was on some other books (*Didachē, Epistle of Barnabas,* etc.).

Towards the end of the second century (170–220) the same agreement shows up more clearly. At the same time it can be shown from the controversy with the Montanists, who through their prophets were spouting a new revelation, that the Church was fully convinced that the age of (public) revelation and of prophecy did not extend beyond the Apostolic Era, and that consequently no book could be admitted as an authoritative source of revelation which the Apostolic Age had not bequeathed for public reading.

The Epistle to the Hebrews was accepted from earliest times by the church at Alexandria as one of the Pauline epistles. Then after it was defended by Origen—who attributed its actual composition to one of Paul's disciples—it spread throughout the whole East. In the West it was not used in public reading before the fourth century. However, SS. Clement of Rome, Irenaeus, and Hippolytus were acquainted with it and thought highly of it.

SACRED SCRIPTURE

The Epistle of James was always accepted in the East by the Greeks. The Latins soon got to know it, but it is missing from the Muratorian Fragment[18] and does not seem to have been used in the churches of Gaul and Africa.

2 Peter was known to SS. Justin Martyr and Hippolytus and perhaps also to St. Irenaeus; Clement of Alexandria wrote a commentary on it, and Origen accepted it as Sacred Scripture.

(3) In the first half of the third century, Origen, having studied the traditions of the churches, called the Gospels, Acts, 13 epistles of Paul, 1 Peter, 1 John, and Apocalypse *homologóumena*. He personally accepted as Sacred Scripture the rest of the books which appear now in the canon of Trent (and a few others also), but at the same time he acknowledged that they were not received by all.[19]

During the same century the *Apocalypse* came under attack. The reasons for the opposition were varied and usually tendentious. It began at Rome with Cajus, a priest, who met with little success. Later the controversy flared up at Alexandria (St. Dionysius, d. 265) and at Antioch (St. Lucian, d. 312), and spread like wildfire throughout the East. In addition, Christians at Antioch, influenced by contact with the Syrians, began to omit some of the Catholic epistles.

(4) In the fourth century (around 325), Eusebius of Caesarea distinguished three classes of books: *homologóumena* (agreed upon, accepted)—Gospels, 14 Pauline epistles, Acts, 1 Peter, 1 John; *antilegomena* (disputed), which seemed to him acceptable —James, Jude, 2 Peter, 2 and 3 John; *notha* (spurious), which should be excluded from the list of the Scriptures.[20] As for the *Apocalypse*, he is not sure whether it should be put in the first or third class. Weighty testimonies of antiquity urged the former classification, but he personally leaned rather to the latter.

In 367 St. Athanasius called all and only the books of the later canon of Trent *kanonizomenoi* (canonized, canonical), and distinguished them from the *apokruphoi* (apocryphal) and even from the *anagignōskomenoi*.[21]

From this time on the doubts and disagreements still remaining in the Eastern churches gradually faded until in the sixth century they had practically vanished.

In the *Latin Church*, disagreement about Hebrews, 2 Peter, 2 and 3 John, James, and Jude continued to the middle of the fourth century. However, the Roman Synod of 382, under Pope Damasus, in its "List of Scriptures of the New and Eternal Testament, which the Holy and Catholic Church receives," enumerated all and only those books later listed by Trent. At this synod were present not only SS. Jerome and Ambrose, but also quite a few Eastern bishops. The canon of Damasus was adopted by St. Augustine, the Councils of Hippo (393) and Carthage (397 and 416), St. Innocent I (405), St. Gelasius (495), etc. We may say, then, that the question of the canon of the New Testament had been definitively settled, though not defined, in the West by the beginning of the fifth century.

28 V. Church's Authority the Only Absolute Proof for a Complete List of Sacred Books

It is not hard to conclude from the foregoing data that the presence of by far the majority of the books in the Tridentine canon can be justified with *certitude* by merely historical arguments. But it would be going too far to make the same claim for all the books, especially those of the New Testament. Let us grant, then, that it is only the authority of the infallible Church which fully guarantees the *complete* catalogue of sacred books. It should occasion no surprise, in view of the fact that our knowledge of early history is relatively incomplete, if we cannot fully appreciate the reasons which led the fathers of the fourth and fifth centuries to give a definitive place in the canon to books about which there had formerly been some dispute. The subsequent universal and constant agreement of the whole Church, viewed in the light of theological principles, fully convinces the theologian that those fathers did not stray from the truth when they formed their judgment. The situation of Protestants is far worse, for since they refuse to admit that Christ established an infallible teaching authority, they have to rely on historical arguments alone to justify their complete canon. No wonder Gore admitted that it was becoming daily more difficult to maintain faith in the Scriptures without faith in the Church.[22]

Notes

1. See J. Balestri, *op. cit* pp., 281–82; CCHS, 11b–c. A comparison may help to make this matter clearer. When the Church *canonizes* someone, it does not thereby *make* him a saint. It merely gives official recognition to the already

SACRED SCRIPTURE

existing fact of his saintliness. Similarly, when the Church canonizes a book, it does not thereby make the book inspired. Rather, it recognizes officially the inspired character of the book. In other words, inspiration is intrinsic to the book while canonicity is extrinsic.

2. See Vacant-Mangenot, DTC s.v. Apocryphes; Robert-Tricot, *Guide to the Bible*, I, 61 ff.; CCHS, 92a ff.

3. It is well to keep in mind the difference in terminology used by Catholic and non-Catholic authors in this matter:

Catholic	Non-Catholic
Protocanonical	Canonical
Deuterocanonical	Apocryphal
Apocryphal	Pseudepigraphic

4. See *Die Studien*, 45, 414; 49, 379; RBibl, (1896), 408 and 575; DTC, II, 1569; J. Balestri, *op. cit.*, p. 286; Hopfl-Gut, *op. cit.*, I, 153.

5. The credal books of the Lutherans contain no list of the sacred books. A list adopted by modern Protestants appears in the *Belgian Confession*, articles 4–6. The Greek schismatics accept just as we do all the deuterocanonical books; but the Russians for the past two centuries have considered apocryphal the deuterocanonical books and passages of the Old Testament. See RBibl (1901), 267; EO (1907), 129 ff.

6. See Cornely, *Introductio generalis in sacram Scripturam* and *Compendium introductionis* (5th ed., 1905); Chauvin, *Leçons d'introduction générale* (1897); Gigot, *General Introduction to the Holy Scriptures* (New York, 1906); Belser, *Einleitung in das neue Testament* (2nd ed., Freiburg, 1906); W. Barry, *The Tradition of Scripture* (1906); T. Zahn, *Geschichte des neutestamentlichen Kanons* and *Grundriss der Geschichte des neutestamentlichen Kanons* (1904); DBV and DTC s.v. *Canon des saintes Ecritures*; Batiffol, RBibl (1903), 10 and 226; *Guide to the Bible, op. cit.*, p. 28 ff.; A. Wikenhauser, *Einleitung in das neue Testament* (Freiburg i. Br., 1953), p. 14 ff.; CCHS, 11a ff.; M. J. Lagrange, *Histoire ancienne du Canon du Nouveau Testament* (Paris, 1933); Hopfl-Gut, *op. cit.*, p. 128 ff.; E. Jacquier, *Le Nouveau Testament dans l'eglise chretienne*, I (Paris, 1911); M. Nicolau, *Sacrae Theologiae Summa*, I (Madrid, 1952), 983 ff.; Robert-Feuillet, *Introduction à la Bible*, I (Tournai, 1959), 31–54.

7. Some, however, are of the opinion that the words of St. Cyril of Jerusalem (*Catecheses* 4. 33 ff.) show conclusively that the Church of Jerusalem did not make *public* use of the deuterocanonical books.

8. Origen, *Commentarium in Matthaeum*, Sermo 46.

9. It is true that some writers of this period accepted also some of the Old Testament apocrypha (*Henoch, Assumption of Moses, Assumption of Isaias*), but actually very few shared this error. It was much more common for the churches to reject such books, knowing as they did that they were not "handed down."

10. *Festal letters* 39
11. *Catecheses* 4. 33–36.
12. For instance, in his *Prologus galeatus* and *Praefatio in Danielem*.
13. *De doctrina christiana* ii. 8. 13.

THE SOURCES OF REVELATION

14. All agree that St. Jerome, captivated by a love for what he called "Hebraic truth," to which he owed a great deal in his emendation of the *text*, accorded an exaggerated authority to rabbinic tradition on the question of the *canon*. And it is worth remembering that this same Jerome, in his search among the earlier fathers for authorities to back up his rejection of the deuterocanonical books, appealed neither to St. Athanasius nor to St. Cyril. See *Studien*, 60, 239–52.

15. Note the qualification, *complete*. 2 Pet. 3:16, for example, hints at a collection of *some* of the Pauline epistles.

16. See especially Zahn, *Grundriss*, p. 15 ff.; A. Wikenhauser, *op. cit.*, p. 16 ff.; CCHS, 16–17.

17. This agreement existed if, as seems likely, 2 and 3 John were customarily added to and included with his first epistle, which was universally accepted. Note: "all the *Greek and Latin* churches"; the Syrian church of Edessa in the second century seems to have recognized only the four Gospels, Acts, 12 Pauline epistles (omitting Hebrews and Philemon), and nothing else. The Peschitto (the Syriac Vulgate) still left out 2 Peter, Jude, 2 and 3 John, and Apocalypse. However, it has been established that St. Ephraem (d. 373) knew and acknowledged at least some of these books.

18. The earliest list that has come down to us, though it need be by no means the earliest written, is the Muratorian Fragment (c. 200) discovered by Muratori in the Ambrosian Library, Milan, in 1740. It contains a catalogue of books which were recognized as authoritative at Rome at the end of the 2nd cent., *viz.* the four Gospels, the Epistles of St. Paul (except Heb), two Epistles of Jn, Jude, Apoc.—CCHS, 17g.

19. He gives a list of all the books of the New Testament in his *Homilia VII in Josue 2*.

20. See HE 3. 25.
21. *Festal letters* 39.
22. *Lux mundi* (London, 1891), p. 283.

Special Bibliography

BALESTRI, J. *Biblicae introductionis generalis elementa*. Rome, 1932. p. 283 ff.

HÖPFL-GUT. *Introductionis in sacros utriusque testamenti libros compendium*. I (Rome, 1940), 128 ff.

LUSSEAU-COLLOMB. *Manuel d'études bibliques*. I (Paris, 1936), 266 ff.

NICOLAU, M. *Sacrae theologiae summa*. I (Madrid, 1952), 983 ff.

ROBERT-FEUILLET. *Introduction à la Bible*. I (Tournai, 1959), 31–54.

ROBERT-TRICOT (ed.). *Guide to the Bible*. Translated under the direction of E. P. Arbez and M. R. P. McGuire. I (Tournai, 1951), 28 ff.

———. *Initiation biblique* (3rd ed.). Paris, 1954.

SACRED SCRIPTURE

Ruwet, J. *Institutiones biblicae.* I (Rome, 1937), 97 ff.
Simon-Prado. *Praelectiones biblicae.* I (Torino-Madrid, 1938), 57 ff.
Wikenhauser, A. *Einleitung in das neue Testament.* Freiburg i. Br., 1953. p. 14 ff.
Zarb, S. M. *De historia canonis utriusque testamenti.* Rome, 1934.

Article II

THE EXISTENCE OF INSPIRATION

I. *The Criteria of Inspiration*
    1. Inadequate criteria:
        a. Holy sentiments engendered by book;
        b. Truth and sublimity of doctrine, etc.;
        c. Direct testimony of the Holy Spirit to reader;
        d. Testimony of hagiographer.
    2. One adequate criterion: divine testimony.

II. PROPOSITION. *All the Books of the Tridentine Canon Are Inspired*
    Proof: 1. Scriptural arguments:
        a. General: from *modus agendi* of Christ and the apostles;
        b. Particular: 2 Tim. 3:15–16; 2 Pet. 1:19–21; 3:15–16.
    2. Testimony of the fathers.
    Corollary: The argument from tradition is not weakened by the fact that we sometimes find the writings of the fathers and the decrees of the Councils attributed to the inspiration and even to the dictation of the Holy Spirit.
    3. Indirect proof based on canonicity.
Corollary: Apostolic origin as a criterion of inspiration.
Scholion: The extension of inspiration to all parts of Scripture.
Corollary: Essentially and accidentally dogmatic passages.

Article II

THE EXISTENCE OF INSPIRATION

We have seen which books the Church reveres as Sacred Scripture, which books it has accepted from earliest times as sacred and canonical. Now we must ask on what grounds it placed them in the canon. The Vatican Council has given the answer:

> But the Church holds these books as sacred and canonical, not because, having been put together by human industry alone, they were then approved by its authority; nor because they contain revelation without error; but because, having been written by the inspiration of the Holy Spirit, they have God as their author and as such, they have been handed down to the Church itself.[1]

Therefore for a book to be considered sacred and canonical, it must be inspired, i.e., written under a divine influence of such a nature that God can and must be acclaimed the Author of that book.

We must find out, then, whether the existence of such an influence can be the object of a valid proof. But first we must set the stage by determining the grounds, i.e., the criterion or criteria which can serve as basis for the proof.

I. The Criteria of Inspiration

1. Protestants in general claim that Scripture is *its own guarantee of inspiration* (*autópistos*).

(a) Some, especially Lutherans, taught that the inspiration of any book could be detected on the basis of its peculiar divine flavor, i.e., on the basis of the holy feelings it engenders in the souls of its readers. (b) Others proposed as criteria of inspiration characteristics intrinsic to the book itself, like the truth and sublimity of its doctrine, the fulfillment of prophecies recorded therein, or the candor of its style. (c) Calvinists claim that the Holy Spirit gives direct testimony to the soul of any reader who has faith. The Holy Spirit who of old inspired the sacred writers to write these words continues from day to day to give individual readers the inspired assurance that what he is reading is the word of God.[2]

It goes without saying that the first and second sets of criteria are inadequate for a sure proof of inspiration. As for the direct testimony given to individual believers by the Holy Spirit—that is a gratuitous and false assumption.[3]

31   2. Once *autopistía* is ruled out, then it follows that the inspiration of Scripture must be proved by testimony of some sort or other. Would the merely human testimony of the sacred writer himself suffice, i.e., the testimony of that man who wrote the sacred book under the influence of the Holy Spirit? Obviously no one other than the sacred writer could possibly observe the fact of divine inspiration. It must be granted that the merely human testimony of the author—even if we possessed such testimony, which we do not—would not suffice to give full certitude. Quite clearly the danger of hallucination is too great in a matter like this for people to place absolute trust in the affirmation of an individual that he had been inspired to write, even if that individual be quite sincere and holy.[4]

32   The only remaining criterion is *divine testimony*, testimony given by an authorized herald of revelation and handed on to us in proper fashion.[5] Now such testimony could have been handed down either in some book of Scripture itself or in other trustworthy documents. Since evidence for the inspiration of at least several books is actually taken from other books of the Bible, it is most important to point out in advance that in this question we use the books of the Bible not as inspired, but as humanly trustworthy historical records only. It would be begging the question in the worst way to seek in Scripture as an inspired document a proof for its inspiration. But there is nothing to prevent one from arguing in the following fashion:

The books of the New Testament are historically trustworthy and so they contain a faithful record of the teaching of Christ and the apostles, whom we know to have been spokesmen for God.

But these books tell us, e.g., that Christ and St. Paul taught that certain books were inspired.

Therefore the inspiration of these books rests on divine testimony given by an authoritative spokesman and promulgated in a trustworthy document.

It is one thing to say that the inspiration of Scripture can, in the final analysis, be validly proved on the basis of divine testimony, and quite another to determine the precise character of this testimony, i.e., to determine whether it was always given explicitly or sometimes contained only implicitly in some other statement. We shall say a bit more on this point later. Moreover, it would be asking too much to demand that the ancient documents on which we base our belief in inspiration should also declare openly that this truth rests on divine tradition. As long as we can show that belief in inspiration was general in the Church from earliest times, we have every right to conclude that it formed part of the legacy of truth left by Christ and the apostles.

II. PROPOSITION. *All the Books of the Tridentine Canon Are Inspired* 33

This is a *dogma of faith,* as we know from the Vatican Council:

> If anyone shall not accept the entire books of Sacred Scripture with all their divisions, just as the sacred Synod of Trent has enumerated them (see n. 783 f.), as canonical and sacred, or denies that they have been inspired by God: let him be anathema.[6]

The *proof* may be lined up somewhat as follows. We shall first give the *scriptural arguments,* which prove the inspiration of several, though not of all, the books. To these we shall add the *nonscriptural arguments,* namely, the statements of the early fathers which, if they are general and unqualified, prove the inspiration of all those books included by them under the heading of Scripture.[7] But if they are qualified and specific, i.e., if they refer directly to only certain particular books, they can still be used as an indirect proof for all the books included in the concept of Scripture, for there can be no doubt that the fathers put all the books of Scripture on the same plane. Finally, we shall corroborate our conclusion and at the same time round out our treatment with an appeal to the *indirect argument* based on canonicity.

THE SOURCES OF REVELATION

34 I. *Scriptural arguments*

1. For the books of the Old Testament.

It is abundantly clear from the New Testament and from other, extra-biblical sources, that at the time of Christ the Jews attributed absolute authority to the books they called Scripture, because they believed them to have been inspired by God. But Christ and the apostles gave positive approval to this belief of the Jews, as regards both the absolute authority of Scripture and the basic reason on which this authority rested, namely, divine inspiration. The conclusion is clear.[8]

The *Major* can be proved in short order by citing the testimony of Josephus, who testifies to the conviction of the Palestinian Jews, and of Philo, who records that of the Hellenistic Jews. Josephus says that the sacred books of the Jews are "rightly believed to be divine" because composed "only by prophets" (men acting under divine inspiration).[9] Philo calls the Scriptures "outstanding oracles which issued from the mouth of the prophets."[10]

Minor. Christ and the apostles gave the fullest recognition to the absolute authority of Scripture. Christ: "*I assure you emphatically: before heaven and earth pass away, not a single letter or one small detail will be expunged from the Law—no, not until all is accomplished.*"[11] "*These events are the fulfillment of what I predicted to you when I was still with you, namely, that anything ever written concerning me, whether in the Law of Moses, or in the prophets, or in the Psalms, must needs be fulfilled*"—Luke 24:44-45. "*Scripture cannot be annulled*"—John 10:34. St. Peter: "*Brothers, it was necessary that the passage of Scripture . . . be realized*" —Acts 1:16. St. Paul argues from the fact that Scripture mentions the promise made to the "seed" of Abraham: *It does not say, "And to his descendants," as if referring to many, but only to one.*[12]

35 Our Lord and the apostles deduce the all-embracing authority of Scripture from the facts that in the Scripture it is God who speaks and that the sacred authors speak in the Holy Spirit, etc. In other words, they *deduce it from the fact of inspiration.* As proof of this we have the manner in which they quote Scripture and the express declaration of St. Paul.

a. *Their manner of quoting Scripture.* Christ: "*In what sense, then,*" he asked them, "*does David, prompted by the Holy Spirit, call him 'Lord,' when he says: 'The Lord said to my Lord?*'"[13] St.

(32)

SACRED SCRIPTURE

Peter: *"Brothers, it was necessary that the passage of Scripture in which the Holy Spirit by the mouth of David spoke prophetically of Judas be realized."*[14] St. Paul: *"We have been called to the apostolate and set apart to proclaim the Good News now made known by God, as he had promised it of old through his prophets in Holy Writ"*—Rom. 1:2. *"And the Scriptures, foreseeing that God would sanctify the Gentiles by faith, announced to Abraham beforehand, 'In you shall all nations be blessed'"*—Gal. 3:8. Here Scripture is used as a synonym for God Himself, its Author.

These passages, of course, prove the inspiration of only a few texts, but in view of the fact that the same authority is attributed to Scripture as a whole, and since very many different citations are introduced by the same formulas, "it is written," "Scripture says," etc., we are justified in concluding that the basic reason for this authority is the same for all the passages cited, namely, divine inspiration.

b. *The express declaration of St. Paul.* The Apostle wrote to Timothy, who had been born in Asia Minor of a Gentile father and a Jewish mother:

> From your infancy you have known the Sacred Writings. They can instruct you for salvation through the faith which is in Christ Jesus. All Scripture is inspired by God and useful for teaching, for reproving, for correcting, for instructing in holiness.—2 Tim. 3:15–16.

The crucial words are, in the original Greek: *pâsa graphḗ theópneustos kaì ōphélimos pròs didaskalían.* . . .

It makes little difference whether the term *pâsa graphḗ* be taken collectively for *all* Scripture or distributively: *any* Scripture.[15] In either case it signifies the whole collection which Timothy had known from childhood on as "the Sacred Writings."

Nor does it make much difference whether, with the Vulgate, one takes the word *theópneustos* in apposition to *pâsa graphḗ*, or, with the original text, as the predicate. In either case, it is clear that this *theopneustía* (divine inspiration) applies to all Scripture and is actually the basis of the latter's usefulness and authority.

The word *theópneustos* (*theós*, God; *pnéō*, to breathe) occurs nowhere else in the New Testament or in the Septuagint. It is found occasionally in the works of profane authors to indicate the action of the gods on men.¹⁶ And so the term *graphḗ theópneustos* can signify nothing other than a writing composed under the inspiration or at the instigation of God.¹⁷ Must this influence be understood as one of such intensity that the Scripture which is its result is truly the word of God and that God is its Author? The word *theópneustos* certainly admits this meaning, and a comparative study of the passages cited above (no. 35) demands it. Furthermore, the real significance of the term *theópneustos* can be clarified from 2 Peter 1:19–21, where the author says of *"prophecy"* or *"prophecy of Scripture"* that it is not the product of a human intellect or will, but that *"men with a message from God spoke as they were moved to do so by the Holy Spirit"* [*allà hypò pneúmatos hagíou pherómenoi elálēsan hágioi theoû anthrōpoi*]. The Holy Spirit so activated, led, moved men that the *"prophecy of Scripture"* was not so much their work as His, relatively speaking.¹⁸

38 Corollary

Which books of the Old Testament are proven to be inspired by the foregoing arguments? *At least* all the protocanonical books, for it can hardly be doubted that the "sacred letters" which the Hellenist Timothy knew from childhood were those of the Septuagint translation, which contained also the deuterocanonical books.¹⁹

39

2. For certain books of the New Testament.

a. In 2 Peter we read:

> And regard the long-suffering delay of our Lord's coming as a means of salvation. Paul, our dear brother, wrote the same things to you according to the wisdom granted him, just as he did in all his letters when speaking of these matters. In his letters there are some passages hard to understand. The unlearned and unsteady twist the meaning of these to their own destruction, as they do also the other Scriptures.²⁰

Evidently St. Peter put some of the Pauline epistles on a par with "the other Scriptures," and so he implicitly affirms that they were written under inspiration.

It is impossible to determine with certitude what "all those epistles" were which St. Peter had in mind.²¹ The very vague manner of expression, "all his letters" seems to hint at something rather general. Do not Peter's words seem to have proceeded from the following conviction, that all the letters which our dearest brother Paul has composed in the exercise of his apostolic office are to be put on a par with "the other Scriptures" and consequently are to be considered as inspired? If this be true, then one would have a hard time finding a reason to prove that St. Peter reached this conclusion about Paul alone and not about the rest of the apostles when they wrote in pursuance of their official function. And so, if I am not mistaken, this passage of Peter's epistle at least suggests the inspiration of all the apostolic writings.

A word of caution is necessary, however. The apostolic origin of 2 Peter cannot be proven with certainty on merely historical grounds. Consequently, he who must rely on historical data alone cannot allege the aforementioned testimony strictly as Petrine. But supplementing the witness of history we have the firm conviction of the primitive Church.

A probable argument for the inspiration of the Gospel of Luke 40
is frequently drawn from these words of St. Paul: "*As the Scripture says, 'Do not muzzle the ox when it treads out the grain,' and 'The laborer is entitled to his support.'*"—1 Tim. 5:18. The words "*the laborer is entitled,* etc." are found in this form nowhere in Scripture outside of Luke 10:7. But in view of the fact that the words, "*You shall not muzzle,*" are taken from Deuteronomy (25:4), we may suspect that the rest of the passage, "*the laborer is entitled,*" is a free interpretation of a passage in the same general context of Deuteronomy (24:14–15).

II. *Non-scriptural arguments* 41

St. Clement of Rome: "You have looked deep into the sacred writings, which tell the truth and proceed from the Holy Spirit."[22] These words must be understood as referring primarily to the Old Testament, but not exclusively. For St. Clement not only cites many New Testament passages but in addition says explicitly of St. Paul: "He was truly inspired [*pneumatikôs*] when he wrote to you."[23]

St. Polycarp speaks of the "Scriptures" in which the Philippians were versed and immediately thereafter cites a Pauline passage, introducing the citation with the words, "So I only say what has been said in the following texts."[24] Evidently he put St. Paul's letters on the same plane as the "Scriptures," the inspiration of which as a whole he certainly acknowledged. The same is true of the epistle attributed to Barnabas, wherein St. Matthew's Gospel is quoted, and again with the introductory formula, "As it is written." (4:14).

St. Justin Martyr (or perhaps another writer of the same period) says of the Old Testament authors that their knowledge of exalted and divine affairs came from no human source, "but from that Gift [the Holy Spirit] which came down upon holy men of that era." Consequently, they had to submit themselves wholeheartedly to the divine influence of the Spirit of God, in order that the divine plectrum itself, coming down from heaven and using holy men as an instrument, like a harp or lyre, might reveal to us the knowledge of divine and heavenly matters. And that is why they are always in common accord, even though "it was at different times and in different places that they passed on to us their heavenly doctrine."[25] Elsewhere St. Justin openly acknowledges the inspiration of the prophets and then indicates that the "commentaries of the apostles" (the Gospels) are considered by Christians as practically in the same class with the "writings of the prophets."[26]

42   Athenagoras says of Moses, Isaias, Jeremias, and others:

> Moses, Isaias, Jeremias, and the rest of the prophets, who, when the Divine Spirit moved them, spoke out what they were in travail with, their own reason falling into abeyance and the Spirit making use of them as a flutist might play upon his flute.[27]

St. Irenaeus: "The Scriptures are perfection itself, in that they are the words of the Word of God and of His Spirit.[28] Of the apostles he says: "They first preached" the Gospel, "and later, in accord with the divine will, they set it down for us in writing that it might serve as the pillar and foundation of our faith."[29] We learn the precise meaning of the phrase, "in accord with the divine will," in another passage, which reads: "The Holy Spirit foresaw that men would distort the truth and so took measures to foil their deceit by saying through Matthew, 'This is the record of Christ's life.' "[30]

St. Theophilus of Antioch, in the course of rejecting an error about the Word of God, says: "And the Holy Scriptures teach us this, as do all the men who were inspired by the Holy Spirit [*pántes hoi pneumatophóroi*], one of whom, John, says, 'When time began, the Word was there.' "[31] The utterances of the prophets and the Gospels are found to be in agreement for the simple reason that they all spoke under the inspiration of the one Spirit of God"; he then goes on to cite some Pauline passages as the "word of God" (*theîos lógos*).[32]

Clement of Alexandria: "I could allege for you numberless scriptural passages, of which not even one pen-stroke will fail of fulfillment, for the Mouth of the Lord, the Holy Spirit, has pronounced them."[33]——"He who believes in the divine Scriptures has an unshakeable proof, the very voice of God who gave them to us."[34]

St. Hippolytus: "Let us understand the holy Scriptures in the sense in which God intended to teach us therein.[35]

Tertullian: "The Apostle [Paul] was moved by the same Spirit who is responsible for all the Scriptures, right back to the very book of Genesis."[36] "If you think that we care nothing for the welfare of the emperors, read the words of God, our [sacred] literature. . . . Pray, it says, for kings and princes" (1 Tim. 2:2).[37] Elsewhere he asserts that the Church of Rome has the same regard for both the Old and the New Testaments: "It combines the Law and the Prophets with the Gospels and apostolic letters and draws thence its faith."[38]

St. Cyprian: "It was necessary, my dearest son, that I accede to your spiritual desire, which begged with most insistent urging for the divine teaching wherewith the Lord has deigned to teach and instruct us by the holy Scriptures.[39]

Origen:

> The just and good God Himself, the Father of our Lord Jesus Christ, gave the Law, the Prophets, and the Gospels. That there was not one Spirit in the men of the old dispensation and another in those who were inspired after the coming of Christ is most clearly taught throughout the churches.[40]
>
> We shall say that we both [Jews and Christians] agree that the books [of the Old Testament] were written by the Spirit of God, but that we part company with the Jews when it comes to the interpretation of those books.[41]

43

Eusebius of Caesarea quotes an early author who attacked the Artemonians (anti-Trinitarians of the beginning of the third cen-

44

tury) "because they boldly impugned the Scriptures. . . . Either they do not believe that the Sacred Scriptures were dictated by the Holy Spirit, in which case they are infidels, or else they consider themselves wiser than the Holy Spirit, and in that case they are just diabolically insane."[42]

St. Cyril of Jerusalem: "These things we learn from the divinely inspired Scriptures of the Old and New Testament." Shortly thereafter he says that the Holy Scriptures were "dictated by the Holy Spirit."[43]

St. Athanasius mentions "divine Scriptures which we have for our salvation." He regrets that some mix apocryphal works in with "divinely inspired Scriptures," and concludes: "Let us be content to be taught by divinely inspired Scriptures, the books of which we have listed above."[44]

St. Basil:

> Do not neglect to read especially the New Testament, because often harm can come from reading the Old. Not that harmful things have been written therein; it is rather that the souls of those who suffer harm are weak to begin with. For all food is fit for nourishment, but it can hurt those who are sick. And so all Scripture is divinely inspired and useful and there is nothing evil therein.[45]

45St. John Chrysostom:

> In the beginning God spoke to men directly, . . . but because they later became unworthy of familiarity with Him, . . . He sent letters to them as to a people afar off. It was indeed God who wrote these letters, but Moses was His postman.[46]
>
> For there is in the sacred letters neither a syllable nor a penstroke in whose depths there is not a rich treasure. . . . For if in worldly transactions documents often depend on one syllable for much of their importance, this is even more true of the divine Scriptures, written as they were by the Holy Spirit.[47]

St. Ambrose, in commenting on the words of Luke 1:1: *Many an attempt has been made before now*, etc., wrote:

> Matthew did not just try, or Mark, or John, or Luke. No, the Spirit of God furnished them with a wealth of words and

SACRED SCRIPTURE

material, and they carried through without any effort the task they had undertaken.[48]

There are many who say that our sacred writers did not write artistically. We offer no objection to this statement, for it was not in accord with art that they wrote but with the grace which surpasses all art: they wrote what the Spirit gave them to write.[49]

St. Jerome:

I have corrected some things in the Latin translation of the Gospels, not because I thought anything needed correction in the words of the Lord or that anything was not divinely inspired, but because I wanted to correct the mistakes of the Latin manuscripts in the light of the Greek.[50]

St. Augustine: 46

Letters have reached us from that city whence we wander [heaven]. These letters are the Scriptures, which urge us to lead good lives.[51]

He [the Son of God], having spoken first through the prophets and then personally, and still later through the apostles—to the extent He deemed sufficient—also produced the Scripture which is called canonical, and it possesses the highest possible authority.[52]

Now even though they [the evangelists] wrote what He indicated and ordered, it must by no means be said that He Himself did not write, since in fact it was a case of His members' putting into operation what they had learned at the dictation of the Head. Whatever He wanted us to read about His deeds and words, He ordered to be written by them as His own hands.[53]

Theodoretus directed this observation against those who claimed that not all the psalms had been written by David:

I have no positive statement to make on this subject. It makes little difference to me whether he wrote all of them or whether others wrote some of them, since in any case they were all composed under the inspiration of the Spirit of God.[54]

St. Gregory the Great: 47

Who the human author of these words [the book of Job] was

is a more than empty question, since we firmly believe that the Holy Spirit is the Author of the book. He wrote those things who dictated them for writing. . . . When, then, we understand the matter, and are convinced that the Holy Spirit was its author, in asking questions about the author, what else do we do than, when reading a letter, make inquiries about the pen? . . . The writers of Holy Scripture, then, since they are moved by the influence of the Holy Spirit, give witness to themselves therein as to other persons. Thus the Holy Spirit spoke of Moses by the mouth of Moses; the Holy Spirit spoke of John through John. Paul, too, intimates that he did not speak from the dictates of his own mind when he says, *"Do you seek a proof that Christ speaks through me?"*[55]

48 Corollary

The argument from tradition is not weakened by the fact that we sometimes find the writings of the fathers and the decrees of the Councils attributed to the inspiration and even to the dictation of the Holy Spirit.[56] For as long as one takes into account, as is only fair, the complete teaching of the fathers and its practical application, it will be easy to see that they did not attribute to the Holy Spirit the canonical books and other writings of purely human origin in exactly the same sense. Take St. Augustine as an example. After having said that St. Jerome wrote "not only under the inspiration but even at the dictation of the Holy Spirit," he adds in no uncertain terms: "I confess to your charity that I have learned to give to only those books of Scripture which are called canonical such reverence and honor as to believe most sincerely that none of their authors could have made a mistake when he wrote."[57]

49 An indirect proof for the inspiration of all the books of both Testaments is based on canonicity.

The question of receiving a book into the canon always involved, in the minds of the fathers, the question of the inspiration of that book. It was not just a matter of whether a certain book was simply useful or pious, but whether it should be added to the list of those books about whose inspiration all were in agreement.

We know, it is true, that the immediate and explicit point of the discussion was sometimes something else, in particular the apostolic origin of a book; but the fundamental issue of the discussion, or of the doubt, was always whether this book was to be classed with the inspired books, both on the score of absolute authority and also on that of the intrinsic reason for that authority, namely, inspiration. We say "also on the score of the intrinsic reason for its authority" because (a) the fathers never give the slightest hint that the ultimate basis of dignity and authority varies for the several books of Scripture. Besides, (b) their reverence for the inspired Scriptures was so great that they would under no consideration put on the same plane with them any ancient book, no matter how true or useful, which they believed had been composed by exclusively human efforts.

Consequently, (1) from the fact that by far the majority of the books were universally accepted without any hesitation or dispute, it follows that their inspiration was always acknowledged by all. (2) From the fact that the fathers were morally unanimous in accepting the rest of the books, at least from the beginning of the fifth century, it follows that the inspiration of these latter was acknowledged at least from that time on as universally as that of the books in the first class.

It will be noted that here, too, we can apply what was said at 50 the end of the preceding article: if one prescinds from the authority of the infallible Church, it is possible to prove with certainty from historical documents alone the inspiration of by far the greater part of the books, but not of all of them. The fathers of the fourth and fifth centuries must certainly have considered adequate the arguments which led them to pass definitive judgment on the inspiration of the deuterocanonical books, but these arguments have been preserved for us only in part. They are evaluated—to the extent that they have come down to us—by biblical scholars, whose business it is to study the teaching of the fathers on *individual* books.

Corollary 51

In the controversies centering around the acceptance of the deuterocanonical books of the New Testament, especially *Apocalypse* and *Hebrews*, the express and immediate issue was generally whether a book could be traced back to one of the apostles. If its apostolic authorship could be ascertained, the book was listed among the Scriptures; if not, it was considered apocryphal. And so the question arises: was the charism of the apostolate considered by the fathers as the criterion of inspiration, and if so, should we so consider it? The exact point at issue is not whether we can determine the inspiration of a given book apart from divine testimony, but rather whether such testimony is already implicitly contained in the apostolic origin of a book, namely: in the fact that a book was composed by an apostle as such, i.e., in the exercise of his apostolic office.

52 The negative opinion is the more common one. However, several authors give an affirmative answer: Lamy, Reithmayr, Ubaldi, Cellerier, Szekely, Schanz,[58] Joüon,[59] and their opinion deserves a fair hearing.

They grant that the apostolate *considered in itself* does not include the gift of biblical inspiration. Most of the members of the apostolic college contributed nothing to the body of Scripture and still they were genuine apostles. They lacked none of the prerogatives which belong essentially to the apostolate. Nor is it antecedently impossible that an apostle should, in the exercise of his office, write something, and do so without being inspired. The hypothetical case of an apostle's speaking or writing on matters of faith or morals without the gift of infallibility would be quite another matter, because this gift is bound up essentially with the apostolate as such.

It is, however, the view of the aforementioned authors that in actual fact the gift of inspiration was *extrinsically* connected with the apostolate, and that, as a result, the apostles were in fact always inspired whenever they wrote anything in the exercise of their apostolic office. It is their opinion, too, that the early Church was aware of this extrinsic but nonetheless real connection and that we have a reflection of this awareness to a certain extent in 2 Peter 3:15–16. If one does not admit the existence and awareness of such a connection, it is difficult to explain satisfactorily the line of argument followed by the fathers.[60] Furthermore, not one of the early fathers seems to have known of *explicit* testimonies for the inspiration of individual books of the New Testament.

53 It is, besides, a well-known fact that unusual gifts of the Holy Spirit were bestowed not only upon the apostles, but also upon many of their immediate fellow-workers—even though in varying degrees. Consequently it should occasion no surprise if the gift of inspiration, too, was granted to certain apostolic men, like Mark and Luke. But since the apostles alone made up the foundation of the Church,[61] the books of their non-apostolic colleagues had to be recommended to the Church as inspired by one of the apostles,

in one way or another. Their books would then have an indirectly apostolic origin. That would explain why from earliest times Mark's Gospel was linked with Peter and Lukes with Paul, and why some fathers even speak of the express approval given these books by one or other of the apostles.[62]

Scholion. The extension of inspiration to all parts of Scripture.   54

In the seventeenth[63] and especially towards the end of the nineteenth century,[64] some writers advanced the opinion that the doctrine of inspiration should be qualified somewhat. They suggested that the divine influence did not affect all genuine scriptural passages indiscriminately, but was limited to those passages which, in the light of the purpose of the Scriptures, should be called primary. These authors were not altogether unanimous in their views, but if one sets aside minor points of disagreement,[65] one finds that they were in general accord on the following basic points. They taught that the sacred writers enjoyed God's help when they wrote on subjects touching religion, faith, and morals, matters directly and necessarily in line with the purpose intended by God. When, however, the hagiographers dealt with other questions, like history, geography, chronology, physical sciences—in a word, profane or merely accessory questions—they did so not with the positive aid of the Holy Spirit, but merely with His permission. The proponents of this restricted view of inspiration acted from the best of motives. They were most anxious to find a way to safeguard Catholic doctrine and at the same time to feel free to admit that some real errors existed in the secondary, non-essential parts of the sacred books. They were well aware of the fact, as we shall point out at length directly, that if the influence of inspiration is such as to make God the real Author of the written word, it necessarily rules out all error.

Leo XIII stated emphatically that no such limitation of inspiration could be admitted on any grounds whatsoever: 55

> But it is absolutely wrong and forbidden either to narrow inspiration to certain parts only of Holy Scripture or to admit that the sacred writer has erred. As to the system of those who, in order to rid themselves of these difficulties (arising from the profane sciences) do not hesitate to concede that divine inspiration regards the things of faith and morals, and nothing beyond,

because (as they wrongly think) in the question of the truth or falsehood of a passage we should consider not so much what God has said as the reason and purpose which He had in mind in saying it—this system cannot be tolerated.[66]

Of course, the supreme pontiff was thoroughly justified in taking this stand. Not to mention many things which might take us far afield, such a limitation contradicts *Catholic tradition*. The fathers, with at least morally universal unanimity, clearly affirm the inspiration of all of Scripture, and consequently exclude any real error from all of Scripture, precisely because they believe it to have been composed throughout under divine inspiration: "for they were unanimous in laying it down that those writings, in their entirety and in all their parts were equally from the *afflatus* of Almighty God, and that God, speaking by the sacred writers, could not set down anything but what was true."[67]

56 The members of the so-called "Liberal School" appealed principally to the following argument. They insisted that inspiration does not extend beyond its purpose, and that its purpose is to teach religion, nothing else.

It must be granted that the special purpose of Scripture is to teach men those abstract and practical truths which will guide them to external life.[68] From this one may rightly conclude that only those matters pertaining by their nature to religion (in which matter, however, are included many historical facts which have an intrinsic tie-up with doctrinal truths) are inspired for their own sake and as a result of God's primary *intention*. But it does not follow that other subjects which by their very nature are not at all or, at most, very remotely related to religion are excluded from the influence of inspiration. For they could have been inspired in line with a *secondary intention*, i.e., *for the sake of the other subjects*, namely, with a view to expressing religious truths more effectively and fittingly. Catholic tradition asserts that this was in fact the way things happened, and one does not have to look very far to find excellent reasons for God's having willed to proceed in this fashion.

57 It is of utmost importance for the authority of Scripture that everything contained therein be acknowledged as inspired. Although in some cases one can tell at a glance what is of religious import and what is not, it is not always easy to determine the limits. That is why if everything were not inspired, the opinion of readers and exegetes would often be uncertain, arguments based on Scripture would be capriciously set aside on the pretext of non-inspiration, etc. If the authority of Scripture was to be incontrovertible it was necessary either to extend inspiration to every single statement or to exclude profane subjects from Scripture altogether. But this latter course would have been extremely inconvenient. Clearly (a) very many things, which appear at first blush to be exclusively historical, play an indirect but very important role in religious instruction, in that they show us how divine Providence prepared for and established the Kingdom of God, directed human affairs, etc., or describe the lives of holy men to serve as an example for us, and of wicked men to serve as a warning. Obviously narratives of this sort could not very well have been composed without constant reference to numberless details like chronology, topography, genealogy, custom, all of them thoroughly secular, but without which the book would be quite dull and so less suited to the fulfillment of its high purpose. (b) It is of no little importance to the defense of truth that the books which record that truth possess a historical authority which can be proved by internal as well as external criteria. And it is precisely the references to secular matters which furnish us with such criteria, for the most part. (c) God's gentle Providence decreed that Scripture be composed in such a way that its books would be not only divine, but at the same time truly human.[69] Accordingly, He accommodated His inspiration to the circumstances of those men whom He chose to be His instruments in the composition of the Sacred Books and also to those of the people to whom the Books were directly addressed. It is quite significant that the actual writing corresponded to external occasions, and that a literary form was chosen which would fit precise circumstances. At times the historical form was called for, at others the didactic, the poetic, the epistolary, etc. This providential arrangement demanded as a consequence that the Holy Spirit inspire the sacred writers to make use of all those elements of composition which men who adopt such and such a literary form customarily employ. Among these elements would be greetings at the ends of letters, personal details concerning material needs,[70] and other things of this type.

The doctrine just set forth does not at all contradict the famous remark of St. Augustine: "The Holy spirit who spoke through them [the sacred writers] had no intention of teaching men those matters [the structure of the heavens, etc.], matters in no wise profitable to salvation."[71] So far was Augustine from excluding profane subjects from the realm of inspiration that he explicitly included them within that realm. One must read the remark just quoted in its context. But since it is not the purpose of Scripture to teach astronomy, etc., he understood well that the sacred authors could have used the ordinary, inexact manner of speaking when they described such things. From this he concluded that in such matters the literal sense of Scripture was not to be insisted upon against well founded opinions of natural science.

58 Corollary

It should be clear from the preceding in what sense and with what justification we distinguish in Holy Scripture passages inspired directly and for their own sake and passages inspired accidentally or for the sake of something else. The former are sometimes called *essentially dogmatic*, the former *accidentally dogmatic*.[72]

Notes

1. Constitution *De fide catholica*, chap. 2 (DB 1787).
2. Calvin held that Sacred Scripture "is *autópistos* [its own guarantee of inspiration], and that there is no need to bolster it with proofs and arguments. The certitude with which it deserves to be accepted by us is based on the testimony of the Holy Spirit"—*Institutes of the Christian Religion*, i. 7. 5. See also the *Belgian Confession*, article 5. Note the ambiguity of the assertion: Scripture is its own guarantee (*autópistos*). All grant that Scripture gets its own intrinsic authority not from the Church or from tradition, but from itself, i.e., from the single fact that it is inspired by God. But the question is whether the divine authority of Scripture *is made known to us* with certitude by the mere reading of Scripture. It is this latter *autopistia* that Catholics deny, not the former.
3. If we allowed the criterion suggested by the Lutherans, any stirring book would be inspired. And how about all those passages in the Bible which are conducive to anything but spiritual exaltation? The subjective character of the Calvinist criterion—which is, to begin with, a completely gratuitous assumption—renders it quite worthless as a norm for discerning the inspiration of any book. The testimony of the hagiographer is an inadequate criterion firstly, because of the very real danger of hallucination involved. Any well-meaning person might feel himself inspired to write a book in God's name. But how could he be sure; how could *we* be sure? And secondly, the fact is that no hagiographer has ever told us that he wrote under inspiration.

SACRED SCRIPTURE

Jeremias comes close when he tells us that God commanded him to rewrite his book after the king had ruthlessly destroyed the first edition. But the mere *command to write* is far from being inspiration, which is a divine influence affecting the *whole process* of writing a sacred book.

4. We have said that the *merely human* testimony of a hagiographer is not enough; for if a hagiographer, whose divine mission was already established on other grounds, testified to his own inspiration, that testimony would not be merely human. We have, however, no such testimony.

5. This is only to be expected, given the fact that inspiration is a supernatural phenomenon. The supernatural cannot be ascertained at all, let alone with sureness, by merely natural means. Our knowledge of even the fact of inspiration must come to us by way of revelation in some guise or other.

The only testimony that abstracts from subjectivism and is truly infallible, universal (*i.e.*, having application to all the inspired books) and at the disposal of all is that of God, which is made known to us through the teaching authority of the Catholic Church. Apart from the insufficiency of all other criteria, it should be clear that the fact of inspiration is a dogma of the Faith and that a dogma of the Faith is not to be believed on merely human testimony. Therefore the fact of inspiration is to be believed upon the authority of God alone.—J.M.T. Barton, "The Holy Ghost," *The Teaching of the Catholic Church*, I (New York, 1949), 170.

6. *Loc. cit.*, canon 2, 4 (DB 1809).

7. Note: "which *those* fathers included under the heading of Scripture." It is of course clear that when weighing the testimony of those fathers who doubted the canonicity of certain books, the reasons for their hesitation must be taken into account.

8. This argument may be presented more completely and perhaps more tellingly as follows:

Using the sacred books merely as historical documents worthy of credence, and prescinding altogether from their inspired character, we can construct an argument which will take us at least part way:

In the time of Christ, Jewish tradition recognized a collection of books as possessing divine authority because they were of divine origin.

But Christ and the apostles approved this tradition.

Therefore Christ and the apostles approved a collection of books as being of divine origin and authority.

However, one must go further in order to *prove* inspiration as a *fact*. All the above syllogism tells us is that certain men accepted certain books as sacred and inspired. To this conclusion one might answer, *salva reverentia*: "So Christ and the apostles approved a collection of books as sacred. So what? What does their approbation mean?" Consequently, using the books still as authoritative historical sources, nothing more, we must prove, as is done in Apologetics, the divine mission and subsequent infallibility of Christ and of His apostles. This puts some teeth into the conclusion. Such a proof is called by theologians a quasi-dogmatic historical argument.

What is to be said, finally, of the sufficiency of this argument? What does it prove? The *fact* of inspiration, nothing more. It will not prove specifically, for instance, the actual inspiration of the *New* Testament or of several books

THE SOURCES OF REVELATION

of the Old Testament. In the final analysis, one must have recourse to Tradition and to the divinely established authority of the Church's *magisterium*.

9. *Contra Apionem* 1. 7–8.

10. *De mutatione nominum,* cited by Franzelin, *De traditione et scriptura* (3rd ed.), p. 324. Indeed Philo thought that even the Septuagint translation was done under inspiration "as if some invisible power dictated to each [translator the proper words]"—*De vita Moysis,* cited by Franzelin, *loc. cit.*

11. Matt. 5:18. The term *Law* is often used to refer to the whole Old Testament.

12. Gal. 3:16; see Heb. 12:26-28, where a very important truth is deduced from the phrase *"yet once again"* (Agg. 2:7).

13. Matt. 22:43; see Ps. 109. What the phrase *to speak in the Spirit* means can be illustrated by the following words of David: *"The spirit of the Lord hath spoken by me, and his word by my tongue"*—2 Kings 23:2.

14. Acts 1:16. The first believers gave expression to the same belief when they prayed: *"Sovereign Master, ... who did say by the Holy Spirit through the mouth of our father, David, your servant: 'Why did the Gentiles rage....'"*—Acts 4:25.

15. Note that in the New Testament the term *Scripture* is often used of an individual passage or sentence of Scripture; see Matt. 15:28; John 13:18; 19:36-37; Acts 1:16; 8:35.

16. See Pesch, *Praelectiones dogmaticae,* I, no. 607.

17. Futile attempts have been made to interpret *theópneustos* in an active sense: "breathing forth God." The form itself is definitely passive, and, with a few—and uncertain—exceptions, all the words of this type into the composition of which *theós* enters as an element have a passive meaning. Thus *theodidaktos*, "taught by God"; *theokinetos,* "moved by God"; *theopemptos,* "sent by God"; *theokletos,* "called by God"; *theodotos,* "given by God," etc. See Bea, *De inspiratione et inerrantia Sacrae Scripturae* (Rome, 1947), p. 3; Höpfl-Gut, *op. cit.,* p. 36.

18. This text is cited only to *illustrate* the meaning of the word *theópneustos,* for *a*) it is not certain that there is a question here of *hagiographers* as such, since it is not improbable that the words are used of prophets in the strict sense, either speaking or writing; and *b*) the apostolic origin of this epistle finds no clear proof in any definite testimony of the Church.

19. See above, no. 15.

20. 2 Pet. 3:15-16. It is not quite clear whether the correct reading is *en pásais taís epistolaís* or *pásais epistolaís.*

21. It is most natural to see here a reference to all the Pauline epistles in the Church's possession at that time. And in fact the more common opinion among Catholics is that 2 Peter was written shortly before the author's death in 66 or 67, and hence after the composition of all the Pauline epistles with the single exception of 2 Timothy.

22. *Epistula I ad Corinthios* 45; ACW translation.

23. *Loc. cit.,* 47; ACW translation.

24. *Epistula ad Philippenses* 12.

25. *Cohortatio ad Graecos* 8; see also 10. On the subject of this work, Dr. Quasten writes as follows:

In his attitude toward Greek philosophy, the author of the *Cohortatio*

SACRED SCRIPTURE

differs markedly from St. Justin. If only for this reason the work cannot be ascribed to the latter. But besides, it is much superior in style and uses a distinctive vocabulary. All this together is enough to prove the treatise nonauthentic. The *Cohortatio* most probably originated in the third century, has thirty-eight chapters and is the longest of the writings falsely attributed to St. Justin.—QP I, 205.

26. *Apologia* i. 36 and 37.
27. *Legatio pro Christianis* 9.
28. *Adversus haereses* ii. 28, 2.
29. *Loc. cit.*, 3. 1.
30. *Loc. cit.*, iii. 16, 2.
31. *Ad Autolycum* 2. 22.
32. *Loc. cit.*, 3. 12 and 14.
33. *Protrepticus* 9.
34. *Stromata* 2.2.
35. *Contra Noetum* 9; see also 11.
36. *De oratione* 22.
37. *Apologia* 31.
38. *De praescriptione* 36.
39. Introduction to *Testimonia ad Quirinum*.
40. *De principiis,* Preface 4; see also 3 and 4. 1 and 6.
41. *Contra Celsum* 5. 60.
42. HE 5. 28.
43. *Catecheses* 4. 33 and 34.
44. *Festal letters* 39; see above, no. 26.
45. *Epistula 42 ad Chilonem* 3.
46. *Homilia 2 in Genesim* 2.
47. *Homilia 21 in Genesim* 1.
48. *Expositio evangelii secundum Lucam* 1. 1.
49. *Epistula 8 ad Justum* 1.
50. *Epistula 27 ad Marcellam* 1.
51. *In Ps. 90 enarratio* 2.1.
52. *The City of God* 11. 3; see *Confessions* vii. 21, 27.
53. *De consensu evangelistarum* i. 35, 54.
54. *Praefatio in Psalmos.*
55. *Moralia* 1, Preface 2–3.
56. See Tertullian, *De cultu feminarum* 1. 3; Augustine, *Epistula 82 ad Hieronymum* 2; Leo the Great, *Epistula* 145, 1.
57. *Loc. cit.*, 3.
58. *Apologie des Christentums,* II (2nd ed.), 608 ff.
59. *Études,* 98 (1904), 80.
60. Did not St. Augustine state explicitly about some apocryphal works: "If these were their [the apostles'] works, they would have been received by the Church of God?"—*Contra adversarium legis et prophetarum* i. 20, 39.
61. See Ephes. 2:20.
62. See Tertullian, *Contra Marcionem* 4. 5, and see also 4. 2; Eusebius, HE 2. 15; 3. 24; St. Jerome, *De viris illustribus* 8. Here is Joüon's view of the matter:

Every time an apostle writes as an apostle, he is inspired. It is not necessary that he do the writing himself. Mark and Luke are personally inspired, but their charism is *objectively* conditional. God's having conferred scriptural inspiration on them and our knowledge of that inspiration rest on the two following conditions: they have reproduced the teaching of the apostles, and it is these latter who are our guarantee of the reliability of that reproduction. The inspiration of the apostles was known *in* their apostolic character, that of Mark and Luke in their derived apostolicity.—*Loc. cit.*, 90.

At the bottom of this suggestion there seems to lurk a confusion between the charism of infallibility and that of inspiration. The end of the latter *is* not precisely to *teach*, but to *record* teaching, as Lagrange very helpfully points out. Inspiration does entail infallibility, but not *vice versa*. See Balestri, *op. cit.*, p. 418 ff.; J. M. T. Barton, *loc. cit.*; S. Tromp, *De Sacrae Scripturae inspiratione* (Rome, 1945), p. 26 ff.; F. Schroeder, *Père Lagrange and Biblical Inspiration* (Washington, 1954); J.-M. Vosté, *De divina inspiratione et veritate Sacrae Scripturae* (Rome, 1932), p. 23 ff.

Another suggestion has been put forward which attempts a different answer.... It is urged that, since the Apostles were sent to teach in the name of Christ and were his ambassadors, whatever they taught was to be received as the word of Christ, ... But why limit their teaching to the spoken word? Were they not just as much the ambassadors of Christ when they wrote as when they spoke? In this way, whatever was written by an Apostle was inspired and, on this understanding, was accepted by the faithful. The writings of Mark and Luke were received because they were considered as coming from Peter and Paul respectively. But, we may ask, is it right to make the transient charisma or gift of inspiration coextensive with the permanent office of apostleship, or to elevate Mark and Luke virtually to the status of Apostles? In fact, it is possible to commit an Apostle's teaching to writing faithfully and yet not be inspired in the true sense of the word.—CCHS, 18c.

See also David M. Stanley, "The Concept of Biblical Inspiration," CTSA, 13 (1958), pp. 65–95.

63. Holden; and later, Chrismann.

64. Lenormant, Rohling, Cardinal Newman, di Bartolo, d'Hulst, Semeria —several of whom subsequently corrected their doctrine.

65. Among minor differences may be mentioned the fact that some of them (di Bartolo, d'Hulst) kept the *term* inspiration for all of Scripture, but distinguished various degrees of inspiration *so as not to admit for merely profane subject matter that influence which would make God the real author of passages dealing therewith*. Actually, this theory of *"mitigated* inspiration" is a denial of that inspiration which the Church teaches and hence differs from the theory of *"limited* inspiration" in name only.

66. Encyclical *Providentissimus Deus*, RSS, p. 23 f.

67. *Loc. cit.*, p. 25; see Corluy, *Science catholique* (1893), p. 481; Fonck, *Der Kampf um die Wahrheit der heiligen Schrift*, p. 21; Pesch, *De inspiratione Sacrae Scripturae* (Freiburg i. Br., 1906), p. 440 ff.; J. Balestri, *op. cit.*, p. 429 ff.; J. M. T. Barton, *op. cit.*, p. 176; CCHS, 37d; DBS, IV, 497 ff.

68. See Rom. 15:4; 2 Tim. 3:15–17.

69. The Greeks had a word for this, too. They called it *synkatábasis*, the wonderful condescension which God reveals in all His dealings with earthbound creatures. If He chooses to communicate with them, it will have to be

in their inadequate language. If He chooses to employ men as instruments of this communication, He owes it to Himself to respect the freedom of will which He has given them, their usual manner of expression, their psychological and cultural equipment. Characteristically, He will do them no violence, but will effect His purpose gently, albeit efficaciously.

With the sole qualification of Teacher of Divine Science, she (the Wisdom of God) came, and established her chair by the side of other chairs; in the public places and crossroads she gathered together all the passers-by without any distinction, and to them she set forth her teaching; she marked out her own definite position, and outside that position she spoke the language of the people, as all great teachers of the human race have done. And if to man, who is all his life but a little child, she spoke in childish terms, and spelled out to him the mysteries of heaven, we really cannot blame her for his own stammering and inconsequence, her whose teaching is so justly pure and lofty. Our own ignorance should be blamed.—P. Lacome, *Quelques considérations exégétiques sur le premier chapitre de la Genèse* (1891), quoted by Lagrange, *Historical Criticism and the Old Testament* (London, 1906), pp. 106–7; see F. Schroeder, *op. cit.*, p. 31. See also J. L. McKenzie, *The Two Edged Sword;* B. Vawter, *A Path Through Genesis;* CCHS, 36j; J. P. Weisengoff, "Inerrancy of the Old Testament in Religious Matters," CBQ, 17 (1955), pp. 128–37.

70. See, for example, 1 Tim. 5:23; 2 Tim. 4:13; Philem. 22.

71. *De Genesi ad litteram* ii. 9, 20.

72. In this matter we should not forget Peters' appropriate reminder (*Unsere Bibel*, p. 53) that, while we admit the inspiration of every part of the Bible, no matter how small, still each item is not inspired, as it were, for itself independently, but as part of a larger unit. The view that considers each verse by itself or in the light of its immediate context only is what Peters calls the atomistic attitude, as contrasted with the modern attitude which rather considers the book as a whole and tries to appreciate the minor parts in their relation to the whole.

Special Bibliography

ARBEZ, E. P.–WEISENGOFF, J. P. Unpublished notes, Catholic University of America, 1953.

BAINVEL, J. *De Scriptura Sacra*. Paris, 1910.

BALESTRI, J. *Biblicae introductionis generalis elementa*. Rome, 1932.

BARTON, J. M. T. "The Holy Ghost," *The Teaching of the Catholic Church*. New York, 1949.

BEA, A. *De inspiratione et inerrantia Sacrae Scripturae*. Rome, 1947.

———. "Inspiration et inérrance," DBS IV. Paris, 1949.

BENEDICT XV. *Spiritus Paraclitus*. Rome, 1920.

BILLOT, L. *De inspiratione*. Rome, 1903.

CHAUVIN, A. *L'inspiration*. Paris, 1897.

CREHAN, J. H. "The Inspiration and Inerrancy of Holy Scripture," CCHS 34 ff.

CRETS, G. J. *De divina bibliae inspiratione.* Louvain, 1886.
DAUSCH, P. *Die Schriftinspiration, eine biblisch-geschichtliche Studie.* Freiburg, 1891.
FEI. *De evangelii inspiratione.* Paris, 1906.
HOLZHEY, K. *Die Inspiration in die Anschauung des Mittelalters.* München, 1895.
HÖPFL-GUT. *Introductionis in sacros utriusque testamenti libros compendium.* Rome, 1940.
HUGON, E. *La causalité instrumentale dans l'ordre surnaturel.* Paris, 1924.
LEO XIII. *Providentissimus Deus.* Rome, 1893.
LEVIE, J. *La Bible, parole humaine et message de Dieu.* Paris-Louvain, 1958.
LUSSEAU-COLLOMB. *Manuel d'études bibliques.* Paris, 1936.
MCKENZIE, J. L. *The Two Edged Sword.* Milwaukee, 1956.
MERK, A. *Institutiones biblicae.* Rome, 1937.
PESCH, CHR. *Zur neusten Geschichte der katholischen Inspirationslehre.* ("Theologische Zeitfragen," 3ᵉ Folge) 1902.
———. *De inspiratione Sacrae Scripturae.* Freiburg i. Br., 1906.
PIUS XII. *Divino afflante Spiritu.* Rome, 1943.
POPE, H. *The Catholic Student's "Aids" to the Study of the Bible.* New York, 1926.
ROBERT-FEUILLET. *Introduction à la Bible.* Tournai, 1959.
ROBERT-TRICOT. *Guide to the Bible.* Translated under the direction of E. P. Arbez and M. R. P. McGuire. Westminster, 1951.
———. *Initiation biblique* (3rd ed.). Paris, 1954.
SCHMID, FR. *De inspirationis bibliorum vi et ratione.* Brixen, 1885.
SCHROEDER, F. *Père Lagrange and Biblical Inspiration.* Washington, 1954.
SIMON-PRADO. *Praelectiones biblicae.* Turin, 1938.
STANLEY, D. "The Concept of Biblical Inspiration," CTSA, 1958.
TROMP, S. *De Sacrae Scripturae inspiratione.* Rome, 1945.
VAWTER, B. *A Path Through Genesis.* New York, 1956.
VOSTE, J. -M. *De divina inspiratione et veritate Sacrae Scripturae.* Rome, 1932.
ZANECCHIA, D. *Divina inspiratio ad mentem sancti Thomae.* Rome, 1899.
———. "Scriptor sacer sub divina inspiratione, responsio ad p. Van Kasteren," *Studien,* 34, 581.

Article III

THE NATURE AND EFFECTS OF INSPIRATION

I. *God Is the Principal Cause or Author of Scripture; Man Is Its Instrumental Cause or Author*
   1. Activity of the principal cause as applied to inspiration.
   2. Activity of the instrumental cause:
      a. Truly human: rational and free;
      b. Suited to individual temperament, education, and other special characteristics.
   3. The effect is to be attributed in its entirety to both causes —but from different points of view.

II. *Analysis of Leo XIII's Definition of Inspiration:*
   1. Inspiration is a supernatural charism influencing the whole writing process.
   2. Influence on author's
      a. intellect: different from revelation;
      b. will: direct, internal, efficacious;
      c. executive faculties.

   Corollary: Did the sacred writers *realize* they were inspired?

III. *Verbal Inspiration*

IV. *First Conclusion: Everything Contained in a Genuine Passage of Scripture Is the Word of God*

V. *Second Conclusion: Everything Contained in a Genuine Passage of Scripture Is Infallibly True*

   Scholion: Inspiration and critical authenticity.

Article III

THE NATURE AND EFFECTS OF INSPIRATION

59 I. God the Primary Author of Scripture; Man the Secondary Author

Once the fact of inspiration is admitted, it follows necessarily that the books of Holy Scripture have *two authors*. They were written by men whom we call hagiographers (sacred writers); but they are still the 'word of God," and so have God or—by appropriation—the Holy Spirit as their Author. The texts cited in the preceding article stated clearly the mutual relationship of the two causes: the Holy Spirit impelled or moved the hagiographer, spoke through the mouth of the hagiographer; the latter spoke in the Spirit, by the Spirit, etc. God then was the cause of Scripture but He used men's services to produce this effect. He was its *principal cause* or *author*, while the hagiographer was its *instrumental cause* or *author*. St. Thomas: "The principal author of Holy Scripture was the Holy Spirit, and man was the instrumental author."[1] Leo XIII advanced the same explanation, teaching that "the Holy Spirit employed men as his instruments."[2] Another way of expressing the same idea is to call God the primary, and man the secondary author.

If this explanation is the right one, then what is known of the relationship of principal and instrumental causes to each other and to their effect can contribute a great deal to our understanding—to some extent at least—of the nature of inspiration and to our formulation of precisely what it is.*

---

* It should be remarked that while the fact of inspiration is a dogma of the faith, the theological explanation of the nature and workings of inspiration is not. It is a human attempt to explain a supernatural phenomenon and, as such, is bound to fall somewhat short of the mark. But the explanation in current vogue, that based on the theory of instrumental causality, has been in possession for centuries now, and it is the most adequate in view of what we know of inspiration from the sources of revelation themselves. It should be noted in addition that the theology of inspiration is, to a great extent, still in the making, although great strides have been taken since the publication of the *Providentissimus Deus*. Before that, relatively little was done on the sub-

SACRED SCRIPTURE

1. It is of the *nature of a principal cause* to *put an instrument to work*. St. Thomas: "An instrumental cause acts by virtue of the motion which it receives from the principal cause."³ It follows as an immediate consequence that they were wrong who so understood scriptural inspiration as to disallow any real action of God, the principal Cause, or of the human author, or to restrict it to just some parts of Scripture. The following opinions must accordingly be rejected. 60

   a. The opinion of Haneberg (1850), who taught that a book written by purely human effort could become Scripture if it was subsequently approved by the Church and included in the canon. The Vatican Council had this opinion in mind when it proclaimed that "the Church holds these (books) as sacred and canonical not because, once composed by purely human endeavor, they were then approved by her authority . . . but, etc."⁴ 61

   b. The opinion usually connected with the names of *Lessius* and *Duhamel* (1587): "Any book (2 Maccabees may be an example) written by purely human effort without the help of the Holy Spirit becomes Scripture if the Holy Spirit subsequently testifies that the book contains nothing false."⁵ These two opinions (a. and b.) are sometimes dignified by the name *subsequent inspiration*, a clear contradiction in terms.

   c. The opinion of *Jahn* (1814), who retained the term "inspiration" because it was in common use but expressed his dissatisfaction with it. To his way of thinking, inspiration should be conceived as a merely negative assistance which neither inspired nor taught anything, but merely kept errors from creeping into the Book. This is known as *negative inspiration*. The Vatican Council seems to have had this erroneous notion in view when it proclaimed: "The Church considers these (books) sacred . . . not just because they contain revelation without error, but because, etc."⁶

   d. The opinion of Bonfrere (1625), according to whom the requirements for inspiration are adequately met if God in some vague, general way moves a man to write such and such an account, hovers over him constantly, always ready to step in should the need arise, and finally does positively intervene as often as His co-author would otherwise have made a mistake of some sort.⁷ This

---

ject. St. Thomas laid the foundations in STh, II—II, q. 173/74, but only in principle, as he was treating prophetic, not biblical, inspiration. (See D. M. Stanley, *op. cit.*)

is called *concomitant inspiration,* and precisely because it is merely concomitant it is not inspiraton at all.

62 2. By its very nature, an *instrumental cause* has a double activity, instrumental and proper, and it performs the instrumental action only through the exercise of that activity which is proper to itself. St. Thomas:

> An instrument has a double activity. One is instrumental, and in accordance with this it acts not by virtue of any power proper to itself, but by virtue of a power transmitted to it by the principal agent. The other is proper to the instrument itself, belonging to it by its own special nature. An axe can split wood precisely because it is an axe, and sharp in the bargain, but it can construct a bed only to the extent that it is used as an instrument for that purpose by an artisan. On the other hand, it performs this instrumental action only through the exercise of its own proper activity, for only by cutting the wood does it contribute to the fashioning of the bed.[8]

Now in the matter under discussion, God decided to use a man as an instrument in writing the word of God—an instrumental activity exceeding man's natural powers. How did the human author contribute to the accomplishment of this design? What was, under God's influence, the activity proper to the human author himself?

63 a. It seems reasonable to suppose that the hagiographers accomplished their divine task by performing some action befitting their nature, an action which was not merely mechanical, but really *human,* i.e., *rational and free.* It would hardly be consonant with God's normal mode of action for Him to do violence to His creatures. And He would if He used men as merely mechanical tools, making use of just their hands and fingers, so that they would copy down the divine message "with their minds in complete disorder, like people in delirium."[9] On the contrary, it is thoroughly in accord with God's gentle providence for Him to make use of a man by adapting to His purpose truly human functions so that, in the case at hand, a sacred writer, under God's active influence, would grasp intelligently the message to be written[10] and then with perfect freedom would proceed to give it written expression. Nor should one be too quick to object that, when God efficaciously moves a man to do something, there is no room left for truly human activity.

For the principle laid down by St. Thomas applies to this process as well as to any other of like nature:

> The motion imparted by the prime mover does not meet a uniform reception in all things moved thereby, but each receives it in its own special way. Consequently, it is by no means antecedently impossible that God should be the cause of an act of free will.[11]

Now if we consult the Scriptures themselves, we find that as a matter of fact the sacred writers did not contribute to the writing of the word of God merely by lending God a helping hand, but by putting at His service their minds and wills. The author of 2 Maccabees writes: *"And all such things as have been comprised in five books by Jason of Cyrene, we have attempted to abridge in one book . . . we have taken in hand no easy task, yea rather a business full of watching and sweat"*—2:24–27. At the end of the book he remarks, in addition, that the imperfect and inadequate presentation of the subject matter is to be attributed to his lack of talent: *"Which if I have done well, and as it becometh the history, it is what I desired: but if not so perfectly, it must be pardoned me"*—15:39. St. Luke, too, affirms that he set about writing his Gospel of his own free will after he had done careful research on the whole subject of Christ's life and work: *"Many an attempt has been made before now to present the drama of events that have come to a climax among us, . . . I, too, after accurately tracing the whole movement to its origin, have decided to write a consecutive account for your excellency."*—1:1–3.

b. It seems quite reasonable to suppose also that the human authors accomplished the task God had assigned them by performing actions proper to themselves, and *in a manner befitting their individual temperament, education, and other special characteristics*. If they did actually work in this fashion, then the genius, temperament, and background of each one of them will shine through the pages of the inspired book, just as the technique of an artist reveals itself in the picture he has drawn. It is possible to tell just from looking at the picture whether the artist used crayon or charcoal, a sharp or a dull pencil.

The facts justify this supposition. St. Jerome: "Isaias' fluent style reveals him as a man of urbane eloquence . . . Jeremias' style is a bit on the rustic side. And such simplicity of speech is due to his having been born where he was."[12] St. Irenaeus remarks that St. Paul often transposed the usual word order "because of the speed with which he wrote and because of the urgency of the Spirit within him."[13] St. Augustine has this to say about the evangelists: "It is clear that, while they all treated the same subject matter, each of them presented it as he remembered it, as it occurred to his mind."[14] St. John Chrysostom, too, explains the apparent discrepancies in the Gospel accounts from the fact that the evangelists did not collaborate on the project, but wrote at different times and in different places.[15] In fact, all exegetes rely on the purpose and the milieu of the sacred writers to explain, for example, why they omit such and such an event or why they relate it in this or that fashion. None of them even dreams of solving such questions by appealing directly to the intention of the principal Author or to the fact of inspiration. Catholic authors use much the same general scientific approach to the Synoptic Question as do rationalists.[16]

And so, even though we may not fully comprehend this mysterious process, still we must recognize the fact that the human authors, under the active influence of the Spirit, performed a genuinely human, personal, individual action, with respect to style and literary form, and to the subject matter of their books. The time-consuming and painful labor mentioned by the author of 2 Maccabees was expended not only in searching for the right words, but also in selecting from his sources of information just the material which would contribute to his purpose.

It follows that the analogies used by the fathers limp rather noticeably, when they describe the sacred writers as the "pens" or the "secretaries" of the Holy Spirit. To a certain extent they were "pens" and "secretaries," because in the actual work of composition they wrote nothing but what God moved them to write; but they were for all of that intelligent and free "pens," and they were not the type of secretary who listens to and transcribes the boss's letters with machine-like, but hardly human, precision.

65 As has just been remarked, the human authors, *in the actual writing of the Sacred Books*, wrote nothing but what God moved them to write. It is not at all necessary that *all* the work of these authors, including that work which contributed even remotely to the final production, should have come under the divine influence.

SACRED SCRIPTURE

The book which I am now writing will be in large measure the end product of study and research done years ago when I wasn't even thinking of writing a book. Still, those studies do not enter immediately into the actual composition of my book. Presuming, then, that the sacred authors, in giving written expression to the word of God, used knowledge and experience acquired in the past, it is still not necessary to extend the influence of the grace of inspiration to those more or less remote preparations. Using an instrument is one thing; getting it ready is another. The preparation of the hagiographer for functioning as a fit instrument of the Holy Spirit has nothing to do with inspiration as such, whether that preparation be natural or supernatural.

3. *What part of the effect*, i.e., *of the finished product*, is to be attributed to the principal cause, and what part to the instrumental? St. Thomas gives the answer: "The same effect is to be attributed in its entirety to the instrument and in its entirety also to the principal agent";[17] but from different points of view.

Some distinguish in an inspired book the *formal part* (the essential contents) and the *material part* (literary form, sentence structure, style, choice of words), attributing at least apparently the former to the Holy Spirit alone and the latter to the hagiographer alone (under negative divine assistance). In view of the principle of St. Thomas just cited, those who make such a distinction do not seem to have a very correct notion of just what inspiration is. An inspired book belongs totally to God and totally to the hagiographer, for the hagiographer contributed nothing to it apart from the influence of the Holy Spirit.[18] But since it is generally admitted that an effect is to be attributed purely and simply to its principal cause and only indirectly to the instrument used in its production, one is justified in calling God alone the Author of Scripture without further qualification.

It does not follow from the foregoing remarks that the obscurities, stylistic imperfections, barbarisms, etc., which can be found in Scripture, are to be attributed to the Holy Spirit. All of these things spring from a lack of perfect clarity in understanding the subject matter, from a lack of perfect order and elegance in arranging and expressing that matter. Since, then, they are not effects but defects, they can be attributed only to a fallible and defective source, and can consequently be traced to the hagiographer alone as their cause. Defects of this sort do not at all thwart the purpose of Scripture, the instruction of the faithful; hence the divine influence does not necessarily prevent them.

It would be quite unrealistic to deny that God could have chosen as His instrument a man of only average talent, endowed with relatively meager literary capabilities. God certainly could have chosen such a man and could have left his intellectual imperfections just as they were without taking steps to correct them. There would be nothing in the whole process unworthy of the God who, as a matter of fact, usually selects the weak things of the world to confound the strong. And if God really did pick out writers who had not too much to recommend them, and if He left them free to do a truly human, personal job, then the aforementioned imperfections were bound to follow. If Menuhin misplaced his Stradivarius and had to give a concert with a run-of-the-mill fiddle, one could hardly expect to hear a flawless performance.

However, while it is quite true that the imperfections of which we have been speaking are not traceable to God as their cause, it would not be quite correct to say that they found their way into His written word apart from His will. For since He freely selected less than perfect instruments and left them less than perfect, the defects in the finished product are indirectly traceable to His permissive will, inasmuch as He directly willed and caused the good to which they came attached.[19]

68 The obscurities and other imperfections presently under discussion are not to be put in the same class as errors in the strict sense. It is not a case of six of one and a half-dozen of another. Whatever is taught or really affirmed in Scripture is affirmed by God. But in all honesty one must admit that if God uses human mouthpieces, He can, without impugning His perfection, deliver a message which will be somewhat lacking in clarity, completeness, and elegance of presentation. On the other hand, the very idea of His teaching a false doctrine is unqualifiedly and absolutely repugnant, involving as it does an intrinsic contradiction. It would mean that God deceived us, lied to us, for in His case the assertion of something untrue would necessarily be a deliberate lie.

69 ## II. Analysis of Leo XIII's Definition of Inspiration

The foregoing considerations should make it easier to understand the description of inspiration given by Leo XIII in the

Providentissimus Deus: Inspiration is that *supernatural action of God on the hagiographers in accordance with which "He so moved and impelled them to write—He so assisted them when writing— that the things which He ordered, and those only, they, first, rightly understood, then willed faithfully to write down, and finally expressed in apt words and with infallible truth."*[20]

"The *action of God* on the hagiographers": this phrase is found equivalently in the words of Leo XIII: "For, by supernatural power, He so moved and impelled them to write, etc." This action, this positive influence, considered from the point of view of its principle, i.e., from the point of view of God, does not differ in any real way from the divine essence and is common to all three Persons alike, but it is usually appropriated to the Holy Spirit. In this discussion it is considered in itself, as it is received by the hagiographer and as it affects him.[21] As such it is a "power or an impression which has God as its source,"[22] existing incompletely and transiently in the hagiographer: a *gratia gratis data*, a charism, belonging to the general category of prophecy.

"*Supernatural*": surpassing the needs or exigencies of a created nature. Although it may be compared to that influence which God as the first Cause exercises on all the actions of secondary causes, it must be clearly distinguished therefrom. For God, as a result of the influence involved in inspiration, is not the *universal* cause of the effect, the written book, but its particular cause (not, of course, as its unique or total cause, but as its partial, its principal cause).

"*He so moved and impelled them to write—He so assisted them when writing.*" These words indicate an influence which both *precedes* and *accompanies* the action of the hagiographer as such, that is, the action of consigning to writing the word of God. This twofold influence is included in the notion of inspiration.

"*. . . that the things which He ordered, and those only, etc.*" This phrase states clearly what God's twofold influence caused in the hagiographers, namely that all those things which God ordered, and only those things, they *rightly understood*, then willed faithfully to write down, and finally *expressed* in apt words and with infallible truth.

Prescinding from the work of preparation, which can vary widely from author to author, the following three elements belong intrinsically to the actual composition of any book: that the author have an intellectual grasp of the matter to be treated, that he have the will to write it down, and finally that he give it written expression, either personally or with the help of a secretary. Keeping in mind all that has been said about the personal activity of the hagiographer, if God is to be the real principal author of the book, it is essential that the instrumental author fulfill the aforesaid three requirements under divine influence. This is why Leo XIII adds this remark to his description of inspiration: "Otherwise, it could not be said that He was the Author of the entire Scripture."

71 ". . . that . . . they, first, rightly understood." Here is the influence of God on the cognitive faculty; this influence is usually called the *illumination of the intellect.*

For the human mind actually to grasp the matter to be written down, two requirements must be fulfilled: (1) that the author have acquired or be now acquiring a knowledge of it; this is called technically the *grasp of the matter (acceptio rerum)*; (2) that his mind form the following judgment: "This matter is to be put into writing"; this is known technically as the *judgment concerning the matter grasped (judicium de acceptis)*. For God to be the principal Author of Scripture, it is not necessary that the hagiographer learn the things about which he is to write in a supernatural manner. He could have learned them by the exercise of his own mental faculties, by perceiving them with his senses, or through the testimony of others, provided that God enlightened his mind to make the following judgment: "These matters are to be consigned to writing." In other words, his reception of the subject matter need not be supernatural; it is enough that the judgment he passes on that matter be supernatural—whatever the source of his knowledge may have been. Consequently, as far as the human mind is concerned, inspiration in itself requires no more than that the hagiographer's intellect, after perhaps extensive and varied research on a natural level, be *raised and aided by divine light to judge that such and such things should be expressed in writing.*[23] It was by virtue of such a *temporary*, not permanent, elevation that God became the principal cause of these judgments and the hagiographer's mind the instrumental cause only.

It is our opinion that the hagiographers, aided by this divine light, passed judgment not only on the subject matter itself, but, in addition, on its arrangement and ordering, on the literary form they were to use, the style and words they would employ. If this be granted, then it seems necessary to hold that the divine light, while affecting primarily the intellect, had some influence on the other cognitive faculties as well, at least indirectly, as aids to the intellect. Such faculties would be, for example, the imagination and memory.

It is obvious that the practical judgment, "This material is to be written down and is to be expressed in this fashion and in these words," includes, or, if you prefer, presupposes a theoretical judgment bearing both on the truth of the matter to be asserted and on the aptness of the terms to be used in the assertion. It is impossible for the divinely aided mind to judge that the matter at hand is to be written and is to be couched in such and such terms without at the same time understanding it *correctly*, i.e., in accordance with truth, and *aptly*, i.e., with proper formulation.

It was affirmed above that inspiration *in itself* does not connote a supernatural acquisition of the matter. Sometimes, though, when there were things to be written which surpassed the hagiographer's natural intellectual powers, then a supernatural acquisition of the matter in question accompanied inspiration. It could likewise happen that the help of divine light sometimes directed even the hagiographer's preliminary research on points which he could have come to know quite naturally. But neither the former nor the latter belongs to the very nature of inspiration; in actual fact, such assistance preceded inspiration itself, chronologically and ontologically—or at least ontologically.

It should now be clear how any supernatural knowledge which is involved in inspiration is to be distinguished from revelation. *Revelation* (in the strict sense) makes known to a man a truth which is altogether unknown or inadequately known, and for this reason it necessarily connotes both a supernatural acquisition of the matter and a supernatural judgment thereof. *Inspiration* as such does not cause knowledge of new truths, it does not increase extensively the hagiographer's theoretical knowledge. Its formal effect is the practical judgment that this truth already known— whether naturally or through a revelation at least logically prior to inspiration—is to be written down. Still, it is not quite clear whether one should say that this supernatural *practical* judgment implicitly contains a similarly supernatural *theoretical* judgment concerning the truth of the matter or that rather it corroborates in a divine way a theoretical judgment already formed by the hagiographer. Nonetheless, insofar as the influence of inspiration affects the intellect, it can be called revelation in the wide sense, i.e., to the extent that we understand by the term "revelation" any divinely caused knowledge. For surely the practical judgment, as it has just been described, would fall in this class. But when all is said and done, it would be much better to keep the two terms, revelation and inspiration, sharply separate. They are too easily confused in the minds of many, and this confusion has been the fruitful source of untold misconceptions and needless difficulties.

73 "*That . . . they . . . willed faithfully to write down.*" This is God's *action on the will*. By it God, who produces all effects efficaciously yet gently, brings it about that the hagiographer wills to write whatever the divine light has shown him must be written, and wills to write it in that fashion in which he has judged it should be written.

This is, furthermore, a *physical* influence which affects the volitional faculty directly. If God moved the will only morally, i.e., by proposing some attractive incentive, then not God but the hagiographer would be the real principal cause of the will act.

The will to write partly precedes and partly follows the intellectual grasp of the matter to be written. First comes the general intention, so to speak, of composing this book. Moved by this intention, the author starts thinking about and lining up the things he will write, and finally decides to write down the individual elements as he has conceived them in his mind. In the case of a sacred writer, not only the final act of the will, which is really not single but multiple, but also that first decision which definitively started the whole chain of mind and will acts, is to be attributed to the influence of God. The fact that some hagiographers undertook the task of writing at the urging and pleas of interested parties alters the situation not a bit. This moral influence of men on the hagiographer's will by no means excludes the physical influence of God. Since He left His instruments free to act in a truly human and personal way, it is altogether in keeping with the notion of inspiration that the individual hagiographer, under the action of God, should make a decision to write which would fit his own disposition and the circumstances in which he lived. Some hagiographers thus decided to write after personal deliberation, while others were prompted by the pleas or advice of those about them.

74 "*That . . . they . . . expressed in apt words and with infallible truth.*" Here is the divine *influence on the external execution* of the

work, on the actual transfer of the matter from the mind of the author to a book by writing—or by dictation to a secretary. This transfer directly involves the executive faculties, the hands, the eyes, perhaps the mouth. For this external work of writing to proceed from God as principal cause, there is no need that He act directly on the executive faculties. By the very fact that these faculties are put into operation at the command of the divinely supported will and under the direction of the divinely enlightened intellect, they really do perform their function as the end result of a divine impulse and as directed by God. It seems superfluous to require a special divine "assistance" for the execution of the work really distinct from the enlightening of the mind and the moving of the will, which latter phenomena would not only precede but also accompany the act of writing. If anyone wants to call the divine influence preceding the external expression "inspiration" and the influence accompanying that expression "assistance," thus distinguishing *in biblical inspiration, inspiration in the strict sense* and *assistance*—understood as a positive help, a real influence—then he is merely quibbling about terminology.

Corollary 75

Did the sacred writers *realize* they were inspired? A natural question. It is certain that such a realization is not strictly demanded by the nature of inspiration. In view of the fact that the divine action itself surpasses sense and even intellectual perception, and since the hagiographers were moved by God to perform an action that was genuinely human, they could have found out only through revelation that they were being inspired. Whether in fact they were always conscious of their situation is not so clear. If it is true, as intimated above, that the primitive Church knew that all writings composed by the apostles in fulfillment of apostolic functions were inspired, then it is all the more to be supposed that the apostles themselves were aware of their personal inspiration. Theologians, with the exception of some recent writers, usually hold as more probable the view that the hagiographers were conscious of the divine influence, on the grounds that this seems more fitting for an intelligent instrument. Others infer from 2 Maccabees 2:20-33; 15:38-40; Luke 1:1-3, that at least these authors were unaware of their inspiration. It would be hard to prove either opinion.[24]

III. The Problem of Verbal Inspiration

76 The solution of the question of *verbal inspiration* is based on the foregoing considerations.

It is possible to distinguish in any book the formal part, the *contents or message*, and the material part, the *words and literary structure*. Those who acknowledge the inspired character of all Scripture necessarily hold that inspiration affects at least all of the formal part, that all the affirmations or judgments contained therein proceed from inspiration.[25] This is called *real inspiration*.[26] But not all are in agreement on the material part. How does inspiration affect the very words used by the author—or does it at all? This is the problem of *verbal inspiration*.[27]

77 *Real inspiration alone.* During the last century there was a strong opinion that the literary form, style, and choice of words were all to be attributed not to God, but to the hagiographer as their principal cause. In this view, God would have, by a negative assistance, guarded against inept expressions and would sometimes have furnished the words themselves, whenever this was required for the accurate formulation of an inspired assertion.[28]

There can be no question of the admissibility of this opinion on dogmatic grounds, for real inspiration together with the assistance just described suffices to justify calling God the Author of all Scripture. Its proponents infer from this that verbal inspiration is a gratuitous assumption. Furthermore, they support their stand by pointing to passages in which the hagiographers are described as working in a perfectly natural way.[29] They appeal also to the fact that their opinion offers an explanation for the diversity of styles and for the literary imperfections we have mentioned.[30]

78 *Verbal inspiration* (in addition to *real*) can be understood in two ways. The term is sometimes used to mean that God dictated every single word, almost like a professor dictating notes, leaving to the writer just the mechanical work of writing. At other times it is used to mean that the same divine influence on the intellect and the will which caused the hagiographer to form a mental judgment of the matter to be written and to will to write it down caused him at the same time to conceive and to will to write that matter in this precise literary form. This influence left to the human authors a genuinely personal activity with regard both to the thoughts which were to be given written expression and, all the more, to the literary form and the specific words they were to use.

Verbal inspiration *in the former sense,* once proposed by many Protestants[31] and by some Catholics, is clearly untenable and is now universally rejected. But taken *in the latter sense* it seems much more probable, and at the present it is finding more and more adherents. That is why we consistently presumed its truth in the foregoing exposition.

This opinion (a) fulfills more adequately the definition of the Vatican Council that the books of our Bible are sacred "because, *written under the inspiration of the Holy Spirit,* they have God for their author." It ties in quite nicely, too, with Leo XIII's assertion that "the Holy Spirit employed men as *instruments*"[32] (b) It corresponds better with the traditional view of inspiration. Although the fathers did not treat this question specifically, most of their remarks are of such a nature that they could hardly be squared with the theory of real inspiration alone—were it the true one. (c) It is more reasonable. Obviously, unless God suspended the laws of psychology, He could not have inspired all the judgments to be expressed without by that very action influencing the choice of words by which those judgments were to be expressed. Finally, (d) it offers a satisfactory explanation for all those characteristics of Scripture to which its opponents usually appeal: the great diversity of style, literary defects, different ways in which the same fact is related or the same speech is recorded, the human toil expended by the writers, etc.

The main *objections* are: (1) The fathers often state that it is not the words of Scripture which count but the meaning they convey. Of course! In our opinion, too (that of verbal inspiration), the words are merely vehicles of thought, and inspiration affects them not for their own sake, but for the sake of the thought they express. (2) If even the words are inspired, then it is only the original autograph which is inspired, and translations of it cannot be called the "word of God" and "Scripture" in the full sense. In answer, it should be pointed out that the words of a translation differ from those of the original only materially, not formally. The meaning they convey remains the same, and so a translation is still unqualifiedly the word of God and Scripture, although not in the same absolute sense as the original text. Is not a sentence of Chrysostom's, translated into Latin, still called the word of Chrysostom, purely and simply? Translations of the original Scriptures are quite accurately described as being "mediately inspired."

IV. All Genuine Scripture Is the Word of God

80

The first conclusion to follow from the correct notion of inspiration is that *everything contained in a genuine passage of Scripture is the word of God*. This conclusion is rather obvious. God is the author of all Scripture and whatever is written in any book is the work of its author. Furthermore, this conclusion, that what is contained in Scripture is the word of God, is stated in the sources of revelation at least as explicitly as is the true notion of inspiration, according to which God is the principal author of Scripture. This furnishes a ready and telling answer against those who try so to water down the formula, "God is the *author* of Scripture" that they succeed only in perverting it.

Now just as any human author can report in his book the words of others, cite letters, or copy historical narratives from other sources without approving or corroborating them, so too could God through His hagiographers. Just as any ordinary author can tell his readers what he once thought on such and such a subject and what he now thinks without asserting that his opinion is necessarily the right one, so, too, God could have the hagiographer describe what he—not as God's instrument, precisely, but as a private individual —felt, thought, feared, etc. That is why all theologians distinguish in Scripture passages which are the words of God extrinsically or *only by reason of their having been written under inspiration*,[33] and those which are the words of God intrinsically, *in themselves,* or by reason of their content. The latter would be those passages which express the meaning of God Himself. It is evident that those statements which are the word of God only extrinsically do not enjoy divine authority, except to the extent that they are approved by Him.

81

It is, however, quite difficult to determine in individual cases just which passages of Scripture are the word of God intrinsically, or which enjoy divine authority by only scriptural approval. Here are some general criteria:[34]

a. *Everything which the hagiographer as such* (i.e., as God's instrument or—what amounts to the same thing—formally as the co-author of this book) *really affirms* and teaches is the word of God intrinsically.[35] But whenever the sacred author reports what he as a private individual felt or said or at present feels or says, we have an intrinsically human word. Examples of the latter would be prayers, curses,[36] doubts,[37] expressions of confidence, of love, of sorrow, advice,[38] greetings, etc.

b. Anything recorded in Scripture as said *by God, by Christ, by angels, or by men actually*[39] *performing a divinely imposed task* (prophets and apostles in the exercise of their office) or *speaking under genuine divine inspiration*, is intrinsically the word of God.

c. Those statements enjoy divine authority which are recorded in Scripture as uttered by men but *approved by God*; approbation by the *hagiographer as such* is equivalent to divine approval.[40] However, general approval of extended discourses does not necessarily include individual statements not contributing to the central theme of such a discourse.

Whether the feelings, emotions, and words of the hagiographer himself as a man (see a. above), by the very fact that they are written under a divine influence, are also approved by *God*, must be determined from the circumstances. It is, of course, clear that the personal sentiments to which, for example, the psalmists gave expression under inspiration, are accordingly approved (unless the contrary is clear in a particular instance), since God's obvious intention in having them recorded was to give people a model and to stir up in them similar sentiments.

For the rest, it should be noted that although God cannot approve anything morally wrong, He could inspire men to record things not quite perfect, and could approve the same, especially in the Old Dispensation, when religious knowledge and standards of morality were as yet quite a bit below the perfection of the Christian Dispensation.[41]

d. When the aforementioned approval is lacking, divine authority cannot be claimed for scriptural statements made by men who were not inspired, pious and holy though they may have been. Nor is the assertion that So-and-so was full of the Holy Spirit in itself a sufficient guarantee that each and every utterance of his is to be considered inspired.[42]

V. All Genuine Scripture Is Infallibly True 82

The second conclusion to follow from the correct notion of inspiration is that *everything contained in a genuine passage of Scripture is infallibly true*. Obviously this assertion applies only to what is intrinsically the word of God or is approved by God, and to the extent that it is so approved. But as applied thereto, the assertion is so certain that one could not deny it without falling into error on a matter of faith. To make a long story short, here are the words of Leo XIII, an authoritative statement of the Catholic position: [43]

> But it is absolutely wrong and forbidden either to narrow inspiration to certain parts only of Holy Scripture or to admit that the sacred writer has erred. . . .
> For all the books which the Church receives as sacred and canonical are written wholly and entirely, with all their parts, at the dictation of the Holy Spirit; and so far is it from being possible that any error can coexist with inspiration, that inspiration not only is essentially incompatible with error, but excludes and rejects it as absolutely and necessarily as it is impossible that God Himself, the supreme Truth, can utter that which is not true. . . . Hence, because the Holy Spirit employed men as his instruments, we cannot, therefore, say that it was these inspired instruments, who, perchance, have fallen into error, and not the primary author. . . . It follows [from the correct notion of inspiration, which the fathers have consistently ratified] that those who maintain that an error is possible in any genuine passage of the sacred writings either pervert the Catholic notion of inspiration or make God the author of such error. And so emphatically were all the Fathers and Doctors agreed that the divine writings, as left by the hagiographers, are free from all error, that they labored earnestly, with no less skill than reverence, to reconcile with each other those numerous passages which seem at variance—the very passages which in great measure have been taken up by the "higher criticism"; for they were unanimous in laying it down that those writings, in their entirety and in all their parts were equally from the *afflatus* of Almighty God, and that God, speaking by the sacred writers, could not set down anything but what was true. The words of St. Augustine to St. Jerome may sum up what they taught:
> "On my own part I confess to your charity that it is only to those books of Scripture which are now called canonical that I have learned to pay such honor and reverence as to believe most firmly that none of their writers has fallen into any error. And if in these books I meet anything which seems contrary to truth, I shall not hesitate to conclude either that the text is faulty, or that the translator has not expressed the meaning of the passage, or that I myself do not understand." [44]

The following remarks are aimed at a correct understanding of the Catholic teaching on the inerrancy of Scripture and at pointing out the way for the solution of difficulties arising from that teaching.

Error in the strict sense, *formal error*, can be found only in an expressed judgment, and is present whenever an author affirms something of a subject which is not verified in that subject, or denies something which is verified therein. Now no author ever expresses a real judgment or really affirms anything, except *when and to the extent* that he intends to affirm it. Obviously the intention we have in mind here is not merely internal, but an intention which the actual words, against the background of the context and other circumstances surrounding their composition, reveal.[45]

Now God is the author of Scripture through the medium of a human author who formed a correct mental concept of, willed to write down faithfully, and expressed fittingly and with infallible truth, all those things and only those things which God ordered. Consequently, whenever there is question of a hagiographer's acting precisely as such, and his literal meaning alone is being sought,[46] we can confidently say that *God willed to affirm or to teach through Scripture all those things and only those things which His secondary author really intended to affirm in the passage under study*—no more, no less.[47]

Now to determine what the secondary author did in fact intend to teach, it is first of all necessary to establish what *literary form* he used. It is evident that statements which would be false in a scientific treatise or in a strictly historical work could not be labeled as errors if the author intended to use everyday language, to write a poetic description, to compose a parable, *midrash*,[48] or apocalypse, to write an idealized history, to record a popular tradition, or to quote a source which may not be reliable in detail, etc.

While it is the Church's right to pass final judgment on everything touching faith and morals, the determination of the literary form falls within the province of the art of literary criticism, the principles of which are too involved to be treated here. However, great care must be taken to *avoid two extremes*. First of all, no book or part of a book which is written in the historical form is to be hastily labeled nonhistorical or historical in the loose sense only, *just because the text presents some problems*. Secondly, *no literary form which is acceptable in itself is to be excluded from Sacred Scripture without further ado just because it does not square with our present moral standards* or is in our opinion not quite seemly. When God took on men to write as His instruments, He took them just as they were and adjusted His influence to their mentality and customs. When He chose a man of the Near East in, say, the fifth or second century B.C., He had him write in the manner in which Near Easterners of the time normally wrote. What we may think today about that manner of writing is quite beside the point.

85 God's purpose in inspiring was not to communicate to men the sum total of all possible truth, but to teach religion. Matters which are not in themselves religious are inspired only for the sake of getting a religious truth across more effectively. It was consequently not at all necessary for the hagiographers to be divinely instructed about non-religious subjects like physics, history, literature, upon which they touched in the course of their writing. They could have entertained ideas on these subjects as imperfect and even as erroneous as were those of their contemporaries, provided that they refrained from making a formal erroneous assertion about them in the sacred text.

86 1. Without doing any harm to the inerrancy of Scripture, the sacred writers could have used all kinds of *metaphors,* of which the oriental genius is so fond, and nothing stood in the way of their sometimes using *mythological beings* as part of their imagery.[49] Can a writer be convicted of believing in myths just because he describes a sot as having sacrificed a bit too generously to Bacchus? They could likewise have used hyperbole, even of the more extensive type.[50] Is a writer guilty of lying or deceit when he says of a secret indiscreetly bruited about through a few villages: "Now the whole world knows it!"?

2. Without the least detriment to the inerrancy of Scripture, the sacred writers could have described natural phenomena according to their *external appearances* and according to the usual manner of speaking based on those appearances.[51] Thus they said, for example, that the sun rose, moved around the earth,[52] that the earth always stood firm;[53] they spoke of the moon as if it were larger than all of the stars;[54] they described the sky sometimes as a tent stretched over the earth,[55] sometimes as a solid roof above which the waters were collected ready to fall during the rainy sea-

son when "God opens the floodgates of heaven."[56] It makes no difference whether the hagiographers recognized these forms of expression as inaccurate and poetical or not. Whatever may have been their own private opinions about the real nature or workings of these things, they certainly did not intend to *teach* anything about them, but rather used common or poetical terms and descriptions as vehicles for the expression of the truths which were the real object of their assertions.

3. In much the same way, when the hagiographers treated *secular subjects*, they could use expressions based on the erroneous opinions of their day. For although it is apparent from these expressions that the sacred writers shared the errors common to the age in which they lived, it does not at all follow that they affirmed these errors in Scripture. If one will only take the trouble to discover the sacred author's intention, he will find that the expression which smacks of error is in reality only the vehicle for the assertion of a truth. It is rather apparent from the description of Genesis 1:3–18 that the author of the creation account considered the sequence of day and night a phenomenon independent of the sun. Nevertheless, what he affirms in these verses is simply this, that all things, light, the sequence of day and night, the sun, etc., owe their existence to God. Several modern exegetes explain Jude 14–15 in somewhat the same manner. It would be difficult to deny that the Apostle used the apocryphal Book of Henoch[57] in writing these verses. It seems perfectly justifiable to conclude that he shared the esteem which his contemporaries held for this book and that he may even have considered it authentic. But strictly speaking, St. Jude teaches nothing in this passage but the following, that the same threat of divine judgment hangs over false teachers as was frequently expressed in the Book of Henoch and attributed therein to this patriarch whom all know as the "seventh after Adam." The very epithet, "seventh after Adam," may well have been taken from the apocryphal work.[58] But one should not be too quick to assert that the word *epropheteusen* (he prophesied) necessarily indicates genuine prophecy; does not St. Paul himself quote a secular author, calling him a "prophet" in the bargain?[59]

With all due reverence for inerrancy, a hagiographer no less than a secular author could *pose as someone else*, so long as he used such a literary fiction for an honorable purpose and not to trick his readers, and so long as he used it in such a way that his readers would not necessarily be duped. On these grounds, recent exegetes hold that while the authors of Wisdom and Ecclesiastes wrote in the name of Solomon, they were in reality anonymous authors of a later age.[60]

89   It is quite certain that the sacred writers did not always approve the contents of the documents they reproduced or explicitly cited in their works. The author of 2 Maccabees relates the death of Antiochus Epiphanes[61] in such a way as to make it clear that the letter of the Palestinian Jews cited by him[62] is to be taken with a grain of salt on this point. The following rule may be safely laid down: *a hagiographer gives no guarantee for the documents and speeches which he quotes quite unqualifiedly* (with no sign of disapproval) *but explicitly, except when and to the extent that he approves them, either formally or equivalently.*

It must be granted that there are in Scripture also tacit or *implicit citations;* in other words, that the hagiographers at times take excerpts from sources or reproduce secular sources without giving any indication of the fact. And one would not be wrong in suggesting that contemporary readers could often have spotted such borrowings much more easily than we can now. It must be acknowledged that the sacred writers could, from time to time, cite implicitly the works of secular authors without giving blanket approval to every statement in the citation.[63] But the presumption will be that they did not cite them in this fashion. That is why the Pontifical Biblical Commission was justified in declaring that one should not appeal to implicit citations in order to solve difficulties involving scriptural inerrancy unless

> it can be proved by solid arguments, first, that the sacred writer really does cite another's sayings or writings; and secondly, that he does not intend, in so doing, to approve them or make them his own, in such a way that he be rightly considered not to speak in his own name.[64]

It should be noted in addition that while apodictic arguments are required for a really certain conclusion, genuinely probable indications may be enough to establish a prudent doubt. In any event, one would certainly exceed all bounds who admitted non-approved citations in the Old Testament so frequently as to undermine thereby the very fabric of sacred history.

SACRED SCRIPTURE

Some Catholic authors claim (a) that some books of the Bible which are to all external appearances historical or prophetic are really so either not at all or only in their broad framework (Job, Judith, Tobias, Jonas, Esther, Daniel);[65] (b) that the first part of Genesis, at least up to the story of Abraham, contains popular traditions, only the substance of which the sacred author intended to approve as true;[66] (c) that in some places, like the book of Judges, we have idealized history, i.e., historical facts, to be sure, but rather freely narrated and artificially arranged, with a view to establishing a definite thesis; (d) that in general the Old Testament was little concerned with strict accuracy in matters of secondary importance and in accessory circumstances, and that in fact it sometimes intended to do hardly anything but report events as they were found in annals and in other sources whose complete veracity it was impossible to check.[67] Finally, (e) some add that even in the New Testament certain historical narratives, at least in matters of detail, betray their dependence on sources or various traditions which the individual sacred authors used, and that the evangelists did not always intend to stamp with the seal of their authority every last detail of events narrated.

Prudent discretion is called for in passing judgment on such opinions, which some defend with great assurance and others bitterly assail. The words of Bainvel are worth recalling:

> Although by means of and subsequent to the decree *Lamentabili* and the encyclical *Pascendi* many obscurities were cleared up and the thoughts of many hearts laid bare, it remains true that, even among outstanding Catholics, several points are not yet quite clear. The difficulty, however, seems to lie in the application of the principles rather than in the principles themselves, in strictly scientific questions of criticism and exegesis rather than in formally theological questions. This difficulty is enhanced by the suspicions of those who, with little knowledge of critical and exegetical matters, start screaming that theological principles are in jeopardy every time a new explanation is suggested, and by the rashness of those who, if a proposal is made by well-informed experts, immediately begin, unlike the experts, to doubt the principles themselves.[68]

It is to be noted, first of all, that there is a great difference between the opinions of Catholics and the claims of Modernists and rationalists on the same subject. Thus, for instance, Lagrange, in setting forth his view of the first chapters of Genesis, teaches that it is possible to distinguish essential and nonessential elements, the doctrine taught and the literary dress in which the doctrine is presented. Actual facts form the basis of that doctrine, but these facts are described in figurative language.[69]

> The first chapter of Genesis affirms and teaches real facts, and it teaches them in the strict sense of the term. This first page of Scripture, then, contains a series of affirmations about real facts, and, as far as the facts are concerned, everything is to be understood quite literally. They are not an allegory, much less a myth born of the author's imagination, . . . but as for a work of six days' duration, this is in our opinion evident allegory.[70]

In the narrative of the first sin, the substance of that narrative is in perfect harmony with the Catholic dogma of original sin, but some details of the story may be interpreted rather freely, since they have no necessary connection with this doctrine and serve merely as a vehicle for its expression.

> Rationalists . . . deny that there is any such thing as revelation or inspiration or Holy Scripture at all; they see, instead, only the forgeries and the falsehoods of men; they set down the Scripture narratives as stupid fables and lying stories: the prophecies and the oracles of God are to them either predictions made up after the event or forecasts formed by the light of nature; the miracles and the wonders of God's power are not what they are said to be, but the startling effects of natural law, or else mere tricks and myths.[71]

Thus Loisy was of the opinion that when Christian exegetes interpreted Sacred Scripture, and especially the Old Testament, they always added something to the strictly literal meaning, and that, as a result, in determining the meaning of the sacred author himself one should ignore traditional commentaries, since these latter incorporated ideas which were the result of centuries of elaboration. This opinion rests on a fundamental error, namely, that something can be historically true but dogmatically false, and *vice versa*.[72]

91a   As a help to the easier avoidance of Modernist errors in the

SACRED SCRIPTURE

matter at hand, the following statements condemned by the decree *Lamentabili* should be very carefully noted:

> 3. "It can be gathered from ecclesiastical judgments and censures passed against free and more learned exegesis, that the faith proposed by the Church contradicts history, and that Catholic dogmas cannot in fact be reconciled with the truer origins of the Christian religion." (DB 2003).
>
> 12. "If the exegete wishes to apply himself advantageously to biblical studies, he should rid himself especially of any preconceived notion of the supernatural origin of Sacred Scripture, and should interpret it just as he would other merely human documents." (DB 2012).
>
> 14. "In many narratives the Evangelists recounted not so much what was true, as what they thought would be more profitable for the reader, even though false" (DB 2014).
>
> 23. "Opposition can and actually does exist between facts which are narrated in Sacred Scripture, and the dogmas of the Church based on them, so that a critic can reject as false, facts which the Church holds as most certain" (DB 2023).
>
> 24. "An exegete is not to be censured who constructs premises from which it follows that dogmas are historically false or dubious, provided he does not directly deny the dogmas themselves" (DB 2024).
>
> 61. "It can be stated absolutely that no chapter of Scripture, from the first of Genesis to the last of the Apocalypse, contains doctrine entirely identical with that which the Church teaches on the same subject, and that, as a result, no chapter of Scripture has the same meaning for the critic as for the theologian" (DB 2061).

91b All agree that both *allegory* and *parable* are of frequent occurrence in the Bible and that, through its minutely accurate description of background details, a parable sometimes uses the historical form so convincingly that it seems to be real history (e.g., the parable of Dives and Lazarus). May not allegory and parable be so extended as to cover a whole book of the Bible? Considering what has been said about the use of literary forms customary among authors of antiquity, there can be good reason to wonder whether a certain narrative is to be understood as strict history, as the words in their obvious sense seem to indicate, or whether in fact the hagiographer, with some special purpose in mind, is only making use of stories whose historical worth he does not guarantee. It is certainly not antecedently impossible for a sacred author to use for his own purposes popular stories, just as he uses everyday forms of speech, metaphors, anthropomorphisms, and the like. It is one thing to use such material as the vehicle for the expression of a truth, and quite another to affirm that the material itself jibes with reality.[73]

Opinions such as the above cannot be effectively and completely refuted in every instance by an appeal to a contrary theological or patristic tradition. In order to prove something on the basis of the way tradition has understood it, one must establish the existence of an at least morally universal agreement and the fact that it is a matter having to do with faith and morals.[74] Even granting such unanimous agreement, it is no easy matter to show that the new opinions in every case of concrete application touch upon matters of faith and morals. It is not enough to say that the fathers did not defend the inerrancy of Scripture in this fashion, for where merely literary questions are involved, the necessary requirements of faith are fulfilled if the inerrancy of Scripture is safeguarded. That it be safeguarded in this or that manner makes no essential difference.

92 On the other hand, and still with an eye on the demands made by the faith, new opinions labor under this serious difficulty, namely, that they must overthrow the legitimate presumption based on the external literary form of the books, on the obvious sense of those books, and on the traditional view of them. Hence they may not be prudently espoused unless they are backed up by good, solid arguments. In matters like these one must be wary of sweeping generalizations which may rest on very shaky foundations. However, in the past half and especially in the past quarter century, Catholic exegetes have come to believe that the good, solid arguments not formerly available are now at hand. An increasingly thorough knowledge of the literary forms of the ancient Near East has been made possible by the discovery of the literatures of those times and places, and, especially under the urging of Pius XII in the *Divino afflante Spiritu,* Catholic scholars have pushed their investigation of the sacred text with vigor, intelligence, and abundant fruit.[75] Their patiently worked out views on the composition of the Pentateuch, of Deutero-Isaias, on the literary forms of Jonas, Tobias, Judith, Daniel, etc., are a real boon to the correct understanding of the word of God, even if they may appear at first blush almost heterodox to those who have not followed recent developments in the field. The solid conclusions reached by Catholic scholars have had at least the tacit approval of the Biblical Commission. And on the occasion of the publication of the new *Enchiridion Biblicum* in 1955, a quasi-official clarification of the status of the Commission's decrees was given by its Secretary and Under-Secretary in the *Benediktinische Monatschrift* and the *Antonianum* respectively. For a splendid discussion of this clarification, see the aforementioned article of E. F. Siegman.[76] Particularly noteworthy are these paragraphs of Father Siegman's article:

> The distinction which Fathers Miller and Kleinhans make between decisions that are in some way connected with truths of faith and morals and those that treat questions of literary and textual criticism is perfectly natural. As Dom Dupont observes, questions of authorship, date of composition, and integrity no longer have the crucial importance attached to them fifty years ago. Today it is clearly seen that these questions are independent of the inspiration and inerrancy of the text. Fortunately, emphasis has shifted to more positive preoccupations, particularly the fuller study of the text itself. Time that a few decades ago was spent in class on introductory problems . . . can now be utilized in reading and explaining the text.
>
> We should not be so naive as to look for a wholesale abandonment by Catholics of the positions enunciated in the Decisions of the Biblical Commission, as a result of the latest statements of the Secretary and Under-Secretary of the Commission. If conservatism in biblical scholarship means clinging doggedly to traditional positions, however convincing the contrary evidence, it can be only stagnation. If, however, conservatism means a reluctance to foresake these positions until the evidence is in, until the atmosphere is sufficiently cleared so that the scholar can see the cogency of the contrary position, then it represents a wholesome current that promotes progress in truth. This is the conservatism which the Church's magisterium expects of us. Dom Dupont closes his analysis with an observation that all Catholic scholars will second: "Let us hope that by their serious and conscientious labor Catholic exegetes will justify the confidence which the Church's magisterium has placed in them."[77]

The following sentence of Leo XIII's in the *Providentissimus Deus* was the occasion of much subsequent wrangling: "The principles here laid down will apply to cognate sciences, and especially to history."⁷⁸ Some understood the Holy Father to mean that, just as the hagiographers followed external appearances in describing natural phenomena, so too, in historical matters, they often followed current opinions and used available sources without bothering to ascertain their objective truth. On this basis they wanted the "principle of the Broad School" to be considered as canonized by Leo XIII. They were, however, mistaken. The words, "the principles here laid down," do not refer specifically to the phrase which mentions the outward appearance of natural phenomena. They refer rather in a general way to the suggestions made about difficulties arising from the physical sciences. It is these suggestions which are said to be applicable to related fields, and, of course, not in the same way to each and every one of them.⁷⁹

93   One simply cannot maintain that the physical sciences and history are essentially the same. If an author is not writing a strictly scientific treatise—and the authors of Scripture certainly were not—then in speaking of natural phenomena he may justifiably be presumed to be using ordinary, rather loose, terminology such as is based on the outward appearance of things. And it makes no difference whether or not he knows that the outward appearance does not correspond to reality. However, if an author relates certain facts in a book whose ultimate aim is religious instruction, but which is at the same time historical, he is certainly presumed to be intent upon reporting objective reality. This one point may be conceded: a sacred writer whose concern in writing books which are really and surely historical is primarily edification and only secondarily historical truth, may quite conceivably have treated historical facts a bit more nonchalantly than an out-and-out historiographer would, or he may have simply recorded certain secondary details as he found them in his sources without meaning to vouch for their reality. This may be granted more readily in the case of the hagiographer, but that is all. For in order to assert with confidence or to regard as probable that such a procedure was actually followed in any given case, one needs solid arguments or at least some genuinely impressive indications. True, some claim that the "law of history" in the early days was simply to relate facts just as they stood in the sources or in popular opinion, *keeping to*

oneself one's personal judgment as to their objective truth. But this cannot be satisfactorily proved, and it does not seem to square with the frank credulity of the ancients. It is, of course, a well-known fact that St. Jerome wrote some things which would give no little support to the claim under discussion if, in the mind of the great Doctor, they had the universal scope which, taken all by themselves, they seem to have.[80] But St. Jerome's teaching, integrally considered, and his constant care to safeguard the objective truth of Scripture even in accessory details certainly do not favor this new school of thought.[81] For the rest, in a question like this, which has not yet been clearly answered, a certain fluctuation of opinion should occasion little surprise.[82]

Quite reasonably, then, the Pontifical Biblical Commission has decreed that books which are generally accepted as historical are to be presumed historical in the strict sense and objectively true until:

> it can be proved by solid arguments that the sacred writer did not intend to give a true and strict history, but proposed rather to set forth, under the guise and form of history, a parable or an allegory or some meaning distinct from the strictly literal or historical signification of the words.[83]

It would seem advisable to view sweeping generalizations with respectful caution and to judge new opinions in the light of their applicability to individual cases, i.e., to see how they work out when applied to individual books of Scripture or to individual passages. This is a task belonging properly to the domain of Scripture scholars. One cannot deny that really solid arguments are often at hand;[84] but in many cases those alleged amount to little more than probable indications, and at times they amount hardly even to that. The experts who are sincerely trying to advance Catholic scholarship in the field of criticism should continue their patient efforts to construct arguments which will support, if at all possible, their respective theories. Meanwhile, both they and professional theologians should refrain from passing judgments which are too absolute and general.

Since the *magisterium* of the Church is the supreme guide in such matters, it may be well to give here the decree of the Pontifical Biblical Commission (June 30, 1909) on the historical character of the first three chapters of Genesis.

(81)

THE SOURCES OF REVELATION

1. *False Exegesis.*—Whether the various exegetical systems, which have been elaborated and defended by the aid of a science falsely so called, for the purpose of excluding the literal historical sense of the first three chapters of Genesis, are based upon solid arguments.

Answer: In the negative.

2. *Historical Character of the Three Chapters.*—Whether we may, in spite of the character and historic form of the book of Genesis, of the close connection of the first three chapters with one another and with those which follow, of the manifold testimony of the Scriptures both of the Old and the New Testament, of the almost unanimous opinion of the Fathers, and of the traditional view which—transmitted also by the Jewish people—has always been held by the Church, teach that the three aforesaid chapters do not contain the narrative of things which actually happened, a narrative which corresponds to objective reality and historic truth; and whether we may teach that these chapters contain fables derived from mythologies and cosmologies belonging to older nations, but purified of all polytheistic error and accomodated to monotheistic teaching by the sacred author or that they contain allegories and symbols destitute of any foundation in objective reality but presented under the garb of history for the purpose of inculcating religious and philosophical truth; or, finally, that they contain legends partly historical and partly fictitious, freely handled for the instruction and edification of souls.

Answer: In the negative.

3. *Historical Character of Certain Parts.*—Whether, in particular we may call in question the literal and historical meaning where there is question of facts narrated in these chapters which touch the fundamental teachings of the Christian religion, as for example, the creation of man, the formation of the first woman from man, the unity of the human race, the original happiness of our first parents in a state of justice, integrity, and immortality, the divine command laid upon man to prove his obedience, the transgression of that divine command at the instigation of the devil under the form of a serpent, the fall of our first parents from their primitive state of innocence, and the promise of a future Redeemer.

Answer: In the negative.

4. *Interpretation.*—Whether, in interpreting those passages of

these chapters which the Fathers and Doctors have interpreted in divers ways without leaving us anything definite or certain, anyone may, subject to the decision of the Church and following the analogy of faith, follow and defend that opinion at which he has prudently arrived.

Answer: In the affirmative.

5. *Literal Sense.*—Whether all and each of the parts, namely the single words and phrases, in these chapters must always and of necessity be interpreted in a literal sense, so that it is never lawful to deviate from it, even when expressions are manifestly used figuratively, that is, metaphorically or anthropomorphically, and when reason forbids us to hold, or necessity impels us to depart from, the literal sense.

Answer: In the negative.

6. *Allegory and Prophecy.*—Whether, granting always the literal and historical sense, the allegorical and prophetical interpretation of certain passages of these chapters—an interpretation justified by the example of the Fathers and the Church—may be prudently and usefully applied.

Answer: In the affirmative.

7. *Scientific Expression.*—Whether, since it was not the intention of the sacred author, when writing the first chapter of Genesis, to teach us in a scientific manner the innermost nature of visible things, and to present the complete order of creation but rather to furnish his people with a popular account, such as the common parlance of that age allowed, one, namely, adapted to the senses and to man's intelligence, we are strictly and always bound, when interpreting these chapters to seek for scientific exactitude of expression.

Answer: In the negative.

8. *Yom.*—Whether the word Yom (day), which is used in the first chapter of Genesis to describe and distinguish the six days, may be taken in its strict sense as the natural day, or in a less strict sense as signifying a certain space of time; and whether free discussion of this question is permitted to interpreters.

Answer: In the affirmative.[85]

It is the task of biblical exegetes to explain in detail the force and meaning of this decree. One thing should be pointed out here, and that is that not all the questions to which the first three chapters of Genesis give rise were solved by the decree just quoted; many points are still under discussion. Moreover, not everything which is not explicitly ruled out is thereby permitted, nor is everything which is not explicitly permitted thereby proscribed.[86]

95 *Scholion. Inspiration and critical authenticity.*

It is one thing to ask whether a book is inspired and another to ask whether it was written throughout by that author to whom it is usually ascribed. The fact of inspiration alone does not *of itself* solve the question of the identity and date of the hagiographer or the question of the process of composition. Was the book written throughout by one man or did several collaborate in its production; was it perhaps given its initial form by one man and then expanded by another, or is its present form, the inspired character of which we believe on faith, the work of a later editor, etc.?[87]

The dogma of inspiration, however, can *indirectly* solve the question of human authorship, or can at least influence that solution.

1. When an inspired author definitely affirms that he or someone else wrote this or that book, his testimony must be accepted as infallibly true, by virtue of inspiration. But mark well the words, "*definitely*—not just apparently—*affirms*"; for (a) it is not impossible that the sacred writer was using the literary device of pseudonymity (the book of Wisdom, for example);[88] (b) in the matter of quotations it may be that the hagiographer was quoting a work under the name currently attached to it without intending to pass judgment on the question of real authorship. Thus, for example, St. Paul's words, "*So Isaias says*"—Rom. 10:16 and 20, and the equivalent expression of John 12:38 are, all by themselves, not enough to solve the question of deutero- or trito-Isaias;[89] nor can one conclude with certainty from our Lord's words alone[90] that the whole Pentateuch as we now have it was written by Moses personally.[91]

2. When an Old Testament text is clearly alleged in the New Testament as a real prophecy, say, of the future Messias, it would be contrary to the doctrine of inspiration to say that this text was not written until after the event prophesied, or that it was not written at the time to which Scripture undeniably assigns it.[92]

3. Since the inspiration of all the sacred books and of all their

SACRED SCRIPTURE

genuine texts is a revealed truth, and since the era of public or Christian revelation does not extend beyond the Apostolic Age, it follows that the doctrine of inspiration itself forbids the attribution of a book or passage of the New Testament to an author who did not live in the Apostolic Age. That is why the decree *Lamentabili* condemned the following propositions:

> 13. "The evangelists themselves and the Christians of the second and third generation arranged the Gospel parables artificially and thus furnished grounds for the meager success of the message of Christ among the Jews"—DB 2013. 15.
> 15. "Up to the time of the defining and establishment of the canon, the Gospels were augmented continually by additions and emendations; hence, there remains in them only a slight and uncertain trace of the teaching of Christ."—DB 2015.

Note well the phrase employed above: the doctrine of inspiration forbids the attribution of any part of the New Testament to an author "who did not live in the Apostolic Age"; it is a deliberately elastic phrase. For it does not seem quite clear whether we can *absolutely* rule out the hypothesis of a canonical book or passage having been written after all the Apostles had died. Granting the truth of the proposition discussed above[93] concerning apostolic origin, or even mediately apostolic origin (in the sense explained), as the criterion of inspiration—do the principles of faith render it absolutely impossible for the Church to have received some book or passage from a charismatic who survived the apostles, but of whose charism of prophecy it had learned previously from the apostles themselves? Since we are in the dark on the precise way in which the divine guarantee of the inspiration of the New Testament books reached the Church, it would seem prudent to refrain from any apodictic judgment in such a matter.[94]

Outside of the cases mentioned under 1, 2, and 3, the doctrine of inspiration does not affect the question of the identity of the human authors of Scripture.

A short postscript: Since no divine (oral) tradition can be established for this question of who the human authors of the sacred books were, the following rule seems reasonable. The question of the identity, etc., of the human authors is in itself a historical one and affects theology and the ecclesiastical *magisterium* only to the extent that it necessarily involves the truthfulness or inspiration of a book.[95] But it would be not at all impertinent to suggest at this juncture that a tradition, even if only historical, as long as it is rightfully worthy of serious consideration, is not to be scuttled just because of the quibbling of a few critics.

Notes

1. *Questiones quodlibetales*, 7, a. 14, ad 5.
2. *Providentissimus Deus*, RSS, p. 24.
3. S.Th., III, q. 62, a. 1.
4. Constitution *De fide Catholica*, chap. 2. Bishop Haneberg of Spires corrected his opinion after the Vatican Council in the fourth edition of his work, *Geschichte der Offenbarung* (1876).
5. A bitter controversy over these and other theses raged during the years 1587–88 between the University and the Jesuits of Louvain. Lessius and Duhamel did not admit the parenthetical remark about 2 Maccabees as their own. In addition, Lessius toned down the meaning of his thesis somewhat in a letter to the Archbishop of Malines. See Dausch, *loc. cit.*, p. 146; Pesch, *op. cit.*, p. 279 ff.; S. Pagano, "Some Aspects of the Debate on Inspiration in the Louvain Controversy," CBQ, 14 (1952), 356 ff.; *ibid.*, 15 (1953), 46 ff.; CCHS, 36c.
6. *Loc. cit.*
7. See Dausch, *loc. cit.*, p. 153.
8. S.Th., III, q. 62, a. 1, ad 2.
9. See *ibid.*, II, q. 173, a. 3, ad 4.
10. The understanding of the matter to be recorded should not be stretched to mean complete comprehension of that matter. All that is required for intelligent authorship is a grasp of the literal meaning of the words in any given context. It should be enough to recall that the intellect of the principal Author is infinite and that of the instrumental author finite. There can be no question of equal comprehension here. St. Thomas accordingly refers to a prophet as an *instrumentum deficiens*, a defective or imperfect instrument relative to the principal Cause. When Isaias, for example, wrote: "*Behold, a virgin shall be with child*, etc." he understood the literal meaning of those words as he wrote them, but not necessarily all the sublime and subtle details of the Incarnation.
11. *De malo* 3, a. 2 *(corpus)*, and ad 4.
12. *Praefatio in Isaiam* and *in Jeremiam*.
13. *Adversus haereses* III. 7. 2.
14. *De consensu evangelistarum* II. 12, 27.
15. *Homilia I in Matthaeum* 2.
16. The Synoptic Problem is basically a literary question. In brief, it arises from the strange combination of resemblances and differences in the first three Gospels (the Synoptics). There is no other group of works in literature with just the same kind of mixture of differences and resemblances. It is this mixture which constitutes the problem. If the three Gospels were completely

different from one another—on the literary level, of course—or if they were all perfectly parallel, there would be no such problem. The differences and similarities—the latter amounting often to *verbatim* identity—show up in the matter selected for treatment by the authors, in the order followed, in the form of language. The question to which scriptural scholars are still seeking a fully satisfactory answer is: what precisely is the interrelationship among the three? When they are alike, who depends on whom? When they differ, what is the source of the divergence? The literature on this problem is mountainous. See B. C. Butler, "The Synoptic Problem," CCHS, 760 ff.; *idem, The Originality of St. Matthew* (New York, 1951), and the critique of this work in CBQ, 15 (1953), 388–92; G. Ricciotti, *The Life of Christ*, translated by A. Zizzamia (Milwaukee, 1949), pp. 126–34; F. J. McCool, "Revival of Synoptic Source-Criticism," TS, 17 (1956), 459–93.

17. *De malo* 3, a. 2 (*corpus*).

18. This statement must be qualified. While the intention—and consequently the meaning—of the principal and instrumental authors are coterminous as far as the literal sense is concerned, the same cannot be said with regard to the typical sense. This latter is a sense peculiar to Sacred Scripture, a sense over and above the literal, a sense intended by the principal Author alone. When the human author described the incident of the brazen serpent in the desert or the institution of the Pasch, he was fully aware of the literal sense of what he was writing, and intended that meaning. But only the divine Author knew that these things were to be understood in a typical sense also, as very real foreshadowings of Christ's saving death on the Cross and of the Eucharist respectively. The explanation of inspiration based on instrumental causality breaks down to a certain extent at this point. See CCHS, 35g.

19. Here is another striking example of the divine condescension. See above, art. II, n. 69.

20. RSS, p. 24.

21. Inspiration is frequently divided as follows:
Active inspiration: with reference to God's activity;
Passive " : " " to the human author's receptivity;
Terminative " : " " to the result—the inspired book.

22. St. Thomas, *Commentarium in I Corinthios* 14:32, lectio 6. From another point of view, inspiration may be predicated of Sacred Scripture *terminatively* to indicate that the Sacred Books, as a result of the aforesaid influence, have God as their author.

23. St. Luke actually resolved to write his Gospel after accurately tracing the whole movement to its origin.—Luke 1:3. That is why St. Jerome remarks: "Therefore he wrote the Gospel on the basis of research, but he composed the Acts of the Apostles on the basis of what he had seen with his own eyes"—*De viris illustribus* 7.

24. To judge from the data at hand, none of the sacred writers seems ever to have realized that God was using him as an instrument. Here again we must distinguish clearly between the awareness of a divine command to write and the awareness of writing under divine inspiration. Some sacred authors were evidently aware of such a command, but there is no evidence that any one of them was conscious of the fact that he was actually writing

under the grace of inspiration. One cannot *feel* grace, and such an awareness would have to be the result of a special revelation, a revelation of which we have no record. See *Guide to the Bible, op. cit.*, p. 16.

25. By *all judgments* is meant not any and every assertion having the logical form of a judgment, but those propositions or series of propositions by means of which *the hagiographer expresses a real judgment*. One who composes a parable, for example, puts many judgments into writing, as far as logical form is concerned, but it may well be that throughout this whole series of propositions he expresses only one or two real judgments.

26. The term "real" is used here in its basic etymological meaning. The Latin word *res* means thing, object, matter, content, and the adjective formed from it, *realis*, would in this context signify "pertaining to the *content* of a writing" as against *verbalis*, "pertaining to the *words* which serve as the vehicle for that content." *Real* inspiration then, would mean inspiration as affecting the *res*, the subject matter, the content, the message, the doctrine; *verbal* inspiration would refer to the divine action as influencing the very words used to express that message.

27. See *Guide to the Bible, op. cit.*, p. 14; Hopfl-Gut, *op. cit.*, p. 69 ff.; E. Hugon, *op. cit.*, p. 51 ff.; C. Lattey, "Two Points of Biblical Introduction," CBQ, 7 (1945), 201 ff.; Pesch, *op. cit.*, p. 459 ff.; DBS, IV, 517 ff.

28. It is clear that in *this* opinion the distinction between *inspiration* and negative *assistance* is not a mere matter of terminology, for it removes the material part of the book from the divine influence, i.e., from inspiration.

29. See especially 2 Macc. 2:24-27; 15:39.

30. See *above*, nos. 64 and 67.

31. The Swiss (Protestant) *formula consensus* (1675) held that even the vowel points and accents of the Hebrew text were inspired and that no barbarisms of language could occur in biblical Greek or Hebrew. See CCHS, 36d. This sets something of a record for extremism and lack of historical realism, since the vowel points and accents were elaborated by the so-called "Masoretic scholars" during the period from the sixth to the ninth century A.D. This formula was subsequently abrogated (1725). See Pesch, *op. cit.*, pp. 212-13.

32. *Providentissimus Deus*, RSS, p. 24.

33. Examples are the words of the wicked in Wis. 2:6 ff.; the Roman rescript in 1 Macc. 8:23 ff.; the letters of the Jews in 2 Macc. 1:1-2, 19; the psalmist's expression of repentance in Ps. 50; the presentiment or surmise of St. Paul in Acts 20:25; the latter's expression of humility in 1 Tim. 1:15: . ."to save sinners. Of these I am at the head of the list."

34. See, for example, F. Schmid, *De inspiratione*, p. 117; Pesch, *op. cit.*, p. 444.

35. This rules out completely the opinion proposed by F. Girard (*Annales de philosophie chretienńe* 1905) and W. McDonald (*Irish Ecclesiastical Record* 1905, 343), who distinguished in at least many passages of Scripture between the hagiographer's meaning and God's meaning, holding the latter, of course, to be infallibly true but granting that the former is sometimes wrong. The example of Caiphas (John 11:51) proves nothing. Caiphas was neither a prophet (STh II-II, q. 173, a. 2 and 4) nor a hagiographer: he was

not taken over by God *as an instrument to speak to the Church*. God brought it about that Caiphas expressed his wicked sentence in those precise terms which, taken all by themselves and apart from the context, express also an idea of God's, an idea quite different from the one in the high priest's mind. But no one would have been aware of this divine arrangement if the Holy Spirit had not revealed it through the evangelist.

36. On the imprecations voiced in certain psalms (e.g., 108), see STh II–II, 25, a. 6, ad 3 and 83, a. 8, ad 1. Furthermore, the literary form must be taken into account, for it would be ridiculous to interpret the ardent expressions of a lyric poem by the standards governing prose. Even inspired 'poets have always enjoyed a like license to use rather bold speech."

37. See, for example, 1 Cor. 1:16.

38. See, for example, 1 Cor. 7:12; 1 Tim. 5:23.

39. Note the expression *"actually* performing," which is not verified of the prophet Nathan, for example, in 2 Kings 7:3.

40. An example is 2 Macc. 12:46.

41. See F. Schroeder, *op. cit.;* J. P. Weisengoff, "Inerrancy of the Old Testament in Religious Matters," CBQ, 17 (1955), 128 ff.; L. Johnston, "Old Testament Morality," CBQ, 20 (1958), 19–25.

42. See, for example, Acts 7:16 and 55.

43. *Providentissimus Deus*, RSS, pp. 23–25.

44. *Epistula 82 ad Hieronyum* 3; see also 5. See De San, *Tractatus de sacra Traditione et Scriptura*, p. 280.

45. It follows that ignorance of these circumstances, to which later readers can easily fall victim, sometimes makes it impossible to pass sure judgment on the author's intention.

46. Note: "whenever there is question of a hagiographer's acting precisely as such," for whenever a hagiographer acts at the same time in the capacity of prophet, it can happen that he understands the literal meaning of his prophecy only inadequately—in fact, quite inadequately. "A prophet's mind is a defective instrument when compared with the principal agent; even genuine prophets do not understand everything which the Holy Spirit intends to convey through their visions or words or even their deeds"—STh II–II, 173, a. 4. Similarly, the hagiographers did not always fully grasp the meaning of the words of God, of Christ, of angels, which they *recorded*. (b) "Whenever his literal meaning alone is being sought"; it can happen that God intends to convey, in addition to the literal sense, a mediate or typical sense—(which we shall see subsequently)—altogether unknown to the hagiographer. Furthermore, (c) it may readily be granted that the sacred writers did not always understand *clearly* the individual elements of a complex truth which they affirmed; it is enough that they understood the whole truth in general.

47. St. Augustine: "In reading Sacred Scripture they desire nothing other than to discover the thoughts and the intention of those by whom it was written and thereby to discern the will of God, in accordance with which we believe these men to have spoken"—*De doctrina christiana* ii. 5. 6.

48. A *midrash* is a biblical narrative developed with great freedom to inculcate a moral truth. It resembles our historical novel.—CCHS, 32h.

49. See, for example, Job 3:8; Isa. 13:21; Jer. 50:39; Judith 16:8.

THE SOURCES OF REVELATION

50. See, for example, Acts 2:5.
51. See *Providentissimus Deus*, RSS, p. 22.
52. See, for example, Jos. 10:12–13; Eccl. 1:5–6; Ps. 18:6–7.
53. Eccl. 1:4; Ps. 92:2; 103:5.
54. Gen. 1:16.
55. Ps. 103:2; Isa. 40:22.
56. Gen. 1:6; 7:11; 8:2; Ps. 148:4; Job 37:18. In somewhat the same way, not precisely the hagiographer, but the divinely appointed lawgiver, following external appearances, forbade the eating of the hare, because it *"indeed chews the cud but does not have hoofs'*—Lév. 11:6; Deut. 14:7; in fact the hare does something which looks very much like rumination, and the distinction of clean and unclean animals was made on the basis of an obvious and apparent criterion—not a scientific one. Kaulen: "The relative truth lies in the fact that the notion of 'ruminant' is taken not in the physiological sense, but rather that the legislators were thinking of animals which, without eating, moved their jaws"—*Katholik* (1868), 1. 19. Hence Maisonneuve was justified in remarking: "There is no more error in this manner of speaking than there is in the language of bishops who, in their Lenten regulations, classify oysters as fish"—Duihle de Saint-Projet, *Apologetique scientifique* (1903), p. 464.
57. In fact the words *"the Lord came,* etc." turn up with almost literal identity in the Ethiopian *Henoch* 1:9. Still, some exegetes suspect that this present reading of the book of *Henoch* was taken from the Epistle of Jude rather than *vice versa*. In their view, the apostle did not use the apocryphal book, but took over an old oral tradition. See A. Charue, "Les epîtres catholiques," SB (Paris, 1946), XII, 565 ff.; R. Leconte, "Les epîtres catholiques," SBJ (Paris, 1953); CCHS, 960a ff.
58. *Henoch* 60:8.
59. Tit. 1:12.
60. See RBibl (1900), p. 375; ThQ (Tubingen, 1900), p. 22; also Kaulen: "The book of Wisdom is an address to the rulers of the earth put into the mouth of King Solomon. . . . It cannot have originated with Solomon"—*Einleitung* (4th ed.), nos. 326–27. "Unless this text as we have it is to be regarded as a reworking of the original in post-exilic style [a supposition which, in the judgment of others, does not suffice to safeguard Solomonic authorship], then Ecclesiastes, like the book of Wisdom, was ascribed to King Solomon *as the most likely champion of the sentiments expressed therein*" —*loc. cit.*, no. 318. See CCHS, 388 b–c; R. Pautrel, "L'Ecclesiasté," SBJ (Paris, 1953).
61. 2 Macc. 9; see 1 Macc. 6.
62. 2 Macc. 1:10 ff.
63. There is an example, it seems, in 2 Kings 24:9 compared with 1 Par. 21:5; and perhaps another in Luke 3:36.
64. Decree of Feb. 13, 1905; see RSS, p. 115; RBibl (1905), p. 161.
65. Actually, in the opinion of Fr. Lagrange and others, the book of Daniel is not prophetic in the usual sense, but is rather an *apocalypse,* in which an unknown author of the age of Antiochus Epiphanes plays the part of Daniel and describes in the style of prophetic visions events which for the

most part have already taken place, but in such a way that he quite frequently gives a truly prophetic picture of the earthly kingdom of the Messias and of his eschatological kingdom as well. See RBibl (1904), p. 494; CCHS, 494g ff.

66. Some take practically the same view of Samson's prodigious feats.

67. The author of 2 Maccabees would clearly indicate such a restricted intention, according to some scholars, in 2:29–31. If this were true, the words of this editor would indicate at the same time that "writers of history" usually wrote with another intention in mind, at least at that time. However, the true sense of the Greek text seems to be the following: "I leave a full description and discussion of the individual facts to the author; I myself am intent on conciseness."

68. *De Scriptura Sacra*, p. 145. The following words of our Holy Father, Pope Pius XII, are quite to the point:

> Let all the other sons of the Church bear in mind that the efforts of these resolute laborers in the vineyard of the Lord should be judged not only with equity and justice, but also with the greatest charity; all moreover should abhor that intemperate zeal which imagines that whatever is new should for that very reason be opposed or suspected. Let them bear in mind above all that in the rules and laws promulgated by the Church there is question of doctrine concerning faith and morals; and that in the immense matter contained in the Sacred Books—legislative, historical, sapiental and prophetical—there are but a few texts whose sense has been defined by the authority of the Church, nor are those more numerous about which the teaching of the Holy Fathers is unanimous. There remain therefore many things, and of the greatest importance, in the discussion and exposition of which the skill and genius of Catholic commentators may and ought to be freely exercised, so that each may contribute his part to the advantage of all, to the continued progress of the sacred doctrine and to the defense and honor of the Church.—*Divino afflante Spiritu*, RSS, pp. 101–2.

See also the letter of the Biblical Commission to Cardinal Suhard, Jan. 16, 1948, RSS, p. 148 ff.

69. RBibl (1897), p. 367 ff.

70. *Ibid.* (1896), p. 393 ff. See Pius XII, *Divino afflante Spiritu*, RSS, p. 97 ff.; Letter of the Biblical Commission to Cardinal Suhard, RSS, p. 150: The question of the literary forms of the first eleven Chapters of Genesis is far more obscure and complex. These literary forms correspond to none of our classical categories and cannot be judged in the light of Greco-Latin or modern literary styles. One can, therefore, neither deny nor affirm their historicity, taken as a whole, without unduly attributing to them the canons of a literary style within which it is impossible to to classify them. If one agrees not to recognize in these chapters history in the classical and modern sense, one must, however, admit that the actual scientific data do not allow of giving all the problems they set a *positive* solution. The first duty here incumbent upon scientific exegesis consists before all in the attentive study of all the literary, scientific, historical, cultural and religious problems connected with these chapters; one should then examine closely the literary processes of the early Oriental peoples, their psychology, their way of expressing themsleves and their very notion of historical truth; in a word, one should collate without

prejudice all the subject-matter of the paleontological and historical, epigraphic and literary sciences. Only then can we hope to look more clearly into the true nature of certain narratives in the first Chapters of Genesis.

See also B. Vawter, *op. cit.*; J. L. McKenzie, *op. cit.*; R.A.F. MacKenzie, "Before Abraham Was . . . ," CBQ, 15 (1953), 131 ff.

71. *Providentissimus Deus*, RSS, p. 10.

72. See Pesch, *op. cit.*, p. 363.

73. See Bainvel, *op. cit.*, p. 152; Lesetre, RpA, X, 678 ff: "Certain people seem sometimes to forget that it would be quite as disrespectful to an inspired author to make an historian of him in spite of himself as to treat as a parable what he intended as real history"; similarly Van Hoonacker, *Les douze petits prophètes*, p. 324.

74. Most of these questions are merely of the literary order, and both the *Divino afflante Spiritu* and the letter to Cardinal Suhard allow the Catholic exegete a great deal of latitude in their investigation. See E. F. Siegman, "The Decrees of the Pontifical Biblical Commission," CBQ, 18 (1956), 23 ff.; J. Coppens, the illustrious Louvain professor, states the matter very clearly and directly:

The difficulties which arise from the authority of the Church and of the Fathers over the Holy Scriptures are normally the result of misunderstanding. The Protestant or independent thinker whom we have in mind does not know, or does not sufficiently consider, the Catholic doctrine in the matter. The authority of the Fathers is rigorously circumscribed by the principles of fundamental theology. It is invoked only in cases, less numerous than our opponents imagine, where there is question of the Deposit of Faith and where the Fathers speak unanimously as witnesses of the Faith, proposing an interpretation in the name of the Church and formally on the plane of divine faith. . . . As for the Magisterium, the supreme ecclesiastical teaching authority, when it claims its right and authority to give a definitive interpretation of the sense of the Holy Scriptures, here too, according to the terms of the Vatican Council, it does so on the plane of faith and in the provinces of morals and Christian dogma.—*The Old Testament and the Critics*, translated by E. A. Ryan and E. W. Tribbe (Paterson, 1942), pp. 142–43.

75. The Encyclical contains the following significant passage:

Let the interpreter then, with all care and without neglecting any light derived from recent research, endeavor to determine the peculiar character and circumstances of the sacred writer, the age in which he lived, the sources written or oral to which he had recourse and the forms of expression he employed.

Thus can he better understand who was the inspired author, and what he wishes to express by his writings. There is no one indeed but knows that the supreme rule of interpretation is to discover and define what the writer intended to express, . . . What is the literal sense of a passage is not always as obvious in the speeches and writings of the ancient authors of the East, as it is in the works of our own time. For what they wished to express is not to be determined by the rules of grammar and philology alone, nor solely by the context; the interpreter must, as it were, go back wholly in spirit to those remote centuries of the East and with the aid of history, archaeology, ethnology, and other sciences, accurately determine what modes of writing, so to speak, the authors of that ancient period would be likely to use, and in fact did use.

For the ancient peoples of the East, in order to express their ideas, did not always employ those forms or kinds of speech which we use today; but rather those used by the men of their times and countries. What those exactly were the commentator cannot determine as it were in advance, but only after a careful examination of the ancient literature of the East. The investigation, carried out, on this point, during the past forty or fifty years with greater care and diligence than ever before, has more clearly shown what forms of expression were used in those far off times, whether in poetic description or in the formulation of laws and rules of life or in recording the facts and events of history.—RSS, pp. 96–7.

76. Among the remarks of Fathers Miller and Kleinhans are the following: Inasmuch as it is a collection of documents which show how Sacred Scripture has always been the primary source and foundation of the truths of Catholic faith and of their progress and development, the Enchiridion renders great service first of all to the history of dogmas. It reflects clearly, moreover, the fierce battle that the Church at all times has had to fight, though with varying degrees of intensity, to maintain the purity and truth of the Word of God. Especially in this respect the decrees of the Pontifical Biblical Commission have great significance. However, as long as these decrees propose views which are neither immediately nor mediately connected with truths of faith and morals, it goes without saying that the scholar may pursue his research with complete freedom and may utilize the results of his research, provided always that he defers to the teaching authority of the Church.

Today we can hardly picture to ourselves the position of Catholic scholars at the turn of the century, or the dangers that threatened Catholic teaching on Scripture and its inspiration on the part of liberal and rationalistic criticism, which like a torrent tried to sweep away the sacred barriers of tradition. At present, the battle is considerably less fierce; not a few controversies have been peacefully settled and many problems emerge in an entirely new light, so that it is easy enough for us to smile at the narrowness and constraint which prevailed fifty years ago.

Finally, the Enchiridion has notable apologetic value, because it bears witness to the Church's untiring vigilance and her perennial solicitude for the Scriptures. She is alert to defend their sacred character and to watch over their correct interpretation. Encyclicals like "Providentissimus Deus" and "Divino Afflante Spiritu" show how she exerts herself to promote in every way possible the solid and fruitful study of Scripture. These Encyclicals present with admirable clarity the basic principles of Catholic interpretation which hold for all times and effectively close the door to subjective and arbitrary expositions. Thus they point out the way to an interpretation and use of Scripture calculated to nourish the life of souls and of the Church as well as to utilize fully the gains made by modern research.—Siegman, *loc. cit.*

77. *Ibid.*, pp. 26 and 29; see also the letter to the Italian Hierarchy under date of Aug. 20, 1941, RSS, p. 129 ff.

78. RSS, p. 23.

79. Benedict XV was quick to point out in the *Spiritus Paraclitus* the error of the so-called "Broad School" and the impossibility of appealing to Leo XIII in support of its untenable position:

Those, too, who hold that the historical portions of Scripture do not rest on the absolute truth of the facts but merely upon what they are pleased to term their relative truth, namely, what people then commonly thought, are . . . out of harmony with the Church's teaching, which is endorsed by the testimony of Jerome and other Fathers. Yet they are not afraid to deduce such views from the words of Leo XIII on the ground that he allowed that the principles he had laid down touching the things of nature could be applied to historical things as well. Hence they maintain that precisely as the sacred writers spoke of physical things according to appearance, so, too, while ignorant of the facts, they narrated them in accordance with general opinion or even on baseless evidence: neither do they tell us the sources whence they derived their knowledge, nor do they make other peoples' narrative their own. Such views are clearly false, and constitute a calumny on our predecessor. After all, what analogy is there between physics and history? For whereas physics are concerned with "sensible appearances" and must consequently square with phenomena, history on the contrary, must square with facts, since history is the written account of events as they actually occurred. If we were to accept such views, how could we maintain the truth insisted on throughout Leo XIII's Encyclical—viz. that the sacred narrative is absolutely free from error? And if Leo XIII does say that we can apply to history and cognate subjects the same principles which hold good for science, he yet does not lay this down as a universal law, but simply says that we can apply a *like line* of argument when refuting the fallacies of adversaries and defending the historical truth of Scripture from their assaults.—RSS, pp. 52–3 [italics ours].

80. For example, *In Jeremiam* 28:10, with reference to Amasias, the *notorious* false prophet, who is called by Scripture simply a "prophet": "As if many things were not said in Sacred Scripture according to the opinion current at the time the facts were recorded, and not according to the objective reality of the matter!" *Adversus Helvidium* 4: "So much so that even the evangelists, expressing public opinion, which is a valid rule of history, called [St. Joseph] the father of our Savior." Elsewhere the holy Doctor, taking the view that Herod only pretended sadness, remarks in commenting on the words, *"the king was greatly disturbed"*—Matt. 14:9: "It is customary in Scripture for the narrator to record the common opinion currently in vogue in his time. So in this instance Herod is said to have been sad because those who were dining with him got that impression. This expert dissembler, this instigator of murder put on a long face, but all the time there was joy in his heart"—*Commentarium in Matthaeum*.

81. See Delattre, *Criterium' de la nouvelle exegese 'biblique*, chap. 2 and 3; Pesch, *op. cit.*, p. 532 ff.

82. See N. Peters, *Theologische Revue* (1910), 334.

83. Reply of June 23, 1905. See RBibl (1905) 321 and note 76 above.

84. Read, for example, Vetter's discussion of the book of Tobias in *Theologische Quartalschift* (Tubingen, 1904–5); see *Revue du clerge français*, Nov. 1, 1908 and 1909, p. 720.

85. RSS, pp. 120–22.

86. See above, no. 92.

87. Therefore, as far as inspiration is concerned, there is nothing to prevent one from accepting the opinion defended by, among others, Happel: "The sacred books of the Old Testament have an inner history. The sacred text underwent many various preliminary alterations and modifications before it finally assumed a fixed norm. This history is not the result of accidental corruption or unauthorized interpolation, but rather the work of authorized, prophetically gifted instruments"—*Biblische Studien* (1901), 27. See C. Stuhlmueller, "The Influence of Oral Tradition upon Exegesis," CBQ, 20 (1958), 299–326.

88. Wisd. 7:1 ff.; 9:8 ff.

89. Note: the question of deutero- or trito-Isaias is not settled *on these grounds alone*. But on June 28, 1908 the Pontifical Biblical Commission issued a decree on the character and the author of the book of Isaias:

3. *Character of the Prophetic Office.*—Whether it may be admitted that the prophets not only as correctors of human wickedness and heralds of the divine Word for the good of their hearers, but also as foretellers of future events, must always have addressed themselves to a present and contemporary and not to a future audience, so that they could be clearly understood by them; and that therefore, the second part of the book of Isaias (chapter 40–66), in which the prophet addresses and consoles not the Jews contemporary with Isaias, but, as one living among them, those mourning in the exile of Babylon, cannot have for its author Isaias himself then long dead, but must be attributed to some unknown prophet living among the exiles.

Answer: In the negative.

4. *Unity of authorship.*—Whether the philological argument, one derived from the language and the style, and employed to impugn the identity of the author of the book of Isaias, is to be considered weighty enough to compel a man of judgment, versed in the principles of criticism and well acquainted with Hebrew, to acknowledge in the same book a plurality of authors.

Answer: In the negative.

5. *Cumulative Arguments against Unity.*—Whether there are solid arguments, even when taken cumulatively, to prove that the book of Isaias is to be attributed not to Isaias alone, but to two or even more authors.

Answer: In the negative.—RSS, pp. 119–20.

But as Auvray and Steinmann observe:

A decision of the Biblical Commission of Rome, under date of June 28, 1908, considered the arguments advanced against the attribution to Isaias of the whole book which bears his name insufficient to modify the traditional teaching. This was a prudent measure which, however, did not close the door to further research. This latter has increased the weight of the reasons brought forward against authenticity. And so more and more Catholic authors are coming to esteem as very probable that the *Book of Consolation* is the work of a disciple of Isaias who lived during the time of the exile.—"Isaie," SBJ (Paris, 1951).

It should be noted that the Commission was understandably concerned about the grounds on which critics rejected Isaian authorship of chap. 40–66. They denied the possibility of supernatural prophecy, and hence deemed it antecedently impossible that a prophet living in the eighth century B.C. could have described in such accurate detail conditions of the sixth century. It goes without saying that modern Catholic views on the authorship of these chapters are based on quite different, more objective, and more truly scientific premises.

90. Mark 10:3–5; Luke 24:44; John 5:39–47.

91. See the decree of the *Biblical Commission,* June 27, 1906, stating that the arguments brought against the Mosaic authorship of the Pentateuch were not sufficient to permit one to abandon the traditional view. See RSS pp. 116–17; RBibl (1906), 349. For recent Catholic views on the Mosaic authorship of the Pentateuch, see CCHS, 1351 ff., and especially R. de Vaux, "La Genese," SBJ (Paris, 1953), pp. 9–21.

What we have said above about the assertions of the New Testament are likewise applicable to conciliar decrees, etc. The Council of Trent (Session IV; see also, the Councils of Hippo and Carthage and the letter of Innocent I in DB 92 and 96) lists several of the sacred books under the names of the authors commonly assigned them. However, it was not the intention of the fathers to pass definitive judgment on the identity of the secondary authors, but only to issue "a *list of the Sacred books,* so that no doubt may arise in anyone's mind as to *which are the books* that are accepted by this Synod" —DB 783.

92. In the decree quoted above *on the character and author of the book of Isaias,* a negative reply was given to the following question:

Whether it may be taught that the prophecies which are read in the book of Isaias, and here and there in the Scriptures, are not real prophecies, but either narratives composed subsequent to the event, or, if it must be acknowledged that something was foretold before the event, that the prophet foretold the same, not from a supernatural revelation of God who foreknows the future, but by conjecturing through a happy sagacity and acuteness of natural intelligence from things that had already happened. —RSS, pp. 118–19.

93. See above, no. 53.

94. In the draft prepared for the Vatican Council on the books of Sacred Scripture, we read: "because they were written as a result of the prompting of the Holy Spirit, they have God for their author, and as such they were entrusted to the Church by the apostles." But since some of the fathers suggested a modification, the "Deputatio de fide" agreed "that those words '*by the apostles*' be omitted; not of course that the words '*and as such they were entrusted to the Church*' give a sense different from '*entrusted to the Church by the apostles.*' For in order for the Church to be able to propose as an obligatory object of faith that such and such a book is inspired, not only must the truth be certain; it must be revealed as well. But that it be revealed it must be found in the Church's deposit, and for it to be found therein, it must have been placed therein by Christ, by the apostles, etc. Still, that the words may be not too restrictive, the Deputatio suggests that the phrase run, '*and as such they were entrusted to it*' the Church"—Coll Lac VII, 72 and 142. See Stanley, *op. cit.*

95. See RBibl (1900), 30; *Civiltà Cattolica* (1903), I, 397; Von Hummelauer, *Exegetisches,* p. 99; Billot, *De inspiratione,* p. 65.

Special Bibliography

In addition to the works listed in the preceding article, see the following:

Auzou, G. *La Parole de Dieu*. Paris, 1956.

Benoit, P. "Note complémentaire sur l'inspiration," RBibl, 63 (1956), 416.

Forestell, J. T. "The Limitation of Inerrancy," CBQ, 20 (1958), 9–18.

Johnston, L. "Old Testament Morality," *ibid.*, 19–25.

Mackenzie, R. A. F. "Some Problems in the Field of Inspiration," *ibid.*, 1–8.

Murphy, R. "The Teachings of *Providentissimus Deus*," CBQ, 5 (1943), 125.

Rahner, K. "Über die Schriftsinspiration," ZkTh, 78 (1956), 137.

Article IV

THE USE OF SACRED SCRIPTURE

1. THE SENSES OF SCRIPTURE

I. *Meaning and Division:*
   1. Literal and typical.
   2. Consequent and accommodated.

II. *The Multiple Literal Sense*

III. *Proof for the Existence of the Typical Sense:*
   1. From the New Testament.
   2. From the fathers.

2. THE INTERPRETATION AND READING OF HOLY SCRIPTURE

Preliminary Considerations:
   a. Protestant and Catholic views on the clarity of Scripture.
   b. The right of the Church to give authoritative interpretations.
   c. Scope and characteristics of an authoritative interpretation.

I. *Scripture Is Not So Crystal Clear that It Can Be the Proximate Rule of Faith for Each and Every One of the Faithful*
   Proof: 1. From Sacred Scripture.
   2. From established facts.

II. *The Authoritative Interpretation of Sacred Scripture Is Within the Competence of the Church's Magisterium*
   Proof: 1. From the institution of a perpetual and infallible teaching office.
   2. From the fathers.

Objections.
Scholion. Dogmatic rules for the interpretation of Scripture.
III. *Principles Governing the Private Reading of Sacred Scripture*

3. The Authenticity of the Vulgate

I. *The Work of St. Jerome*
II. *The Decrees of Trent*
III. *Detailed Study of These Decrees*
IV. *The Substantial Fidelity of the Vulgate to the Original*
V. *Corollaries*

Article IV

THE USE OF SACRED SCRIPTURE

This article will treat of the *senses, interpretation,* and *reading* of Sacred Scripture, and the *authenticity of the Vulgate.*

1. THE SENSES OF SCRIPTURE

98 **I. Notion and Division of Various Senses of Scripture**

The sense of Scripture is the meaning which the text expresses as intended by the Holy Spirit. We say "as intended by the Holy Spirit" because He alone is simply and without qualification the Author of Scripture. Furthermore, it follows from the relationship existing between the instrumental and principal authors that the sense which the hagiographer wished to express and did in fact express is always that intended by the Holy Spirit. But it does not follow that the human author always had an adequate comprehension of the whole sense intended either directly or, especially, indirectly by the Holy Spirit.[1]

99 **1. It is customary to distinguish the literal sense and the typical sense.**

The *literal* (historical) *sense* is that which the words themselves in this precise context directly express. It makes no difference whether the words be taken in their proper or non-proper (metaphorical) signification.

> The figure [of speech] itself is not the literal sense, but that which is expressed by the figure. When Scripture speaks of God's arm, the literal meaning is not that God has such a bodily member, but rather the idea suggested by this member, namely, the power to act.[2]

What is true of metaphors is equally true of parables, allegories, and the like, and so, to discover the true literal sense, it is not always enough to subject individual sentences to grammatical analysis. Rather the whole context, immediate and remote, must be taken into account, as well as the literary form of the book.

The *typical* (mystical, spiritual) *sense* is that which the words express, not directly, but through the medium of the objects which they directly signify. God,

> the Author of the universe, can use not only words to signify something, but can establish objects also as figures. Accordingly truth is expressed in Scripture in two ways. One way is that whereby words signify objects; this is the literal sense. The other way is that whereby objects are used as figures of other things; this is the spiritual sense.[3]

Note that the typical sense is grounded on the literal and necessarily supposes it. Hence there is no room for confusion, "since the senses are not multiplied as if one word signified many things. It is rather that the things signified by the words may be signs of other things."[4]

2. It is usual to mention at this point the consequent sense and the accommodated sense.

The *consequent sense* is the truth which the words of Scripture, at least all by themselves, do not formally express, but which can be legitimately deduced from a scriptural statement by a process of reasoning.[5] But if a conclusion of this sort should be so intimately and obviously included in the words of Scripture that, all things considered, the Holy Spirit clearly intended to suggest it to His readers, then that conclusion is a true sense of Scripture and is in fact included in the literal sense. On the other hand, if it be merely a conclusion based on the words of Scripture, true though it may be, it can be called only loosely a sense of Scripture.

The *accommodated sense* is a sense not intended by the author of Scripture, but rather one given a scriptural expression by someone else because the situation described or the words themselves seem currently applicable to a similar situation. It is, therefore, not a sense of Scripture at all, but merely the application or accommodation of a scriptural passage to something quite foreign thereto.[6]

II. Can the Literal Sense Be Multiple?

With regard to the literal sense, which is present in every passage of Scripture, authors have often discussed the *possibility of its being multiple*. There is no question here of an uncertain sense which leaves room for various probable explanations, nor of the implicit or consequent sense, nor of the fact that prophecies have been at times so worded as to be only imperfectly applicable to the type but perfectly to the antitype.[7] The point at issue here is whether the hagiographer, or at least the Holy Spirit, intended to convey several distinct meanings by one and the same word. St. Augustine is the only one of the fathers to give an affirmative answer:

> When someone says, "He [the author of the Pentateuch] meant what I think he meant," and another, "No, it is rather my interpretation which catches his meaning," I think I can say with all reverence, "Why cannot you both be right, if the meanings you propose are true?" And if someone should propose a third or a fourth meaning, or even if someone should find an altogether different truth in these words, why may he not be believed to have discerned all of these meanings, he through whom one and the same God accommodated the sacred words to the understanding of many, who would find therein true, albeit divergent meanings?[8]

St. Thomas once followed this opinion:

> It does not surpass belief that Moses and other authors of Sacred Scripture were favored by God with the ability to understand and to express in one phrase different truths accessible to human understanding, and in such a way that any one of these truths would be the author's meaning. Hence even if scriptural exegetes see in an expression truths which the author did not understand, doubtless those truths were understood by the Holy Spirit, who is the principal Author of Sacred Scripture. Any truth, then, which can be ascribed to Sacred Scripture in a given context is its meaning.[9]

But in the *Summa*, the holy Doctor clearly leans to the other opinion and adds just this one brief remark, that plurality of meaning is not unfitting, since God comprehends all things by one simple act of His intellect."[10]

By far the more common opinion, and surely the correct one,

holds that there is only one literal sense in any one passage of Scripture.[11] In any event, the controversy is of no great importance, since the passages where the context would allow several different senses are few indeed.[12]

III. Proof for Existence of the Typical Sense of Scripture 104

The following remarks will help to explain the typical sense. It is altogether clear that God, in inspiring a writer, *could* have at times intended, in addition to the literal sense, a spiritual sense as well. For God to have had this intention, it is enough that He inspired the description of something ordained by Him in advance as the figure or type of something else. Since the typical sense, when it turns up, is contained directly not in the words of Scripture but in the objects which they signify, it need not have been known to the hagiographer, nor can one expect to discover it simply by reading the sacred text.

Although the Church has given no explicit definition on this matter, *there is no doubt that some passages of Scripture contain a typical sense*. The following arguments may be adduced as proof of this.

1. **The New Testament** (a) clearly considers many things in the Old Testament to have been types or figures of things to come;[13] (b) it often asserts that statements of the Old Testament have been fulfilled in events of the New, statements which, in their literal sense, had no reference to such events;[14] (c) at times it even affirms explicitly that such and such a thing happened "that Scripture might be fulfilled" when the passage referred to literally signifies something else, e.g.:

> When they came to Jesus, they saw that he was already dead. So they did not break his legs, . . . In fact, these incidents took place that the Scripture might be fulfilled: "Not a bone of his shall be broken."[15]

Now to try to explain *all* these instances, or *nearly all*, as mere accommodations or literary applications would be to do open violence to the sacred text, and to offend against the analogy of faith in the bargain.* Clearly the understanding of the Church,

---

* The "analogy of faith" may be defined as the harmony of any given doctrine with other revealed truths. See M. Nicolau, *Sacrae Theologiae Summa*, *op. cit.*, p. 1086.

THE SOURCES OF REVELATION

which no one can just blithely deny, considers that the Old Law as a whole was by the will of God a figure and a prophecy of the New. This truth cannot be maintained if everything which the New Testament, taken in its obvious and natural meaning, explains as a type, is stripped of all the characteristics of a real type (i.e., of a figure predetermined by God). It may be granted that the apostles and other New Testament authors could at times use Scripture in the merely accommodated sense, and it is quite true that in some instances it is difficult to determine precisely whether they are using accommodation or the strictly typical sense. But it would be an unwarranted extreme to toss out all genuine typology.

105 no sense, however, is New Testament typology to be equated with the procedure of rabbinic authors of those days and later, who forced upon the words of Scripture completely foreign and painfully twisted meanings, practicing a truly "creative exegesis." Considering the procedure of the apostles, it seems thoroughly admissible that the Jews who were their contemporaries were well aware of the typical relationship of the Old Testament to the Messianic Kingdom. But while the secular authors just mentioned fell into all sorts of weird subtleties by applying soundly solid principles immoderately and even ineptly, the hagiographers, thanks to the guidance of the Holy Spirit, were able to stay within reasonable bounds.

2. The Fathers unanimously acknowledged the typical sense of Scripture, and from earliest times displayed a great fondness for it.

106 The question of *whether a given passage of Scripture has a typical sense* can be answered with complete certitude only on the basis of divine testimony. Such testimony is at hand, however, as often as it can be definitely established that Christ, the apostles, or the sacred writers of the New Testament really explained an Old Testament text in the genuinely typical sense. But given the typical character of the Old Testament as a whole, the mere comparison of Old Testament events, etc., with those of the New can give sufficient grounds for establishing some typical meanings with more or less convincing probability. It seems likely that even the apostles and other sacred writers of the New Law did not always learn of the typical senses which they used through a revelation in the strict sense, but rather by means of a comparison such as the one just mentioned. But since they were guided by the light of inspiration in making this comparison or at least in passing final judgment on it, they were safe from error. The fathers, on the other hand, did not enjoy such guidance, and so were liable to error in their personal explanations. Note: "in their *personal* explanations;" for whenever they are morally unanimous in suggesting the typical sense for a specific passage, even though that sense was not indicated in the New Testament, they should rather be considered as witnesses to divine tradition on the point. For the rest, what has been said above about the hagiographers of the New Law holds good also for the fathers and the liturgy of the Church: it is quite often difficult to decide whether they are giving a real typical meaning to a passage or are using accommodation only.

2. The Interpretation and Reading of Holy Scripture

107 Ever since the days of Luther, *Protestants* have extolled the *transparent clarity* of Scripture. They acknowledge, of course, that there are very many things in the Bible which are unintelligible without the help of scientific exegesis; they admit that not every single passage of doctrinal or moral import is clear just as it stands. But they insist that the faithful who read through the whole Bible with serious concentration and attention find so easily therein the path of salvation, i.e., the doctrines necessary for salvation, that there is not the slightest need for the teaching of the Church or of its priests. They attribute this ease of understanding above all to the Holy Spirit, who dwells in the heart of each of the faithful and whose unction all have received.[16] Consequently they not only urge with insensitive insistence that all indiscriminately read the whole Bible, but teach besides that every private individual is free to hold his own personal interpretation of Scripture in preference to the judgment and preaching of the Church.[17]

108 *Catholics* do not deny that certain basic teachings can be found in Scripture with little difficulty, especially by those who, with a thorough grounding in the principles of the Christian religion, follow the analogy of faith. They hold, however, (a) that the authoritative determination of the meaning of Scripture in matters of faith and morals belongs, according to the arrangement of Christ Himself, to the teaching office of His Church and that, consequently, no one is ever free to depart from the meaning which the Church has always held; and (b) that the suitableness of this arrangement, in fact its relative necessity, rests on the fact that not

even in matters of faith and morals is Scripture so crystal clear that it can serve as the proximate rule of faith for each and every one of the faithful.[18] They add, finally, (c) that while the private reading of Sacred Scripture is in itself most helpful indeed, it is not necessary, and can be controlled by the Church as the circumstances of the times or of certain locales demand.

The *Vatican Council:*

> Repeating the same decree [of Trent], We declare that this was its intention: that in matters of faith and morals which play a part in the development of Christian doctrine, that must be accepted as the true sense of Sacred Scripture which Holy Mother Church held and holds; for it is her right to judge concerning the true meaning and interpretation of Holy Writ and, therefore, no one may give Sacred Scripture a meaning which would run counter to this meaning or even to the unanimous agreement of the fathers.—DB 1788.[19]

That this decree is not merely disciplinary but dogmatic as well is clear from its subject matter and from the position it holds in the decrees of the Council.

109 An *authoritative* or dogmatic interpretation is one which is its own guarantee of credibility because issued by the divinely established teaching office of the Church. It can be merely authoritative,[20] or it can be infallible. The latter alone binds absolutely and, in the present discussion, has the chief claim to our attention. To an authoritative interpretation is opposed a *private* or scientific one, which is based exclusively on hermeneutical rules and personal erudition, and can be relinquished without any injury to the duty of religious obedience.

An authoritative interpretation is *limited* by its very nature to "*questions of faith and morals,* questions which play a part in the structure of Christian doctrine." Merely profane matters do not come within the province of the teaching authority of the Church.[21] The Councils of Trent and of the Vatican make this limitation sufficiently clear.

Note that an authoritative interpretation is limited to "*questions of faith and morals,*" but not to passages or texts which touch upon such questions. Inspired texts as such are matters of faith and morals by a twofold title. The first is their subject matter and the second is the fact of their inspiration. With regard to the latter, some passages are frequently called "accidentally" inspired texts in that they are classed as matters of faith and morals simply because they are inspired, and consequently fall within the province of the Church's teaching power only insofar as the fact of their inspiration must be defended along with its necessary sequel, inerrancy.[22]

Note, finally, the following phrase: "questions which play a part in the *structure* of Christian doctrine." It is, of course, clear that the structure of Christian doctrine is built not of doctrine alone (theoretical and practical) in the strict sense, but also of many historical facts without which Christian doctrine would lack foundation, defense, backing. Therefore texts wherein facts of this sort are recorded are subject to the interpretation of the Church not only by reason of their being inspired but also because of their very subject matter. But if at times it is doubtful whether or not such and such a matter contributes to the building up of Christian doctrine, then, in the final analysis, one must accept the decision of the Church, which certainly can determine infallibly the scope of its jurisdiction.[23]

I. *Scripture Is Not So Crystal Clear that It Can Be the Proximate Rule of Faith for Each and Every One of the Faithful*   110

Proof:

1. From *Sacred Scripture*. St. Peter says of the Pauline epistles:

In his letters there are some passages hard to understand. The unlearned and unsteady twist the meaning of these to their own destruction, as they do also the other Scriptures—2 Pet. 3:16.

These last words show that there is question here of an understanding so erroneous as to constitute an obstacle to salvation. The apostles themselves needed the interpretation of our Lord on many points:

He then gave them the key to the understanding of the Scriptures.— *Ibid.*[24]

As a proof to the contrary one may not appeal to Ps. 18:8-9; 118:105 and 130; Prov. 6:23. These passages do not refer directly to Scripture, much less to the whole Bible, but to divine doctrine and precepts in general.[25]

2. From established *facts*. Vincent Lerins wrote that the "authority of the mind of the Church" was necessary

> because, due to the profundity of Scripture, not all understand it in exactly the same sense, but the same words are interpreted in one way by one and in another way by another, with the apparent result that almost as many meanings can be wrested from it as there are men. Novatian interprets it one way, Sabellius another way, Donatus another, Arius another, Nestorius another.[26]

And were not the errors of Sabellius, Arius and Nestorius obstacles to salvation? Then there are the well-known words of the Reformed theologian Samuel Werenfels (d. 1740) concerning Scripture: "This is the book in which everyone seeks his own dogmas and in which everyone finds his own dogmas."[27] Finally, more recently, Dr. Bavinck could write: "The doctrine of the clarity of Scripture undoubtedly carries with it serious dangers. Because of it Protestantism has been split up to the point of desperation."[28]

Consider, furthermore, the history of the controversies that have engaged both Catholics and Protestants, controversies over the true meaning of Scripture carried on vigorously by men who were, most of the time, very sincere and quite concerned about their salvation. In the light of this, it is easy to see that the text of 1 John 2:20, 27, where we read that the faithful have been anointed by the Holy One and know all things, so that they need no one to teach them, has been sadly misunderstood by Protestants, as if each individual Christian were promised the Holy Spirit so that he could correctly understand Sacred Scripture with no help from the Church.[29] Would it be correct to conclude that all those who fell into error through infidelity or folly had not received the Holy Spirit? Could one sustain the thesis that all the disputes, especially among Protestants, were concerned with matters not necessary for salvation? And how many dogmas are there which in fact all Protestants agree can be found in Scripture?

111   The obscurity of Scripture finds easy *explanation* in the fact that it contains mysteries and very profound truths, and in the further fact that it was written many centuries ago by men who differed greatly from one another and especially from us, who are

so far removed from them in genius and disposition, men who used oriental languages and forms of speech and made frequent reference to circumstances about which we have only a hazy notion or even no notion at all.

From another point of view, this obscurity is *not without its advantages:* **112**

> God so disposing, as the holy Fathers commonly teach, in order that men may investigate them [the Scriptures] with greater ardor and earnestness, and that what is attained with difficulty may sink more deeply into the mind and heart, and most of all, that they may understand that God has delivered the Holy Scripture to the Church, and that in reading and making use of His Word, they must follow the Church as their guide and their teacher.[30]

Even if Scripture were much more clear and evident than it actually is, it would still be morally necessary to have an interpreter or at least a defender of its authentic meaning. It would be morally impossible to compose any book about religious and moral subjects with such unmistakable clarity as to leave no room for questions and disputes, at least after a lapse of time.

II. *The Authoritative Interpretation of Sacred Scripture Is* **113**
Within the Competence of the Church's Magisterium

This is a dogma of faith from the Vatican Council, as quoted above.

Proof:

1. *From the institution of a perpetual and infallible teaching office,* which has been proven elsewhere. Clearly, if Christ instituted a living and perpetual teaching office to preserve His teaching whole and entire and to preach it authoritatively, He certainly did not intend to leave the interpretation of Scripture in matters of faith and morals to the whim of everyone and anyone. This conclusion would follow with even more urgency if there were any truth to the Protestant claim that Scripture is the sole source of revelation. For then, with Scripture removed from its competence, there would be nothing left for the *magisterium* of the Church to teach. Again, if Christ endowed the Church's teaching office with the gift of infallibility, so that all might safely learn of their faith

from it, He certainly did not promise the Holy Spirit to each individual believer in the sense that anyone at all could interpret Scripture for himself independently of and even in opposition to that *magisterium*.

2. From *the fathers*. St. Irenaeus: "Where the charisms of the Lord are, there it is that one must learn the truth, from those among whom is found the apostolic succession. For they explain Scripture for us without the slightest risk [of error]."[31] Tertullian: "Where the truth of Christian discipline and belief clearly appears [i.e., where the true Church clearly appears], there the truth of scriptural exegesis and of all Christian tradition will be."[32] Vincent Lerins: "It is gravely necessary that the interpretation of the prophets and apostles follow the direction set for it by ecclesiastical and Catholic understanding of them."[33]

114 Protestants *object* that the Catholic teaching on scriptural interpretation (a) sets the Church, i.e., mere men, above the word of God; (b) stifles freedom of conscience and of exegesis; (c) handcuffs biblical studies.

a. In its belief and in its preaching the Church is guided by the word of God and thus is subject to that word. But it is superior to the personal, fallible interpretation of individuals, and this is true not because it is a society made up of men, but because, thanks to the help of the Holy Spirit, it is kept from error in understanding and preaching Christian doctrine.

115 b. Granted the divine institution and infallibility of the Church's magisterium, an authoritative interpretation no more hinders the legitimate exercise of freedom than does revelation itself. If the rights of men are not impugned by the duty of accepting a doctrine revealed in Scripture or elsewhere, how would those rights be injured by the duty of accepting a divinely true explanation of that same doctrine? Is freedom of conscience or of theological knowledge lessened by the exclusion of error?

116 c. The Catholic doctrine does not at all handcuff biblical science. Far from it!

> A wide field is still left open to the private student, in which his hermeneutical skill may display itself with signal effect and to the advantage of the Church. On the one hand, in those passages of Holy Scripture, which have not as yet received a certain and definite interpretation, such labors may, in the be-

nignant providence of God, prepare for and bring to maturity the judgment of the Church; on the other, in passages already defined the private student may do work equally valuable, either by setting them forth more clearly to the flock and more skillfully to scholars, or by defending them more powerfully from hostile attack.*

If biblical studies among Catholics sometimes lagged rather badly, the blame lay with the unfavorable conditions of the times or with the indolence of men. One often hears the complaint that a feeling of security about having the essential truths well in hand can encourage natural laziness. But there is certainly no necessary connection between the two conditions. When all is said and done, to display a lack of brilliance and enthusiasm in scriptural studies is a lesser evil than to black out with the smoke of incessant

---

* *Providentissimus Deus*, RSS, p. 15. See E. F. Siegman, *loc. cit.*; J. Coppens, *op. cit.*, p. 139 ff.; after discussing in detail the various ecclesiastical directives affecting exegesis, especially the decrees of the Biblical Commission, Fr. Coppens concludes:

Hence we are in a position to reply to the difficulties proposed by independent exegetes. It cannot be denied that the Church has placed restrictions on scientific exegetical research. Nevertheless this strict regulation has worked out to the advantage of scholars. It put them on their guard against the fascinations of a system whose weaknesses the investigations of Protestant and independent savants have since disclosed. Catholic workers were accordingly spared the heavy penance which so-called liberal exegesis has had to perform in burning what it once adored, and in returning to positions which it should never have abandoned. While time is decanting the too rich wine of criticism, the Church is adapting her positions to meet what many consider the no longer debatable results of progressive scholarship. If the development thus nursed along can continue prudently and without that rash enthusiasm which vitiates all causes, even good ones, Catholic exegesis will soon have drawn profit from the positive results of historical criticism, the results which have withstood the wear and tear of time and the process of checking and rechecking. Thereafter nothing will prevent it from feeling perfectly at ease in scientific circles.

We can, it therefore appears, give an adequate answer to those who persist in throwing up to us as objectionable the ecclesiastical directives on scientific exegesis. They have no right to picture these decrees as so many petrified texts, destined to collectivize and standardize exegetical research once and for all. The pronouncements made no pretense to infallibility and their prime purpose was to regulate instruction. Promulgated in strict dependence on the scientific movement, they cannot and must not pretend to be independent of it. On the contrary, living interpretation, of course under the control of the Church, must be applied to clear up and adapt their meaning. In the period of crisis, as we have seen, such interpretation was restricted; it can be allowed more freedom now that we live in a time of peace and harmonious development.

THE SOURCES OF REVELATION

wrangling religious truth dealing with matters of even the greatest moment.

117 *Scholion. Dogmatic rules for the interpretation of Scripture*

The doctrine just explained furnishes a clear basis for some rules to be followed in the private interpretation of Holy Scripture. They are called dogmatic rules in contradistinction to the merely scientific rules of hermeneutics.

1. In passages inspired for their own sake, that meaning must always be maintained which *the Church by solemn decision or by its ordinary and universal magisterium has declared to be the true one*. Leo XIII:

> Wherefore the first and dearest object of the Catholic commentator should be to interpret those passages which have received an authentic interpretation either from the sacred writers themselves, under the inspiration of the Holy Spirit (as in many places of the New Testament), or from the Church, under the assistance of the same Holy Spirit, whether by her solemn judgment or her ordinary and universal *magisterium*—to interpret these passages in that identical sense, . . .[34]

Strictly speaking, it is superfluous to restrict this rule to "passages inspired for their own sake," since a definition of the Church, solemn or not, is not given for the meaning of other passages. The limitation was included, however, in order to make the following distinction clear: it is one thing for the Church to make a *specific* declaration about the meaning of a passage in its ordinary and universal teaching and to insist in the same way that that meaning be maintained; and quite another for it to *accept* just incidentally the obvious meaning of a passage on the basis of a universally admitted scientific opinion.

It would not be out of place to mention here that only a defined interpretation must be accorded absolutely firm assent, but that even a merely authoritative interpretation must be accepted with due reverence.[35]

118 2. In passages inspired for their own sake that meaning must always be maintained which the fathers declared with moral *unanimity* to be the true one. The reason behind this is that the unanimous agreement of the fathers is a sure indication of the

(112)

SACRED SCRIPTURE

Church's tradition, as will be explained in the next chapter of this treatise.[36] Leo XIII:

> The holy Fathers . . . are of supreme authority, whenever they all interpret in one and the same manner any text of the Bible, as pertaining to the doctrine of faith or morals; for their unanimity clearly evinces that such interpretation has come down from the Apostles as a matter of Catholic faith.[37]

Again it must be remarked that only the morally unanimous agreement of the fathers binds one absolutely. However, an interpretation backed up by the authority of even quite a few of the fathers is not to be brushed aside lightly.[38]

On the other hand, when there is question of a merely secular matter, the fathers' understanding of it, even though they may be unanimous on the point, does not bind a Catholic exegete. Leo XIII:

> Hence, in their interpretations, we must carefully note what they lay down as belonging to faith, or as intimately connected with faith—what they are unanimous in. For "in those things which do not come under the obligation of faith, the saints were at liberty to hold divergent opinions, just as we ourselves are," according to the saying of St. Thomas.*

---

* *Loc. cit.*, pp. 22–23. Fr. Coppens has a very lucid statement of this matter:

> The difficulties which arise from the authority of the Church and of the Fathers over the Holy Scriptures are normally the result of misunderstanding. The Protestant or independent thinker whom we have in mind does not know, or does not sufficiently consider, the Catholic doctrine in the matter. The authority of the Fathers is rigorously circumscribed by the principles of fundamental theology. It is invoked only in cases, less numerous than our opponents imagine, where there is question of the Deposit of Faith and where the Fathers speak unanimously as witnesses of the Faith, proposing an interpretation in the name of the Church and formally on the plane of divine faith. If, by way of exception, the authority of one or several of the Fathers is sufficient, it must be clearly proved that they were directly commissioned by the Church, or that they manifestly represent the mind of the Church in matters of divine faith. As for the Magisterium, the supreme ecclesiastical teaching authority, when it claims its right and authority to give a definitive interpretation of the sense of the Holy Scriptures, here too, according to the terms of the Vatican Council, it does so on the plane of faith and in the provinces of morals and Christian dogma.—*Op. cit.*, pp. 142–43.

119 In passages inspired for their own sake, should there be no authoritative interpretation and no unanimity on the part of the fathers, then one must always *look to the analogy of the Catholic faith.* Leo XIII:

> In the other passages the analogy of faith should be followed, and Catholic doctrine, as authoritatively proposed by the Church, should be held as the supreme law; ... Hence it follows that all interpretation is foolish and false which either makes the sacred writers disagree one with another, or is opposed to the doctrine of the Church.[39]

The analogy of faith renders *negative* service to the exegete, by keeping him from giving an interpretation which would be incompatible with the Catholic faith. In addition, it sometimes gives him *positive* help, by showing him the way to discover more easily the true meaning of a passage.[40] Thus, for example, the Catholic teaching on oaths smooths the way for an explanation of our Lord's words in Matt. 5:33–37.

120 Even in those passages which were only "accidentally" inspired, one may *never* admit an interpretation which would run counter to the Catholic teaching on the inspiration and inerrancy of all Scripture. The very reverend secretary of the *Deputatio fidei* appointed to draw up the decrees of the Vatican Council wrote:

> As to interpretations dealing with truths of history, I say that such interpretations either do not contravene the dogma of the inspiration of Scripture and of all its parts or do contravene this dogma. In the former case, these interpretations are of course open to free discussion; in the latter case, if such an interpretation of a historical truth runs counter to the dogma of inspiration, it then involves a matter of faith and so the Church surely has the right to pass judgment on it.[41]

For the rest, one can readily agree with Granderath, who holds that an exegete is blameworthy who, even in matters of this sort, would *lightly*, i.e., without a really probable reason, depart from the obvious meaning and the common view held by the fathers, or would part company with them in such a way as to be, without a justifying reason, *the cause of scandal* to Christian people. Such an interpretation—even granting that it might be correct—would certainly tend to lessen the reverence due to Scripture and could therefore be censured as "offensive to pious ears."[42]

III. Principles Governing the Private Reading of Sacred Scriptures

121

1. The reading of Sacred Scripture *is not necessary* for the individual faithful—certainly not by necessity of means, since they can obtain outside of Scripture not only an adequate but even an abundant knowledge of doctrines about faith and morals. Nor is it necessary by divine command, for certainly no such command can be proved to exist. The appeal to the following words of our Lord is of no avail:

> "You have the Scriptures at your finger ends (ereunate), since you think you have in them a source of eternal life; and, in fact, they are my standing witnesses"—John 5:39.

For (a) the context seems to call for taking the verb *ereunate* as the indicative rather than the imperative: (b) even granting that it is the imperative, the text still proves nothing. From the fact that Christ directs the Jews, in this case the Scribes and Pharisees, to the writings of the Old Testament that they may learn therein of His divine mission, it does not at all follow that He wished to bind all men to the reading of Sacred Scripture. St. Augustine's words are worthy of note:

> The man who is solidly grounded in faith, hope, and love, and remains unshakably rooted therein, needs the Scriptures only for the instruction of others. And in fact many people live by these three virtues out in the desert, far from access to the sacred books.[43]

2. The reading of Scripture is in itself most *advantageous*, for

122

All Scripture is inspired by God and useful for teaching, for reproving, for correcting, for instructing in holiness—2 Tim. 3:16.

But in view of the obscurity of Scripture, a certain amount of *risk* is always mixed in with the advantages. There is always the chance that the unlearned will misunderstand it and so be sidetracked into error. That is why the Church, to which Christ entrusted the control of spiritual goods, should be praised rather than blamed when it takes steps to neutralize whatever danger may be lurking in the shadows. One such step would be to prescribe that those of the faithful who want to read the Scriptures must use a version with good explanatory footnotes. For the rest, anyone who is familiar with the Bible knows full well that not all the books offer equal advantages or the same chances of error.[44]

3. It may happen that the aforesaid *danger*, which in itself is not so very great for adults sincerely devoted to the Church and well instructed in Christian principles, may, however, *as a result of special circumstances of time and place, grow so imminent that the indiscriminate reading of Scripture might have to be considered harmful rather than helpful.* When this happens, the Church acts according to its rights and very prudently in the bargain if it forbids the ordinary faithful to read the Scriptures and reserves the privilege to those alone for whom it would be really profitable.[45]

4. The foregoing observations explain why *the Church's discipline* in permitting or urging the reading of Sacred Scripture *has not always been the same.*

Before the thirteenth century there was no prohibition or restriction;[46] in fact many of the fathers heartily recommended the reading of the Bible. There were, it is true, many sects which misused Scripture, but this misuse was generally limited to just a few passages.

From the thirteenth century to the Reformation there were some partial and local prohibitions.[47]

At the time of the Reformation, the Reformers began to use Sacred Scripture, "crystal clear and sufficient by itself alone," as their chief weapon in the battle to overthrow the tradition and the hierarchy of the Church. Pius IV countered in 1564 by approving and promulgating the *fourth rule of the Index,* which forbade anyone to read the Bible in the vernacular except those who, on the advice of their pastor or confessor, obtained written permission from the bishop or the inquisitor. The reason for the prohibition was expressed as follows: "Since experience has made it clear that, if Bibles in the vernacular are allowed to circulate out of control, more harm is caused than good, and this because of the rashness of certain people, etc." Sixtus V and Clement VIII reserved the granting of the permission just mentioned to the Holy See and the

Sacred Congregation of the Index. When the danger died down, this law was toned down considerably by the decree of Benedict XIV (apparently) and by gradually changing custom, and was finally restated as follows by Leo XIII.

Present-day legislation on private Bible-reading: [48] **124**

a. Editions of the *original text,* of the *ancient Catholic versions* and of *other versions in languages other than the vernacular* which are published by non-Catholics may be read *only* by those who are engaged in theological or biblical studies, *provided,* however, that doctrines of the Catholic faith are not attacked in the introduction or notes. All may use the same versions if they are published by *Catholics.*

b. No translation in the *vernacular,* even though done by Catholics, may be used unless *approved by the Holy See* or *edited under the watchful eye of the bishops and furnished with notes* taken from the fathers of the Church and from learned Catholic authors.[49]

c. Translations in any vernacular whatsoever which have been made by non-Catholics may be used *only* by those who are engaged in theological or biblical studies, with the proviso mentioned above under (a).

St. Pius X praised and granted indulgences to the Italian Society of St. Jerome, which strives to promote the reading of the Gospels in Christian homes by making the historical books of the New Testament available at a very low price. In fact, the pontiff remarked: The Gospel "is, of all books, the one from which humble souls can obtain instructions which are useful and, at the same time, attractive."[50] And the words of our late Holy Father, Pius XII, are most eloquent:

> If these things which We have said, Venerable Brethren and beloved sons, are necessary in every age, much more urgently are they needed in our sorrowful times, when almost all peoples and nations are plunged in a sea of calamities, when a cruel war heaps ruins upon ruins and slaughter upon slaughter, when, owing to the most bitter hatred stirred up among the nations, We perceive with greatest sorrow that in not a few has been extinguished the sense not only of Christian moderation and charity, but also of humanity itself. Who can heal these mortal wounds of the human family if not He, to whom the Prince of the Apostles, full of confidence and love, addresses these words:

"Lord, to whom shall we go? Thou hast the words of eternal life."

To this Our most merciful Redeemer we must therefore bring all back by every means in our power; for He is the divine consoler of the afflicted; He it is who teaches all, whether they be invested with public authority or are bound in duty to obey and submit, true honesty, absolute justice and generous charity; it is He in fine, and He alone, Who can be the firm foundation and support of peace and tranquility: "For other foundation no man can lay, but that which is laid: which is Christ Jesus." This the author of salvation, Christ, will men more fully know, more ardently love and more faithfully imitate in proportion as they are more assiduously urged to know and meditate the Sacred Letters, especially the New Testament, for, as St. Jerome the Doctor of Stridon says: "To ignore the Scripture is to ignore Christ"; and again: "If there is anything in this life which sustains a wise man and induces him to maintain his serenity amidst the tribulations and adversities of the world, it is in the first place, I consider, the meditation and knowledge of the Scriptures."

There those who are wearied and oppressed by adversities and afflictions will find true consolation and divine strength to suffer and bear with patience; there—that is in the Holy Gospels—Christ, the highest and greatest example of justice, charity and mercy, is present to all; and to the lacerated and trembling human race are laid open the fountains of that divine grace without which both peoples and their rulers can never arrive at, never establish, peace in the state and unity of heart; there in fine will all learn Christ, "Who is the head of all principality and power" and "Who of God is made unto us wisdom and justice and sanctification and redemption."[51]

The rich stream of biblical literature aimed at encouraging and helping the faithful in their reading of the Bible bears abundant testimony to the Church's attitude in this regard.[52] Eloquent witness, too, is borne by the constant efforts being made to render the sacred text itself intelligible and enlightening by making it available in readable, scientifically solid, modern translation. Not to mention the outstanding European works of this kind, we might recall those of the Confraternity of Christian Doctrine, of Monsignor Knox, and of Fathers Kleist and Lilly.[53]

Corollary

1. It is hardly necessary to point out that Protestant Bible Societies[54] have been condemned over and over again by the Church in no uncertain terms. Aside from the dangers which lurk in indiscreet reading of Sacred Scriptures, there are also the following reasons: (a) These societies are founded squarely on the heretical principal that Scripture is the unique and proximate rule of faith; (b) no legitimate authority guarantees the trustworthiness of the translations they hand out; (c) they often use the distribution and sale of Bibles as a cover-up for efforts to wean simple folk from the Catholic Church.[55]

2. An antiquated fable has it that Luther and the Reformers in general resurrected Scripture out of the accumulated dust of centuries. Since there are still many who believe this old wives' tale, it will help to add here some data on *Catholic versions* of Sacred Scriptures *in the vernacular,* published *in printed editions* before the Reformation.

A *German* translation of the whole Bible was published at Strasburg in 1466. By 1500 it had gone through fifteen editions.

An *Italian* translation of the whole Bible was published at Venice in 1471. By 1500 it had gone through nine editions.

A *Bohemian* translation of the New Testament came out in 1475, of the whole Bible in 1488 and again in 1489.

A *Dutch* translation of the Old Testament was published at Delft in 1477. The psalms were not included in the first editions, but followed in 1480. A Dutch translation of the whole Bible was published at Louvain and Antwerp in 1518 and again in 1525.

A *French* translation of the whole Bible came out in 1477; there were three editions prior to 1500.

A *Spanish* translation of the whole Bible by Boniface Ferrer was published at Valencia in 1478.

A translation in *Limousine* was published at Valence in 1478.

Meanwhile the Latin version of the whole Bible, which was printed at Mainz, 1450–1455, and was in fact the first book printed with movable type, went through fifty-six printings.

And no mention has been made here of the many editions of just parts of the Bible.

THE SOURCES OF REVELATION

3. THE AUTHENTICITY OF THE VULGATE[57]

127 Thus far the discussion has centered on the inspired Scriptures as a whole, prescinding from the concrete form in which the Latin Church has used them for many centuries. Now attention must be focused on the authority enjoyed by that form or edition to which a universal custom of long standing has given the name of the "old and vulgate edition" or, more simply, the Vulgate.

I. St. Jerome and the Vulgate

The *Vulgate* owes its origin to St. Jerome, who, from 383–405:
(a) *Made a new translation from the original* of all the protocanonical books of the Old Testament (except the Psalter) together with Tobias and Judith; (b) *polished up* the "Old Latin" translation of the Psalter and of the whole New Testament, the former on the basis of the *Hexapla* of Origen,[58] the latter on the basis of the original Greek; (c) *took over without alteration* from the Old Latin the remaining deuterocanonical books of the Old Testament and the deuterocanonical sections of Esther and Daniel.[59]

Jerome's Vulgate, at first received enthusiastically by some and bitterly attacked by others, gradually and almost imperceptibly elbowed out the Old Latin version, so that, by at least the middle of the seventh century, it was accepted universally.[60] St. Isidore of Seville (d. 636): "All the Churches in general make use of" the version of St. Jerome, "for the reason that what it expresses is closer to the truth and its wording is clearer."[61]

The Vulgate certainly does not achieve the apex of perfection, but its excellence is nonetheless acknowledged by many non-Catholics and rationalists.[62]

128 ### II. Council of Trent and the Vulgate

The *Council of Trent,* session 4, 1546, *practically canonized the Vulgate* by a twofold decree, at first rather indirectly, but later quite specifically. For a correct appreciation of this decree, three things must be distinguished:

a. The Vulgate *version*, which came from the hands of St. Jerome.

b. The Vulgate *edition* which at the time of the Council had been "approved by continuous use throughout so many centuries in the Church itself." There was no question of any single codex, as the Vulgate existed in innumerable codices, both in handwriting and in print, which the western Church had been using for many centuries and was using at that very time. Those numerous codices, even though containing the work of Jerome in substance, were far from agreeing with that work in every detail. A great number of false readings had slipped in as a result of the carelessness of copyists and of the rash boldness of self-appointed correctors. The Fathers of Trent were well aware of this sad state of affairs, and in that same fourth session decreed:

> "that hereafter Sacred Scripture, and especially this aforementioned venerable Vulgate edition, be printed as correctly as possible"—DB 786.

The result of this decree was:

c. *The Sixto-Clementine* Vulgate, i.e., that edition of the Vulgate which, by order of Sixtus V and Clement VIII, was published in 1592. Efforts were made in its preparation to eliminate the false readings and mistakes caused by errant correctors. This is the edition which, by law, has served and still serves as the model for all other editions of the Vulgate.[63]

Again, the decrees of Trent speak of the *Vulgate edition* such as it is described under b. above; in fact, considering the time at which the decrees came out, they can have had no other in mind.

III. Analysis of Trent's Decrees on the Vulgate 129

The *decrees of Trent* are as follows:

> If anyone should refuse to accept these books [just listed], whole and entire with all their parts, as they are customarily read in the Catholic Church, and as contained in the old Latin Vulgate edition, as sacred and canonical, . . . let him be anathema.—DB 784.
>
> Furthermore, this sacred Synod, in the conviction that no little advantage can accrue to the Church of God, if it be made clear just which one of all the Latin editions of the sacred books currently in circulation is to be considered authentic, has decided and does herewith decree that the aforementioned old Vulgate edition, which has stood the test of centuries-long usage in the Church in public readings, disputations, sermons, and instructions, be accepted as authentic, and that no one, for any pretext whatsoever, may dare or presume to reject it.—DB 785.

130   Consider first the second decree. Setting aside for the moment the question of the juridical force of the word *authentic*, the general meaning of the decree is that, of all existing Latin versions, the Vulgate alone is chosen as the *public text* or, as modern parlance would put it, the *official text* of the (western) Church. This text must be used in every *public exercise of the Church's teaching power*, and no one may, in performing a function of this sort, either refuse under any pretext to use it, or substitute for it another Latin version.[64]

Clearly, then, the decree is primarily disciplinary, not dogmatic. Absolutely speaking, there is nothing to prevent the Church from choosing at some later date another version as authentic in place of the Vulgate. However, the decree does imply or suppose a *dogmatic fact;*[65] for in passing this law the Council really, even though implicitly, guaranteed the doctrine of the whole Vulgate, to the extent that is well within the province of the Church's magisterium, i.e., all the Vulgate's teaching in matters of faith and morals.

The basic dogmatic fact, then, on which this decree rests, is this: *in no passage does the Vulgate differ from the original text in such a way as to teach error in a religious matter*. But since to call for the universal use of a version which would be orthodox indeed but substantially untrustworthy as a translation would be for all practical purposes tantamount to adulterating the sources of revelation, the further dogmatic fact on which the law of Trent is based is this: *the Vulgate edition is an at least substantially faithful translation*. On the other hand, since it is abundantly clear from the *Acta* of the Council that the fathers of Trent were well aware that the Vulgate as they then possessed it was in sad shape,[66] it is quite *certain that they did not guarantee its absolute or integral fidelity to the original*.

Clearly, then, the choice of the Vulgate as the Church's public text actually did confer upon it *authenticity* or authority, in accordance with which it can stand on its own two feet as the word of God without recourse to the original text. But this authority must be recognized as primarily and immediately *dogmatic*, not critical. Surely the Council's intention was not precisely to proclaim that the Vulgate is a perfect rendering of the original Scriptures *in every single detail*, but rather that the Vulgate never *sets forth in*

SACRED SCRIPTURE

any passage whatsoever a doctrine which is not truly and surely Catholic.

The reason for the fathers' choice of the Vulgate as the authentic text and the argument on which they based their conviction of the complete orthodoxy and substantial fidelity of this edition, is made clear by the decree itself: 131

> "the old Vulgate edition, which has stood the test of centuries-long usage in the Church."

Considering its infallibility, it was simply impossible for the Roman Church together with the whole western world to have used for so many centuries a version devoid of the above mentioned qualities.

IV. Substantial Fidelity of Vulgate to the Original Bible   132

There remains the question of the *extent of the "substantial" fidelity* to or conformity with the original which we must attribute to the Vulgate in accord with the principles of Theology.

To answer this question we must look a bit more closely at the first decree of the Council as quoted above, which is more surely *dogmatic*. By virtue of this decree "these books, whole and entire with all their parts, as they are customarily read in the Catholic Church, and as contained in the old Latin Vulgate edition" must be accepted "as sacred and canonical," or, in other words, as inspired.[67] Since no one claims that the Vulgate itself was written under inspiration, it is evident that the books which make it up can be considered inspired by no other title and to no greater extent than that they are in conformity with the original text. It follows that the decree under consideration indirectly but nonetheless truly guarantees the fidelity of the Vulgate translation. But the question is: *To what extent?*

The decree says first of all *"these* books," i.e., those just listed. It is accordingly most certain that no book which is contained in the Vulgate is not inspired, no matter how short that book may be.

The decree says further: *"whole and entire."* It is accordingly certain that the individual books of the Vulgate integrally or *completely throughout* mirror the individual books of the original. However, the term "whole and entire" all by itself may be understood in a less restricted sense. If a copyist accidentally or carelessly leaves out two or three sentences which are not precisely essential, or takes it upon himself to add a few glosses which are not out of line with the tenor and theme of the book, he can still be said to have copied the whole book. Again, in the present instance the word "whole" must be taken less strictly, as indicating only substantial integrity. This is clear from the fathers' frank recognition of the poor condition of the Vulgate, and from the qualifying phrase, "with all their parts, etc." It would have been pointless to add these words if the fathers had meant the term "whole" in the strict sense.

133 The decree says, finally, "with *all their parts*, as, etc." All agree that the term "part" need not be understood as referring to every single word, every single sentence, including those having nothing to do with faith or morals. The reason for this general agreement is the oft mentioned defectiveness of the extant Vulgate. But the precise force of this phrase is still a matter for discussion.

It seems clear from the *Acta* of the Council (to the extent that they are known) that the phrase was added to safeguard the deuterocanonical passages, especially those of the New Testament, which the Protestants were rejecting. Still, the fathers were loath to specify those passages,[68] and chose a noncommittal formula instead. That formula is, in our opinion, to be understood as follows. Individual passages are to be considered inspired if it can be established that they have been in constant and universal use in the Church. The Vulgate (in the sense explained in 128b) is the witness to this use, not the only witness or one that, all by itself, would compel assent, but certainly the principal one.

It is our opinion, then, that by virtue of the phrase "with all their parts, as, etc." one must consider inspired the *deuterocanonical parts of the New Testament* (which the Council had in mind above all) and *any single passage whose constant and universal use has been established.*

Others, however, are of a different mind. A few think that this phrase offers guarantee for no specific passage but only vaguely for all whose use, as explained above, has been established.[69] Some hold that the phrase covers *only the deuterocanonical passages and no others.*[70] Quite a few are of the opinion that it has in view *every single passage* (i.e., every directly dogmatic passage) *which was definitely in the Vulgate edition* (i.e., in all or practically all copies thereof).[71]

V. Corollaries 134

1. It may help to indicate briefly how much of a difference can be admitted between the Vulgate and the original text even in independently dogmatic passages, without running counter to the decrees of Trent.[72]

a. One may admit that some text or other which was in the original is missing from the Vulgate.

b. One may admit that the Vulgate text sometimes differs from the original in manner of expression, i.e., that the same point of doctrine is taught in both, but in different ways.

c. One may admit that some passage or other (setting forth orthodox doctrine) is now in the Vulgate but was not to be found in the original.[73] An argument based on such a text would not have force as a proof from Scripture, but it would be valid as a proof from Tradition. The fact that a teaching of this sort is found in the venerable Latin Vulgate is a sure proof that it is genuinely Catholic.

It is clear from the foregoing that the Council of Trent gave 135 the Vulgate no preeminence whatsoever over the original texts, not even over those texts as they existed at the time of the Council. The Church does not for a moment doubt the substantial integrity of the original texts (or of the Septuagint and other reputable ancient versions), since it used them for its revision of the Clementine Vulgate.[74] Neither does it discourage their use even in matters of doctrine, nor does it consider such use a waste of time. On the contrary, it approves it heartily:

> For, although the meaning of the Hebrew and Greek is substantially rendered by the Vulgate, nevertheless, wherever there may be ambiguity or want of clearness, the "examination of the older tongues," to quote St. Augustine, will be useful and advantageous.[75]

As things stand, the Vulgate (along with oral Tradition) suffices for the development of Christian doctrine. For a fuller and more accurate understanding of the meaning of Scripture, for a stronger defense and more profound explanation of that doctrine, recourse to the original texts is often very helpful and sometimes quite necessary.[76]

Notes

1. See *above*, no. 83, n. 46.
2. S.Th. 1, q. 1, a. 10, ad 3.
3. St. Thomas, *Quodlibetales*, 7, q. 6, a. 14.
4. S.Th. 1, q. 1, a. 10, ad 1.
5. See C. De Vine, "The Consequent Sense," CBQ, 2 (1940), 145 ff. An example of such a process would be the following:
Christ was a real man.
But a real man has a body and a soul.
Therefore Christ has a body and a soul.
6. If the proper precautions are observed, there can be no serious objection against using Scripture in the accommodated sense for the edification of the faithful, etc. Care must be taken, however, that no meaning foreign to the text be suggested or recommended as a true sense of Scripture. See Bainvel, *Les contresens bibliques des Predicatêurs*. The following story from the life of St. Francis de Sales will illustrate what is meant by the accommodated sense. Once, when the bishop was ill, his doctor set about applying some rather mysterious therapy. When the patient asked for an explanation, he answered, "*What I do thou knowest not now; but thou shalt know hereafter*"—John 13:7. As the story goes, St. Francis took umbrage at such a flippant use of the word of God. Countless instances of accommodation are to be found in the Church's liturgy, but here, of course, the procedure is employed with great reverence. The New Testament writers themselves not infrequently accommodated Old Testament quotations to analogous situations. It is, then, a licit procedure in itself, but private individuals should use it with extreme caution, for fear of suggesting to untrained minds that such a meaning is truly the sense of a given passage of Scripture. As Pius XII wrote in the *Divino Afflante Spiritu:*

> Let priests . . . confirm the Christian doctrine by sentences from the Sacred Books and illustrate it by outstanding examples from sacred history and in particular from the Gospel of Christ Our Lord; and—avoiding with the greatest care those purely arbitrary and far-fetched adaptations, which are not a use, but rather an abuse of the divine word—let them set forth all this with such eloquence, lucidity and clearness that the faithful may not only be moved and inflamed to reform their lives, but may also conceive in their hearts the greatest veneration for the Sacred Scripture.—no. 50, RSS, p. 103; see also no. 27, p. 93 f.

7. See G. Gietmann, "Der mehrfache Sinn der heiligen Schrift," ZfKTh, (1903), 381; for the view of St. Thomas, see the article by Blanche in *Revue Thomiste*, 14, 192; see also A. De Guglielmo, "Dan. 5:25—An Example of a Double Literal Sense," CBQ, 11 (1949), 202 ff.
8. *Confessions* 12. 31; see *De doctrina Christiana* iii. 27, 38.
9. *De Potentia* 4, 1 (corpus); see *In II sententiarum* d. 12, a. 2, ad 7.
10. STh 1, q. 1, a. 10; see also *Quodlibetales* 7, q. 14, a. 16.

SACRED SCRIPTURE

11. See, for example, Beelen, *Dissertatio theologica de multiplici sensu literali*.

12. Proponents of the multiple sense appeal especially to Ps. 2:7 (see Heb. 1:5; 5:5; Acts 13:33) and to John 11:50–53 (which passage is definitely not apposite.)

13. See, for example, Rom. 5:14; 1 Cor. 5:7; 10:6 and 11; Gal. 4:24; Heb. 7:3; 9:9; 1 Pet. 3:21.

14. See, for example, Matt. 2:17 (Jer. 31:15); Matt. 3:3 (Isa. 40:3); Matt. 27:9 (Zach. 11:12–13; Jer. 32); Acts 1:16–20 (Ps. 68:26; 108:8).

15. John 19:36 (Exod. 12:46; Num. 9:12); see, for example, Matt. 2:15 (Osee 11:1), although this may be rather a good example of the use of accommodation; Matt. 13:35 (Ps. 77:2); John 13:18 (Ps. 40:10).

16. See, for example, 1 John 2:20 and 27; Jer. 31:31–34.

17. See, for example, Bavinck, *Gereformierde Dogmatiek*, I, 394–99.

18. See A. J. Cotter, "The Obscurity of Scripture," CBQ, 9 (1947), 453 ff.; J. T. Forestell, "The Limitation of Inerrancy," CBQ, 20 (1958), 17–18; R. A. F. MacKenzie, "Some Problems in the Field of Inspiration," *ibid.*, 1–8.

19. The Council of Trent (Session 4) had used the *negative* form, forbidding anyone to explain Scripture in a sense *contrary* to that held by the Church. Some inferred from this that it is wrong to give Scripture a meaning by which a dogma of the Church would be ruled out or denied, but that it is not necessary to accept the meaning proposed by the Church. Thus, for example, one would be free to say that the text of Jas. 5:14 makes no reference to Extreme Unction, as long as he admitted that Extreme Unction was a true sacrament of the New Law. In order to obviate any such perverse interpretation, the fathers of the Vatican Council changed the negative form to the *positive*, and in so doing gave a clearer picture of the true mind of the Council of Trent.

20. See the treatise on *Christ's Church*, nos. 79, 180, 198.

21. See *ibid.*, no. 85.

22. See *Coll. Lac.* 7, 226 and 240.

23. See Mangenot in DBV III, 619 for an account of recent controversies on the authoritative interpretation of Sacred Scripture.

24. Luke 24:45; see Acts 8:30–31.

25. Likewise, Protestants gain little profit from an appeal to St. John Chrysostom, who does in fact emphatically extol the clarity of Scripture (*Homilia 3 de Lazaro* 2 and 3; *Homilia 3 in 2 Thessalonicenses* 4) but nonetheless urges that for the more difficult passages the faithful consult the more learned and ask their priests for help. And when he treats the words, "*You search the Scriptures*," he says quite frankly: "For what is said in the prophets concerning Christ does not lie on the surface in clear view, but is very deeply hidden, like a treasure of some sort"—*Homilia 41 in Joannem* 1.

26. *Commonitorium* 2.

27. *Dissertatio variorum argumentorum*, II, 391.

28. *Gereformierde Dogmatiek*, I, 396 ff.

29. The true meaning in the context is: You have been sufficiently instructed by the preaching of the apostles and the anointing of the Holy Spirit, through which you received and hold fast to the faith, and you have no need

to learn from Antichrists. See SB XII, 532 ff.; Mollat-Braun, "L'evangile et les épîtres de saint Jean," SBJ (Paris, 1953), pp. 218–19; CCHS, 957 a–b.

30. Leo XIII, *Providentissimus Deus*, RSS, p. 14.
31. *Adversus haereses* iv. 26, 5; see 33. 8.
32. *De praescriptione haereticorum* 19; see 37–39.
33. *Commonitorium* 2.
34. *Loc. cit.*, p. 15.
35. The submission due to a merely authoritative *magisterium* will be discussed in the treatise on *Faith*.
36. Notice that, strictly speaking, this second rule is already included in the first.
37. *Loc. cit.*, p. 16.
38. See Leo XIII, *ibid.*
39. *Loc. cit.*, p. 15.
40. One may judge from this how far they stray from the truth who demand that an exegete approach Sacred Scripture unencumbered by dogma, shackled by no fixed belief, so that he may seek his doctrine in Scripture alone! This demand, which, moreover, not even Protestants themselves acknowledge (Bavinck, *op. cit.*, I, 399), is ruled out of court by Catholic principles on the relationship of Scripture to the Church.
41. *Coll. Lac.* 7, 240.
42. See *Der Katholik* (1898), 2, 396.
43. *De doctrina Christiana* 39, 43.
44. See A. C. Cotter, "The Obscurity of Scripture," CBQ, 9 (1947), 453 ff.; CCHS, 10b ff.
45. From what was just said above in paragraphs 1–3, one can easily understand how justified the Church was in proscribing certain propositions of Quesnell and of the Synod of Pistoia. See DB 1429–35 and 1567.

Undoubtedly the Divine Scriptures have been given to the whole Church and to all the children of the Church for their instruction. The Bible is certainly an ordinary and universal means of instruction, but at the same time there is no universal precept, either divine or apostolic, that all the faithful—every man, woman and child—should personally read the Bible. Heaven is open to illiterates. It is the doctrine of the Bible that matters, not knowledge of the letter. Those who teach religion—the pastors of the Church—should know the Book, but the faithful may, according to circumstances, know and live the faith which the Bible teaches without having spelled one sentence of its pages. Even in this present age of paper and of printing numberless Catholics live admirable and even sublime lives of faith, hope and charity without any direct reading of Holy Writ. They nourish their minds with the substance of the Bible through the liturgy of the Mass, through the mysteries of the Rosary, through the prayers which they know by heart, and through the sermons which they hear. Just as in countries which have an old traditional culture illiterate peasants can have an exquisite refinement of soul and manners, so also bookless peasants who have lived in the stream of Christian tradition can have all the grasp of faith and right living which are necessary for any, even the highest, degree of sanctity.

This is not a defense of illiteracy, but a warning against exaggerations. Self-instruction through reading must always be built on a basis of oral instruction received in the home, the school and the Church. The extent to which this supplementary aid can be used will depend on the available supply of books and on the ability of persons to read them fruitfully. Now these two things have varied considerably at various times. Some knowledge of this variation of conditions—varying book facilities and varying spread of education—is necessary, in order to understand the wise providence of the Church in regard to the Bible at different times. We must also keep in mind that whenever or wherever reading endangers the purity of Christian thought and living—the *unum necessarium*—it has to be wisely restricted.—CCHS 10b.

46. There is no basis for the accusation that Gregory VII forbade the Bohemians to use Scripture; see ZfKTh (1901), 746.

47. Moved by the disturbances of the Cathari, the Synod of Toulouse in 1229 put a ban on Sacred Scripture, and the Synod of Tarragona in 1233 forbade clerics as well as laymen to use the Romance version (see Hefele, *Conciliengeschichte* [2nd ed.], V, 982 and 1037). Because of the activities of Wyclif and his followers, the Synod of Oxford in 1408 banned English translations, but not all of them—only those which lacked ecclesiastical approval. See Hefele, *op. cit.*, VI, 985; *Stimmen*, 66 (1904), 351; CCHS 10c.

48. See *Decreta generalia de prohibitione et censura librorum*, I, chap. 2 and 3.

49. As a matter of *fact* the Apostolic See does not usually approve translations which have no explanatory notes.

50. See *Civiltà Cattolica*, 18, 12 (1903), 736. Benedict XV seconded the approval of his predecessor; see *Spiritus Paraclitus*, RSS, p. 63. Leo XIII had granted indulgences for the daily reading of the Bible; see CCHS 4h.

51. *Divino afflante Spiritu*, nos. 56–58, RSS, pp. 104–106.

52. To cite but a few such works, we might point to the following as excellent examples: C. Charlier, *La lecture'chretienne de la Bible* (Maredsous, 1957; J. L. McKenzie, *op. cit.*; B. Vawter, *op. cit.*; A. Jones, *Unless Some Man Show Me* (New York: Sheed & Ward, 1951); Dom Van Zeller's works on the prophets; *A Catholic Commentary on Holy Scripture* (London: Thos. Nelson & Sons, Ltd., 1953); see also the recent survey by H. Duesberg, "Horoscope du Mouvement Biblique," NRT, 79 (1957), 3 ff.

53. See the splendid article by W. Leonard and B. Orchard, "The Place of the Bible in the Church," CCHS 1 ff.

54. See *Kirchenlexikon* under the word *Bibelgesellschaften;* CCHS 10e ff.

55. The words of Perthes, a Protestant, are quite to the point: "If Catholics employed the means which Protestant Bible Societies use to bring Bibles to Catholics, we would label those means as Jesuitical proselytizing tricks"— cited by Hettinger, *Apologie* (7th ed.), IV, 494.

56. See F. Falk, *Die Bibel am Ausgang des Mittelalters* (1905), p. 91; *Kirchenlexikon* under the word *Bibelübersetzungen*, where there is also a treatment of translations done in manuscript before the invention of printing. Concerning these latter, Schanz has this to say:

"The first translations into the vernacular go back much further than was formerly supposed, and they are not to be attributed to heretical, for instance Waldensian, influences"—*Apologie* (3rd ed.), II, 682. For the view that Wycliffe was not responsible for the English translation of the

THE SOURCES OF REVELATION

Bible, see *Stimmen,* 66 (1904), 345; but see CCHS 29e ff.; H. Pope, *English Versions of the Bible* (St. Louis: Herder, 1952).
With the invention of printing by Johann Gutenberg in 1450, editions of the Bible appeared in rapid succession. In the first fifty years there were 124 of them. Between 1452 and 1522 (the year that Luther began his translation) fourteen complete editions of the Bible in High German appeared at Augsburg, Basle, Strasbourg, and Nuremberg; five in Low German at Cologne, Delf, Halberstadt, and Luebeck. During this same interval there were 156 Latin, six Hebrew, eleven Italian, ten French, one Flemish, one Limousine, one Russian, and two Bohemian editions. Almost all of these were sponsored and approved by the Catholic Church.
This much should suffice against the charge that the Church kept the people in a state of Biblical starvation, and that this was especially the case before the Reformation. England, indeed, may have been slow in the sense explained above; for historically speaking she has generally been a generation behind the Continent in her ideas. On the Continent, vernacular versions had long had wide manuscript circulation, and had come from the printing presses in goodly numbers before Luther's Bible was published.—CCHS 4g.

57. See Franzelin, *op. cit.*, theses 18 and 19; Vercellone, *Sulla authenticità delle singole parti della Bibbia volgata* (1866); *Revue du clergé français* (1895); RBibl (1895). 649; J. -M. Voste, "The Vulgate at the Council of Trent," CBQ, 9 (1947), 9 ff.; CCHS 27 eff.

58. Origen's *Hexapla* was the first attempt at a critical emandation of the Septuagint. It gets its name from the fact that it was arrannged in six parallel columns. For details, see CCHS 8b.

59. St. Jerome made extensive corrections of the Old Latin Psalter *(Roman Psalter),* then amended it further *(Gallican Psalter),* and finally made a completely fresh translation from the Hebrew. However, it is not this last translation, but the second emendation, the *Gallican Psalter,* which found its way into the Vulgate.

60. In some parts of the sacred liturgy, particularly in those sung by the choir, the use of the pre-Jerome (Old Latin) translation continued for quite a while longer, and still continues to a certain extent. Notice the differences between Ps. 94 in the (pre-Pius XII) Invitatory at Matins (Old Latin), and in the third nocturn for the feast of the Epiphany (Vulgate).

61. *De ecclesiasticis officiis* i. 12, 8.

62. Keil: "His translation surpasses all ancient versions in accuracy and fidelity"—*Einleitung*, p. 572. De Wette-Schräder: "By virtue of his careful accuracy he produced the most excellent work of the sort that all of antiquity has to offer"—*Einleitung*, p. 59 Bleek-Wellhausen: "The work in general is always acknowledged by impartial judges as very excellent"—*Einleitung*, p. 598. Teuffel: "Jerome's translation of the Bible is a masterpiece in its field" —*Römische Literaturgeschichte* (3rd ed.), p. 1023 (cited by Cornely, *Introductio*, I, 429 and Schanz, *Apologie* [3rd ed.], II, 682).

63. A short while before, in 1578, the Sistine Edition of the Septuagint had been published at Rome by order of Sixtus V, and in the introduction was printed an Apostolic Brief which decreed "that the Old Testament in the Septuagint version, thus revised and corrected, be accepted and retained by

all, and used especially with a view to the (better) understanding of the Latin Vulgate and the ancient fathers. All are forbidden to dare make any further changes in this new Greek edition by adding or expunging anything." The fathers of Trent had sincerely wanted an edition of the *Hebrew Bible*, revised by authority of the Holy See. But this desire was not satisfied. For the story behind the *Clementine Vulgate*, see Bellarmine's *Prefatio ad lectorem*.

A reconstitution of the text of St. Jerome according to the modern canons of textual criticism could scarcely be expected at this period. Nevertheless the third Congregation of Cardinals appointed to prepare the new emended edition under the presidency of Cardinal Carafa in 1586, if we may judge from the record of their labours preserved in the Codex Carafianus, would have produced an excellent critical text had not Sixtus V rejected their corrections and himself prepared the Sixtine edition of the Vulgate, published at the new Vatican Press in 1590. This edition, recognized as needing correction even by Sixtus himself, was almost immediately withdrawn from circulation. The new and final edition of Clement VIII in 1592, prepared by Toletus, left much to be desired from the critical point of view. It was not until 1907 however that an official revision of the Vulgate text was undertaken by Pius X. The Benedictines to whom the work was assigned have already published an excellent text with a full critical apparatus of Gen-Kings. More recently Pius XII ordered the preparation of a new Latin version of the Psalter from the original texts, published in 1945, and permitted the use of this version in the daily recitation of the Breviary.—CCHS 28c.

See also J. -M. Vosté, *loc. cit.*

64. It will be easy to appreciate the usefulness, in fact the moral necessity, of such an arrangement, if one considers the fact that during the years 1515–1550 there were published at least 181 editions of different versions either of the whole Bible or of different parts thereof. See Hurter, *Theologiae dogmaticae compendium* (8th ed.), I, no. 178. On the use of the Vulgate in the public exercise of the Church's teaching power, see the citation from Pius XII, *Divino afflante Spiritu*, n. 76 below; also the letter of the Biblical Commission to the Italian hierarchy, RSS, p. 139 ff.; the decree of the Biblical Commission on the use of versions of Sacred Scripture in the vernacular, under date of Aug. 22, 1943, RSS, p. 146, and CCHS 53e for a review of Vosté's comments on this latter decree.

65. See the preceding treatise, *Christ's Church*, no. 89.

66. See Theiner, *Acta*, I, 65 and 70. The fathers were reluctant to mention the faultiness of the Vulgate in the *decree* itself lest they give the faithful an occasion of scandal and heretics an opportunity for further detraction. The theologians who were in the Roman curia at first gave no approval to the decree as drawn up by Trent, because of the faults (of the Vulgate), which they too recognized. So the three papal legates wrote from Trent to Rome "that all were in agreement on regarding the Vulgate as the safest [translation], *because it was the only one which, over such a long span of time, had not had to be censured for heresy,* even though it appears to differ in some passages from the Hebrew, and although its style is not of the purest and not even always free from barbarisms and solecisms"—Pallavicini, *Histoire du Concile de Trente*, VI. 17, 15. It may help to add here the words of Andrea

Vega, who took part in the Council of Trent as a consulting theologian: the Council "wanted it to be considered authentic to this end, *that all might be sure that it was tainted by no error such as might furnish a basis for some erroneous doctrine of faith and morals*, and that is why it decreed that no one should, under any pretext, dare reject it. And that this was the mind of the Synod, and *that it intended to decree nothing further*, you can deduce from the words themselves and from the other usual approbations of the Council" —*De justificatione*, XV, 9, cited by Cornely, *loc. cit.*, p. 446. See also the letter of Cardinal Bellarmine, April 1, 1575, in RBibl (1908), 103.

67. See the Vatican Council, constitution *De fide catholica*, cap. 2. For the rest, since the Vatican Council made no new decrees concerning the *extent* of inspiration and the *authenticity* of the Vulgate, but wished simply to restate the doctrine of Trent, it is enough to speak of the Tridentine decrees alone. See Coll Lac VII, 123, 141, and 1621.

68. In the general assembly seventeen fathers wanted explicit mention of the Gospel passages to be made in the decree; thirty-four voted against it; some wanted a special decree drawn up later on this point, but this was never done. See Theiner, *Acta*, I, 71–77; M. Nicolau, *Sacrae Theologiae Summa, op. cit.*, p. 1035 ff.; J. Balestri, *op. cit.*, p. 216, ff.

69. So, for example, Anton von Scholz, as cited by Peters, *Grundsätzliche Stellung*, p. 23.

70. So, for example, Fonck: "The Council declares all inspired books sacred and canonical in that form and integrity in which they were used in the Church from antiquity; it is therefore forbidden to reject whole books (*libri ipsi*), essential parts (*integri*), or the disputed parts mentioned (*cum omnibus suis partibus*)"—*Der Kampf*, p. 44.

71. So Franzelin, *De Traditione et Scriptura*, thesis 19, and his followers.

72. The very rigorous decree of the Sacred Congregation of the Council, Jan. 17, 1576, which is considered apocryphal by many, but which was discovered in 1890 by Battifol, does not, according to Pius IX, apply except to the extent that it prohibits any assertions attacking the Vulgate in matters of faith and morals. See Franzelin, *loc. cit.*, (3rd ed.), p. 563.

73. This third assertion is not admitted by those who share Cardinal Franzelin's views. The words of Fr. Vosté are worth quoting at this point:

As a version, the Vulgate is a human work, although made by a holy Doctor specially guided by God; and as a human work, it contains perfectible translations, more or less inexact, as well as errors in names and numbers. It is a Christian version, that is, a Christian *interpretation;* therefore it sometimes renders a text in a more explicitly messianic sense; . . . Sometimes, it introduces certain so-called translations, which are really new creations; . . . Perhaps you will ask me: "How can the Vulgate be called authentic, if it contains such evidently free and erroneous translations, even in doctrinal matters?" I reply: Because the Vulgate contains two elements, which a good theologian, when quoting it, should always distinguish accurately; firstly, the genuine inspired word of God, wherever it perfectly agrees with the original (and this is the ordinary case); secondly, the testimony of ecclesiastical tradition only, wherever it departs from the original. In the first case, the theologian will be able to cite the text of the Vulgate as a proof from Sacred Scripture; whereas in the

SACRED SCRIPTURE

second case, he must speak of a proof from tradition.—*Loc. cit.*, pp. 19–20. The same may be asserted today as regards preaching, according to the grand example of our Holy Father, who in his estimable discourses never quotes a biblical text which is not proved to be consonant with the original Hebrew or Greek.—*Ibid.*, p. 24.

74. See *Praefatio ad lectorem*. This one thing is true, that the Church *does not go surety* for the complete orthodoxy and substantial integrity of the Hebrew text, and no wonder: did it not cease to be used publicly in the Church almost from the very beginning?

75. *Providentissimus Deus*, RSS, p. 13. See also *Divino afflante Spiritu*, RSS, pp. 88–89.

76. For a recent statement of the mind of the Church in this matter, the words of Pius XII cannot be surpassed:

Nor should anyone think that this use of the original texts, in accordance with the methods of criticism, in any way derogates from those decrees so wisely enacted by the Council of Trent concerning the Latin Vulgate. It is historically certain that the Presidents of the Council received a commission, which they duly carried out, to beg, that is, the Sovereign Pontiff in the name of the Council that he should have corrected, as far as possible, first a Latin, and then a Greek, and Hebrew edition, which eventually would be published for the benefit of the Holy Church of God. If this desire could not then be fully realized owing to the difficulties of the times and other obstacles, at present it can, we earnestly hope, be more perfectly and entirely fulfilled by the united efforts of Catholic scholars. And if the Tridentine Synod wished "that all should use as authentic" the Vulgate Latin version, this, we all know, applies only to the Latin Church and to the public use of the same Scriptures; nor does it, doubtless, in any way diminish the authority and value of the original texts. For there was no question then of these texts, but of the Latin versions, which were in circulation at that time, and of these the same Council rightly declared to be preferable that which "had been approved by its long-continued use for so many centuries in the Church." Hence this special authority or as they say, authenticity of the Vulgate was not affirmed by the Council particularly for critical reasons, but rather because of its legitimate use in the Churches throughout so many centuries; by which use indeed the same is shown, in the sense in which the Church has understood and understands it, to be free from any error whatsoever in matters of faith and morals; so that, as the Church herself testifies and affirms, it may be quoted safely and without fear of error in disputations, in lectures and in preaching; and so its authenticity is not specified primarily as critical, but rather as juridical.

Wherefore this authority of the Vulgate in matters of doctrine by no means prevents—nay rather today it almost demands—either the corroboration and confirmation of this same doctrine by the original texts or the having recourse on any and every occasion to the aid of these same texts, by which the correct meaning of the Sacred Letters is everywhere daily made more clear and evident. Nor is it forbidden by the decree of the Council of Trent, to make translations into the vulgar tongue, even directly from the original texts themselves, for the use and benefit of the faithful and for the better understanding of the divine word, as We know to have been already done in a laudable manner in many countries with the approval of the Ecclesiastical authority.—*Divino afflante Spiritu*, 20–22, RSS, pp. 90–91.

Special Bibliography

BALESTRI, J. *Op. cit.*, pp. 423 ff.

BROWN, R. E. *The Sensus Plenior of Sacred Scripture.* Baltimore: St. Mary's University, 1955. pp. 1–28.

COPPENS, J. *Les harmonies des deux testaments.* Tournai-Paris, 1949.

FULLER, R. C. "The Interpretation of Holy Scripture," CCHS 39b ff.

HÖPFL-GUT. *Op. cit.*, pp. 423 ff.

ROBERT-TRICOT. *Guide to the Bible, op. cit.*, pp. 504 ff.

―――. *Initiation biblique* (3rd ed.). Tournai: Desclée et Cie., 1954.

CHAPTER II

Sacred Tradition

I. 1. *Definition: Objective Oral Tradition Is that Collection of Speculative and Practical Truths Communicated* viva voce *to the Church by Christ and the Apostles as Organs of Revelation, to be Safeguarded Until the End of Time*
   2. *Further Specifications:*
      a. dogmatic;
      b. divine or divine-apostolic;
      c. ecclesiastical vs. mundane;
      d. apostolic vs. post-apostolic.

II. *The Protestant Position*

III. *The Catholic Dogma on the Origin, the Preservation, and the Value of Tradition*

IV. 1. *The Precise Question at Issue in the Controversy with Protestants: Does the Church Draw the Christian Revelation which It Must Teach from Scripture Alone?*
   2. *This Question Divisible Into the Two Following:*
      a. Are the truths actually contained in Scripture known by the *magisterium* from this source alone?
      b. Is all of Christian revelation to be found in Scripture?

V. *Some Necessary Distinctions:*
   1. inherent Tradition;
   2. declarative Tradition;
   3. constitutive Tradition.

VI. *All Agree, More or Less, on the Existence of Inherent or Declarative Tradition, but Not on that of Constitutive Tradition. The Controversy, then, Centers on Two Issues:*

THE SOURCES OF REVELATION

1. Is Tradition to be considered *a distinct source* even for those truths formally contained in Scripture?
2. Does Tradition *go beyond the data of Scripture?*

CHAPTER II

Sacred Tradition

I. Notion and Division of Tradition 136

We turn now to the other source of Christian doctrine, *Tradition* in the strict sense, or *oral Tradition*. It may be defined as that collection of speculative and practical truths communicated *viva voce* to the Church by Christ and the apostles, acting as organs of revelation, to be safeguarded until the end of time. The precise designation of this tradition is objective oral Tradition.[1]

Tradition as studied in the following pages is called dogmatic from the point of view of its subject matter, and divine or divine-apostolic from the point of view of its origin. It is called *dogmatic* because the truths it contains, whether practical or speculative, constitute the object of divine and Catholic faith. It is called *divine* or *divine-apostolic* to distinguish it, on the one hand, from ecclesiastical traditions, which are precepts and customs long observed in the Church but post-apostolic in origin, and, on the other, from human-apostolic traditions, which trace their origin to the apostles indeed, but not in their capacity as channels of revelation, but rather as the Church's first pastors.[2] Note, however, that divine tradition is sometimes called *ecclesiastical* in contrast to merely mundane traditions, and *apostolic* in contrast to those which are of later vintage.

II. Protestant Viewpoint on Tradition 137

All Protestants, claiming as they do that Scripture is perfect by itself and all-sufficient, deny the existence of Tradition in the Catholic sense.

They grant, of course, that the first Christian communities got their faith by the oral preaching of the apostles and of their fellow-workers, and that the immediately following generations had a very high regard for oral tradition, at that time easily accessible, and even that they had little notion of the need for the New Testament

Scriptures. They grant, too, that not everything Christ and the apostles did and taught was recorded in Scripture. But they insist (1) that once Scripture was completely written, it contained everything necessary for salvation, and (2) that the *other things,* a knowledge of which would be interesting from an historical rather than a religious point of view, *passed into oblivion* after a short time, to such an extent that it was *impossible* to ascertain their apostolic origin. In apostolic times, then, the genuine apostolic Tradition was joined with what was written down so as to form one body of Scripture, and so, soon after the apostolic era, Scripture took its permanent place as the *one* source of Christian revelation.[3]

Still, there are some Protestants who do not spurn all tradition. They admit that the religious teaching of the Scriptures is preserved also in the works of the fathers, in the practice and the liturgy of the Church, and in the living convictions of generations of Christians. But this tradition (a) is really *inherent* in Scripture and only *explanatory* of Scripture, since it contains the same truths as Scripture and at most expresses them more clearly and explicitly. Besides, this tradition (b) is founded in its entirety on Scripture and flows from it. These people refuse absolutely to admit a Tradition distinct from Scripture, a so-called "constitutive" Tradition, one which discloses teachings not contained in the Sacred Books.[4]

138 III. The Catholic Dogma on Tradition

The Catholic doctrine was defined by the Council of Trent in these words:

> The council is aware that this [Christian] truth and teaching are contained in written books and in the unwritten traditions that the apostles received from Christ himself or that were handed on, as it were from hand to hand, from the apostles under the inspiration of the Holy Spirit, and so have come down to us. The council follows the example of the orthodox Fathers and with a loyalty and reverence equal to that with which it accepts and venerates all the books both of the Old and the New Testament, since one God is the author of both, it also accepts and venerates traditions concerned with faith and morals as having been received orally from Christ or inspired by the Holy

Spirit and continuously preserved in the Catholic Church. . . . Moreover, if anyone does not accept the books [of Sacred Scripture] . . . and knowingly and willfully spurns the traditions previously mentioned: let him be anathema.[5]

This definition states the origin, the preservation, and the value of traditions.

1. The origin of traditions: The apostles received them either from the very lips of Christ or at the dictation of the Holy Spirit. This "dictation" is not to be understood in a crassly mechanical sense, but as including all the ways in which a truth can be revealed to men by God. These traditions are said to have been received "from the apostles *themselves*," in contradistinction to the apostles' successors in the pastoral office. To these latter "the Holy Spirit was promised not that they might make known new doctrines revealed to them by Him, but that they might with His help reverently safeguard and faithfully teach the revelation handed down through the apostles, that revelation which makes up the deposit of faith."[6] Furthermore, the truths which the apostles received at the dictation of the Holy Spirit are included under the term "Christian doctrine" or "revelation," both because they form the complement of what Christ personally taught, and because Christ Himself said: *"But when he, the Spirit of truth, has come, he will conduct you through the whole range of truth. What he will tell you does not originate with him; no, he will tell you only what he is told . . . for he will draw upon what is mine and announce it to you."*—(John 16:13–14).

2. The *preservation* of the traditions: ". . . have come down to us . . . continuously preserved in the Catholic Church."—*Ibid.*

3. The *value* or dignity of the traditions: ". . . with equal loyalty and reverence . . . it also accepts and venerates traditions . . ."—*Ibid.* Although traditions, from the point of view of the words or the form in which they are expressed, are inferior to Scripture, they are, from the point of view of their subject matter or content, equal to Scripture as the word of God.

Tradition may be *defined* as follows: *the collection of revealed truths which the Church has received through the apostles in addition to inspired Scripture and which it preserves by the uninterrupted continuity of the apostolic teaching office.*

139 IV. The Precise Point at Issue in the Controversy with Protestants

The state of the question.

A few preliminary remarks will contribute to a clear understanding of the controversy with Protestants on the subject of Tradition.

1. The question is not primarily whether everything which one must know in order to be saved is contained in Scripture as we now have it, but whether the *magisterium* of the Church draws the Christian revelation which it must preach *from Scripture alone,* whether it could and should draw upon this source exclusively.

Attention is focused on the "*magisterium* of the Church" because it was established in the treatise on the Church that the preaching of the Church's *magisterium* is the proximate rule of faith for each person in the age in which he lives. Consequently, Scripture—setting aside the question of its being the only source of revelation—is at any rate only the remote rule of faith.

The question is concerned with that "*Christian revelation* which the Church must preach." In addition to what is necessary for each of the faithful to order his life aright or for the Church to carry out its mission successfully, Christian revelation contains much that is only useful. Now it has never been proved that our Lord wished the Church to preserve only what is necessary. He willed that it should faithfully safeguard *His whole doctrine.* "*Initiate all nations to discipleship: . . . and teach them to observe all the commandments I have given you*" (Matt. 28:20). "*The Holy Spirit, whom the Father will send in my name, will teach you everything*" (John 14:26). "*There is still much I might say to you; but you are not strong enough to bear it at present. But when he, the Spirit of truth, has come, he will conduct you through the whole range of truth*"[7] "*And I will ask the Father, and he will grant you another Advocate to be with you for all time to come, the Spirit of Truth*" (John 14:16).

Note, however, that "the whole doctrine of Christ," in the sense explained above, i.e., inclusive of those things which the apostles learned through the Holy Spirit, does not include every single word and deed of Christ and the apostles. In fact, many words and deeds of our Lord Himself, and, even more so, of the apostles, could have passed into oblivion without the loss of anything *taught, commanded,* or *instituted* by Christ or by the Holy Spirit.[8]

Granted, then, that those things which everyone must explicitly believe are to be found in Scripture, it does not at all follow that the rest are matters of historical, rather than of religious, interest. For (a) many of these other things are necessary for the Church to be able to carry out its mission successfully, and (b) whatever Christ revealed, even things which are merely useful, must be faithfully treasured by the Church and believed implicitly by all and explicitly by those who have knowledge of them.

V. Some Necessary Distinctions

The question of whether the Church's magisterium draws revelation from Scripture alone is divisible into two others. The first would be: *Whether those things which are actually contained in Scripture are drawn or known by the Church's magisterium from Scripture alone.* The second would be: *Whether all of Christian revelation is to be found in Scripture.* The former question has to do with the relationship to Scripture of inherent and declarative Tradition (in the Protestant sense). The second is concerned with the existence of declarative Tradition (in the usual Catholic sense) and of constitutive Tradition.

It must be pointed out that "declarative Tradition" can be understood in two ways. *Protestants* admit declarative Tradition only to the extent that it expresses in a clearer and more distinct *manner* a doctrine rather vaguely or implicitly but still *formally* contained in Scripture. In this view, declarative Tradition contains nothing which, when one comes right down to it, cannot be known and proved from Scripture alone. *Catholics,* on the other hand, understand by the term "declarative Tradition" also, and, in fact, especially, that tradition which *objectively* or materially complements the teaching found in Scripture, i.e., in all the passages containing matter pertinent to a specific subject. It complements Scripture by offering more information than the latter does on the same subject. As a result, one and the same point of doctrine which in Scripture is either only hinted at or only partially taught may, thanks to this Tradition, be known with certitude and completeness.

When all is said and done, declarative Tradition, in the sense admitted by Protestants, is, strictly speaking, the same as inherent

Tradition. And, to the extent that it actually goes beyond the data of Scripture without proposing a doctrine altogether foreign to it, it is as a matter of fact constitutive. Accordingly, nothing is lost by replacing the threefold distinction with this twofold one of *inherent* and *constitutive* Tradition.

141 With regard to *the former question:* Protestants conceive of inherent Tradition as completely dependent on Scripture as on its origin. It "flows from Scripture," they say, and consequently they do not consider it a separate source. Catholics look upon Scripture and inherent Tradition as *two distinct sources* for the same truths. In fact, they affirm not only that the primitive Church generally[9] received from Christ and the apostles those truths which are contained more or less clearly in Scripture in two ways: primarily by oral preaching and secondarily in inspired Scripture. But, conscious of the fact that, in preserving the doctrine of Christ, the Church enjoys the gift of infallibility, they hasten to add that these truths are drawn from a twofold source and are known in two ways by the present-day *magisterium* as well. These two sources, these two ways, are the safely preserved oral preaching of the apostles and inspired Scripture. They admit, of course, that the inspired books did in fact contribute a great deal, indeed a very great deal, to the safeguarding of apostolic preaching, just as, from another point of view, Tradition played a most important role in the preservation and understanding of the Scriptures. But they do not agree that inherent Tradition is so dependent on Scripture that the truth it contains today must be traced back ultimately to Scripture alone.

142 With regard to *the second question,* one fact must be heavily underscored. The controversy between Catholics and Protestants on the matter is by no means limited to those points of doctrine of which Scripture has nothing to say. For there are really very few such points, as one can easily verify by looking at any handbook of Theology. He will not find therein many theses which take their proof from the data of Tradition alone without an appeal to Sacred Scripture for at least the first steps of the demonstration.

VI. Controversy Has Two Facets

The controversy about Tradition, then, comprises two issues: (1) whether Tradition is to be considered *a distinct source* even for those truths formally contained in Scripture; (2) whether Tradition *goes beyond the data of Scripture* by giving more information than Scripture about some matters contained in the latter, or even by teaching some points of doctrine about which Scripture is completely silent.

With the ground thus broken, Article I will treat of the existence of Tradition in the sense already explained; Article II will discuss the various media and documents in which Tradition is preserved; Article III will take a closer look at some specific records of Tradition.

Notes

1. See above, no. 3.
2. See the treatise on *Christ's Church*, no. 33.
3. See, for example, Bavinck, *Gereformierde Dogmatiek* I, 401–415.
4. The writings of such men as Bultmann and Cullmann have sparked an increasing awareness in Protestant circles of the weighty role which Tradition played in the early development of Christian doctrine. The discussions carried on in various Ecumenical Movement congresses have deepened this awareness. This is at least a step in the right direction, but the issue is still confused to a great extent. Protestants are apparently afraid of falling into the Orthodox extreme of equating Tradition with traditions, of putting liturgical and disciplinary customs on a par with genuine revealed truths. And, of course, both Protestant and Orthodox theologians still shy away from any notion of a divinely established *magisterium* as the organ of Tradition. For a good review of the situation as it stands today, see J. Daniélou, *art. cit.*
5. DB 783–784; see the Vatican Council, constitution *De fide catholica*, CH. 2, DB 1787; and the Second Council of Nicaea, sess. 7: ". . . accepting everything whatsoever the holy Catholic Church has accepted from antiquity, written or no" (DB 302–304).
6. See the Vatican Council, constitution *De ecclesia*, ch. 4, DB 1836.
7. "The whole range of truth" does not signify all possible truths of any kind whatsoever, but the whole body of truths which God had determined to reveal to His Church on earth. Since, however, all those truths are conducive to salvation, although in different ways and degrees, "the whole range of truth" is usually interpreted to mean "all salutary truths."
8. One may judge from this the sense in which the following Protestant claim may be admitted and in what sense it is to be rejected: "The revelation of Christ was richer than the doctrine of the Church in a quantitative, not in a qualitative sense."
9. Note the qualification, "generally"; for it is not certain that the apostles handed down to the Church *no* truth by means of Scripture alone.

Special Bibliography

BAINVEL, J. V. *De magisterio vivo et traditione.* Paris, 1905.
BILLOT, L. *De sacra traditione contra novam haeresim evolutionismi.* Rome, 1904.

BOUYER, L. *The Spirit and Forms of Protestantism.* Translated by A. V. Littledale. Westminster, Md., 1956.
BURKE, E. "The Scientific Teaching of Theology in the Seminary," *CTSA Proceedings.* New York, 1949.
DANIÉLOU, J. "Ecriture et Tradition dans le dialogue entre les chrétiens séparés," *La documentation catholique,* LIV (1957), 283 ff.
DEJAIFVE, G. "Bible, Tradition, Magistère dans la théologie catholique," NRT, 78 (1956), 135–151; see TD, 6 (1958), 67 ff.
DIECKMANN, H. *De ecclesia.* Friburg i. Br., 1925.
DIEKAMP, F. *Theologiae dogmaticae manuale.* Tournai, 1949.
GEISELMANN, J. "Das Missverständnis über das Verhältnis von Schrift und Tradition und seine Überwindung in der katholischen Theologie," *Una Sancta,* 2 (1956), 131–150; see TD, 6 (1958), 73 ff.
LERCHER, L. *Institutiones theologiae dogmaticae.* Innsbruck, 1951.
PARENTE, P. *Theologia fundamentalis.* Rome, 1950.
SALAVERRI, I. *Sacrae theologiae summa.* I, Madrid, 1952.
SCHRADER, C. *De theologico testium fonte deque edito fidei testimonio seu traditione commentarius.* Paris, 1878.
SMITH, G. (ed.). *The Teaching of the Catholic Church.* New York, 1949.
TANQUEREY, A. *Synopsis theologiae dogmaticae.* Paris, 1949–1950.
WINKLER, M. *Der Traditionsbegriff bis Tertullian.* Munich, 1897.

Article I

THE EXISTENCE OF SACRED TRADITION

PROPOSITION: *Tradition Exists as a Source of Revelation Distinct from Scripture and Goes Beyond the Data of Scripture*

    Proof: 1. From Sacred Scripture (limitations of this proof);
            2. From the testimony of the early fathers:
               a. written testimony;
               b. practical testimony;
               c. objections based on some remarks of the fathers.

Article I

THE EXISTENCE OF SACRED TRADITION

143 PROPOSITION. *Tradition Is a Source of Revelation Distinct from Scripture and Goes Beyond the Data of Scripture*

This is a *dogma of faith* from the Council of Trent as quoted above and from the Vatican Council.[1] The first part of the proposition states the existence of Tradition in general and consequently includes inherent Tradition; the second part refers specifically to constitutive Tradition.

Proof:

1. From *Sacred Scripture*.

a. The books of the New Testament furnish an adequate proof for the existence of *Tradition in general* by showing that written books were not to be the sole source of revelation. Christ personally established a permanent living *magisterium* to be heeded by all and gave not the slightest intimation that books were to be written or that they would one day constitute an exclusive source of information.[2] St. Paul refers the faithful to doctrines taught by word of mouth: *"I praise you because you bear in mind all that I taught you and cling to the traditions precisely as I passed them on to you"* (1 Cor. 11:2). *"So then, brothers, stand firm and hold fast to the traditions which you have learned from us by word or letter."*[3] This same Paul advises the bishop Timothy to safeguard the "deposit," *"that noble trust,"* and to *"hold to the form of sound teaching"* which he had heard from his teacher. And when he felt his last days drawing near (2 Tim. 4:6), he commanded Timothy to hand on this oral teaching to trustworthy men who were fit to teach others: *"O Timothy, guard what has been entrusted to you, and keep free from profane novelties in speech and the contradictions that come from so-called knowledge"* (1 Tim. 6:20). *"In the faith and love that are in Christ Jesus, hold to the form of sound teaching which you have heard from me. Guard that noble trust with the aid of the Holy Spirit, who dwells in us"* (2 Tim. 1:13–14).

SACRED TRADITION

"And what you have heard from me in the presence of many witnesses, commend to trustworthy men who will be competent in turn to teach others" (2:2). Here is proof first of all for the fact that in apostolic times oral Tradition was a source of faith, and indeed the chief source. These texts show, secondly, that this arrangement continued into the immediately succeeding generation. A final conclusion is certainly not unwarranted, namely, that the same rule was to retain its force permanently. Indeed, an arrangement honored and sanctioned by the apostles was by its very nature permanent, or at least could be altered only by apostolic authority. There is, however, not the slightest indication that the apostles ordered or ever foresaw any such change.

b. The existence of Tradition as a source distinct from Scripture may be considered a proven fact. The next question is whether this tradition is inherent only or constitutive as well. Admittedly the existence of *constitutive* Tradition (subsequent to the completion of the Scriptures) cannot be proven positively and compellingly from Scripture. But it would be unfair of our adversaries to demand such a proof of this point. On the other hand, Catholics have every right, in view of the preceding considerations, to ask Protestants to prove from Scripture itself the nonexistence of constitutive Tradition. It is consequently worth the trouble to show that *neither the words nor the general tenor* of Scripture lend support to the Protestant position. (i) Nowhere in the books of the New Testament is it said or intimated that the sum total of faith is contained or would be one day contained in Scripture. (ii) The books of the New Testament were composed by hagiographers who did not consult one another on the matter, but who wrote as occasion demanded, for special reasons and to answer special needs. A general statement to the effect that the later books were written as supplements to the earlier would be, consequently, quite untrue.[4] All agree that no single book contains the whole of Christian doctrine, and so if in the ensemble they did cover it all, this would be quite accidental as far as the hagiographers were concerned. But was such a rounding out of the record perhaps intended by the Holy Spirit, the principal author of all the books? An affirmative answer would have some foundation if the Sacred Books made up one organic whole. But in view of the fact that they reveal no such systematic unity, the supposition is really quite groundless. It follows, then, that Protestants, who insist that nothing but Scripture must be believed with divine faith, thereby admit that their basic principle, the all-sufficiency of Scripture, at least lacks divine backing. And it is of no avail to seek refuge in philosophical arguments and claim that it would be unworthy of God to write a Scripture which would not contain the whole of revelation. What would be so unseemly about God's providing for the needs of the Church partly by Scripture and partly by a Tradition safeguarded with the help of the Holy Spirit?

145 2. *From the testimony of the early fathers.*

a. With reference to the *first part of the proposition,* i.e., the existence of Tradition, it is a solidly established fact that no one in the first centuries of the Church's existence taught that the teaching arrangement set up by the apostles was altered shortly after their death. On the contrary, the earliest fathers, though not treating specifically the question of a single or double source of revelation, held oral Tradition in the highest esteem and recommended it no less than they did Scripture.

St. Clement of Rome:

> The Apostles preached to us the Gospel received from Jesus Christ, and Jesus Christ was God's Ambassador. . . . And so, after receiving their instructions and being fully assured through the Resurrection of our Lord Jesus Christ, as well as confirmed in faith by the word of God, they went forth, equipped with the fullness of the Holy spirit, to preach the good news that the Kingdom of God was close at hand. From land to land, accordingly, and from city to city they preached, and from among their earliest converts appointed men whom they had tested by the Spirit to act as bishops and deacons for the future believers . . . and afterwards laid down a rule once and for all to this effect: when these men die, other approved men shall succeed to their sacred ministry.—ACW trans.[5]

Eusebius has this to say about St. Ignatius Martyr:

> Although he was being led through Asia under the unrelenting vigilance of guards, he nonetheless managed to urge the churches of each city he entered that they beware, above all else, of the vicious views of heretics, and he exhorted them to cling tenaciously to the traditions of the Apostles which, corroborated as they were by his testimony, should in his opinion

SACRED TRADITION

be committed to writing that future ages might have more certain knowledge of them.[6]

St. Ignatius insinuates elsewhere that it is characteristic, not of a true Christian, but rather of a heretic to insist on written testimony for his faith and to quibble about the meaning of Scripture.[7] Papias of Hierapolis (c. 150 A.D.) wrote in the Introduction to his book on the *Interpretation of the Words of the Lord:*

> I shall not hesitate to set down for you, along with my interpretations, all the information[8] I have ever carefully gathered from the presbyters. I carefully committed it to memory and vouch for its truth. In fact, unlike most people, I did not care for men who gave the longest accounts, but for men whose teachings were true; nor yet for men who reported the commandments of others, but for such as related those given by the Lord to be believed and stemming directly from the Truth. But when someone turned up who had been closely associated with the presbyters, it was the words of the presbyters that I would ascertain . . . I simply took for granted that book knowledge would not help me so much as a living or still surviving voice.[9]

When the Gnostic heresy was raging, Hegesippus (c. 160 A.D.), with a view to learning the tradition of the churches, approached many bishops and finally the Bishop of Rome: "In each of the episcopal lines of succession and throughout each of the cities the same doctrine is held as that taught by the Law, the Prophets, the Christ."[10]

In their polemic against the Gnostics, St. Irenaeus and Tertullian quite frankly recognize Tradition as a distinct source of revelation, and indeed the chief source. St. Irenaeus:

> When they are refuted by the Scriptures, they take to maligning the Scriptures themselves. . . . But when we refer them to that tradition which originates with the apostles and which is preserved in the churches through the succession of the presbyters, they attack the tradition, claiming that they themselves are wiser not merely than the presbyters but even than the apostles. [However] anyone who wants to see the truth can look to the tradition of the Apostles which is clearly manifested throughout the whole world; and we can list those who were set up as bishops in the different churches as well as their successors

(149)

right down to our own time, men who neither taught nor knew anything like what these [Gnostics] are raving about. For if the apostles had known secret doctrines which they were in the habit of teaching to the "perfect" clandestinely and apart from the rest,[11] they would most certainly have communicated these things to those to whom they were entrusting the churches themselves.

And he adds that it suffices to seek out the tradition held by the Church of Rome,

> for with this Church, because of its more efficient leadership, all churches must agree. . . . Since therefore we have such weighty proofs [of apostolic tradition], there is no need to seek among others the truth which it is so easy to obtain from the Church: since the apostles, like a rich man depositing his money in a bank, entrusted to her in abundance everything pertaining to the truth. . . . And if a dispute should arise over some point or other, should we not have recourse to the most ancient churches, in which the apostles were actively interested, and find out from them what is certain and clear with regard to the point at issue? What if, in fact, the apostles had left us no Writings? Would it not be necessary to follow the line indicated by the tradition which they handed down to those to whom they entrusted the churches?[12]

147 Tertullian says that heretics "should not be admitted to any discussion of the Scriptures,"[13] but that they should be admonished on the basis of Tradition:

> The Lord Jesus sent the apostles to preach. . . . Now what they actually preached can, as I must here likewise prescribe, be proved only by those very same churches which the apostles themselves founded by preaching to them both *viva voce*, as they say, and later by letters. Such being the case, it is consequently certain that any doctrine which agrees with [what is held by] these apostolic churches, moulds and original sources of the faith, must be considered the truth, undoubtedly containing that which these churches received from the apostles, the apostles from Christ, and Christ from God; but any other doctrine must be presumed false, since it smacks of opposition to the truth of the churches, of the apostles, of Christ, of God.[14]

He considers it impossible for the tradition of the churches to have strayed from the truth, both because of the assistance of the Holy Spirit and because they never could have agreed together so to err:

> Come now! Would they all have fallen into error? Would the steward of God, the Vicar of Christ [the Holy Spirit] have neglected His duty by allowing the churches to understand and believe otherwise than what He Himself taught the apostles? Is it likely that so many and such outstanding churches would all have strayed into the one [false] faith? No chance happening ever has the same outcome in the case of many different individuals. A doctrinal error in so many different churches would of necessity have taken different forms. But when unity exists amid diversity, this can be the result, not of error, but only of tradition.[15]

The Greek fathers are of like mind. Origen:

> Since there are many who think they share the mind of Christ and yet some of them think differently from their predecessors, let the preaching of the Church be held fast, that preaching which has been handed down from the apostles through the ranks of succession and perdures in the churches to the present day. That alone is to be believed as the truth which varies in no wise from ecclesiastical and apostolic tradition.[16]

St. Gregory of Nyssa: "It suffices as proof of our thesis that we have a tradition coming to us from the fathers, like a legacy handed down from the apostles through the saints who followed them in succession."[17]

b. With reference to *the second part of the proposition,* i.e., that Tradition goes beyond the data of Scripture, *theoretical* testimony regarding oral Tradition's surpassing Scripture objectively, i.e., from the point of view of the truth contained therein, does not exist, as far as I know, before the time of Tertullian. The earliest fathers frankly acknowledge Tradition as a source distinct from Scripture and esteem it as a source more practically valuable than the latter. They thus offer not the slightest support for the Protestant principle of the self-sufficiency of Scripture;[18] but they do not seem to have touched on the question at issue from the theoretical

(151)

angle. The following fathers do not treat it specifically, either, but they do brush against it in other contexts

Tertullian, writing on a matter of discipline (that a Christian should not wear a military decoration), has this to say:

> Let us inquire, therefore, whether tradition, unless it be written, should be accepted. Certainly we shall say that it ought not to be accepted if we can allege as precedent no cases of other practices which we justify without any written document, but solely on the grounds of tradition and because of the approval of subsequent custom.

Then, after mentioning several Christian customs, he concludes:

> If you demand scriptural justification for these and other such practices, you will find none. Tradition will be held out to you as their author, custom as their consolidator, and faith as their observer.[19]

Admittedly, Tertullian does not speak directly of traditions—either of theoretical traditions or of those concerned with dogmatic practices. But since among examples of non-written customs he alleges the following: "We make offerings for the deceased and in honor of the eternal birthdays (of the martyrs) on their anniversary days," and since the offering of the Eucharistic sacrifice for the dead and in honor of martyrs certainly involves a genuinely dogmatic Tradition, and an oral Tradition to boot, it is fair to conclude that he too recognized dogmatic traditions which were not contained in Scripture.

Origen: "The Church received from the apostles the tradition that baptism is to be administered to infants, too."[20]

St. Basil:

> Of the beliefs and practices [disciplinary regulations] preserved in the Church, some we possess from teaching handed down in written form; others we have received as delivered to us in a mystery from the tradition of the Apostles, and both of these have the same force as far as religion is concerned.[21]

It makes no difference that St. Basil immediately gives examples of disciplinary traditions,[22] for in view of the fact that he expressly

SACRED TRADITION

distinguishes "beliefs" and "practices," the principal affirmation must be understood as applying to both.

St. Epiphanius:

> There is need of tradition also; for not everything can be found in Scripture. That is why the most holy apostles left some things in writing and others in tradition. Paul affirms this very fact as follows: "*as I handed it on to you.*" Likewise in another passage: *This is my teaching and thus have I handed it on to the churches.*" Similarly: "*If you continue to cling firmly to it, as I preached it to you—unless your faith has all been for nothing.*"[23]

St. John Chrysostom, in his explanation of St. Paul's words *"Stand firm and hold fast to the traditions which you have learned from us by word or letter,"* says:

> It is therefore clear that [the apostles] did not teach everything in epistolary form, but that they taught many things besides in unwritten form, and these things, too, are worthy of acceptance. Wherefore we should consider the tradition of the Church also as worthy of belief. If there is a tradition, look no further.[24]

St. Augustine appealed to apostolic Tradition in favor of the validity of baptism administered by heretics and of the efficacy of infant baptism.[25]

The nub of the question being considered exclusively here is not whether everything which individual fathers considered as apostolic Tradition actually belongs to apostolic or even divine-apostolic Tradition, but whether the testimony of these fathers really proves that they admitted the *existence* of some *dogmatic* traditions not contained in Scripture.

Far outweighing any theoretical testimony in both antiquity and in unmistakable universality is the *practical testimony* of all the fathers and of the whole Church, even in the earliest years. To mention only one example out of the many which could be alleged, the four Gospels and many other books of the New Testament were accepted as inspired without any backing from Scripture and hence on the basis of Tradition alone.

c. By way of *objection*, our adversaries cite several passages in

(153)

which the fathers, by affirmative or exclusive statements, urge the completeness and self-sufficiency of Sacred Scripture.

Since it would take forever to treat each such passage individually,[26] it will be enough to give here the principles for the solution of this difficulty. (a) The fathers quite frequently mean not absolute but relative sufficiency, in the sense that Scripture suffices for a knowledge of those things which must be expressly believed by each and every one of the faithful, or that it sufficed to settle a particular case in which they were involved. (b) When they rule out all other arguments except those based on Scripture, they have in mind only philosophical reasoning, apocryphal books, false prophecies, and spurious traditions; or if they rule out even the very Tradition of the Church, they do so only for reasons of methodology, led on by the exigencies of controversy to select a basis of argument common to themselves and their antagonists. (c) At all events, the fathers mean that Scripture is an adequate source only if one presumes the preaching and interpretation of the Church. But it is one thing to proclaim the complete self-sufficiency of Scripture all by itself, and quite another to affirm the adequacy of Scripture as received from the hands of the Church and clarified, not to say enriched, by the light of ecclesiastical Tradition. The fathers found many things in the Scriptures with the latter qualifications for which they would not have found sufficient backing in Scripture purely and simply. Recall the many instances in which they were satisfied with mere hints in the text and their readiness to admit the typical sense. There are really very few things which cannot be squeezed from Scripture by this method. But (d) it should occasion no surprise if the fathers, who were blissfully unaware of the Protestant error, but did have the deepest reverence for Scripture, now and then made statements which must not be taken with strict literalness. The following remark of Augustine may be applied in this case: "When engaged in discussion within the confines of the Catholic Church, he had no thought of his meaning being misconstrued. . . . When it was not yet you outsiders who were party to the debate, he could speak more freely."*

---

* *Contra Julianum* i.6, 22. Clearly the statements of the fathers on this point are not always to be pressed. Take the example of St. Vincent Lerins, who says that "the canon of Scripture is perfect and is completely self-

SACRED TRADITION

Notes

1. Constitution *De fide catholica*, ch. 2; DB 1787.
2. See Matt. 28:19–20; Luke 16:15–16; Acts 1:8; 9:15.
3. 2 Thess. 2:15; see Rom. 16:17; Phil. 4:9; Col. 2:7; 1 Thess. 4:1–2; 1 John 2:21–24.
4. Bainvel was right when he said that the books of the New Testament were written rather "that the things which had been taught orally might be recalled to mind, that the absence of a living teacher might be compensated, and that errors and false teachers might be refuted when they arose (*loc. cit.*, p. 23).
5. *Epistula I ad Corinthios* 42, 1–44. 2. Harnack: "The whole Catholic notion of Tradition is rooted ultimately in that sentence formulated long ago by Clement of Rome" (*Dogmengeschichte* I [3rd ed.], 154).
6. HE 3. 36.
7. *Epistula ad Philadelphenses* 8.
8. In the Greek: *kai hósa;* it may be supposed that Papias had treated in an earlier section the utterances of our Lord which are recorded in Scripture. See Funk, *Patres apostolici*, II (2nd ed.), 351; or perhaps the *kai* merely reinforces the preposition *syn* in *synkatataxai*, cf. Kleist in ACW 6 (Westminster, Md., 1948), 206, n. 7.
9. Fragment 2, ACW trans.
10. In Eusebius, HE iv. 22. 3.
11. The Gnostics, of course, appealed to a secret tradition.
12. *Adversus haereses* 3. 2–4.
13. *De praescriptione* 15.
14. *Ibid.*, 21.
15. *Ibid.*, 28.
16. *De principiis,* preface 2.
17. *Oratio 3 contra Eunomium.*
18. See, for example, Bavinck, *op. cit.*, I, 405.
19. *De corona militari* 3–4.
20. *In epistulam ad Romanos* i. 5, 9.
21. *De Spiritu Sancto* 27, 66; see 29, 71: "Most of the mysteries (*tà pleísta tôn mystikôn*) are accepted by us without any written evidence."
22. Furthermore, he alleges as an example, "also the very anointing with oil" (the use of chrism in Confirmation).
23. *Haereses* 61, 6; see 75, 8.

---

sufficient, indeed more than sufficient" (*Commonitorium* 2 and 29). And yet in the same work he records the fact that the validity of baptism administered by heretics has been upheld by Tradition alone. Bavinck himself writes that while the fathers extolled the completeness of Scripture, they nonetheless recognized Tradition as well and did in fact admit therein an element incompatible with the Protestant view of the all-sufficiency of Scripture.— (*op. cit.* I, 409).

THE SOURCES OF REVELATION

24. *Homilia 4 in 2 Thess* 2; see *Homilia 3 in 2 Tim.*

25. See *De baptismo* ii, 7, 12; iv. 24 and 31; v. 23. 31; *De Genesi ad litteram* x, 23. 39.

26. Several such passages are discussed by De San, *De traditione et scriptura*, p. 66; see also Franzelin, *De traditione*, thesis 19; Danielou, *loc. cit.*; Salaverri, *Sacrae theologiae summa*, I, 755; Lercher, *Institutiones theologiae dogmaticae*, I, 319.

Article II

THE PRESERVATION OF SACRED TRADITION

I. PROPOSITION 1. *The Chief Means or Organ for the Preservation of Tradition Is the Unbroken Continuance of the Apostolic Teaching Office*
   a. This is the means clearly willed and directly established by Christ.
   b. This means offers absolute certitude of the safe preservation of the whole deposit of faith and hence of Tradition also.
   c. In any particular case, for a complete theological solution of the question whether a doctrine is part of divine-apostolic Tradition, it is enough to show that this doctrine is clearly and explicitly taught by the Roman Catholic episcopate as one which much be believed with divine faith.

   Scholion. The merely natural value of the Catholic *magisterium* as a factor in the preservation of Tradition.

II. PROPOSITION 2. *Ancient Documents of Various Kinds Help the Living* Magisterium *in Striking Fashion to Preserve Tradition*
   a. Apostolic Tradition found its way into writing from earliest times.
   b. The documents of Tradition are the following:
      1. creeds and definitions of faith;
      2. acts of the councils and of the supreme pontiffs;
      3. liturgical books;
      4. acts of the martyrs;
      5. writings of the fathers and of theologians;
      6. records of Church history;
      7. works of Christian art.

   Scholion. The theological value of documents of Tradition in general. The canon of St. Vincent.

Article II

THE PRESERVATION OF SACRED TRADITION

152   Oral tradition, say the Protestants, is very susceptible to corruption, and so after the charism of truth had accompanied the apostles to the grave, Scripture stood alone as a reliable source of revelation. This raises the question of how traditions could have been safeguarded and passed along to us. The most important fact to remember in this discussion is that when all the apostles had died, the charism of revelation did indeed die with them, but not the charism of truth, the gift of infallibility. Furthermore, the preservation of Tradition does not deserve to be painted in such dark colors as an almost impossibly difficult feat. Really, Tradition must not be thought of as a long, confused conglomeration of statements which depend on human memory for continued existence, but rather as a compendium of Christian faith and living which is included for the most part in the day by day profession of that faith, in liturgical and disciplinary custom, and in Christian practices themselves and finds varied and gradually clearer expression as the needs of times and locales demand.

Furthermore, the search for the *means* by which the apostolic Tradition was safely preserved will involve a simultaneous search for the *criteria* in the light of which genuine traditions are distinguished from their counterfeit.

153   PROPOSITION 1. *The Chief Means or Organ for the Preservation of Tradition Is the Unbroken Continuance of the Apostolic Teaching Office*

The unbroken continuance of the apostolic teaching office in concrete terms is nothing other than the living and enduring *magisterium* of the Church.

This is the means clearly willed and directly established by Christ. For He arranged for the unending continuance of the Petro-apostolic College upon which He laid the duty and the authority to preach His entire doctrine, and He saw to it that there would always be at hand in the Church a body of authoritative teachers hierarchically interrelated: the Roman Catholic episcopate. He saw to it, too, that the Holy Spirit would always assist this enduring *magisterium* by steering it away from error and by guiding it to the truth.

This means offers, in the light of Catholic principles, absolute certitude of the safe preservation of the whole deposit of faith and hence of Tradition also. This certitude is based on what was said elsewhere about the Church's infallibility. Still it is worthwhile to recall that both Irenaeus and Tertullian, who insisted specifically on the Church's Tradition in their polemic against the Gnostics, appealed directly to the assistance of the Holy Spirit joined with apostolic succession.[1] Protestants, therefore, have no right to say that the early fathers acknowledged just the historical and not the dogmatic authority of tradition.

In any particular case, then, for a complete theological solution of the question whether a doctrine is part of divine-apostolic Tradition, it is enough to show that this doctrine is clearly and explicitly taught by the Roman Catholic episcopate as one which must be believed with divine faith.* It makes no difference at what point in history a proposition of this sort achieved full clarity of expression, whether in the fourth or only in the twelfth century, for the charism of truth is perennial, like the *magisterium* itself. How it can happen that the Church's magisterium *clearly and distinctly* proposes certain things as objects of faith only after several centuries will be explained in the Treatise on Faith, in the section dealing with the development of the Christian faith, i.e., dogmatic progress.

The same treatise will explain the various ways in which a proposition is made clear and explicit by the Church. Meanwhile, we should like to mention here one way which is sufficient to produce the above effect: an *ex cathedra* pronouncement of the Roman pontiff alone, who enjoys the absolute fulness of supreme jurisdiction over the whole Church.[2] As things stand, in virtue of the fact that the assistance of the Holy Spirit has been promised both to the Supreme Pontiff both as head of the bishops and to the college of bishops when they are united with that head, it is impossible for a

154

---

* "For a complete *theological* solution" or, if you prefer, for a full dogmatic solution. It is one thing to solve a question by the principles of faith, and quite another to solve it from those of history.

majority of the bishops to disagree with a pronouncement of the Roman pontiff. Irenaeus had expressed this clearly enough in the second century: "For with this Church, because of its more efficient leadership, all churches must agree, that is to say, the faithful of all places, because in it the apostolic tradition has been always preserved by the [faithful] of all places."[3]

155 Furthermore, the clear and distinct preaching of the Roman Catholic episcopate necessarily strikes a responsive chord in the common faith of the churches, which is, as it were, an echo of its voice. It was not to the *magisterium* alone, but to the universal Church that the privilege of infallibility was promised, although not to both in the same way, for the churches are infallible in their belief for the reason and to the extent that they follow the teaching of the infallible *magisterium*.[4]

It follows that the common faith of the churches is also a touchstone of genuine tradition—not an independent touchstone, it is true, but still certain and, in fact, infallible.*

156 *Scholion. The merely natural value of the Catholic magisterium as a factor in the preservation of Tradition.*

The unbroken succession of the Catholic episcopate is an *absolute* guarantee of the safe preservation of Tradition because it can count on God's promise of infallibility. But if that organization established by Christ be considered *inadequately*, i.e., from the point of view of its external element alone and prescinding from the assistance it gets from the Holy Spirit, it must still be acknowledged as a very apt and morally safe means of preserving Tradition. For the Catholic episcopate (a) has always been made up—for by far the most part—of mature men, outstanding for holiness and learning, who have consistently safeguarded the original deposit of faith with unflagging solicitude and have always had a horror of heresies. Now (b) they have never treated any part of our sacred doctrine as a secret, esoteric tradition, but have taught all of it

---

* Note: "the common *faith*," not just any common persuasion. Whether or not a common persuasion is really divine faith, i.e., the assent to truth based on the authority of God revealing, is more readily ascertained from the fact and the manner of the *magisterium's* teaching than from the simple fact of the common agreement of people. Hence, even from this point of view, the criterion of clear and actual teaching is worth more than the criterion of the common faith of the churches.

publicly and openly, with the result that any change would have been immediately detected by the people and would have been an affront to their common faith. Furthermore, (c) the individual bishops and their churches have always religiously cultivated mutual union and intercommunication, both among themselves and especially between themselves and the Church of Rome.[5] As a consequence, any doctrinal corruption which might sneak in here or there could not go unnoticed for long, but was soon corrected or was punished by the excommunication of those who insisted on fostering it. Finally, (d) the living *magisterium* has never been without various aids connatural to its needs, as will be pointed out in the next proposition. Anyone who gives all these factors the consideration they deserve will find it hard to deny that the agreement of the Catholic episcopate or, what amounts to the same thing, the agreement of the individual churches on a point of doctrine as revealed, even from a merely natural standpoint, proves the apostolic origin of this doctrine with moral certitude, or at least furnishes the basis for a most valid presumption in favor of such origin.

Notice, too, that the early fathers themselves, even back in their times, either explicitly or at least in practice, indicated the agreement of the churches as the sure criterion of a genuine tradition. Irenaeus uses the agreement of the churches to put dissident sects to shame:

> The Church, although scattered throughout the whole world, still carefully preserves the faith as if she were gathered under one roof. She likewise believes these points [of doctrine] as if she had but one soul and one heart, and she preaches them and teaches them and hands them down with perfect harmony, as if she had but one mouth.[6]

Tertullian insists on the impossibility of agreement in error:

> Come now! Would they all have fallen into error? . . . No chance happening ever has the same outcome in the case of many different individuals. A doctrinal error in so many different churches would of necessity have taken different forms. But when unity exists amid diversity, this can be the result, not of error, but only of tradition.[7]

THE SOURCES OF REVELATION

157 PROPOSITION 2. *Ancient Monuments of Various Kinds Help In Striking Fashion the Living Magisterium to Preserve Tradition*

When Protestants say that oral Tradition cannot help becoming corrupt, they not only deny the charism of infallibility, but in addition they apparently suppose that oral Tradition as understood by Catholics leaves no room for aid from written records. They are mistaken. In the early ages the Church's authoritative teachers taught Christian doctrine not only by word of mouth, but when the occasion presented itself, they also set that doctrine down in writing. Other Christians did the same, moved by a desire to explain or defend in writing the Church's teaching or to describe Christian institutions, rites or customs. They gave expression to their faith not with paper and ink alone, but in inscriptions, sculpture, and painting. The heretics themselves and other of the Church's antagonists sometimes outlined her doctrine in their works. Clearly, then, all these things, to the extent they have been preserved, furnished subsequent ages with a valuable means for ascertaining and spreading the tradition of the Church more easily.[8]

158 The monuments of tradition are, for all practical purposes, the following: (a) creeds and definitions of faith; (b) acts of the councils and of the supreme pontiffs; (c) liturgical books; (d) acts of the martyrs; (e) writings of the fathers and of theologians; (f) records of Church history; (g) works of Christian art.

Now these means were not furnished directly by God, but (a) they do follow *connaturally* upon the existence of the Church as a visible society. In every society carefully composed documents of this sort are put in permanent form and are consulted by men of later ages with a view to preserving the bond of unity linking them with those who have gone before. The more important documents had as authors those who in their day were members of the Church's official teaching body. Such documents are (b) *morally necessary* because, when God promised the aid of the Holy Spirit, He had no intention of dispensing the beneficiaries of this promise from using the natural means at their disposal. On the contrary, He sees to it that such means are at hand and are not neglected.[9] However, (c) they are only *aids*, since they are at the service of the living magisterium in much the same way as a book is at the service of a professor or as a document is at the service of an historian.

Scholion. The theological value of monuments of tradition in general. **159**
The canon of St. Vincent.

1. On the basis of the foregoing remarks, it is easy to solve the question of the value of ancient monuments as a whole for the identification of a genuine tradition. Their value is proportionate to the proof they offer for the fact that at one time or other the ecclesiastical magisterium was in morally unanimous agreement on some doctrine or other as revealed. They constitute a compelling argument, then, (a) whenever they bear witness to a solemn definition of the infallible magisterium concerning a revealed truth; (b) whenever they offer sure proof for the morally universal agreement of the world-wide magisterium on a doctrine as revealed. To secure this effect it is enough at times to have monuments which may be few in number but which are known, because of special circumstances, to represent the belief of the universal Church.

On the other hand, when the available monuments are not of sufficient weight to prove the agreement of antiquity, or when they positively show that this agreement did not exist at one time, one may not immediately jump to the conclusion that this doctrine does not belong to apostolic Tradition. In the first case, there could have been a quite explicit and clear agreement without its being proved in written documents, since not everything found its way into writing and not everything which was ever written has been preserved. As for the second case, it must be pointed out that not everything which is formally contained in apostolic Tradition was always *clearly and explicitly* taught in the Church. There is a very real progress in the knowledge and formulation of Christian revelation, a point which will be taken up expressly in the Treatise on Faith. Again, a full explanation of matters contained in the deposit of revelation only rather vaguely or implicitly is not usually worked out without some discussion, and such discussion can sometimes go on for quite a while. In the case of truths like this, the one sure and reliable criterion of Tradition is the gradually growing and, finally, perfectly harmonious agreement of the living magisterium, to which the Holy Spirit was promised not only for the material safeguarding but also for the explanation of Tradition. The documents of antiquity then, are of value to the extent that they show that the luxuriant tree of present-day belief grew to its present estate, under the tender care of authorized gardeners, from the seed of the ancient faith.

160   2. It is in the light of the above that judgment must be passed on the canon drawn up by Vincent Lerins (434 A.D.), which came in for a great deal of abuse at the hands of our adversaries, especially at the time of the Vatican Council. The canon reads as follows: "Great care is to be taken that we hold that which has been believed everywhere, always, and by all, for this is truly and properly Catholic."[10] Vincent's intention was to give private individuals a criterion for discerning the truth in the case of a controversy which had just arisen and had not yet been solemnly decided by the magisterium.

He enunciated the following principles: (a) if only a few disagree, one must follow the morally unanimous agreement of the churches as currently expressed: *"agreement of totality"*; but (b) if quite a few disagree (so that at the present time no morally unanimous consent is discernible), one ought to stand by the agreement which obtained before the controversy arose: *"agreement of antiquity."*

Now this rule of thumb, while it is sometimes hard to apply, is quite all right in the affirmative sense: when agreement on a doctrine as revealed either exists at present or existed formerly, it must certainly be followed. But it is *not* valid in the exclusive sense: it is not antecedently impossible to have a "truly and properly Catholic," i.e., a revealed, doctrine on which explicit agreement does not exist at the present time and did not formerly exist. St. Vincent himself certainly did not mean his canon to be taken in the exclusive sense, since in the same work he clearly acknowledges and, in fact, praises highly the development of faith by a progressively more distinct and lucid teaching of age-old truth.

It should be noted in addition that Vincent did not understand his canon, even in the affirmative sense, as requiring absolutely unanimous agreement,[12] and even less did he propose it as a norm for the acceptance or rejection of the living magisterium's doctrinal decisions. Any appeal to his authority on the part of the Old Catholic sect is, accordingly, misguided and pointless.

It may of course seem surprising that St. Vincent did not refer his readers to the judgment of the Roman pontiff. But it must be remembered, in the first place, that he was dealing with the case of a fresh controversy about which no solemn decision had as yet been issued. Recall, too, that at that time the doctrine of the infallibility of the Roman pontiff had not yet received the full and brilliant scientific treatment which later ages were to give it. Present-day Catholics are quite familiar with the fact that this prerogative belongs to the pope himself as distinct (but not separate) from the episcopal college; but those of an earlier age were more inclined to consider the supreme pontiff as he is conjoined with the body episcopal.[13] It is largely a question of emphasis.

Notes

1. St. Irenaeus: "Wherefore one should obey the presbyters who are in the Church, those who enjoy apostolic succession; those who, along with apostolic succession, have received the sure charism of truth, according to the good pleasure of the Father" (*Adversus haereses* iv. 26, 2; see iii. 24, 1). For Tertullian, see *above*, no. 147.

2. Protestants, of course, draw from this the following conclusion: therefore the Roman pontiff is the master of tradition, and can foist his whims on all Catholics under the false title of divine Tradition. Not at all! Catholics believe that matters of faith are defined by a solemn pronouncement of the supreme pontiff *because they are divinely certain* and that a pope speaking ex cathedra is preserved by the assistance of the Holy Spirit from all error in recognizing and in explaining the truth (whether he does so in writing or orally).

3. *Adversus haereses* iii. 3, 2.

4. See *Christ's Church*, no. 77.

5. Harnack testifies to the fact that such intercommunication was not lacking even in the first centuries:

> The journeys of leading Christians teach us how active personal communication and contact were in the first centuries. Because of this the Roman community stepped into the foreground in startling fashion: it was the destination of most Christians whom we know as travelers. . . . Here, too [in the exchange of letters], the Roman community stands in the foreground. . . . In fact, up until the time of Constantine, at any rate until about the middle of the third century, the centripetal forces became stronger than the centrifugal, but Rome was the center of those forces: the Roman community was *the* Catholic community. It was not only the symbol and representative of unity, but to it above all others do we owe thanks for that unity.—*Mission und Ausbreitung des Christentums in den ersten drei Jahrhunderte*, pp. 269–72.

6. *Adversus haereses* 1. 10, 2.

7. *De praescriptione* 28.

8. Even Holy Scripture itself is a great help to the Church's magisterium; in fact it renders boundlessly outstanding service to the preservation of Tradition (inherent and declarative in both senses). But since this fact is obviously clear and beyond all cavil, theologians usually do not mention

Sacred Scripture in this context, lest they appear to put divine books and human documents on the same level.

9. See *Christ's Church*, no. 99.

10. *Commonitorium* 2; see W. Reilly, *Etude sur la regle de foi de s. Vincent de Lerins* (1902).

11. But this will so happen only if we follow totality, antiquity, agreement [later, in his summation, he explains: "We have said that the agreement of totality as well as that of antiquity should be taken into account" (ch. 29)]. But we shall follow *totality* in this way, by confessing that this one faith is the true one, which the whole universal Church *confesses* (ch. 2). What if some new contagion should try to infect the whole Church at once? In that case it will be similarly prudent to stick to *antiquity*, which is altogether secure from seduction by any novel deceit (ch. 3).

12. See ch. 2 and 28.

13. Hence Vincent writes in the following strain about the resistance shown by Pope St. Stephen to St. Cyprian:

> Then the holy martyr Pope Stephen, bishop of the Apostolic See, together with the rest of his colleagues indeed, but even more than all of them, put up stiff resistance, considering it justified, I suppose, if he outstripped all the others in devotion to the faith as much as he surpassed them in authority of position.—Ch. 6.

Article III

SOME SPECIFIC DOCUMENTS OF TRADITION

I. *The Symbols of Faith:*
   1. The Apostles' Creed;
   2. The Niceno-Constantinopolitan Creed;
   3. The Athanasian Creed.

II. a. *The Writings of the Fathers:*
   1. What is a "father of the Church"?
   2. What is a "doctor of the Church"?
   3. What are "ecclesiastical writers"?

   b. *The Authority of the Fathers:*

   PROPOSITION: The unanimous agreement of the fathers on a doctrine as revealed is a sure argument for divine Tradition.

   Proof: 1. from the conviction and practice of the infallible Church;
   2. theological argument.

   Corollaries.
   Remarks on the interpretation of the fathers' writings.

   c. *The Fathers and Secular Matters*
   Scholion. The authority of theologians.

Article III

SOME SPECIFIC DOCUMENTS OF TRADITION

Since space does not permit a treatment of each of the several documents, we shall have to rest content with a few brief remarks about the symbols of faith (creeds). This will leave room for a somewhat more detailed study of the writings of the fathers and theologians.

161 **I. The Symbols of Faith**

Symbols of faith is the term generally used to indicate brief summaries of the truths of faith; more developed formulae are called not symbols but *professions* of faith. The name seems to have originated in the fact that the faithful were distinguished from other people by such a formula as by a sign (*symbolon*)[1] or mark of identification.

There are three symbols which the Greeks, too, and several Protestants share with Catholics: the *Apostles' Creed*, the *Nicene Creed* (or, more exactly, the Niceno-Constantinopolitan), and the *Athanasian Creed*.

1. The Apostles' Creed. There is no doubt that all the doctrine contained in this symbol is apostolic, but there is some question about the formula itself.[2]

On the testimony of Ambrose,[2] Jerome,[3] Rufinus,[4] and Leo the Great,[5] there was a strong opinion about 400 A.D. that the baptismal symbol which the Roman Church kept inviolate and to which other western churches made some additions, had been composed by the apostles. Rufinus bases his view expressly on the tradition of the ancients: "our elders tell us";[6] and his subsequent remarks are of such a nature that they could easily have given rise to the idea that each of the apostles contributed a single phrase to the formula.[7]

However, the fathers just mentioned were speaking, not of the text in common use today, but rather of the older text which read as follows:

(168)

I believe in God, the Father almighty; and in Jesus Christ, His only Son, our Lord, who was born of the Holy Spirit and of the Virgin Mary; crucified under Pontius Pilate and buried, He arose from the dead on the third day; He ascended to Heaven; He sits at the right of the Father; from here He will come to judge the living and the dead. And in the Holy Spirit, the holy Church, the remission of sins, and the resurrection of the body.

162 The commonly accepted text, called also the Gallican, turns up first in a sermon of Caesarius of Arles (d. 543).[8] It is the common opinion of scholars that it took form in southern Gaul in the fifth century. The Roman Church took it over in the seventh or eighth century.

The older text, called also the Roman, certainly goes back to the middle of the second century in substance (i.e., in its over-all structure and in all the articles except perhaps the last three).[9] Many think it probable that it goes back to the beginning of this century, right back to the apostolic age itself. But, for lack of documentary evidence, this cannot be proven positively. This older Roman text is certainly the archetype of all western creeds and probably of all oriental ones as well.

But the opinion which attributes the composition of this formula to a joint council of the apostles is today rejected by many, even Catholic, critics, on the grounds that it finds no sufficient proof in the testimony of the ancients, and especially because no trace of a uniform creed can be found among the ancient eastern churches. The nucleus of the whole formula, however, the profession of baptizing in "God, Father, Son, and Holy Spirit," is justifiably considered apostolic.

Whatever one may think of the origin of the verbal formula, the authority of the creed as such is unshakable in the face of its approbation and centuries-old use in the universal Church.

163 2. **The Niceno-Constantinopolitan Creed.** The basis of this symbol is the old text of the Apostles' Creed, which (a) the Nicene fathers (325 A.D.) elaborated in order to give more distinct expression to the consubstantiality of the Word.[10] Later, (b) the fathers of Constantinople (381 A.D.) accepted with little change[11] a creed which was very much like the Nicene, but in which the divinity of the Holy Spirit was more plainly indicated.[12] It had the approval of the universal Church from at least the sixth century on.

This creed began to be used in the Mass during the sixth century in the east and shortly thereafter (589 A.D.) in Spain, where the phrase "and from the Son" was added to the words "who proceeds from the Father." Gaul and Germany followed suit in the eighth century. The Roman Church adopted this custom along with the phrase "and from the Son" only in the time of Benedict VIII (1012–1024).

164 3. **The Athanasian Creed,**[13] or the "Quicumque," composed in the style of a psalm, contains a more accurate exposition of the mysteries of the Trinity and of the Incarnation.

Scholars have ascertained that this symbol was not composed by Athanasius and was not completely Greek in origin; the Greeks became acquainted with it quite late. It seems to have been composed in Gaul in the fifth century and somewhere in the region of Arles. Künstle has attempted to demonstrate that it was an exposition of the true faith aimed at the Priscillian heresy.

"The Belief of Athanasius," as it once used to be called, began to be used in the Divine Office around the end of the eighth century, came to be known as a symbol in the tenth, and was considered a solid rule of faith in the universal Church from at least the thirteenth century on.

165 The chief *professions* of faith are (a) the profession of Trent, prescribed by Pius IV, to which Pius IX made a few additions after the Vatican Council; (b) the profession prescribed for the Greeks by Gregory XIII; (c) the profession prescribed for Oriental Catholics by Urban VIII and Benedict XIV; (d) the profession of faith and the oath against Modernism, prescribed by Pius X.[14]

II. a. The Writings of the Fathers

166 1. **What constitutes a father of the Church?** The title *fathers* in the broad sense indicates ecclesiastics who, in the early ages of the Church, recorded Catholic doctrine and explained and defended that doctrine by their writings. Thus it embraces the fathers strictly so called, the doctors of the Church, and those who are generally referred to as ecclesiastical writers.

1. In the strict sense, the fathers of the Church are those who are outstanding for orthodoxy, holiness, and antiquity, and are *acknowledged* as such by the Church.

Their *orthodoxy* is not destroyed by a few errors in matters which at the time they wrote had not yet been worked out clearly, as long as they had a truly Catholic attitude and generally treated Christian doctrine correctly. Their *holiness* of life won for them the special illumination of the Holy Spirit, and resulted in their edifying the Church not by their words alone, but by their example as well. Final judgment on soundness of doctrine and on holiness belongs to the Church. Consequently no one must be considered a qualified and, as it were, authoritative witness to Catholic tradition if the Church does not acknowledge him as such. This acknowledgment is made in different ways, as for instance, when they are cited as fathers by councils or by a supreme pontiff, or when they are praised in the Roman Martyrology as "eminent for holiness and learning," or when the Church agrees in practice that they are worthy of the title. It is customary to call fathers of the Church only those who stand out as witnesses of Christian *antiquity*. The limits of this antiquity are not rigidly fixed. They are usually extended in the Greek Church to include John Damascene (d. 754), and in the Latin Church to take in Gregory the Great (d. 604) or, better, Isidore of Seville (d. 636).

But if the title of "father" is used in a little wider sense to indicate a group other than the Scholastic theologians, then Bernard of Clairvaux has the distinction of being called "the last of the fathers."

Several fathers were bishops, but not all. Ephraem the Syrian (d. 373) was a deacon; Justin Martyr (d. c. 165) and Prosper of Aquitaine (463) were laymen.

2. **The title "doctors of the Church"** applies to those who were outstanding for orthodoxy, learning, and holiness, and have been *honored with this title* by the Church.

Since the work of a doctor is more directly concerned with explaining doctrine than with merely witnessing to it, antiquity is not required in this case but rather an *outstanding erudition* in the field of theology. The title of doctor, at least in recent centuries, is bestowed upon certain men in very explicit fashion, either by pontifical decree or by the granting of the liturgical Office of Doctors to be used on their feasts by the universal Church.

The great doctors of the Latin Church are customarily listed as four: Ambrose (d. 397), Jerome (d. 420), Augustine (d. 430), and Gregory the Great (d. 604).[15]

The great *ecumenical* doctors are listed in the liturgical books of the Greeks as three: Basil (d. 379), Gregory Nazianzen (d. 390), and John Chrysostom (d. 407).

The other doctors are: Hilary of Poitiers (d. 366), Athanasius (d. 373), Ephraem (d. 373), Cyril of Jerusalem (d. 386), Cyril of Alexandria (d. 444), Peter Chrysologus (d. 450), Leo the Great (d. 461), Isidore of Seville (d. 636), Venerable Bede (d. 735), John Damascene (d. 754), Peter Damian (d. 1072), Anselm of Canterbury (d. 1109), Bernard (d. 1153), Anthony of Padua (d. 1231), Thomas Aquinas (d. 1274), Bonaventure (d. 1274), Albert the Great (d. 1280), John of the Cross (d. 1591), Peter Canisius (d. 1597), Robert Bellarmine (d. 1621), Francis de Sales (d. 1622), Alphonsus Liguori (d. 1778).

168 3. *Ecclesiastical writers*, in the technical sense of the term, are those who once brilliantly illumined the Church with their writings, but are not classed among the saints or may even have left the Church—in a word, all those whom the Church does not recognize as authoritative witnesses to its tradition. Such are, for instance, Tatian, Athenagoras, Minucius Felix (towards the end of the second century), Tertullian (d. after 220), Clement of Alexandria (d. 215), Origen (d. 254), Arnobius (d. after 304), Lactantius (d. about 320), Eusebius of Caesarea (d. about 320), Rufinus (d. 410), Theodoretus (d. 458), Dionysius, called the Areopagite (d. about 500), etc.[16]

169 b. The Authority of the Fathers

In this discussion, the term "fathers" will be taken in its broad sense. Still, real fathers and doctors will be accorded more weight than ecclesiastical writers, and of the latter group those who left the Church will be considered only to the extent that they are in agreement with genuine fathers.

PROPOSITION. *The unanimous agreement of the fathers on a doctrine as revealed is a sure argument for divine Tradition.*

The *agreement* must be morally unanimous. But the fact of such agreement may be determined indirectly as well as directly, for example, (a) when all *subsequent* fathers are in accord, those, namely, who lived after a doctrine began to come under attack or to receive more specific attention; or (b) when *many* fathers of *different* times and countries agree, with no opposition from the others; or (c) when only *a few* fathers come to the defense of a doctrine, but in such *circumstances* as to make it clear that they speak, as it were, in the name of the whole Church, as in the case of Augustine against the Pelagians or of Sophronius against the Monothelites.

The agreement must be about a doctrine *as revealed*. The fathers can assert this not only explicitly but also in equivalent terms, as, for example, when they use the formula, "we believe with the Catholic Church," or when they propose a doctrine as one which must be believed by everyone or openly declare an opposite opinion heretical, etc. As long as they unanimously teach something as a doctrine which must be believed, it makes no difference whether they are acting as witnesses only or as doctors as well, by declaring what is the authentic meaning of ancient tradition. For then when they teach and clarify as well as give witness, they are the spokesmen of the Church and can be said to be acting as authoritative teachers. On the other hand, when they are carrying on research, suggesting opinions or hesitating, they are clearly speaking as private teachers.

This proposition is *certain* and, in fact, is partially defined by the Councils of Trent and of the Vatican in what they have to say about the interpretation of Scripture.[17]

Proof: 170

1. From the *conviction and practice of the infallible Church,* which has always proclaimed the teaching of the fathers to be its own, and has always consulted them when there were controversies to settle. The fathers and doctors themselves give historic proof of this fact, for when they were alive, they consistently taught that the teaching of the fathers who had preceded them must be followed.[18]

2. *Theological argument.* The agreement of the fathers reflects the agreement of the ecclesiastical magisterium. During their lifetime they were the Church's spokesmen: many of them held authoritative positions in that very magisterium and the rest wrote at least under the watchful eye of the Church and with its approval. After their death they were acknowledged by the Church as qualified witnesses of Catholic tradition.

171 It is frequently *objected* that the Antenicene fathers were in sympathy with the error of Chiliasm (the more subtle type) and with Subordinationism. This objection will not hold water. (a) Many did look with favor on Chiliasm, but by no means all—not even a moral majority. Besides, its chief supporters did not propose this doctrine as a matter to be believed by all with the sureness of faith. Justin:

> I admitted to you formerly that I and many others are of this opinion, but on the other hand, I indicated to you that there are also many Christians of pure and pious mind, who are not of the same opinion.[19]

(b) It is simply not true that all or even many Antenicene fathers were Subordinationists, although some of them, while holding to the essentials of the true doctrine, did stray somewhat from the truth in secondary points, and were not quite accurate especially in the matter of terminology. More about this in the Treatise on the Trinity.

In developing this thesis, we have been speaking of the *theological* authority of the fathers when they are in agreement. But from a merely historical point of view as well, the agreement of the fathers, especially if it can be established not indirectly and by inference but directly, must be taken as a morally certain criterion of the truth.[20]

172 Corollaries

1. If the fathers are in common accord in defending some doctrine which, by the nature of its subject matter, can be classed with doctrines of faith or morals, and if they propose it *to be held as true* without making it sufficiently clear that they consider it revealed, their agreement must be taken as a sure criterion of at least its theological truth, although perhaps not of its revealed truth.[21]

2. The authority of one or of a few fathers is not compelling, even in a strictly theological matter, for as individuals they were not infallible. And no one of them has received such approval from the Church as to make every single statement of his an object of obligatory belief. In fact, there can be found hardly one who did not err at one time or other, at least in less important matters.[22]

But if some of them spoke in such fashion that in the circumstances they can be said to have spoken in the name of the Church, then they must by all means be followed as far as the substance of their teaching on the point is concerned. But as far as their treatment of accessory questions or their more detailed explanations are concerned, the words of Pope Celestine I may serve as a guide: "The deeper and more difficult parts of secondary questions which they who combatted heretics treated in great detail we do not dare brush aside disdainfully, but neither do we consider it necessary to assent to them."[23]

Still, in matters of faith and morals, the authority of even individual fathers is to be held in high regard, and all the more, the more outstanding they are for learning, holiness, antiquity, and especially for the approval and commendation they have received from the Church.

173 A few remarks on the interpretation of the fathers. (a) Since in the light of theological principles it is antecedently impossible that there be agreement in favor of a matter of faith in one age and against it in another, and since what is theologically impossible cannot be critically true, we must rule out, first of all, any interpretation according to which all or many fathers of an earlier age could be said to disagree with those of a later age in a matter of faith or morals. (b) Even in the case of individual fathers or doctors, no real error is to be admitted in matters which have been explicitly taught by the Church right from the beginning or at least from a very early age. How could the Church have recognized a man as a witness of its tradition if he had subscribed to heretical doctrine? Still, if he had a substantial understanding of the true doctrine, he may quite possibly have expressed confused concepts, scientific explanations which were not quite correct or consistent, and especially he may have used inaccurate or careless terminology which may at times seem to lend support to a heresy of a later age. (c) In matters which were not clearly and explicitly contained in the Church's articles of faith until much later, it is even easier to admit error on the part of individual fathers. But since on Catholic principles later agreement could not have been reached if the seeds of the same doctrine, anticipations of it, as it were, had not been in existence earlier, it is quite reasonable to expect that vague, indecisive passages in earlier works will be cleared up in the light of later agreement. (d) In the case of the

fathers as in the case of all other authors, and this is especially true of some of them, attention must be paid to the rhetorical or polemical emphasis of their writings. As is often the case in literature in general, their real meaning must at times be gleaned not from their words alone, but also from the attendant circumstances: the people they are addressing, the error they are attacking, and the like. Often, too, a puzzling passage must be cleared up by reference to other passages where they treat the same subject more clearly.

It follows from this that a truly scientific interpretation of the fathers is not merely a matter of following the rules of philology and lexicography, and that those "critics" who shun the light furnished by the common conviction of the Church of the father's day or of later ages quite often risk missing the author's meaning by sticking too exclusively to the letter. On the other hand, those theologians who, by failing to take sufficient account of human foibles and of the obscurity to be expected in questions not yet thrashed out, are determined to defend every statement of the fathers, difficult or no, come hell or high water, show little respect for the rights of truth and bring discredit on their science.

174 c. The Fathers and Secular Matters

4. In *merely secular matters* the fathers have no special authority. No matter how staunchly unanimous their agreement may be on such points, the conclusion reached by Melchior Cano still holds good: "The authority of the saints, be they few or many, when brought to bear on matters which fall within the province of natural reason, does not furnish certain proof, but is only as valid as the reasoning process on which it is based."[24]

175 *Scholion. The authority of theologians.*

The term "theologians" signifies those writers of the post-patristic period and especially of the period following the twelfth century who produced more systematic works on sacred doctrine under the aegis of the Roman Catholic episcopate. More systematic works, indeed, for the theologians "undertook a task of great magnitude, namely, to harvest with reverent care the abundantly rich sheaves of doctrine from the extensive writings of the holy fathers, to bind them together and to store them in one place for the use and convenience of later ages."[25] In addition, they strove to clarify, to recommend, and to defend revealed doctrines with the aid of philosophical reasoning to a greater extent than the fathers had done. The theologians succeeded the fathers as witnesses of revelation although they did not enjoy the same authority. In the first place, by far the majority of the fathers were bishops, but this is not true of theologians. Again, the Church, which gave its official approval in at least general fashion to the fathers and doctors, even as individuals, does not recognize individual theologians as witnesses of its tradition, but reserves this recognition rather for schools of theologians (Thomists, Suarezians, Scotists, Salmanticenses, etc.).

However, *the unanimous and constant agreement of theologians on a doctrine as revealed is a sure criterion of divine tradition.* This fact is established (a) by the authority of Pius IX: "The actual submission which must be given to divine faith" is not restricted to matters which have been solemnly defined, but "must be extended to those matters also which are proposed as divinely revealed by the magisterium of the universal, world-wide Church, and which are consequently maintained as part of the faith by Catholic theologians in universal and constant accord."[26] (b) By *theological reasoning* (hinted at in the words of Pius IX). The bond between theological schools and the Church's magisterium is so intimate that those things which theologians with morally universal unanimity—and not during just a short period but over a considerable span of time—teach as matter calling for the firm assent of faith could not but coincide with what is taught by the ordinary and universal magisterium of the Church. Would not the Catholic episcopate be clearly derelict of duty if it winked at an error in faith taking root and growing apace throughout Catholic schools? Would not an error tacitly approved by the protracted silence of the Church's pastors end up by poisoning that Church quite thoroughly? On the other hand, how explain the constant unanimity of so many sincere and learned men if not by the fact that they follow either the Church's public, day-to-day teaching or at least the mind of the Church, the "Catholic sense"?

Whenever theologians, with this same unanimity, teach a doctrine belonging by its subject matter to faith and morals as true and as demanding the assent of everyone, but without calling it a revealed doctrine, their teaching is a reliable criterion of *theological truth.* Care must be taken, however, not to confuse such decisive and solid agreement with *conjectural* agreement, i.e., agreement on an opinion as such. This latter is not very common, and can be recognized by its very fluidity.

Notes

1. See Bardenhewer, *Geschichte der altkirchlichen Literatur*, I, 68; DTC, I, 1660 ff.; Vacandard, *Etudes de critique* (1905), p. 3; J. Quasten, *Patrology*, I, 23 ff.
2. *Epistula* 42, 5.
3. *Contra Joannem Jerosolymae* 98.
4. *Commentarium in Symbolum*, 2–3.
5. *Sermo* 96, 1; *Epistula* 31 *ad Pulcheriam* 4.
6. *Loc. cit.*
7. See the sermon of Pseudo-Augustine 240 (ML 39, 2189).
8. *Sermo de symboli fide et bonis operibus* (244, one among the spurious sermons of Augustine, *loc. cit.*, p. 2195), where, however, the following words are still wanting: "Creator of heaven and of earth." The older text clearly consisted of twelve articles. In the presently accepted text St. Thomas preferred to distinguish fourteen articles (S.Th 2–2ae, q. 1, a. 8).
9. In the opinion of some, the creed which was in use in the Roman Church around the year 150 is to be reconstructed as follows:
   I believe in one God, Father almighty, and in Jesus Christ His Son, our Lord, who was born of a virgin, was crucified under Pontius Pilate, rose from the dead on the third day, ascended into heaven, sits at the right hand of the Father, whence He shall come to judge the living and the dead; and in the Holy Spirit.
10. See Hefele, *Conciliengeschichte*, I (2nd ed.), 314.
11. *Ibid., II* (2nd ed.), 10.
12. This can be found in Epiphanius *Anchoratus* 121.
13. See DTC, I, 2178; K. Künstle, *Antipriscilliana* (1905).
14. DB 994, 998, 1459, 2145.
15. In 1298 Boniface VIII extolled these men as "outstanding doctors of the Church" (in the decretal *Gloriosus* 3, 22).
16. For information on these writers see the recognized works of patrology, like Fessler-Jungman, *Institutiones patrologiae*; Bardenhewer, *Geschichte der altkirchlichen Literatur; Patrologie* (2nd ed.); Battiffol, *La litterature grecque* (3rd ed.); Rauschen, *Grundriss der Patrologie*; Cayre, *Manual of Patrology*; Quasten, *Patrology*; Kihn, *Patrologie*; Altaner, *Patrologie* (2nd ed.).
17. See above, no. 103.
18. Some examples of this can be found in Pesch, *Praelectiones dogmaticae*, I, no. 576 ff.
19. *Dialogue with Trypho* 80; see De San, *De traditione*, pp. 183 ff., where there is a discussion also of those fathers who were of the opinion that the beatific vision would be postponed until the time of the general judgment (p. 194).
20. See Augustine *Contra Julianum* ii. 10, 37.

21. See *Christ's Church,* and especially the Treatise on Faith, in the article entitled "Theological Truths."

22. And so Augustine writes: "I do not accept Cyprian's views on the baptism of heretics because those views are not accepted by the Church for which St. Cyprian shed his blood" (*De baptismo* 2, 3). St. Thomas: "One must stand by the authority of the Church rather than by that of Augustine or Jerome or any doctor at all, because the very teaching of Catholic doctors gets its authority from the Church" (S. Th., 2-2ae, q. 10, a. 12). In this connection the following condemned proposition also could be cited: "Whenever anyone finds a doctrine with clear backing in the works of Augustine, he can hold and teach it unconditionally, without the slightest regard for any pontifical Bull" (DB 1320).

23. *Epistula 21 ad episcopos Galliae;* DB 142.
24. *De locis theologicis,* VII, 3.
25. Encyclical *Aeterni Patris.*
26. *Epistula ad archiepiscopum Monaci,* 1863; DB 1683.

Introduction

The Notion and Division of Faith

I. *A Generic Notion of the Term Faith:*
   1. Sometimes refers mainly to the *will* and designates:
      a. faithfulness
      b. trust
   2. Usually refers to the *intellect* and designates:
      a. any kind of assent in obscure matters;
      b. a firm assent in moral or metaphysical matters grounded only on subjective attitudes;
      c. a firm assent given because of someone's testimony.
      (1) This is the genuine notion of faith.

II. *Faith In the Strict Sense of the Term Differs From:*
   1. Opinion, experience, understanding, or knowledge.
   2. St. Thomas on the difference between faith and all other intellectual assents.

III. *The Cooperation of the Will Is Necessary for an Assent of Faith*
   1. The intellect is reluctant to assent to what it does not see and the very nature of faith precludes its seeing.
   2. The will cooperates in overcoming the natural reluctance of the intellect, but this cooperation is not a blind impulse of the will.

IV. *Faith Is Categorized in Accord with the Type of Testimony Upon which It Rests as:*
   1. Human faith.
   2. Divine faith.
   3. Ecclesiastical faith.

V. *The Vatican Council's Definition of Divine Faith*
   1. Comparison of Vatican Council's definition with that

INTRODUCTION

given by St. Thomas, and the descriptive definition given by St. Paul.
2. St. Thomas's explanation of St. Paul's description of faith.

VI. *Various Divisions of Divine Faith:*
1. *Merely divine faith* vs. *divine-catholic faith.*
2. *Formed* or living faith vs. *unformed* or dead faith.
3. *Explicit* faith vs. *implicit faith.*
4. *Actual* faith vs. *habitual* faith.

Divine Faith

177 The preceding treatises (*The True Religion, Christ's Church, The Sources of Revelation*) dealt with the objective foundations on which all sacred doctrine rests: the fact of a revelation made by Christ, the Church He established to safeguard and expound that heavenly revelation, and Scripture and Tradition the twin storehouse from which the Church draws its teaching. To round out fundamental theology we must now examine the subjective means, or the personal act by which individual men lay hold of the truths revealed by Christ and offered to them by the Church from Scripture and Tradition. This act is known as the assent of divine faith. More briefly, it is called simply *faith*.

Introduction

The Notion and Division of Faith

I. Variant Usage of the Term "Faith"

A generic notion of faith. The word *faith* is used with a bewildering variety of meanings. So true is this that one writer at the beginning of the twentieth century, with some justification, called it "a nest of equivocations."[1]

1. Sometimes the term faith refers mainly to the *will*. In this usage it designates:

a. *Faithfulness,* or on unswerving determination to keep one's promises. It may even signify the promise itself. Here are two examples of such usage: "*Will their unfaithfulness nullify the faithfulness of God?* (fidem Dei-tēn pistin tou theou)."[2] "*But refuse to enroll younger widows, because when they wantonly turn away from Christ, they wish to marry; thus they incur condemnation because they have broken their prior pledge*" (pledge-*primam* fidem *irritam fecerunt-hoti* tēn prōtēn pistin ēthetēsan).[3]

b. *Trust* engendered by another's power and goodness, or trustworthiness. So, for example, the rebuke of our Lord to Peter: "*How little faith you have!*", he said to him; "*what made you doubt?*" (*Modicae* fidei, *quare dubitasti*-oligopiste, *eis ti edistasas*)[4] refers mainly—though not exclusively—to a lack of trust. This was the connotation stressed by the early Protestants when they claimed that the faith which justifies a man is primarily "faith in God's promises." In other words, justifying faith is that by which a man trusts with absolute assurance that his personal sins have been forgiven and that eternal justice and salvation have been bestowed upon him by God because of the merits of Christ.[5]

2. Most of the time the term faith refers directly to the *intellect* and is used in one of the following ways:

a. For *any kind of an assent* to one side of a question, particularly in *obscure matters.* This is the explanation for Paul's axiom: "*Everything which is not of faith is a sin*" (Kleist-Lilly; "*Every act that does not proceed from conscientious conviction is sinful"—omne autem quod non est ex* fide, peccatum est—*pan de ho ouk ek pisteos hamartia estin*).⁶ Again the term faith may be used of the assent given to something evident from the first principles of reason. Using the term this way some of the Greek fathers speak of faith as 'prior" to knowledge.—But these last two examples are exceptional cases.

b. Sometimes—in philosophical and religious literature—the term faith is used to signify a firm assent in metaphysical or moral matters; but an assent which ultimately rests on *subjective* attitudes, or on proofs that appeal to the *heart*. Such proofs are according to Kant: the irresistible demands of the practical reason (moral conscience, a categorical imperative); according to neo-criticism (Renouvier): an inclination of "the whole man," i.e., intelligence, will, emotions, as modified by various internal and external circumstances; according to the Scottish school (Reid): a common instinct of human nature and the agreement of mankind which issues therefrom; according to Jacobi and the Sentimentalists: a kind of instinctive spiritual feel for suprasensible realities; according to Balfour: the demands of the common good, or the necessity of rationally vindicating the religious, moral and social sphere, without which human life would lack all value and society itself soon crumble.

Since neither purely subjective attitudes—no matter how explained—nor utilitarianism, either public or private, can offer grounds for genuine certitude, as any critical mind can see, the "faith" described by such writers tends to end up as a necessary consequence in skepticism.⁷ Still some French apologists (the Immanentists) display a predilection for such a volitional approach and even Cardinal Newman may be said to have looked on such an approach favorably at times.⁸

c. Finally, the term faith is used to designate a *firm assent of the intellect given because of someone's testimony*. This is the genuine notion of faith in the strict sense, as is proved in the field of philosophy.⁹

180 **II. How Faith Differs from Other Intellectual Acts**

Faith in the strict meaning of the term differs:

a. From *opinion*. Opinion means the intelligence inclines to one side of a question, but with some fear of the opposite side being true. Opinion signifies, then, an assent of the mind which is hesitating, not firm. Still, in everyday usage we must admit, people frequently do say, "I believe," when they mean: "it is my opinion that."

b. From *experience, understanding, knowledge*. In all such learning processes the mind yields its assent because of arguments or evidence that is *intrinsic* to a given proposition. In other words, the mind assents because of the very evidence for the truth that is offered to it: evidence which is lucidly clear to either the mind or the senses, regardless of whether it be had first-hand or second-hand. In faith, on the contrary, the mind yields its assent because of an argument or motive that is *extrinsic* to the proposition itself, namely because of someone's *testimony*.

St. Thomas sums up neatly the difference between faith and all other intellectual assents in these words: "faith goes beyond opinion in that it clings to something firmly; it stops short of knowledge in that it assents to what it does not see."[10]

III. Cooperation of Will Needed for Faith 181

Since the intellect, by its very nature, cannot be constrained to give its assent unless it clearly sees the intrinsic truthfulness of a proposition—and such evidence for the truth is missing in the act of faith—it follows that the assent of faith takes place only under a command from the will. That is why faith is defined as: *an act of the intellect firmly assenting to a truth, given because of someone's authority and at a command from the will*. The will does, then, cooperate effectively in producing an act of faith; but this is not a blind impulse of the will, nor is the will-act the final explanation for the assent. In the act of faith a man's will only orders the assent *because* his intelligence has already acknowledged the authority (competence and truthfulness) of the witness and judged that it is reasonable to accept the authority's word on the matter. In the intellectual act of faith, therefore, even though no *constraining* evidence is at hand there is not lacking *sufficient* reason for assenting with certitude.

IV. Different Types of Faith 182

Since faith is an assent given because of the authority (competence) of a witness, the type of faith varies in accord with the type of authority at hand. That is why we distinguish three kinds

INTRODUCTION

of faith: human, divine, and ecclesiastical. (a) *Human faith* rests upon the authority of a man; (b) *divine faith* upon the authority of God; (c) and *ecclesiastical faith* upon the infallible authority of the Church. By ecclesiastical faith we mean the assent we give to truths which, while belonging to the sphere of faith and morals, have not been formally revealed but which have been sanctioned by a definitive judgment on the part of the Church. Actually it is disputed whether such assents may not belong to the realm of divine faith: a number of theologians think they do and describe them as "indirectly of divine faith" (*fides mediate divina*); many others say no: they are simply assents of ecclesiastical faith. This point is discussed *ex professo* later. (See nos. 246–250.)

183   **V. The Church's Definition of Faith**

Here is the *definition of divine faith* as stated by the Vatican Council:[11]

> Because man completely depends on God as his Creator and Lord and because created reason is completely subject to Uncreated Truth, when God reveals anything we are bound to give him, by faith, the complete submission of our intelligence and will. Now the Catholic Church asserts that *this faith*, "which is the beginning of human salvation" (*see* DB 801), *is a supernatural virtue whereby, under the stimulus and assistance of God's grace, we believe the matters revealed by Him are true*—not because we see their intrinsic truthfulness through the natural light of reason—but *because of the authority of God himself who reveals them*, and who can neither deceive nor be deceived. [Translation and italics ours.]

The council's words refer directly to the *habit of faith*, which is a permanent quality inclining us to make acts of faith. Since the nature of a habit is made known in the act that flows from it, the above description can equally well serve as a definition of the *act of faith*, if in place of the words "a supernatural *virtue*" you substitute, "a supernatural *act*."

The shorter definition by St. Thomas is in perfect conformity with the one above: "an act of the intellect assenting to divine truth, under the command of the will, itself moved by grace."[12] If it is of the very nature of faith to enable us "to believe *as true*"

(188)

those matters God has revealed, St. Thomas correctly defines faith as an act of the intellect since the goal of the intellect is truth.[13]

It is helpful to add, as does the Vatican Council itself, the sublime saying of St. Paul: "*Faith is the foundation* [substance] *of the blessings for which we hope, the proof of the realities which we do not see.*"[14] St. Thomas explains[15] St. Paul's saying this way:

> The relation of the act of faith to its end, which is the object of the will, is indicated by the words: *Faith is the substance of things to be hoped for*. For we are wont to call by the name of *substance* the first beginning of a thing, especially when the whole subsequent thing is virtually contained in the first beginning. For instance, we might say that the first self-evident principles are the substance of science, because, namely, these principles are in us the first beginnings of science, the whole of which is itself contained in them virtually. In this way, then, faith is said to be the *substance of things to be hoped for*, for the reason that in us the first beginning of things to be hoped for [i.e. the Beatific Vision] is brought about by the assent of faith, which contains virtually all the things to be hoped for.[16] For we hope to be made happy through seeing the unveiled Truth to which our faith cleaves, as was made evident when we were speaking of happiness.
> The relationship of the act of faith to the object of the intellect, considered as the object of faith, is indicated by the words, *evidence of things that appear not*, where *evidence* is taken for the result of evidence. For evidence induces the intellect to adhere to a truth, and so the firm adhesion of the intellect to the nonapparent truth of faith is called *evidence* here. Hence another reading has *conviction*, because, namely, the intellect of the believer is convinced by divine authority, so as to assent to what it sees not.
> Accordingly, if anyone would reduce the foregoing words to the form of a definition, he may say that *faith is a habit of the mind, whereby eternal life is begun in us, making the intellect assent to what is non-apparent.*" (Translation from Pegis, *Basic Writings of St. Thomas* [New York, 1945] II, 1095–96; italics ours.)

VI. Terminology Describing Various Facets of Divine Faith 184

Division of divine faith. Since we are here concerned solely with the faith by which one believes, we omit here the division of faith into *subjective* and *objective*. Faith in the objective sense

INTRODUCTION

means simply the truth which is believed or even the entire gamut of all revealed religion.[17] But faith in the *subjective** sense is divided into:

a. *Merely divine faith* and *divine and Catholic faith* (or simply: *Catholic* faith). Merely divine faith is concerned with revealed truths which are known to man apart from any proposal of them by the Church; divine and Catholic faith deals with truths which are both revealed and proposed as such by the Church for our belief. Merely divine faith and divine-Catholic faith differ from one another purely accidentally, since the fashion in which revealed truths become known to us does not change the nature of faith in itself.

b. *Formed* or *living* faith and *unformed* or *dead* faith. Living faith means that which is accompanied by charity; dead faith that which exists apart from charity. Briefly, living faith is faith as found in a man in the state of grace; dead faith is faith as found in a man in the state of mortal sin. Charity is said to give life to or to inform faith not in the sense that charity is an intrinsic form or constitutive element of faith, for even dead or unformed faith is real faith and possesses all the elements required for the nature of faith.[18] Charity, then, is a form which perfects faith only extrinsically; in other words, it is necessary to produce acts that are *meritorious* in the strict sense of the word.

Although unformed faith is dead in the sense explained above (i.e., unproductive of meritorious acts) it does not follow that it is completely dead (i.e., totally unproductive), since it can and ought to exercise its power in the production of works that prepare or dispose one for justification.

c. *Explicit* faith and *implicit* faith. By the former we assent to a truth in itself, that is, as known in its own proper terms; by the latter we assent to a truth which is not itself expressly known but is contained in some other truth that is explicitly believed. For example, anyone who acknowledges that he believes whatever the Catholic Church proposes for belief, or who explicitly professes his belief in the necessity of grace for each and every salutary work, implicitly believes in the necessity of grace for the beginning of faith.[19]

---

* Subjective here has no connotation of a purely personal attitude, of something without objective foundation. It is used here in the literal meaning of the word: the faith which is found in a living *subject*.

INTRODUCTION

d. *Actual* faith and *habitual* faith. The former is a transient act of the intellect, the latter a permanent quality or habit from which the act is elicited.

The foregoing divisions may be put into a schema as follows:

FAITH
- a
  - *Merely divine* faith: . . . rests on God's authority apart from a proposal of a truth by the Church.
  - *Divine-Catholic* faith: . . . rests on God's authority and is given after a proposal of a revealed truth by the Church.
- b
  - *Formed* or *living* faith: . . . faith as found in a man in the state of grace.
  - *Unformed* or *dead* faith: . . . faith as found in a man in the state of mortal sin.
- c
  - *Explicit* faith: . . . directed to a truth as known in its own terms.
  - *Implicit* faith: . . . directed to a truth not known in its own terms but as contained in some other truth.
- d
  - *Actual* faith: . . . a transient act of the intellect by which a person says: "I believe."
  - *Habitual* faith: . . . a permanent quality or virtue or habit which disposes the intelligence to be ready to make an act of faith whenever necessary or useful.

Notes

1. "Every generic notion of faith is necessarily a nest of equivocations" (Gaudeau, *Le Besoin de croire* [1889], p. 18).
2. Rom. 3:3.
3. I Tim. 5:12.
4. Matt. 14:31.
5. See *Heidelberg Catechism*, question 21. Protestants, at least the original ones, distinguished three types of faith: *historical faith,* meaning the acceptance of whatever God has revealed as true; *faith in miracles,* meaning the type of faith which moves God to work a miracle; *faith in promises,* or special faith, meaning complete assurance about one's own justification.
6. Rom. 14:23.
7. See Beysens, *Criteriologie,* p. 240.

INTRODUCTION

8. See *De Katholik*, 115 (1899), 182.

9. See Beysens, *loc. cit.*, p. 307; in English see Phillips, *Modern Thomistic Philosophy* (Westminster, Md., 1945), II, 11.

10. St. Thomas, Ia–IIae, q. 67, a. 3, *corpus*.

11. Constitution, *On Faith*, ch. 3; DB 1789.

12. St. Thomas, IIa–IIae, q. 2, a. 9, *corpus*.

13. It should be clear, therefore, that not faith but rather charity which flowers from the root of faith is being described by those who say: "Faith . . . is the act by which a man offers himself to God to live really and eternally in Him." (Laberthonniere, *Le realisme chretien et l'idealisme grec.* Paris, 1904, p. 98.

14. Hebrews 11:1: *estin de pistis elpizomenon ypostastis pragmaton elegkos oy blepomenon.*

15. St. Thomas, IIa–IIae, q. 4, a. 1, *corpus*.

16. Elsewhere the holy doctor writes: "For just as substance is the foundation for all other entities, so faith is the foundation of the whole spiritual house" (*In III Sent.* d. 23, q. 2, a. 1). Others explain the passage this way: "the substance of things hoped for"—that by which the things to be hoped for are proven to us, are made certain for us.

17. For example the *Athanasian Creed* is speaking of this objective faith when it states: "This is the Catholic faith, which unless a man faithfully and firmly believes, he cannot be saved."

18. See the *Council of Trent:* "If anyone says that when grace is lost by sin, faith is also always lost at the same time, or that the faith which remains is not true faith, granted it be not living [faith], or that he who has faith without charity is not a Christian, let him be anathema." (Session VI, On Justification, canon. 28; DB 838.); *Vatican Council:* "Faith itself, even if it does not work through charity, is itself a gift of God (see Gal. 5:6), and its act is a work which pertains to salvation." (Constitution, *On Faith*, ch. 3; DB 1791).

19. Consequently they pervert the notion of implicit faith who use the term to indicate the *good will* by which a man begins to wait for the supernatural aids God bestows to help our insufficiency; "From the time that a man ceases to pretend to be self-sufficient, it matters little whether one knows or does not know how to name God: one accepts Him and awaits Him: one has implicit faith" (Laberthonniere, *Le probleme religieux*, p. 26).

CHAPTER I

The Object of Divine Faith

Article I

THE FORMAL OBJECT OF DIVINE FAITH

I. *Meaning of the Phrase: "Formal object of faith":*
   1. Warning: the term "motive" of faith must not be mistaken for anything in the purely subjective or psychological order.

II. *What the Formal Object of Faith Is Not:*
   1. It is not the attractiveness or usefulness of the truths to be believed.
   2. Is it not clear-cut evidence of the truthfulness of the revealed propositions.

III. *The Formal Object of Faith Is the Authority of God Revealing:*
   1. *Meaning* of phrase: "authority of God revealing."
   2. *Proof* of proposition:
      a. Church's Magisterium; Scripture; Tradition.

IV. *Theological Dispute Over Whether Revelation Itself Constitutes Part of Faith's Formal Object, or Is Simply a Condition Sine Qua Non*
   1. Three viewpoints briefly examined.

V. *The Church's Proposal of Revealed Truth Does Not Pertain to the Formal Object of Faith*
   1. Some theologians have mistakenly thought the contrary.
   2. A refutation of that viewpoint.

VI. *Corollary for Everyday Life:*
   1. Children and uneducated people should be instructed that their faith rests not on the word of pastors, or nuns, but exclusively on God's authority.

CHAPTER I

The Object of Divine Faith

Faith has a twofold object: a *material* and a *formal* object.*
The material object is a technical term used to describe what
English usage would call the "subject matter," or "content," or
"field" of faith. It means simply the data of revelation. The formal
object is a technical term used to describe the factor which specifies
or differentiates the act of faith from all other types of intellectual
assent.

In Article I we shall discuss the formal object of faith, for on it
depends the whole nature of faith and all its properties. In the
remaining articles we shall discuss the subject matter or the material object of faith. Thus in Article II we consider the material
object of *merely divine faith;* in Article III the material object of
divine and Catholic faith. Article IV discusses the question of
growth or increase of the material object of divine and Catholic
faith, or what is known as "dogmatic progress." Finally, as a kind
of appendix to faith, we shall discuss, in Article V, *"theological
truths"* and, in Article VI, *"theological censures."*

---

* The terms *matter* and *form* belong strictly to the Aristotelian hylemorphic
theory about the structural principles of all natural bodies. By *analogy* these
terms have been extended to all the branches of philosophy (and also to
various sections of theology) to designate anything that is analogously conceived of as actualizing or determining. (On this point see Maritain, *An
Introduction to Philosophy* [New York, 1933] p. 252.) For their specific
application to the act of faith, see Brunsmann–Preuss, *Fundamental Theology,*
IV (St. Louis, 1932), 205–207.

Article I

THE FORMAL OBJECT OF DIVINE FAITH

185 I. Meaning of Formal Object of Faith

The formal object of faith (*objectum formale, quo*) is that means which enables the intellect to reach its subject matter; that factor on account of which the assent of the intellect is given, and that which, finally, illumines or "informs," or clothes the material object in such a way as to make it apt to incite the intellect to produce an act of faith. Briefly, it is that objective factor or cause which moves the intelligence to yield its assent. That is why the formal object can be and often is called the *motive of faith*, provided one understands by the term "motive" an *objective* motive force which informs and specifies the assent, and by which we are here and now (*immediate*) moved to yield our assent to some revealed truth. For the term, "motive of faith," is frequently used in a much looser sense to indicate all the factors or causes that concur, even remotely, in the production of an act of faith: either by getting us *ready* for faith, as does a study of the "motives of credibility"; or by making the act of faith seem *attractive* to us, such as the moral goodness of subjecting oneself completely to God; or by *commanding* that we produce an act of faith, as the will: or by *helping* us to produce the very act of faith, as, for example, God's grace; or by giving *direction* to our faith, as, for example, the proposal of some truth by the Church for our belief. All these factors will be discussed more at length in the course of this treatise.

186 II. Rejection of False Notions of Formal Object

First of all this much is certain: there has to be something which really deserves the name *formal object*, or some objective motive, for if the assent of the mind were to rest merely on subjective dispositions, it would neither deserve the name faith, nor could it stand up under critical analysis.

Furthermore, from the genuine notion of faith in general, as described above, it is certain that the formal object is *not* any kind of goodness or usefulness of the truths to be believed. That is why the opinion defended by Lederer,[1] and indeed alleged as St. Thomas' own opinion, cannot be held. In this opinion the intellect assents to Christian truths because it judges that these truths lead one to supernatural happiness. Desire for the salvation promised by Christian doctrine can be a motive for *inquiring* whether that doctrine deserves to be embraced because of the proofs alleged in its behalf. Once that question has been answered satisfactorily the same desire can be a motive on account of which the will orders us to give our assent, but in no way can it be the formal motive of the assent itself.

Finally, from the same correct notion of faith it is clear that the formal motive of assent is not clearcut evidence of the truth; otherwise the assent would not be faith, but knowledge.

III. The Formal Object of Faith Is the Authority of God Revealing   187

This is a *dogma* of the faith defined by the Vatican Council[2] and was quoted above. Authority arises from a combination of *knowledge and truthfulness* and that is why the Vatican Council added to the definition these words: "because of the authority of God Himself revealing, *who can neither deceive nor be deceived.*" Since the Church plainly juxtaposes this authority of God to evidence of the truth, the authority of God must necessarily be understood of God's authority taken formally *as a witness*. A witness differs from a teacher in this, that a witness testifies merely to the existence of a fact, while a teacher in addition lays open the reason or explanation for the fact. Consequently the phrase "of God revealing," cannot be taken to mean revelation in a loose sense, or natural[3] revelation, because in that area God is not acting as a witness, but is teaching.

The proposition is proven from:

1. *Sacred Scripture:*

a. When Nicodemus, puzzled by Jesus' assertion that it was necessary to be "born again" to enter the kingdom of heaven, showed his reluctance to accept the doctrine by stating: "How are such things possible?," Jesus did not explain the mystery—He simply appealed to his own divine authority:

"You are a teacher in Israel" Jesus, answered him, "and do not understand things like this! I tell you the plain truth; we speak of what we know, and testify to what we have seen; but you all refuse to accept our testimony! If I have told you of earthly things and you refuse to believe, how will you believe if I should tell you of heavenly things! Of course, no one has ever ascended into heaven; but mind—there is one who has come down from heaven, the Son of Man, whose home was in heaven!"—John 3:10.

b. John the Baptist told his followers not to be disgruntled over the rising popularity of Jesus as though it were an injury to himself. Jesus is the "bridegroom"; he, John, is only the "friend of the bridegroom." Commenting on this incident the evangelist points out that Jesus' doctrine is from heaven and should be accepted on the testimony of Jesus alone:

He who comes from above is above all; he who is sprung from the earth is earthly through and through, and his speech savors of the earth. He who comes from heaven is above all: what he has seen and heard—that is the sum of his testimony; yet no one accepts his testimony! Everyone who accepts his testimony thereby puts his seal upon the truthfulness of God; for he who is God's ambassador proclaims God's message—John 3:31-34.

c. Jesus, in arguing with the Pharisees, justifies His doctrine against the Rabbinic argument that He was a "lone witness" by asserting He indeed has another witness—the Father for whom He is acting as an ambassador:

Once more Jesus addressed them. He said, "I am the light of the world. He who follows me will not walk in the dark, but have the light of life." "You testify in your own case," the Pharisees said to him; "your testimony is not valid." Jesus answered the charge. "Suppose" he replied, "I do testify in my own case: my testimony is valid even then, for I know where I came from and where I am going; but you do not know where I came from or where I am going. You judge according to outward appearances: I judge no one. And even if I judge, my judgment conforms to rule, for I am not alone. No, there are two: I and the Father, whose ambassador I am. Even in your own Law it is laid down that the testimony of two men is valid. I am the witness in my own case, and the Father, whose ambassador I am, witnesses in my behalf."—John 8:12–19.

d. *"If I speak the truth, why, then, do you not believe me? He who is sprung from God gives ear to God's message. You do not give ear, because you are not sprung from God."*— John 8:46–47.

e. *For this too we give unceasing thanks to God, that when you received the word of God's message from us, you welcomed it, not as a human message, but, as it truly is, the message of God . . .* —I Thessalonians 2:13.

f. *We accept the testimony of men, but the testimony of God has much greater authority. This is, in fact, the testimony of God: He has testified concerning his Son. He who believes in the Son has within himself the testimony of God. He who refuses to believe God treats him as a liar, because he does not believe the testimony that God has given concerning his Son.*—I John 5:9–11.

2. From *Tradition:*

St. Chrysostom: "This is faith when we believe those things which are not seen, and we focus our attention on the grandeur of the one who has promised. Let us also learn to believe the statements of God."[4]

Leo the Great: "It is divine authority which we believe."[5]

St. Thomas: "In faith if we consider the formal reason of the object it is nothing other than the First Truth; for the faith we are talking about does not assent to anything unless it has been revealed by God. Consequently faith rests on divine Truth itself as on a medium." Again: "The very testimony of the First Truth is related to faith the way a principle is to the demonstrative sciences."[6]

IV. Is Revelation Part of Faith's Formal Object? 188

While all theologians, at least since the Vatican Council, teach that the authority of God revealing is the formal object of faith, they are still divided on the question of whether or not revelation itself should be considered a real part of, that is, a constitutive element of the formal object.

Some hold that God's authority, that is, God's knowledge and truthfulness, constitutes the total motive of faith, whereas revelation or God's testimony is only a condition *sine qua non.*

Many others hold that the total motive of faith arises from a combination of both authority and revelation, but in such fashion that the revelation is a *subordinate element* and a sort of material element which is informed by God's authority. Here is their position: God's knowledge and truthfulness viewed simply in themselves certainly deserve our complete submission and they achieve this much: they make us ready to believe in case God should speak. But, viewed purely abstractly, they neither move us to make an act of faith nor can they move us to do so, unless God has first made known His thoughts to us by the act of revelation.

Finally, other theologians solve the problem by distinguishing between *active* revelation and *passive* revelation. Active revelation means the very act of the will by which God destines His thoughts to reach us, or the act by which He wills that His thoughts should become known to us. Passive revelation means the very activities and signs which disclose the divine truth to the external world. These theologians teach, then, that active revelation is indeed a constitutive element of the formal object of faith whereas passive revelation is only a condition requisite for practical application. They say: the knowledge and truthfulness of the God who is directing His thoughts to us really moves me to believe just as soon as I become aware of the divine truths by means of external or passive revelation.

This view has much to commend it because it sticks to the formula of the Vatican Council without intermingling in the motive of faith (which is a theological virtue) anything created, since active revelation is not really distinct from God Himself.

189 V. Church's Teaching Is Not Part of Motive of Faith

Some have thought that even the Church's proposal of the revealed truth, especially if it be viewed as a kind of continuation of the divine testimony, pertained to the formal object of faith. They are mistaken. The proposal of a truth by the Church is nothing more than the normal means by which the truths contained in the treasury of Scripture and Tradition are made known to us in secure fashion so that we may cling to those truths exclusively because of the authority of God revealing. Consequently when

Augustine says: "I would not believe the gospel unless moved to do so by the authority of the Catholic Church,"[7] he does not mean that the Church's authority is the motive or formal reason why we believe the gospel. He simply means that the Church's authority is the normal means for knowing what should or should not be accepted as belonging to the gospel.

We used the phrase *"normal* means," that is to say, in the present order of providence. For even though it is morally impossible to know the *entire* Christian revelation without the help of the Church, it does not follow that it is impossible to know this or that individual truth without her assistance.

There is some justification for speaking of the Church's proposal of divine truths as a kind of continuation of divine testimony; but it is a continuation really distinct from the external divine testimony which established the deposit of the faith. If one subscribes to the opinion which excludes even passive revelation from the motive of faith, much more obviously should any continuation of it by the Church be excluded as part of the motive of faith.

VI. Corollary for Everyday Life 190

Since an act of divine faith absolutely requires "that a revealed truth be believed on the authority of God revealing," children and uneducated people who would accept the dogmas of the faith *exclusively* because of the authority of their parents or of a parish priest, would not produce an act of *divine* faith. Consequently the faithful should be instructed on this point. But take care not to exaggerate the matter. It is not at all necessary to advert explicitly to the formal object every time one makes an act of faith; what suffices is an habitual knowledge of the authority of God as the motive of faith. Such habitual knowledge is certainly present if the faithful when directly questioned why they believe such or such a doctrine, immediately know to reply: "because God who is truthful has said so." And it does not really make much difference if they should reply: "because the Church teaches it"; since they know that the Church is the guardian and teacher of God's truth.

Notes

1. See ThQ (1901), p. 232, and (the same author) in the work *Ein sehr notwendige Reform auf dem Gebiete Katholische Lehre und Praxis,* 1905.
2. See chap. 3, canon 2: "If anyone says that there is no distinction be-

tween divine faith and natural knowledge about God and morals and, therefore, that for divine faith it is not necessary that revealed truths be believed on the authority of God who reveals them, let him be anathema." (DB 1811; transl. TCT 70.)—We omit here any discussion of the conflicting opinions of some of the more ancient theologians. Cajetan, for example, held that the divine essence was the formal object of faith, William of Paris held that it was God's supreme dominion, Banez and Sÿlvester Maurus that it was to be found at least partially in the light of faith, either habitual or actual, and Ripalda held that for revelations containing promises it consisted in God's fidelity. For information on these viewpoints see Wilmers, *De fide*, p. 44 ff.

3. See the treatise on *The True Religion*, no. 12.
4. *In Genesim homiliae* 36.6.
5. *De Nativitate*, Serm. 7, 1.
6. S. Th., II–II, q. 1, a. 1; *De veritate*, q. 14, a. 8, ad 16.—*Truth*, the conformity of the intellect with the thing (i.e., extramental reality) is formally found in the intellect. *In God* there is formal truth, in fact truth at its supreme level because His intellect knows all things most perfectly just as they are. But since God is identical with His own act of understanding, we say correctly: *God is truth*. Furthermore, God is called the *first truth* because in the created intellect there is truth only insofar as, through the light received from God, it imitates the divine knowledge. See St. Thomas, I, q. 16, a. 5. For a discussion of the various kinds of truth, "ontological," "moral," and "logical," see Phillips, *Modern Thomistic Philosophy*, II, 116–124.
7. *Contra epistulam manichaei quam vocant fundamenti* 5.

Article II

THE SUBJECT MATTER OF MERELY DIVINE FAITH

I. *Which Truths—Viewed Abstractly—Belong to the Province of Divine Faith?*
   General Principle: *all and only those things which have been revealed by God* constitute the province of faith.
   1. Meaning of the term 'revelation" in this context.
   2. The precise way in which truths must be contained in the sources of revelation in order to constitute an object of faith:
      a. *formal* containment vs. *virtual* containment;
      b. *formal* containment includes both *explicit* and *implicit* revelation.
         (1) various ways in which a truth may be implicitly contained in the sources of revelation.
      c. virtual containment signifies that a proposition rests upon one revealed premise and one rational premise and issues therefrom as a necessary conclusion.
         (1) difference between a purely *expository* and an *inferential* syllogism.

II. *It Is Certain that All Matters Formally Contained in the Sources of Revelation, Whether Explicitly or Implicitly, Form the Subject Matter of Divine Faith*

III. *It Is Disputed Whether Matters Contained in the Sources of Revelation Only Virtually Belong to the Province of Divine Faith*
   1. First opinion: unqualifiedly denies.
   2. Second opinion: unqualifiedly affirms.
   3. Third opinion: states that virtual containment suffices provided the Church defines the matter.
   4. Refutation of the second and third opinions.

IV. *A Special Question Concerning Propositions Contingently Contained in Revelation, Dependent Upon the Fulfillment of a Condition*

V. *There Exists a Hierarchical Order Among Various Truths Revealed by God:*
   1. *Primary* object of faith: truths about God Himself.
   2. *Secondary* object: truths about means leading man to God.
   3. *Accidental* object: matters not directly belonging to religion but contained in Scripture nonetheless.
      a. The vast difference there is between the secondary object of faith and the merely accidental object.

VI. *Divine Faith Is Concerned with God in Three Ways:*
   1. It is *about* God.
   2. It is *given to* God.
   3. It *leads to* God.

VII. *Are Private Revelations Part of the Field of Divine Faith?*
   1. Meaning of private revelation.
   2. Private revelation *can* and *ought* to be believed with divine faith by those who directly receive such revelations and are certain of their divine origin.
   3. The rest of the faithful may remain non-commital towards them.
   4. What the Church's *approbation* of private revelations signifies.

Article II

THE SUBJECT MATTER OF MERELY DIVINE FAITH

In this article we wish to find out which matters, *viewed purely abstractly* (secundum se), belong to the province of divine faith. In other words, which truths can and ought to be believed by us with an act of divine faith *on the supposition* that we are sufficiently aware of their existence.

I. Rules for Determining the Field of Faith 191

From the matters already discussed, the following general principle flows spontaneously: *all and only those things which have been revealed by God* form the subject matter (material object) of divine faith. This is clear from the fact that all and only these matters fall under the formal motive of faith which is the authority of God revealing.

Please notice, though, that the term revelation is *not* here taken in its restricted* sense as juxtaposed to "inspiration." It is taken in the full extent of its proper[1] meaning, that is, as signifying a divine utterance or testimony. Taken this way, 'revelation" includes even such matters as the sacred writers already knew by natural means before committing them to writing under the influx of divine inspiration. Surely if all the matters affirmed in the Scriptures by the sacred writer, acting in his official capacity, are intrinsically the word of God, there can be no doubt that they fall under the authority of God speaking. In Scripture, God, the principal author, speaks through the sacred writer to the Church;[2] consequently it is correct to say that God is revealing *to us* whatever He truly affirms therein.

With this fact taken for granted and prescinding for the time being from any discussion of *private* revelations, the whole question about the material object of divine faith may be reduced to this

---

* The restricted sense of 'revelation" means the disclosure by God of truths *previously unknown*. See above, no. 72.

DIVINE FAITH

question: in what precise way must a truth be *contained* in the sources of revelation in order to be *regarded as revealed?* For as soon as you have something truly revealed, you necessarily have a material object of faith.

192   A truth may be contained in the sources of revelation either *formally* (strictly) or only *virtually* (potentially).

1. A truth is said to be formally contained if the very truth itself and through itself is disclosed therein, whether it be disclosed directly or indirectly (i.e., contained in *two revealed* premises from which it issues as a conclusion).

2. A truth is said to be only virtually contained, if the truth itself is not there disclosed in itself, but rather is contained in *only one* of two premises (one of which is revealed, the other known naturally) from which it is deduced.

Formal containment in the sources of revelation. Something formally contained may be there in either of two ways: *explicitly* or *implicitly*.

a. It is explicitly contained if the sources of revelation express the proposition under scrutiny in so many words, in its very own terminology, and consequently in absolutely clear and unmistakable fashion.

b. It is *implicitly* contained (in vague fashion—*in confuso*) if the sources of revelation do not disclose the proposition in such open fashion, not in its own precise terms, but still do make it known in *equivalent* terms. The various ways in which a truth may be implicitly contained in the sources of revelation is explained in the following particular rules.

1. If the *very thing defined* is explicitly contained in the sources of revelation, then its *definition* is implicitly contained and vice versa. Take for example the proposition: "Christ is a man"; is it not truly synonymous with this: "Christ is a rational animal?" Similarly those scriptural passages which explicitly describe the Father, or the Son, or the Holy Spirit as engaged in some divine and intelligent activity, implicitly contain the proposition: "the Father, Son and Holy Spirit are divine Persons." Again the words: "I and the Father are one thing (unum)," implicitly contain the doctrine of the consubstantiality of the Father and Son. Again those passages which speak explicitly of the external rite and effect of baptism implicitly contain the proposition: "Baptism is a sacrament."

2. If a *physical whole* is explicitly contained in the sources, each

and every one of its *essential* parts, and also those *integral* parts without which the whole could not exist, are revealed implicitly. Under the proposition: "Christ is a man," are there not formally contained the propositions: "Christ has a rational soul," "Christ has an organic body, . . . a head, heart, brain, lungs, blood?"

3. If *two premises* are explicitly contained in the sources, they implicitly contain the *conclusion* (not formally, of course, as a "conclusion," but as objective content or material) drawn therefrom. For example, if these two premises are explicitly revealed: "Grace is required for each and every supernatural work"; and "The beginning of faith is a supernatural work"; you have implicitly contained: "Grace is required for the beginning of faith."

4. If the sources of revelation in *different places* explicitly contain all the *various elements*, out of which some *collective truth* arises by correlating those elements, the collective truth is itself implicitly contained in the sources. That is how the following proposition is contained in the sources of revelation: "There are seven sacraments of the New Law: baptism, confirmation, etc." The same holds true of the individual elements. If the *collective truth* itself is explicitly contained in the sources of revelation, its *various elements* are contained there implicitly. So, for example, when revelation explicitly affirms: "It is appointed unto men once to die and after this the judgment," it implicitly teaches: "It is appointed for Harry Smith and Joe Jones to die and to be judged."

In addition to the above rules, theologians generally also add this one:

5. If the sources of revelation explicitly affirm something about a *logical whole* or a universal subject (i.e., in universal propositions), they implicitly teach the same truth about the various species or the various individuals which clearly fit under that subject. So, for example, when revelation explicitly affirms: man is mortal, but his soul is immortal, it implicitly teaches: Peter is mortal, but Peter's soul is immortal.

Finally, even though the above rules (and others like them, but of lesser importance) are extremely useful for determining what truths are formally but implicitly contained in the sources of revelation, they are not rigorously self-sufficient by themselves. One must also study carefully what was the *intention* of the speaker—an intention which may be made clear from the concrete circumstances under which he spoke.

For it can happen that a speaker intends to imply something more by his words than the words themselves reveal, if viewed abstractly. If such an intention is clearly present from the circumstances, one would certainly have to say that the speaker's deeper meaning is implicitly contained in the actual words uttered even though that meaning overflows the rules of purely grammatical analysis. The supreme rule of correct interpretation is this: The speaker may be said to have disclosed by his words whatever, analyzing the circumstances rightly, he is judged to have *willed* to manifest by his words. When Stalin asked sardonically, in reference to having the pope consulted in world affairs, "how many battalions has he?", no one thought he wanted an inventory of the Swiss Guard.

194 *Virtual containment* in the sources of revelation. A truth is said to be contained only virtually in revelation when the proposition in question is deduced from a revealed premise with the aid of some rational premise through a syllogism that is not purely expository or purely explanatory. Virtual revelation is thus technically described as a *theological conclusion.*

A syllogism is purely expository or merely explanatory whenever the premises are simply judgments of *identity*; judgments in which the predicate simply gives a definition, complete or incomplete, of the subject. In other words, the predicate expresses some *essential* note of the subject. If, for example, someone says: "Christ is a man, but a man is a rational animal, therefore Christ is a rational animal" —the syllogism is purely expository or merely explanatory. For in the premises: "Christ is a man" and "Man is a rational animal," the predicate lays bare a note that is strictly essential to the subject. You have not simply an explanatory but an *inferential*, or illative, syllogism when the premises express more than simple judgments of identity. In other words, when the predicate expresses some feature or note that is *extra-essential* and yet true of the subject. For example, if someone says: "Christ is a man, but man laughs"; or: "Man needs food to live"; or: "Man *needs air* or he will die" (*therefore*, "Christ laughed" . . . "needed food" . . . "needed air") —he is constructing an *inferential* syllogism. "To laugh"—meaning the type of laughter which is an expression of rational delight— or "To need food" or "To need air" are not essential notes though they are proper characteristics of human nature.

II. All Formal Revelation Belongs to the Field of Faith 195

It is *certain* that all matters *formally* contained in the sources of revelation, whether *explicitly* or *implicitly*, are the material object of divine faith. There is no doubt that they have been revealed by God, that is, truly disclosed to us. That statement holds even for matters implicitly contained in revelation: for if it be true that "the Gospel is found not in the words of Scripture but in their meaning, not in scrolls containing pen-scratches, but in the key of intelligence,"[3] we definitely must conclude that God willed to make known to us every truth whose meaning is either synonymous with or formally included under some truth which the very words of revelation express in unmistakable fashion.

On this principle all theologians are agreed, even though they may disagree sharply at times as to whether this or that truth should be rated as formally implicitly revealed, or only "virtually" revealed—as we shall soon see.

III. Disputed Whether Virtual Revelation Belongs to Faith 196

It is *disputed* among theologians whether matters which are contained in the sources of revelation *only virtually* should be reckoned as part of the material object of divine faith or not.

The first view,[4] (which is also the more common and, in our estimation, the correct one) *unqualifiedly denies* this. Here are the arguments for this opinion: 1. Only a truth disclosed to us by God can be believed by divine faith; but a truth which is only virtually revealed has *not itself* been disclosed to us by God, since it is a truth *different* from the truth contained in the sources of revelation. 2. The only truth which can be an object of divine faith is one accepted exclusively on the authority of God revealing. But a virtually revealed truth is not accepted exclusively on God's authority; for it is a real conclusion drawn from two premises, only one of which has been revealed. But a conclusion whose truthfulness is made known to me partly by divine revelation and partly by the light of reason cannot be accepted by me *exclusively* on God's authority: a conclusion always follows the weaker premise. Briefly, I accept a theological conclusion partly because of God's authority and partly because of my own reasoning process; hence not solely on the authority of God revealing.

197   The *second* opinion[5] *unqualifiedly affirms* that virtual revelation is a part of the object of faith, provided one is dealing with theological conclusions that are certain and uncontested. Here is the argument for this view: God both knows and approves all the conclusions that may be legitimately deduced from His utterances and furthermore knows that men will some day draw such conclusions; therefore He has revealed those conclusions no less than truths formally implicitly revealed.

Answer: The question is not: did God *know* and approve of such conclusions: rather it is, did God *disclose* them to us by speaking to us, that is, did He *intend* to disclose them. That point is not proven; in fact for many conclusions there would be good reason to deny that such was God's intention. Do you think that God in saying: Christ is a 'man,' really intended to disclose to us that Christ used to laugh or had a sense of humor? or needed air to breathe? This second opinion seems to be pretty largely abandoned today. It smacks of confusing God's knowledge with His deliberate testimony.

198   The *third* opinion[6] makes a *distinction*. It teaches that mere virtual containment does not by itself suffice for a truth to be believed by divine faith; but that it does suffice if the Church should define the matter

In maintaining the latter viewpoint, however, different authors give different explanations. Some say: whatever the Church defines, regardless of *how* it be contained in revelation, is always an object of divine faith, for even though the immediate motive for assenting is the infallible authority of the Church, the final motive is the authority of God, through whose testimony we have learned about the Church's infallibility. According to these authors, therefore, the real explanation (*ratio formalis*) why a theological conclusion defined by the Church should be accepted by divine faith is to be sought not in the virtual revelation of antiquity, but in the contemporary testimony of the Church. This testimony is, according to their viewpoint, really *divine* testimony. This third opinion, if understood in this fashion, does indeed argue logically from its premises; but one of those premises is, in our opinion, false. It is a gratuitous assumption to state that the Church's testimony is God's testimony, as we shall see later on in discussing ecclesiastical faith.

Others[7] say: a definition by the Church proves beyond a doubt that God willed that at least this particular conclusion should be quarried from His testimony and should be held by divine faith. In other words, God *willed* to communicate this conclusion by His word and consequently truly 'revealed" it.

Answer: 1. When the Church simply defines a proposition which is rated as only virtually revealed, it does follow that God wills us to accept that proposition because of the authority of the Church, for He wants us to listen to the Church; it does not follow that God wants us to believe the proposition as something communicated to us *by His very own word.*

2. It can happen that some proposition hitherto considered by many theologians to be merely virtual revelation may be defined by the Church in such a way that she proposes it for our belief as a *revealed truth* [8] In this case we know by that very fact that it was formally contained in the sources of revelation. It should be obvious that a definition by the Church does not *change* the relationship which obtains between a given proposition and the sources of revelation. Consequently when the Church takes some truth formerly thought to be simply a theological conclusion and proposes it as a revealed truth to be believed by divine faith, you can draw only one of two alternative conclusions: either you must concede that that truth was always formally contained in the sources of revelation and in this case you subscribe to the first opinion; or else you are forced to admit that virtual containment by itself suffices for a matter to be believed by divine faith, and thus you fall back into the second opinion.[9]

IV. Do Contingent Propositions Belong to Revelation? 199

A special question arises in regard to propositions whose inclusion in revelation hinges upon the fulfillment of a condition. Briefly, some important particular propositions are contained under universal propositions or collective truths (themselves formally revealed) but *dependently* upon the fulfillment of some condition. If it is absolutely *certain* that the condition has been fulfilled, do such propositions form part of the object of divine faith?

I say: "*dependently* upon the fulfillment of some condition," because propositions which are directly and unmistakably seen to be included under some formally revealed universal proposition or some collective truth pose no difficulty at all.[10] For example, the following propositions that are implicitly revealed can be believed by divine faith: Peter sinned in Adam; Peter will be judged; Peter will rise from the dead. It is obvious that this man whose name happens to be Peter is unmistakably included in the universal propositions: all men sinned in Adam; all men will be judged; all men will rise from the dead.

I say: "if it is absolutely *certain* that the condition has been fulfilled, for if the fulfillment of the condition is not established in such a way as to remove completely all danger of being mistaken, such a particular proposition cannot be believed by divine faith. That is why the Real Presence of Christ under *this* or *that* host, the justification of this *particular* child recently lifted out of the baptismal font, are not usually thought to be believable by divine faith because the fulfillment of the condition (that this particular host was properly consecrated; that this child was validly baptized) will not be absolutely verifiable by the faithful.[11]

200 The particular propositions we are concerned with here are, above all, ones like the following: "Pius XII holds the primacy over the universal Church"; "Pius XII when speaking ex cathedra is infallible";[12] or, "The Council of Trent was infallible"; or "The Vatican Council was infallible."

All theologians admit that the following universal propositions are formally revealed: "Peter and all his successors possess the primacy"; "Peter and all his successors are infallible"; and: "the Church's magisterium (i.e., an ecumenical council) is infallible." But the particular propositions in question which are included under those universal ones dependently upon the fulfillment of some condition are: "Cardinal Pacelli was legitimately elected to take Peter's place"; "the Council of Trent, or the Vatican Council, was truly an ecumenical council." That these conditions have been fulfilled are absolutely guaranteed by *ecclesiastical* faith as founded on the conviction and practice of the universal Church.

It is quite commonly taught, particularly by the more recent theologians, that the particular propositions we have been discussing should be considered to be formally revealed and consequently able to be believed by divine faith. The real explanation for this teaching seems to come down to this: God's purpose in revealing propositions of the type under discussion was not that they should be simply acknowledged in a general way, but rather that they might be believed by each generation of men in all their particular determination; in other words, so that the men of every generation might know with divine certitude which individual they should cling to as the supreme shepherd of souls, and above all from which man they should receive the norm of their faith. Even granted that the particular propositions we have been discussing can be considered, if the matter be viewed purely in abstract fashion, conclusions from revelation, they are conclusions which God willed to disclose to us and consequently, viewed concretely, they ought to be considered formally implicitly revealed. From another viewpoint there is good reason for saying that the total *motive* for my assenting to the fact that Pius XII is infallible when speaking ex cathedra is simply and solely the divine revelation made about St. Peter as living in all his successors; whereas the certitude about the fact that Cardinal Pacelli was legitimately elected to fill Peter's position is merely a *prerequisite condition*.[13]

Finally, the question is of little *practical* importance since the particular truths we have been discussing must be held at least by ecclesiastical faith as *infallibly true*.

V. Hierarchical Order of Revealed Truths 201

Up to this point we have simply inquired: Which truths are formally contained in the sources of Christian revelation and consequently constitute the material object of divine faith? Now since the authority of God revealing applies with equal vigor to all and every truth formally contained in the sources, all of them deserve equal faith and must be held on to with the same degree of firmness. But if one looks to the *goal* of revelation and of faith, which is eternal life or the beatific vision of God, one can easily see that there is a *sort of hierarchy* among the various revealed truths. That is why we may distinguish the material object of faith into three categories: the "primary," "secondary," and merely "accidental" objects of faith.

The *primary* and principal object (object or subject of attribution) is God Himself, our supernatural goal; for all the rest of the truths "do not fall under the assent of faith except insofar as they bear some relationship to God, namely insofar as through some of the works of God a man is helped on his way to the enjoyment of God."[14]

The *secondary* object are all the revealed truths about the *means* by which men are orientated toward God and are helped toward the attainment of their goal; truths, for example, about the humanity of Christ, about the universal economy of His kingdom on earth, about the relationship of various kinds of creatures to God, moral precepts, and so forth. Finally, among all the matters which belong to the secondary object of faith not all stand in the same rank since some contribute immediately, others remotely, and still others only very remotely to our knowledge of the means which lead us to the vision of God.

The *accidental* object of faith comprises all such matters as do not directly (*per se*) belong to religion, and yet nonetheless are contained in Scripture: matters falling under inspiration only *accidentally.*

202 Notice what a vast difference there is between the secondary object of faith and the merely accidental object. The *secondary objects* of faith are bound up with the primary object intrinsically. They have been revealed by God's direct intention, that is, with the intention of making them known to us: consequently together with the primary object they constitute faith's *proper* subject matter; together with the primary object they make up "the matters of faith and morals that pertain to the building up of Christian doctrine," the things with which faith is essentially concerned. Still, each pertains to faith's proper subject matter in its own way: for the primary object is concerned solely with the *goal*, whereas the secondary object is concerned with the *means* to the goal. Contrariwise, the *accidental* objects of faith have only an extrinsic and purely circumstantial connection with faith's proper subject matter. For they were not revealed by God's direct intention, but only accidentally, that is, they were revealed not so that they should be known for their own sake, but simply that because of them religious truths might be disclosed more fittingly and harmoniously. They belong to religion not by reason of their content, but only by reason of the person uttering them, and consequently they fall under the field of faith only by *accident.*

203 **VI. How Faith Is Totally Dependent on God**

From what has been discussed in this article and the preceding, one can see that our faith tends towards God in three ways:[15] our faith is *about* God, it is *given to* God, and it *leads us to* God (*credimus Deum; credimus Deo; credimus in Deum.*)

(214)

Our faith is *about* God because from the viewpoint of the material object God himself is the primary object of our faith, and to Him all the rest is referred. Our faith is *given to* God because God is the formal object of faith: we accept things as true solely because He says so. Our faith *leads us to* God because God is the goal towards which we walk by faith. Still, we do not really and perfectly walk towards God except through faith that is accompanied by charity. That is why St. Augustine says: "If you move towards Him by faith, you do believe Him; but not everyone who believes Him moves immediately toward Him. What is it to move towards Him by believing? It is believing with love, it is believing with choice, it is believing by becoming incorporated in His members."[16]

VII. Do Private Revelations Belong to the Field of Faith? 204

One question remains. Are matters made known through *private revelation* part of the object of divine faith and of the science of theology? A private revelation is one which is directed to individual men and precisely as individuals, in such fashion that in these matters at least they are not set up to act as messengers of God to the Church. The goal of private revelation is private spiritual direction for either the recipients of the revelation or for certain other people. St. Thomas says: "In every age there have always been some who possessed the spirit of prophecy, not indeed for the sake of establishing new doctrines for the faith, but for the sake of giving direction to human actions."[17]

Even though a number of theologians have denied the point, it seems indisputable that even a private revelation—at least if it is concerned with matters bearing some relationship to God as our goal—*can* be believed by the same virtue of faith by which we believe a truth publicly revealed. Of course this is on the supposition that the divine origin of the revelation can be proven with certitude, which will not be the case very frequently except perhaps for those who directly receive it and a few other people. Granting that the divine origin of the revelation can be established with certainty, the question arises whether such revelations not only can be believed but *ought* to be believed. Briefly we think the answer is this: such a revelation ought to be believed both by the one who receives it and by those for whom it is destined: the rest of the faithful cannot outrightly deny it without some sort of sin; yet on the other hand they do not seem obliged to believe it. They can, consequently, remain noncommittal about it.

As for the *approbation* of the Church which has sometimes been given to private revelations, Cardinal Franzelin writes:

> The Church's judgment has as its goal not to propose such revelations to the faithful to be accepted by divine faith, but simply to declare: (a) in these revelations there is *nothing which is opposed* to the Catholic faith, or to good morals, or to Christian discipline; (b) there are sufficient evidences of its reality so that these revelations may be piously, prudently, and without superstition accepted on human faith, and that they may be read for the edification of the faithful; (c) once the Church has granted such approval, or even if she has not yet given any judgment so long as there is strong evidence for the genuineness of the revelation, it is certainly not right to condemn such revelations."[18]

Notes

1. We say in its *proper meaning*, because what is called "natural" revelation has already been ruled out and, even more obviously, so has revelation in the "modernist" sense of the term. The modernist concept was described in proposition 20 of the decree *Lamentabili* as follows: "Revelation cannot mean anything more than a man's acquired consciousness of his relationship to God" (DB 2020). See also proposition 22; DB 2022.

2. This teaching was attacked—without any solid foundation for doing so —by Bonaccorsi, *Questioni Bibliche* (1904) p. 214.

3. Jerome, *In epistulam ad Galatas commentarii* I. 11–12.

4. Held, for example, by the Salmanticenses, *De fide*, disput. I, dubium 4, §4–7; Kilber (*Theologia Wirceburgensis*), *De virtutibus theologicis*, disput. II, cap. 1, art. 3; Billot, *De virtutibus infusis* (4th ed.), thesis XIII, pp. 252–255; J. Aldama (*Sacrae theologiae summa*, vol. 3) *De virtutibus infusis*, nos. 149–155. Aldama also cites in favor of this opinion: Pesch, Hugon, Schultes, Lennerz, *et alii*. See *ibid.*, no. 150c).

5. So, for example, Vásquez, *In I partem summae theologiae*, disp. 5, cap. 3. The famous name of Melchior Cano is sometimes cited as favoring this opinion, but, according to Aldama and P. Marín-Sola, this is a big mistake— Cano belongs with the authors cited above in note 4. On this point see Aldama, *op. cit.*, no. 150, footnote 3.

6. So, for example, Suárez, *De fide*, disp. 3, s. 3, no. 11; De Lugo, *De fide*, disp. 1, s. 13, no. 272. Among modern theologians favoring this opinion, Aldama cites the following: Schiffini, Grandmaison, Minges, Gardeil, Beraza. See Aldama, *op. cit.*, no. 150b).

THE OBJECT OF DIVINE FAITH

7. So, for example, Wilmers, *De fide*, p. 249.

8. So, for example, before the definition of the Immaculate Conception of the B.V.M. as a dogma, many theologians while granting the truth of the doctrine thought that it was only *virtual* revelation. This is even truer of the Assumption. Before the bull *Munificentissmus Deus* so fine a theologian as Diekamp (3rd rev. edition by Hoffman) as late as 1949 classified the doctrine of the Assumption with the technical note of: *"sententia pia et probabilissima!* See *Theologiae manuale dogmaticae*, II (3rd rev. ed.) 431 and 433.

9. Even though we do not accept the explanation offered by the learned Wilmers, our position is not far apart from his own as regards the *fact* itself. For he writes: "the arguments which make us certain [that this truth which seems to be only virtually contained in the sources of revelation is actually directly revealed] come down to this: to showing that a point which, considered purely abstractly, is only virtually revealed, can, if you consider all its attendant circumstances, God's purpose in speaking and the explanation added by the apostles (i.e., if you *consider the matter concretely*) may be said to be directly revealed" (*loc. cit.*, p. 252). Absolutely right! I would like to add: but the Church can define matters of this sort as something to be believed by *divine faith* just as often as she is convinced *from the circumstances* that God really intended to reveal the matter.

10. See above no. 193.

11. That is why St. Thomas writes: "The faith of the believer is not directed to these (particular) species of bread and wine, but to this (truth) that the real body of Christ is present under the visible appearances of bread whenever it is correctly consecrated" (St. Thomas, II–II, q. 1, a. 3, ad 4). Actually, the faithful daily recite this prayer: "I believe that you are really present *here*" and so they unqualifiedly acknowledge the presence of Christ under this particular host as true. It is perfectly right for them to do so; for —apart from truly extraordinary circumstances—we neither doubt nor would we have any sensible reason for doubting the validity of the act of consecration. All the same, since the faithful have, as a matter of fact, only a human-moral certitude about the fact of a valid consecration whereas the act of divine faith requires a metaphysical-moral certitude, the judgment, "Christ is really present under *this* host," is not a judgment of *divine* faith except under an interpretative condition about the validity of the consecration. But it does not follow that an act of *adoration* towards Christ as present under this particular host is also interpretatively hypothetical. For the exercise of a moral virtue all that is required is a sure *practical judgment* as to the goodness of the action, which—prescinding from extraordinary cases in which there could be some reason for prudent doubt—is not at all lacking in this case. See De Lugo, *De fide*, disp. 1, no. 320.

12. See DB 673; 674; 1831.

13. See, for example, Franzelin, *Thesis de ecclesia*, p. 200.

14. St. Thomas, II–II, q. 1, a. 1, *corpus*.

15. *Ibid.*, q. 2, a. 2.

16. *Tractatus 29 in Joannem* 6. It is clear that the formula *to believe in* ("credere in"—"faith *leads us to* God"), in the sense explained above, can be used with reference to God alone. Occasionally, however, the formula is used

DIVINE FAITH

with another connotation. See St. Thomas, II–II, q. 1, a. 9, ad 5; Heinrich, *Dogmatica theologia*, I, no. 60, viii.

17. St. Thomas, II–II, q. 174, a. 6, ad 2. Indirectly, however, private revelations can benefit the whole Church. For it can happen that because of them the rulers of the Church are stirred to scrutinize the sources of public revelation more diligently, and to ponder more deeply about the needs of the faithful. If as a result of such pondering there arise some doctrinal or disciplinary decrees, the private revelation will have served as an occasional or alerting (impulsive) cause; but the very matter of the decrees themselves will always be based on either public revelation or on rules of Christian prudence. So the private revelations made to St. Margaret Mary were an occasional cause for the spread of devotion to the Sacred Heart; but the deep doctrinal truth on which the devotion rests and which the rulers of the Church were set to pondering about is the mystery of the hypostatic union: the heart of Jesus Christ is truly adorable because it is the heart of God.

18. *De traditione* (3rd ed.), p. 277. See Benedict XIV, *De canonizatione sanctorum*, I. II. cap. 32, no. 11; see the decree of the Sacred Congregation of Rites (May, 1877) mentioned in the encyclical *Pascendi* slightly before the end of it.—Worth reading on this matter of private revelations is Meschler, "Über Visionen und Prophezeiungen," *Stimmen aus Maria-Laach*, 14 and 15 (1878).

Article III

THE SUBJECT MATTER OF DIVINE-CATHOLIC FAITH

I. *Which Truths Constitute the Province of Faith for the Entire Catholic World?*
    1. *General Principle:* All the truths proposed by the Church's *magisterium* for our belief as divinely revealed.
        1. Explanation of the principle:
            a. the phrase, "as divinely revealed";
            b. the phrase, "proposed for our belief."

II. *The Two Ways in which the Church Proposes Truths for Our Belief:*
    1. By *solemn decrees;*
    2. By her *ordinary and universal magisterium;*
    3. Explanation of each type of teaching.
    Corollary: A comparison of the ordinary and solemn *magisterium.*

III. *Notion and Division of Dogmas:*
    1. What is a dogma?
    2. Necessary vs. useful dogmas.
    3. Formal vs. material dogmas.
    4. Doctrines considered "proximate to faith."

Article III

THE SUBJECT MATTER OF DIVINE-CATHOLIC FAITH

The preceding article dealt mainly with the question: which matters belong to the province of divine faith viewed in itself (*quoad se*). In other words, which truths can and ought to be believed by an act of divine faith on the supposition that we are sufficiently aware of their revealed character. Here the point of inquiry is: Which truths constitute the material object of faith *for us*, i.e., for all of us Catholics viewed in group-fashion; which truths are believable in *catholic* fashion (katolikos), i.e., ought to be believed by all the members of the Church with an act of divine-catholic faith.

205 **I. Field of Catholic Faith Determined by the Church**

PRINCIPLE: *The subject matter of divine-catholic faith are all those truths proposed by the Church's magisterium for our belief as divinely revealed.*

Note the phrase: *as divinely revealed*. To meet this requirement the truths must: (a) be contained in *public* revelation, the depositories of which are Sacred Scripture and divine-apostolic tradition. What was committed to the guardianship and teaching of the Church is public revelation alone. Consequently private revelations, even if they be genuine, are excluded from the object of divine-catholic faith. (b) It is more probable—in accord with what was explained in the preceding article about "virtual" revelation—that the truths must be contained in the sources of revelation *formally*.[1]

Note the phrase: *are proposed for our belief*. This means: (a) a *clear* and *unmistakable* proposal; one which removes any doubts on the part of the Church viewed as a single organism and, consequently, any doubts on the part of all Catholics sufficiently instructed to make a judgment of this sort. The Church does indeed, by the very fact of faithfully safeguarding the whole deposit of Christian revelation, propose in some fashion all the truths contained in that deposit; but the proposal of some of these truths may be done only in implicit or obscure fashion, as we shall see in the next article. But a merely implicit or obscure proposal of a truth is normally not sufficient to make the entire membership of the Church reach certitude about the revealed character of such a truth. In such cases, the lack of knowledge or the hesitation on the part of many Catholics should be attributed not so much to the ignorance of the individual as to the obscure presentation of the matter by the magisterium. It means: (b) a *definitive* proclamation which amounts to a real law demanding an absolutely firm assent on the part of every Catholic. Only a proposal of this sort is infallible.

The principle laid down above is contained almost verbatim in this declaration of the *Vatican Council:*

> By divine and Catholic faith everything must be believed that is contained in the Written Word of God, or in Tradition, and that is proposed by the Church as a divinely revealed object of belief either in a solemn decree or in her ordinary, universal teaching. DB 1792; TCT 66

The principle is *proved* by the fact that our Lord Himself established the teaching of the Church as the proximate norm of belief.

II. Ways in Which the Church Proposes Revealed Truths 206

A proposal of revealed truth by the Church, such as we have described above, can, according to the Vatican Council, take place in either of *two* ways: either by a *solemn decree,* or by the Church's *ordinary and universal teaching.*

1. Under the formula *solemn decree* are included the following: (a) definitions made by the pope when speaking ex cathedra; (b) definitions made by particular councils which have either been ratified by the pope in solemn form,[2] or accepted by the universal Church.[3] The term "definition" covers creeds and professions of faith which have been edited or solemnly approved by the supreme magisterium of the Church. Finally, please note the term *definitions.* In the very dogmatic decrees issued by councils and popes it often happens that matters are mentioned which are by no means meant to be defined: for example, historical observations,

the motives behind the promulgation of the definition, etc. No assent of faith is exacted for such matters. As for points adduced by way of explanation, or as a genuine proof of the truth defined, one must examine whether they were adduced with the intention of defining them, or merely authoritatively.

207   2. The exercise of the *ordinary and universal magisterium* includes the whole gamut of diverse actions by which the pope and bishops dispersed around the world, either by themselves or through various kinds of helpers, continuously expound doctrine on faith and morals. This teaching is exercised first of all by *explicit* teaching, either oral or written. Secondly it is also exercised by *implicit* teaching through the practices and liturgy of the Churches, by the promulgation of laws, by the approval of customs, by the recommendation of devotions, by the approval of books, and so forth.[4]

Clearly if a truth is capable of being declared an object of divine-catholic faith through the force of this ordinary and universal teaching, there is required such a proposal as is *unmistakably definitive*. The proposal must be of such a nature that without any misgivings it is proven that the doctrine in question is taught throughout the entire world as revealed and, consequently, as something necessarily to be believed by every Catholic. Now since a definitive proposal of this sort must blossom forth from countless activities which individually are neither definitive nor infallible, the existence of such a proposal (with the exception of some fundamental truths) is frequently enough not too obvious. The major signs of such a proposal are these: that the truth be taught throughout the world in popular catechisms, or, even more importantly, be taught by the universal and constant agreement of theologians as matter belonging to faith.

207a   The reason we prefer the agreement of theologians to the agreement of catechisms is that the latter, by the very fact of being intended for popular instruction, usually make no distinction between matters which must be held by *divine-catholic* faith and those which must be held by *ecclesiastical* faith, or simply as *theologically certain*. Furthermore, a papal document designates, as we have, the agreement of theologians as a sign of a definitive proposal by the Church. Listen to Pius IX: "By divine faith are to be believed those things which, through the ordinary teaching of the whole Church throughout the world, are proposed as divinely revealed and, as a result, *by the universal and constant consent of Catholic theologians* are held to be matters of faith." (Letter to Archbishop Scherr of Munich, 1863) DB 1683; TCT 180.

At this juncture many theologians teach that the ordinary and universal magisterium proposes for our belief *all matters which are so clearly contained in Sacred Scripture that their containment is immediately obvious to anyone reading it*. The Church, they say, obviously holds Scripture up to us as the Word of God; therefore, it equally obviously holds up to us whatever is lucidly contained in Scripture. I decided to omit this theological opinion: first, because of the practical difficulty of determining what is *"lucidly"* contained and what is not; secondly, and more importantly, because of a theoretical difficulty. According to Catholic principles, the *proximate rule* of the faith is the teaching of the Church, through which the *remote* rule, Sacred Scripture, is to be applied to us. But the aforesaid opinion inverts this order of things and makes Scripture the proximate rule of faith. You ask: "What does the Church's teaching hold?" and the reply comes back: "Consult the clear words of Scripture!" It is true that *such matters as are per se religious* and are lucidly contained in Scripture will *also* be clearly contained in the daily teaching of the Church; but it is an error to conclude: to find out the clear teaching of the Church, among other means, you should have recourse to Scripture.

Some Distinctions About Church's Ordinary Teaching 208

Furthermore, even in those very truths which the ordinary and universal magisterium unmistakably inculcates, there is sometimes room for questioning whether all the elements of that teaching are meant to be inculcated with equal force. For example, the following doctrines have always been unmistakably proposed by the ordinary magisterium: that God created our first parents by forming their bodies from the slime of the earth and from the rib of the man; that Adam sinned in tasting the forbidden fruit at the urging of the serpent; that God in punishment for mankind's sins caused a deluge over the entire earth; that Christ will come one day as the judge upon the clouds of heaven, etc. Do you think that the definitive intention of the magisterium bears with equal force upon the *mode* of the bodily formation and on the *very fact* of creation? With equal force upon the *external description* of the sin of our first parents and upon the *sin itself?* With equal force upon the *universality* of the flood and upon the *manifestation of Divine justice?* With equal force upon the *circumstances* of the heavenly spectacle and upon the *actual return* of the judge? Even upon a priori grounds an affirmative answer would have little probability to it, seeing that the circumstances described contribute either nothing at all or very little to religion. Actually, if one checks history, he will find that at least a number of the circumstances enumerated have been called into doubt by one or another of the fathers of the Church, or by excellent theologians, without their teaching ever being considered in the slightest heretical. That is why today we see more liberal interpretations of these accidental elements are tagged even by theologians who have a penchant for strictness not as "heretical" but as "rash" or, at a maximum, as "erroneous." Consequently even the strictest theologians interpret the ordinary and universal magisterium in such fashion as to admit in it different degrees, formerly not so clearly distinguished, but now after more diligent examination clearly discerned. For they hold that the substance of the doctrines proposed must be believed with absolutely certain faith, whereas the circumstances are not imposed with the same rigor. These circumstances were and still are preached as the *obvious* sense of Scripture. But if the obvious meaning of Scripture should not be abandoned apart from necessity, it does not directly follow that it must always be retained with an assent of Catholic faith.

208a New Light from Biblical Research

Actually the immense flowering of Catholic biblical research during the past fifty years has done much to eliminate unnecessary bewilderment on the part of the ordinary Bible reader trying to reconcile his own reading of the "obvious" meaning of Scripture with the findings of modern science. This bewilderment has been caused by an almost total ignorance of what is meant by "scriptural inerrancy," "inspiration," and "revelation." It has been further nurtured by a failure to enter sympathetically into the mentality of the ancient Semitic world, a lack of knowledge of ancient languages and history, a total unawareness of literary genres, and a lack of theological insight into what in the Bible pertains to "matters of faith and morals" and what is merely "accidentally inspired." Such readers, lacking both biblical and theological training, when coming across ancient cosmological viewpoints, unconsciously reflected by the sacred writers, have taken such viewpoints to be a revelation by God on matters of science.[5] Hence a whole rash of unnecessary problems, concordism and the like.

Here it is important to note that this immense biblical harvest has received its major impetus from the ordinary magisterium itself —from the popes who have exhorted the exegetes to plunge into the arduous task of solving scriptural difficulties and to take advantage of the new techniques and data provided by archeology, oriental linguistics, ethnology and other modern sciences. While the Church from the encyclical *Providentissimus Deus* of Leo XIII down to the *Divino Afflante Spiritu* of Pius XII has insisted that the exegete keep his eyes on the traditional teaching of the Church, the exegetical work of the fathers, and the analogy of faith, it has at the same time been extremely careful to safeguard the liberty of the exegete and to protect him from ill-tempered attacks inspired by an ignorance of the nature of his work. No one has stated this point more clearly than Pius XII. After pointing out what an immense vista of scriptural labor still lies open to scientific investigation, how many problems yet remain to be solved, the pope gives this fatherly warning to nonbiblical scholars:

> Let all the other sons of the Church bear in mind that the efforts of these resolute laborers in the vineyard of the Lord should be judged not only with equity and justice, but also with the greatest charity; all, moreover, should abhor that intemperate zeal which imagines that whatever is new should for that very reason be opposed or suspected.—*Divino Afflante Spiritu* 47; RSS p. 101.

It is true that a few years later the same pontiff had to issue a warning (*Humani generis*) to a few* exegetes and theologians who, misunderstanding the liberty afforded them, questioned not merely details connected with divinely revealed truths, or the language in which certain divinely revealed truths are enunciated, but the

---

* The pope makes it plain in this encyclical that the aberrations he is condemning were peculiar to a relative handful of exegetes and theologians: "Truly, We are aware that the *majority* of Catholic doctors, the fruit of whose studies is being gathered in universities, in seminaries and in the colleges of religious, *are far removed from those errors*. . . . But We know also that such new opinions can entice the incautious; and therefore we prefer to withstand the very beginnings rather than to administer the medicine after the disease has grown inveterate" (*Humani generis* 40; NCWC trans., italics added).

DIVINE FAITH

very substance of clearly known dogmas like: the personal character of angels, the concept of original sin, the satisfaction offered for us by Christ, and the real Presence of Christ in the Eucharist.[6] Still, the rebuke itself witnesses to the matter here under discussion. The pope rebuked such exegetes and theologians not for attempting to discriminate about the precise way in which the ordinary magisterium was inculcating revealed truths, but precisely for failing to have any sense of discrimination: for endangering the very deposit of the faith rather than for elucidating nonessential details connected with dogmatic truths only by way of accidental inspiration; and, above all, for disregarding the ordinary magisterium as the proximate norm of the faith:

> In interpreting Scripture, they will take no account of the analogy of faith and the Tradition of the Church. Thus they judge the doctrine of the Fathers and of the Teaching Church by the norm of Holy Scripture, interpreted by the purely human reason of exegetes, instead of explaining Holy Scripture according to the mind of the Church which Christ Our Lord has appointed guardian and interpreter of the whole deposit of divinely revealed truth.—*Humani generis* 22; NCWC trans.

209 Corollary. Comparison of ordinary and solemn magisterium.

If one compares[7] the teaching done through the ordinary and universal magisterium with that done by a solemn decree, it is quite clear that the first method is the *original, normal,* and *connatural* way of proposing revealed truths; whereas the second is the *unusual* but much more *clear-cut* method. For in a solemn decree it is easier both to discern a definitive intention on the part of the magisterium and to gauge more accurately the limits and precise meaning of the doctrine itself. Still, the relative ease of learning the Church's teaching through solemn decrees should not blind the theologian to the importance and reverence due to the ordinary magisterium even when the latter is exercising its function not at its maximum power but simply authoritatively. As Pius XII reminds us in the encyclical *Humani generis:*

> Nor must it be thought that what is expounded in encyclical letters does not of itself demand consent, since in writing such letters the Popes do not exercise the supreme power of their teaching authority. For these matters are taught with the or-

dinary teaching authority, of which it is true to say: "He who hears you, hears me"; and generally what is expounded and inculcated in encyclical letters already for other reasons appertains to Catholic Doctrine.—*Humani generis*, 20; NCWC trans.

The Church makes use of a solemn decree for one of two reasons: first, and most often, for reasons of *necessity:* namely, when doctrinal innovations have been fostered either by heretically-minded, or at least rash and querulous men, and such errors have to be repelled with all possible clarity and energy. So the divinity of Christ had to be defended against the attacks of the Arians by the Council of Chalcedon; the dogmas on grace and the sacraments had to be promulgated against the attacks of the original Protestants; so too, the nature of faith had to be protected against the attacks of the Rationalists by the Vatican Council. Secondly, and more rarely, the Church makes use of a solemn decree for reasons of greater *usefulness.* When, for example, some truth formerly disputed but now clarified and universally admitted is raised to the dignity of a Catholic dogma.[8] So, for example, the doctrine of the Immaculate Conception once obscured in the western part of the Church during the medieval era, was promulgated as a dogma of divine and Catholic faith many centuries later by Pius IX. The doctrine of papal infallibility, once obscured by the Western Schism, was promulgated by the Vatican Council. In recent times for the glory of God, the glory of Mary, and the usefulness of the faithful, the doctrine of Mary's Assumption into heaven, while it had never been disputed, was raised to the dignity of a Catholic dogma by the solemn definition *Munificentissimus Deus* by Pius XII in November, 1950.

III. Notion and Division of Dogmas 210

1. A dogma (*dogma, dokeo*) in the strict and customary[9] meaning of the term is *a truth revealed by God and proposed as such for our belief by the Church.* This means a clear-cut proposal, as we have previously explained. If the proposal is made by a solemn decree it is labeled a *defined* dogma; if proposed by the ordinary and universal magisterium it is described as a *nondefined* dogma, i.e., not defined solemnly. A dogma in the sense just explained is exactly the same as: *a truth of Catholic faith.*

It should be clear, then, how far some writers at the turn of this century strayed from the truth in maintaining that the intention of the Church in defining dogmas was not to propose a speculative truth for our intellectual assent, but simply to hand down a *practical regulation*, or a directive for leading a religious life. So, for example, the dogma of the Real Presence would strictly amount to this: one should *behave* towards a consecrated host the way one would behave towards Christ if He were visible.[10] This error was condemned in the decree *Lamentabili*, proposition 26: "Dogmas of the faith are to be held only according to their practical meaning, that is, as preceptive norms for action, but not as norms for believing."

The major dogmas are called *articles of faith*. In St. Thomas' opinion these articles call for separate elaboration, or are distinguished insofar as they pose some special difficulty: "Since faith deals with truths that surpass the comprehension of reason, wherever a new truth incomprehensible to reason occurs, there a new article is required."[11]

211   2. From the viewpoint of the obligation binding all Catholics to believe some truths of the faith in *explicit* fashion, dogmas may be divided into "necessary" and "useful."

Necessary dogmas are those which must be known in their own proper terms and believed in explicit fashion by all. They are necessary either by necessity of *means* because knowledge of those truths is necessary for a rational adult to orientate himself towards his supernatural goal; or by necessity of *precept,* because a knowledge of them is required to lead a worthy Christian life in accord with the ordinary status of the faithful.

Useful dogmas are those which the normal run of the faithful may be unaware of without thereby endangering their salvation or causing any harm to the leading of a Christian life. Still the faithful must hold these dogmas by *implicit* faith; that is, by assenting to all the truths which the Church proposes for belief. Such dogmas are usually ones that pertain to a more perfect knowledge, both deeper and wider, of revealed truth, and also pertain to a defense of the faith.*

It should be quite clear that this distinction between "necessary" and "useful" dogmas is miles apart from the teaching of some

---

* In modern times, with the emphasis on the apostolate of the laity, this seems to call as a practical corollary for a better instruction in theology.

Protestants who, following the lead of Pierre Jurieu (d. 1713) distinguished between *fundamental* and *nonfundamental* articles.¹² The fundamental articles had to be believed by everyone, but the nonfundamental or indifferent articles could either be denied or doubted if one chose to do so. Such denial would not harm the integrity of the faith or endanger one's salvation. Contrariwise, the Catholic Church teaches that all dogmas without exception must be believed by Catholics with at least implicit faith. One may not pick or choose among them. One may not believe in heaven while rejecting belief in hell, or reject Mary's Assumption while admitting her Immaculate Conception. But Catholics are not all obliged to *know* all dogmas in explicit terms.

3. The term *dogma* is fairly frequently used in a looser sense to describe every revealed truth, or rather (so as to exclude private revelations) every truth contained in Scripture or Tradition. Dogmas taken in this looser sense of the term may be divided into:

a. *Formal* dogmas or dogmas known to us (*quoad nos*). This category is identical with dogma taken in the strict sense as described above.

b. *Material* dogmas or dogmas in themselves (*quoad se*). This means a revealed truth which has neither been solemnly defined by the Church, nor clearly taught by the ordinary and universal magisterium. It is, consequently, a truth about whose revealed character disputes can take place even within the boundaries of the Church. Material dogmas are also described as *definable* truths of the faith, or truths held by *theological faith*. A material dogma can and ought to be believed with an act of *divine* faith by one who has certitude about its revelation; it cannot, however, be believed with an act of *divine-catholic* faith.

4. A doctrine considered by the common consent of practically all theologians as revealed, even though its *proposal* as such by the Church is not completely evident is called a truth *proximate to faith* (fidei proxima). Such a truth is described by other technical labels which are practically synonymous: *pertains to faith* (ad fidem pertinens), *certain by faith* (fide certa), and *others*.

Notes

1. No wonder, then, the decree *Lamentabili* condemned proposition no. 22: "the dogmas which the Church holds as revealed are not truths which have come down to us from heaven, but are a kind of interpretation of religious

DIVINE FAITH

experiences which the human mind has, by immense effort, excogitated for itself."

2. Note the phrase: *in solemn form*. Particular councils are normally approved only in "simple" form, whether it be a generic approbation or even a specific one. Benedict XIII solemnly approved the Council of Embrun (held in the year 1727; condemnation of the Jansenist Soanen). See *Coll. Lac.*, I, 636.

3. Such as the decisions of the II Council of Mileve (416) and the Council of Carthage (418) against the Pelagians.

4. See A. Vacant, *Le magistere ordinaire* (1887); Bellamy, *La theologie catholique au XIX siecle*, p. 233. In English a brief but excellent discussion of the ordinary magisterium and its workings is given by E. Burke, "The Scientific Teaching of Theology in the Seminary," CTSA (1949) pp. 139–143.

5. For an excellent elucidation of the problems mentioned above—circumstances of Adam's sin, universality of Flood etc.—see Bruce Vawter, *A Path Through Genesis* (New York, 1956) and Hauret, *Beginnings: Genesis and Modern Science* (Dubuque, 1955). For more technical treatment see *CCHS*, *Bible de Jerusalem* (introduction) and other scientific commentaries.

6. Cf. *Humani generis* 26.

7. For brief, recent article comparing the teaching of the ordinary magisterium with the solemn magisterium see *Ami du clergé* (July, 1957). This is a summation of a longer article in *Revue Thomiste*.

8. See Bellamy, *op. cit.*, p. 236.

9. I say: "most customary use of the term," because some of the older theologians frequently use the term to designate *any* truth which the Church sanctions by an infallible judgment: both those which are "revealed" and those which, though not revealed, are so intimately bound up with revelation that a denial of them would endanger the whole deposit of the faith and which, consequently, fall within the orbit of the secondary object of infallibility. Such truths, passed on infallibly as *true* but not as *revealed* should, in our opinion, be classified as of *ecclesiastical* faith and so are not dogmas in the strict sense of the term. See below, the *ex professo* discussion of ecclesiastical faith.

10. So wrote E. Le Roy in *Quinzaine* (April 16, 1905). He went on to add that this practical rule, if it is to be rational and of use for salvation, presupposes in the host itself a mysterious "reality," and consequently that the dogma of the Real Presence *implicitly* obliges one to acknowledge this reality. But at the same time he made such a distinction between the understanding of the dogmatic formula proposed by the Church and faith in the hidden reality as to amount to this: each man is free to interpret the dogmatic formula in his own way provided he leaves intact the practical rule and, as a consequence, the underlying reality. (This position is technically known as "religious pragmatism.")

11. *Compendium theologiae*, cap. 246; *see also*, S. Th., II–II, q. 1, aa. 6, 8, 9. Other theologians use the term *articles of faith* to designate truths which must be believed by all Catholics *explicitly;* still others use it to designate all the truths contained in the Apostles Creed, and so on.

12. See *Christ's Church*, no. 104.

Article IV

INCREASE OF THE SUBJECT MATTER OF CATHOLIC FAITH OR "DOGMATIC PROGRESS"

I. *Explanation of What Is Meant by Dogmatic Progress:*
   1. *Absolute,* or objective progress; this signifies that the deposit of the faith is itself increased. God reveals truths not hitherto disclosed.
   2. *Relative,* or subjective progress: no new truths are revealed; believers simply grow in their knowledge of the original deposit of the faith through the clearer, more explicit teaching of the Church.
   3. Absolute progress occurred from the time of Adam till the Apostles; after the death of the Apostles there can be no objective increase in faith, only a relative progress in our grasp of the deposit of the faith handed down once for all.

   PROPOSITION 1: After the death of the Apostles the material object of faith did not increase objectively, nor will it ever so increase.

   Proof: 1. The sources of revelation themselves definitely exclude new public revelations which would either
      (a) establish a new *economy;*
      (b) proclaim *new truths,* with the Christian economy remaining unchanged.

   PROPOSITION 2: After the death of the Apostles the material object did increase and still can increase in a relative sense.

   Proof: 1. From the *magisterium.*
      2. Theological argument:
         (a) some truths are contained in sources of revelation only in *obscure fashion;*
         (b) the Church *did not* in *its first beginnings*

(231)

DIVINE FAITH

proclaim these obscurer truths in clear and unmistakeable fashion;

(c) the Church, with the passage of time, *did proclaim* some of these truths in clear-cut fashion for our belief;

(d) the same process can occur in the future in regard to other truths contained obscurely in the deposit of faith.

Corollary: There was nothing remiss in the Church's teaching during the periods in which some of these obscure truths remained in obscurity.

Scholion I. A fuller explanation of what is meant by relative progress.

Question 1: In what does this progress consist?
Question 2: What were the occasions of this development?
Question 3: What is the efficient cause of this progress?
Question 4: Does this progress not imply change?

Corollary: Cardinal Newman's theory of doctrinal development.

Scholion II. False theories of dogmatic progress.
1. Harnack's theory:
   (a) exposé and rebuttal.
2. Anton Günther's theory:
   (a) exposé and rebuttal.
3. Alfred Loisy's theory:
   (a) exposé and rebuttal.

Article IV

INCREASE OF THE SUBJECT MATTER OF CATHOLIC FAITH OR "DOGMATIC PROGRESS"

The number of dogmas we must believe can be increased in a twofold way: God may publicly reveal truths which He had not formerly made known; or, truths which He had formerly made known but which had not yet been clearly proposed by the Church may later on be clearly proposed by her and thus made easily knowable by all her members in explicit fashion. 213

In the first case, the very deposit of the faith is increased: the number of dogmas themselves (*quoad se*) is increased and thus you have progress in the revealed doctrine itself. Technically this is called objective progress, or *absolute* progress.

In the second case the deposit of revelation is not itself increased; it is simply better understood. The number of dogmas in our regard (*quoad nos*) is increased and thus you have progress not in the revealed doctrine itself but in the Church's proposal of it and in our understanding. Technically this is called subjective progress, or *relative* progress. Briefly, no new truths are added, we simply grow in our knowledge of the contents of doctrine already revealed because of clearer, more explicit teaching of that doctrine by the Church.

Everyone knows that under the Old Testament dispensation, both before the promulgation of the Mosaic Law and even during the epoch of the Law, there was real objective progress in faith. God, with the passage of time, gradually disclosed more and more truths, particularly truths about the Messias and His kingdom, which he had not disclosed in ages past. St. Gregory the Great says: 214

> With the passage of time the knowledge of our spiritual forebears increased. For Moses was better instructed than Abraham, the prophets were better instructed than Moses, and the Apostles were better instructed than the prophets in the knowledge of the omnipotent God.[1]

Again, everyone knows that objective progress, in fact the most brilliant and fruitful progress took place with the institution of the New Testament. The main herald of this revelation was our Lord Himself, and secondly the apostles. An examination of our Lord's own words[2] would hardly allow one to maintain the position that the Holy Spirit on Pentecost Day did not teach the apostles any new truths, but merely recalled and explained these truths which Christ had already taught and which the Old Testament contained. As to whether even after Pentecost the apostles continued to learn new truths from the Holy Spirit, theologians disagree. The negative opinion,[3] unless it be made with very careful qualifications, can hardly be sustained. Still it does seem more probable that most of the revelations made to the apostles after Pentecost looked primarily to an explicit and well-rounded grasp and application of matters which they had already learned in some fashion earlier.

215 Even though the deposit of revelation did increase objectively or absolutely from the time of Adam to the time of the apostles, it is still customary to say that the *gist* of revealed religion has always remained the same. By the *gist* or substance of revelation we mean the two most fundamental articles of the faith: the existence of God and His providence in the supernatural order. For all the rest of the matters which, with the passage of time, were revealed are in some fashion contained in these two truths: that is, they are contained in *ontological* fashion, not logical (so that without explicit, new revelations they could not be extracted from those two truths):

> In the divine "being" are included all the things which we believe to exist in God eternally and in which our final happiness consists. And in the belief in God's "providence" are included all the things that God has actually arranged in time for man's salvation, all the means which are the way to happiness.[4]

After the death of the last apostle any *objective* increase in faith is excluded, but not subjective or relative increase. The latter, however, has to be very carefully distinguished from the rationalist conception of an "evolution" of doctrine. Many non-Catholics subscribe to such a rationalist theory of evolution of doctrine (i.e., some doctrines disappear as the ages go by because they are no longer compatible to man's intellectual progress). In fact, even a few

THE OBJECT OF DIVINE FAITH

Catholics are not sufficiently removed from such a conception, as was brought out clearly by the encyclical, *Humani generis*.

PROPOSITION 1. *After the death of the apostles the material object of faith did not increase objectively, nor will it ever so increase.*

216

Theological label. Even though the thesis has never been defined in these exact terms, it is so clearly contained in the theoretical and practical teaching of the Church that it deserves to be classified as: *de fide.**

Proof of proposition. The thesis is proved by the fact that the sources of Christian revelation definitively exclude any new public revelations which would: (1) refer to setting up a new economy to supplant the present one; or, (2) simply increase the deposit of the faith with the present economy remaining unchanged.

1. Exclusion of a new economy.

Sacred Scripture: (a) describes the economy established by Christ as the "fullness of the times,"[5] "the last era,"[6] "the consummation of the ages,"[7]; (b) it plainly teaches that the economy established by Christ is eternal, changeless, and perduring right up to the Day of Judgment and the end of the world.[8]

The same doctrine is taught by the earliest *fathers*, especially Irenaeus and Tertullian (while he was still a Catholic) against the Gnostics and the Montanists.

2. Exclusion of new truths increasing the deposit, while the Christian economy remains unchanged.

Sacred Scripture: (a) nowhere gives even the tiniest hint that we should still look for a new revelation; (b) it quite clearly teaches that all salvational truth[9] was bestowed on the apostles themselves personally; consequently, (c) it insists on just one point for the apostles' successors: they should guard the deposit of the faith, they should persevere in the truths they have learned, they should valiantly defend the faith handed down once and for all.[10] The point is hammered home even more forcefully by *Tradition*, which from the very earliest days was willing to follow only

---

* See the Council of Trent, session 4; Vatican Council, constitution, *De Ecclesia*, chap. 4: "For the Holy Spirit was not promised to Peter and his successors so that by His revelations they might propose new doctrine but that by his assistance they might jealously guard and faithfully explain the revelation or deposit of the faith handed down by the apostles" (DB 1836).

the doctrine of the apostles, and always considered any novelty in matters of faith to be a clear hallmark of heresy.[11]

217 PROPOSITION 2. *After the death of the apostles the material object did increase and still can increase in a relative sense.*[12]

This proposition is *certain* and clearly taken for granted in this declaration by the Vatican Council:

> Therefore, let there be growth . . . and all possible progress in understanding, knowledge, and wisdom whether in single individuals or in the whole body, in each man as well as in the entire Church, according to the stage of their development; but only within proper limits, that is, in the same doctrine, in the same meaning, and in the same purport.—DB 1800; TCT 80. [The words are originally from Vincent of Lérins.]

To bring out clearly the truth of the proposition we need only show: (1) that some truths are contained in the sources of revelation in obscure fashion; (2) that the Church did not immediately at its very beginnings proclaim such truths in clear and unmistakable terms; (3) that the Church, with the passage of time, did propose some of those truths in a clear-cut way for our belief; (4) that the same process can occur in the future in reference to other truths.

218 **1. Some truths are contained in the sources of revelation only in obscure fashion.** Although all revealed truths deserve the same assent of faith, they are not all equally necessary to know. God, who in the supernatural order as well as in the natural behaves with a kind of exuberant generosity, has revealed in addition to those truths necessary for leading a worthy Christian life, many other truths a knowledge of which is useful, in varying degrees, but not necessary. Now truths necessary for everyone to know ought to have been taught by the Apostles clearly and in explicit terms. That is why they are explicitly contained in the sources of revelation and have been proposed in unmistakable terms by the Church in every age, at least in their essentials. Of course, more scientific expositions of necessary dogmas do not have to be known by all.

As for the nonnecessary dogmas—those which pertain to a more exact and deep understanding of the Christian religion and its defense—it would not be surprising to find that some of them should be handed down by the apostles in rather obscure fashion, or in implicit terms, or, at least, in less clear-cut terms. This point appears quite plausible when one recalls that Christ Himself promised that the Spirit of truth would always be with His Church to help the successors of the apostles to understand revealed doctrine correctly and to explain it more distinctly in accord with the needs of various ages.

Depth of dogma and method of apostolic preaching prevented explicit presentation of the entire gamut of revelation.

As a matter of fact it was impossible for the apostles themselves to enunciate in explicit and unmistakable terms all the Christian truths in all their multiple facets, not because the apostles lacked a perfect grasp, in their own way,* of those truths (indeed, they

---

* Notice the words: ". . . a perfect grasp, *in their own way.*" Theologians hold it as certain that the apostles themselves knew the entire gamut of Christian revelation more perfectly than any Father or theologian of the Church, so that they clearly and fully grasped it as *a kind of concrete and complex reality*. But it does not follow that the apostles had at their finger-tips: (a) a *distinct*, articulated knowledge of the individual elements of each and every dogma; or (b) a *systematic* or scientific knowledge of dogmas; or, (c) a knowledge of the *abstract formulae* which scientific theology would excogitate later on. Labeyrie's discussion of this point is illuminating: "The apostles possessed a perfect and extremely penetrating knowledge of revelation, and not simply a vague and confused knowledge such as our evolutionary suppositions might lead us to believe. The truths they personally sowed throughout the world were destined to nourish everywhere the faith of all generations. Their mission required full light. For how could they ever have said or written the profound and divine words which the greatest minds will never finish sounding, if they themselves had had of their very own doctrine only dim glimpses akin to those of children learning their catechism? Their knowledge, however, was not theology. It was living possession and akin to the experience of a concrete and real truth in its inexhaustible richness; it was neither deduction, nor analysis, nor purely speculative abstraction." (*La science de foi*, p. 321).

Perhaps an analogy would be of help here. Compare the knowledge a skilled biographer would possess of a famous scientist or statesman with the knowledge possessed by his wife. A biographer (particularly one writing some years after the death of a famous man), no matter how painstaking his research or his reflections, no matter how scientific his assessment of the material to hand would still never get to know his subject as fully or as deeply as the woman who had shared his life for thirty or forty years. The wife might be utterly incapable of doing the scientific work required to produce a definitive biography; for all that, by her intimate, day-to-day sharing of the great man's most secret thoughts and her affectionate contemplation of him she would possess a far fuller, sharper, more penetrating knowledge of the man than all footnote chasers for generations to come.

We might remark, in passing, that even some Catholic writers today, try-

had infused knowledge of them) but because both the very nature of the doctrine and the method of apostolic preaching blocked any such exposition.

a. *The very nature of the doctrine:* the divine dogmas are so profound that the human intelligence, even when copiously illuminated by supernatural light, cannot immediately and singly grasp and distinctly explain all their facets; they are so fruitful that they possess widely divergent applications for varying conditions and needs that were to arise throughout the centuries. Besides, the dogmas in multiple ways touch upon human sciences which had not even been thought of during the lifetime of the apostles, and they are opposed, directly or indirectly, to the most variegated kinds of errors which human ignorance or malice would conjure up over the course of the centuries.

b. *The method of apostolic preaching* also stood in the way of any such absolute exposition. It was popular not scientific in character. It was not a systematic presentation, but accommodated to the pressing necessities of varying times and locales; finally, it was not only theoretical but practical inasmuch as it proposed many truths not so much in explicit formulas as by examples, laws and institutions. For the rest, it should be obvious from all the pages of the New Testament that Christ's method of teaching and the method of His apostles was not this: to teach some dogma and then analyze it in all its ramifications and explain it in every detail. They were preaching to people; not instructing theologians.

From another viewpoint it was very fitting that many truths or facts of revelation should be disclosed in rather obscure fashion; in fact, even that they should be buried deep in the depths of the Christian deposit. Why? Because by this economy divine revelation became like a fertile field which both brings forth abundantly food necessary for spiritual life, and also, the more intensely it is cultivated by men, continues to yield even more abundant fruit of truth. In this way the magnificence of the divine gift is beautifully brought home to us, and at the same time God leaves room for the bent of human curiosity which, however much it may progress in

---

ing to assess the "psychology" of the apostles some two thousand years afterwards, are guilty of neglecting this most fundamental fact of life—*the primacy of living, personal contact* over historical and linguistic tools. If they seem to minimize the grasp the apostles had of our Lord's teaching it may well be that they have unconsciously granted a superiority to the examination of dead documents by scientific tools to living contact with a living teacher.

THE OBJECT OF DIVINE FAITH

assimilating divine truth, always finds still more left over for its investigation.

2. The Church did not immediately after the death of the apostles preach in clear and unmistakable terms the truths which were contained only obscurely in the sources of revelation. 219

Granted that the first generation of Christians did not themselves receive from the apostles an explicit and detailed knowledge of some dogmas, this assertion offers no difficulty. One would hardly expect the rulers of the Church, when as yet no controversy had arisen and there was no urgent necessity, to give a detailed explanation of matters which they themselves had received only in implicit fashion from the apostles. It should cause no one surprise, then, that the sort of truths we are discussing for some time, shorter or longer, should have been proposed by the Church only implicitly, or not too obviously, or with not too great insistence. But if the Church herself did not teach those truths in clear-cut fashion the natural conclusion anyone will arrive at is: the faithful of that era, for the most part at least, did not have too clear or distinct knowledge of such truths—granted that clear and distinct knowledge was even at that time at least physically possible. But do not jump to the conclusion that the Church was therefore derelict in her duty of teaching. If a "less obvious revelation' and "implicit faith" sufficed for truths of this sort why would not—speaking *per se* and abstracting from special circumstances—implicit *teaching* suffice?

That the Church's teaching was, as a matter of fact, not always too obvious is clearly shown by some of the statements of the fathers of the Church. These statements while directly proving that the Church's preaching was not always clear indirectly prove the prior point: that implicit teaching sufficed for such matters. 220

Origen distinguished between doctrines which are "most openly preached in the churches," which "have been defined in the Church's preaching," about which "there is complete unanimity in the whole Church": and other doctrines which "have to be sought for to the best of one's ability from Sacred Scripture and have to be investigated with wise analysis"; in which "there is not yet a clear-cut knowledge"; which "are not made known by obvious preaching," and about which "it is not evident in ecclesiastical preaching that the doctrine is being taught."[13]

Augustine distinguishes between "an error which can be tol-

(239)

erated in questions that have not been diligently investigated and which have not yet been fully stabilized by the authority of the Church," and errors which are intolerable, "which threaten to undermine the very foundations of the Church."[14] In another place he writes: "There are some matters about which even the most learned and best defenders of the Catholic rule [of faith] sometimes disagree among themselves, and one expresses better and more truly some point than another man. But the matter we are now dealing with [original sin and the baptism of children] belongs to the very foundations of the faith."[15]

Leo the Great distinguishes between that "which the Lord wanted no one in His church to be ignorant of" and "some little portions of our faith which may be less lucidly clear."[16]

Thomas Aquinas writes:

> It must be observed that in matters of faith some have not been made perfectly clear by the Church. Just as in the primitive Church it was not perfectly and distinctly declared that those men who had been converted from Judaism were not held to observe the requirements of the Law; and in the time of Augustine it had not yet been clearly declared that the soul did not originate by traducianism . . . but there are other matters which pertain to the faith as something already passed upon by the Church.[17]

221 3. **Over the course of the centuries the Church has proposed in clear-cut fashion many truths which had been only obscurely revealed.** History itself witnesses to the truth of this assertion in unmistakable terms. Everyone knows that certain dogmas, afterwards defined by the Church, were once, within the boundaries of the Church and without any injury to the Catholic profession of faith, called into question and disputed. Who does not know that even learned and saintly men hesitated over truths of this sort, or were even doubtful, or, even opposed them? Take, for example, St. Cyprian on the question of rebaptizing heretics; St. Augustine on the question of the origin of the human soul; St. Thomas on the Immaculate Conception. All the while, all of them, both those who judged the matter correctly and those who fell into error—all confessed that neither side of the question had been clearly and manifestly taught by the Church.

Actually, the saying of Vincent of Lérins has often been verified: "O strange turn of affairs, the originators of the same opinion are judged to be Catholics while the followers are called heretics; the teachers are absolved, the disciples are blamed; the writers of the books will be the sons of the kingdom, but their promulgators will end up in hell."[18] Why is this? Because while the former category were making their mistakes, the teaching of the Church was not yet clear and obvious, but afterwards it did become so.

Corollary 222

Although the phenomenon just described happened fairly often, no one should jump to the conclusion that prior to a solemn *definition* the Church's proposal of doctrine was not sufficiently clear most of the time. Quite the contrary is true. Most of the truths afterwards solemnly defined were, prior to that time and even from the very beginning of the Church, preached with sufficient clarity through the ordinary and universal magisterium. Why, then, did the Church afterwards take the further step of solemnly defining these truths? She did so to vindicate them against doubts raised by heretical-minded or rash men, or those which arose because of evils rampant in various eras or places.

4. The Church in the future will be able to preach in more clear-cut fashion some truths which are even now not so clearly enunciated. 223 Surely, the Church can do in the future what she has done in past ages, if there are even now objectively present in the sources of revelation some truths which have not yet been perfectly settled and explained. That such truths exist will not be easily denied by anyone who has even a nodding acquaintance with the controversies of theologians about subtler points of revealed doctrine. Finally, Leo XIII in urging exegetes to make an untiring study of Sacred Scripture says:

> A wide field is still left open to the private student, in which his hermeneutical skill may display itself with signal effect and to the advantage of the Church. On the one hand, in those passages of Holy Scripture which have not as yet received a certain and definite interpretation, such labors [i.e., by Scripture scholars] may, in the benignant providence of God, prepare for and bring to maturity the judgment of the Church.—*Providentissimus Deus;* RSS, p. 15.

DIVINE FAITH

The same point has more recently been alluded to by Pius XII in his encyclical, *Divino afflante Spiritu:*

> No one will be surprised, if all the difficulties are not yet solved and overcome; but that even today serious problems greatly exercise the minds of Catholic exegetes. We should not lose courage on this account; nor should we forget that in the human sciences the same happens as in the natural world; that is to say, new beginnings grow little by little and fruits are gathered only after many labors. Thus it has happened that certain disputed points, which in the past remained unsolved and in suspense, in our days, with the progress of studies, have found a satisfactory solution. Hence there are grounds for hope that those also will by constant effort be at last made clear, which now seem most complicated and difficult.—RSS, p. 100.

224 Scholion 1. A fuller explanation of what is meant by relative progress.

Having established the fact of subjective growth or relative progress, we need now to explain its genuine nature, the way it works, and its causes a bit more fully.

We ask: 1. *In what does that progress consist?*

It consists mainly of three things: in a *more finished* exposition of dogmas the gist of which had always been taught explicitly; in the *explicit* proposal of dogmas which had formerly been taught implicitly in other dogmas; in the *clear-cut proposal* of dogmas which formerly were proposed in less obvious fashion.

For with the passage of time the Church began:

a. *To determine more accurately the meaning* and *to express in more scientific terminology* dogmas which she had formerly taught explicitly indeed but in *more popular language and consequently more vaguely.* From the very beginning, for example, the Church professed her belief in one God who is Father, Son, and Holy Spirit; but little by little she explored this dogma more deeply and enunciated it more brilliantly by professing unity of nature, trinity of persons, the consubstantiality of the Son, the divinity of the Holy Spirit, etc. Similarly, the Church always explicitly believed that Christ was true God and true man, but the philosophical concepts and technical terms expressing the same doctrine "one person in two natures," only a later age would expound.

It was this more lucid type of explanation that Vincent of Lérins so ardently longed for when he wrote:

> O doctor, if a divine gift has fitted you out for the task, carve out the precious gems of the divine dogma. By your exposition may that be understood more lucidly which formerly was more dimly believed. Through you may posterity bless as understood what antiquity venerated though not understood. But teach the very same truths which you have learned: so that when you say something in a new way, you do not say something altogether new.*

b. The Church began to *propose explicitly and distinctly* those truths which she formerly proposed more implicitly. She did so either (a) by *articulating* individually *the various constitutive elements of some complex dogma;* or, (b) by *stating in various particular propositions what she formerly included under one universal proposition.*

So, for example, the reality of a real body and a rational soul, of two wills and two kinds of activity in Christ; the immunity of the Blessed Virgin from all actual sin and even from original sin; the particular rights and privileges of the supreme pontiff are all constitutive elements of the following complex dogmas: that Christ is true God and true man; that the Blessed Virgin was full of grace and was linked to Christ in the work of our redemption; that Peter is the foundation of the Church and the shepherd of all the sheep.

Vincent of' Lerins refers to this sort of progress in these words:

> May the religion of souls imitate the process of bodies which even though, over the course of years, they may evolve and extend their members, still remain the same bodies which they were before. There are just the same number of joints in little children as in the grown men, and if in their place arise those members which appear at a maturer age, they were already accounted for in the power of the seed, so that nothing new is afterwards brought to maturity in old men which was not already priorly present though hidden. So, too, it is fitting that

---

* *Commonitorium* 22. The understanding here spoken of means such understanding as is possible when dealing with mysteries, i.e., that a revealed truth may be grasped with clearer and more distinct (but still only *analogous* concepts) thus removing further the appearance of a contradiction between the mystery and the principles of reason—a *negative* understanding.

DIVINE FAITH

the dogma of the Christian religion should follow the laws of progress so that, with the years, it may be consolidated, and broadened with time, and made more noble with age, and yet remain still uncorrupted and undefiled.[19]

226 c. The Church began to propose in *clear terms* and with *systematic presentation* what formerly she had inculcated mainly *by practice* and *custom*.

So, for example, the dogmas on the validity and necessity of infant baptism; on the validity of baptisms administered by heretics; on the characters conferred by the sacraments; on the Real Presence of the whole Christ under each sacramental species and under each individual part of them, were, for the most part, during the first centuries enveloped and hidden in the customs and practices of the churches,—from which hidden condition, under the direction, so to speak, of the "Catholic sense"[20] they emerged into clear-cut teaching. The same process, in a sense, is observable in the dogma of papal infallibility, which Christian antiquity venerated much more by deeds than by words.

Of this type of progress, Vincent of Lérins writes: "Finally what else has [the Church] ever struggled to do by the decrees of her councils except to see that the very same thing she taught earlier in more casual fashion should now be taught more insistently; that the very same thing she reverenced in earlier days more quietly should afterwards be venerated with much more care."[21]

227 Corollaries

a. We said above that relative progress consists *principally* in three things: the finished exposition of the popular, the explicitation of the implicit, and the theoretical teaching of what was held by practice and custom. Still, we do not mean that the whole of dogmatic progress—a very complex matter—is completely accounted for by these three factors. Besides these, one might mention the solution of doubts, the clear refutation of new errors, the application of revealed principles to new situations of human life; furthermore, one could mention the teaching on matters not themselves revealed but intimately bound up with revealed data, the systematic arrangement of all the doctrines into a unified system, the more systematic defense and scholastic penetration of dogmas, etc. But all these points, insofar as they are really different from the three listed above, pertain more to the *science of theology* than to relative progress in Catholic *faith* itself. Furthermore, between strictly "dogmatic" progress and progress in "theology" there is this big difference: *theology* "assimilates" to itself and incorporates in its system even matters which are *not* revealed: presuppositions, conclusions, applications, and illustrations of dogma; whereas *dogmatic progress,* even when it uses concepts and terminology borrowed elsewhere, adds nothing whatsoever—so far as *the truth itself* that is so conceived and expressed—to revelation. To say that the Father and Son are "consubstantial" does not add one iota to the revealed truth that the Father and Son are "one thing." It simply expresses it in more precise terminology.

b. Neither should one think that the three modes of progress indicated above take place separately; as a matter of fact they usually *blend together* in different ways with the result that the knowledge and proposal of the same dogma frequently makes progress in all three ways mentioned. Finally, the first mode of progress occurs in all the dogmas, granted in different measure; but not so the other two. **228**

c. We have proceeded along purely intellectual lines in describing dogmatic progress. There is no other way for a theologian to describe it, seeing that the whole business tends to a fuller knowledge of truth. For all that, we do not mean to imply that only speculations of the intellect contribute to this progress; actually the whole Christian life and practice contributes to it. Finally, from another viewpoint, notice that *religious* progress is not finished and completed simply by "dogmatic" and "theological" progress.

We ask: 2. *What were the occasions and process of this development?* **229**

a. Most of the time the *occasions* of dogmatic progress were the rise of controversies and the attacks of heretics. St. Augustine writes:

> Many matters belonging to the Catholic faith, during the time that they were being stirred up by the hot restlessness of heretics, were both scrutinized more diligently and understood more clearly and taught more insistently in order to defend them against them: and thus through the enemy's attack there arose an opportunity for learning.[22]

Elsewhere he writes:

There were many well-versed in understanding and explaining the Scriptures hidden in the ranks of God's people who did not bring forth solutions to the more difficult questions so long as no slanderer was attacking. You do not think that the Trinity was perfectly thrashed out, do you, before the Arians started carping? You do not think that penance was thoroughly discussed, do you, before the attacks of the Novatians? So, too, baptism was not perfectly discussed before the Rebaptizers started contradicting at the gates: not even on the question of the very unity of Christ [i.e., unity of Person] was doctrine so accurately expressed as it has been expressed except after that separation [urged by Nestorius—i.e., two Persons in Christ] began to disturb the weak brethren.[23]

Similarly, *St. Gregory the Great* writes: "Holy Church is always instructed more deeply in her own doctrine while she is being attacked by the questions raised by heretics."[24]

Finally, we should note, there are also other occasions for dogmatic progress: first of all, the native bent of the human intellect which reflects upon the truth received by faith and tries in its own small way to penetrate it better, and, in diverse eras and circumstances applies its acumen more intensely now to this, now to that part of the deposit of faith. Then, too, advances in the natural sciences, and particularly in philosophy, offer an occasion for progress. For the better educated the human mind is, the more is it ready to elucidate dogmas. Thirdly, we must not forget the love and devotion of the faithful which, for example, in the discussions on the Immaculate Conception, gave quite a bit of impetus to the studies of the theologians. But all these factors are not merely "occasions"; they are also partial causes.

230   b. The *process* by which dogmatic progress takes place can be fairly varied. But if one examines those dogmas which historically exhibit the most increase in knowledge and teaching, one can generally distinguish a *triple stage*.

In the first stage of the process, the dogma is contained in the Church's teaching implicitly or only in some practice. Consequently it is indeed implicitly *believed* by all Catholics, but is *known* by most of them only rather vaguely. They scarcely pay any specific attention to the doctrine, since the question has not directly been posed. The consequence is that the monuments of tradition left over from this stage or period contain very few testimonies, or none at all, about our doctrine that are *explicit, clear,* and *obvious.*

In the second stage, the matter begins to be subjected to deliberate scrutiny and thus, regardless of the exact cause, there arise hesitation and controversy as to whether the doctrine should be understood this way or that, whether it is contained in the sources of revelation, etc. Then arguments are adduced, first of all speculative ones: reasons of fitness, the connection of the truth with other doctrines, etc. Then, because of the lack of an explicit and obvious tradition, a far greater obscurity than formerly casts its pall over some minds which finally results in real doubts. It is not surprising if in circumstances of this sort some theologians, even the best of them, should call the truth into doubt or even attack it, without, of course, any detriment to the Catholic faith, since they have no intention of abandoning the proximate rule of faith—the teaching of the Church—which, nonetheless, is not yet obvious enough in the matter to hand. Something more, it can happen that in some *particular* churches or in *some* theological schools, the true tradition may fade into oblivion and some false ideas be temporarily introduced.[25] Still, an erroneous doctrine never prevails in the *universal* Church; rather, under the gentle direction of the Holy Spirit a more accurate analysis of the matter little by little clears up the difficulty, puts the darkness to flight until finally:

In the *third stage,* with the questions clarified and the judgment of the Church brought to maturity, the truth is rendered absolutely certain either through the now universal consent of the ordinary magisterium, or even through a solemn definition. Thus it is unmistakably proposed for belief and becomes explicitly believed throughout the entire Church.

Corollary 231

The special science devoted to an orderly exposition of the way a truth was revealed by God, of how, from the beginning down to our own day, it was grasped, discussed, explained, defended and finally defined, is called the *History of Dogmas.* It is easy to see that the history of dogmas, provided it be animated by Catholic principles, is extremely useful both for understanding and defending the Catholic faith.[26] Some moderns, however, make the blunder of thinking that it can almost serve as a substitute for systematic theology, or think that at least the role of scholastic theology should be diminished.

232 We ask: 3. *What is the efficient cause of this progress?*

The principal efficient cause of this progress in ecclesiastical teaching and in the understanding of the faithful is the authoritative magisterium of the Church (working under the assistance and direction of the Holy Spirit). To this are joined, as secondary causes, the labors of individual experts, and theological schools; in a word, theological studies.

Surely, Christ in handling over the deposit of the faith to His Church did not hand down a dry collection of formulae. Rather, He gave a sort of treasury containing truths of enormous depth and fruitfulness, and He established the apostles and their successors as both guardians and *teachers* of this deposit. But it is the task of doctors or teachers to make plain what is obscure, to make explicit what is implicit, and to refute false interpretations by those who deny Christ's truths, etc.

Since, however, the magisterium of the Church does not receive any new revelations, in carrying out its task it must make use of human means: a positive search of the sources of revelation together with theological ruminations. This labor is carried on for the most part by the theologians *insofar as they are helpers of the authoritative magisterium*. So even though the theologians usually prepare the way for progress in faith by their studies, it is not they themselves but the authoritative teachers (the pope and bishops) who must be rated as the major cause of such progress. This is so first because the theologians, most of the time, only begin their studies at the order of or with the approval of the bishops; secondly, and more importantly, because their explanations and solutions are judged by the episcopacy. Finally, their viewpoints do not exercise any influence on the Church's teaching except insofar as they are welcomed by the episcopacy. The episcopacy generally does so by favoring, or commending a doctrine, then by giving it still clearer approbation, and finally by giving it definitive sanction. With good reason, therefore, the decree *Lamentabili* condemned the following proposition of the Modernists: "In truths that are to be defined the teaching and the learning Church collaborate in such a way that there is nothing for the teaching Church to do except to sanction the commonly accepted theories of the learning Church" (DB 2006). Still, the authentic teachers themselves in this matter of progress are not left to their own intellectual acumen, but are helped by the Holy Spirit Himself who was promised to them and whose assistance brings it about that "the most intense sort of speculation will never end up in any error."[27]

The Teaching Church Itself Learns. You can see that the teaching Church, over the course of the centuries till the present has itself been learning, and can in the future keep on learning, not indeed by any receptance of brand new truths, but by a fuller and more accurate understanding of the ancient deposit of the faith. And it will do so by human means and with the help of men, but under the assistance, in fact under the leadership of the Holy Spirit. Surely if the magisterium of the Church in any given era had had an explicit and lucidly clear understanding of all dogmas, how could you explain that the public teaching of the Church was at some particular time and for a long time not very obvious about certain portions of doctrine which would be defined in later ages? Do you think that the Church's magisterium deliberately kept closed lips when there were serious and long-drawn out controversies going on? **233**

The assistance of the Holy Spirit does not, of course, make the authoritative teachers of the Church omniscient—not even in the matter of Christian revelation; but it does render them infallible. It brings it about, in other words, that *when* they clearly propose some doctrine to be believed they will never err since the gentle providence of God so arranges matters that they will not be lacking in explicit and clear knowledge at least at that time when the good of the Church demands it.

We ask: 4. *Does this progress not imply change?* **234**

First of all it is certain that the progress we have described does not imply any change in the revealed doctrine *itself*, since, as has been said, the Church cannot propose anything to be believed by divine faith which has not been contained in the sources of revelation from the very start.

But neither does it imply any real change in the *teaching* of the Church or in "Catholic" faith (viewed objectively); rather, it signifies an organic explanation or evolution of that same teaching and of that same faith. Certainly the Church has never proposed a brand-new truth to be believed, i.e., one that was not genuinely lying hidden away in her ancient teaching; nor has she ever proposed a different meaning for any dogma; nor has she ever retracted any dogma, or quietly pushed it aside; but in preaching the *very same deposit* of truth she began to teach some portions of it more accurately, more explicitly, more openly, more insistently. Furthermore, those fuller explanations were most of the time defined for the very purpose of preventing that ancient faith from being corrupted.

Just as a mature man is not another person than the small knobby-kneed boy he once was, granted that his individual limbs have increased in strength and power, and just as the objective faith held by the learned theologian is not a different belief than that of the simple peasant, granted that almost all of the same truths are more accurately and more explicitly known by the theologian, so, too, the teaching of the Church, granted it has been made more explicit and in that sense "evolved" over the course of the ages, always remains the very same because it has always been amplified in the same sense and with the same purport: "Indeed it pertains to progress that each thing should be amplified in itself, whereas it pertains to change that something should be mutated from being one thing into being something different."[28]

It may be helpful to add that just as the nature and character of a given person is more easily and more strikingly known from the mature man than from the small child, so the whole power and perfection of the Christian deposit is more clearly known from the polished teaching of the contemporary Church than from the preaching of the primitive Church which was, in a number of points, as yet rather obscure and implicit. Now if that be true of the living teaching of the Church such as it actually took place in the first centuries, how much more true will it be of that same teaching as we excavate it only very imperfectly through a historical examination of the relics and monuments that remain of it!

235 Corollary

Cardinal Newman, in order to show (against the Anglicans) that the multifaceted progress—not only dogmatic, but theological, liturgical, and social—which historically took place in the Roman Catholic Church is a true, organic, or vital process and not a corruption, laid down and applied seven criteria for distinguishing a legitimate evolution from a corruption.[29]

These criteria are:

a. *Conservation of the same type,* or of the same general physi-

THE OBJECT OF DIVINE FAITH

ognomy, as a result of which the present-day Church possesses the same qualities and is subject to the same *calumnies* as the Church of the first centuries.

b. *Continuity of the same fundamental principles* which are applied in every doctrine and in practice.

c. *The power of assimilation.* This means the Church incorporated into herself (i.e., imbued with her own spirit and put to her own use) whatever she found to be good or true in the world around her, and especially the philosophy of the Greeks and the ritual of the pagans.

d. *Logical consistency* in virtue of which doctrines made explicit at a later era and customs that later came into vogue very harmoniously blend in both with her principles and with one another.

e. *Anticipation of future events.* This means that sometimes there are found among the ancient Christians dim foreshadowings or beginnings of doctrines and practices of later ages.

f. *Preservative addition to antiquity.* This means the new additions did not take away or diminish, but rather corroborated and strengthened matters which were already held much earlier. So for example the cult of the Virgin Mary enhances rather than obscures the cult of Christ.

g. The *inexhaustible vigor* with which the Church in evolving her doctrine, her worship, and her organization neither perishes nor grows old, but acquires new strength in marching onward.

Scholion 2. False theories of dogmatic progress: 236

Worlds apart from the *relative* (subjective) progress admitted by Catholics are certain frankly rationalistic theories (such as those of Harnack and Sabatier) and theories imbued with rationalism and subjectivism (Gunther and Loisy) which are much noised about in modern times. Of these theories we shall now give a brief account.

I. **Harnack's theory.**[30] The essence of Christianity, and in fact of religion itself in the strict sense, is faith (in the Kantian sense) in God as a Father. Jesus, prior to all others and much more perfectly than all other men, realized this. But Christ's own religion *lacked all dogma* and consisted entirely in a filial relationship to God, intimately experienced, and in love of our neighbors. But from the time of St. Paul to the beginning of the fourth century dogma

(251)

grew up, i.e., dogmatic Christianity was prepared and sanctioned: the Christians gathered together their conceptions about God, the universe, the goal of existence, the economy of salvation under certain articles which, attributing to divine revelation (inspired Scriptures and divine tradition), they considered to be the sumtotal of the Christian religion and thought that belief in these articles was necessary for salvation.

This evolution should be attributed to some historical causes but also, and more importantly, to a Hellenizing mentality which transformed the gospel into a religious philosophy. In the meantime Christianity created for itself a system of sacraments and then, in imitation of the Roman Empire, a social and hierarchical organization, the Catholic Church. During succeeding centuries dogma *was enlarged*: though, indeed, the theologians are said to have explained the ancient doctrines more "explicitly," as a matter of fact by their very own speculations they *invented new doctrines* which the ecclesiastical authority then put on the same level as the dogmas under the guise of Tradition. For Catholicism always finds a way to proclaim the immutability of its dogmas and at the same time still manages to accommodate its dogmas to the needs of the times, by changing the meaning of the truths with very subtle distinctions. Now even though that dogmatism was a *kind of progressive corruption of Christianity*, it did not completely destroy faith or the principles of the gospel. What is more, some of the proclaimers of dogma did attempt a return to the genuine gospel: St. Augustine, and above all, Luther. The work that the former had hardly begun was not completed by the latter. That work must now be accomplished, especially by the aid of the history of dogmas, so that the minds of Christians may be freed from the iron yoke of dogma and may return to the purity of the gospel which is: living faith in God, in the God who instructed us through the man Jesus how to love God and our fellowman.

This is the only way that the split between Christianity and the world, between faith and science can be healed, and it is on only this condition that educated men will ever become religious.

2. August Sabatier's[31] **position is essentially that of Harnack's.** It differs from it only in these points: (a) he explains the origin and increase of our dogmas more on *psychological* grounds than historical circumstances; (b) he considers that dogmas are necessary at every state of human evolution so that men, through these dogmas, may give expression to their religious sense (their dependence on God and need of God) so that we should not strive to have a religion completely without dogma; what we should strive for is to give equal valuation to all the dogmas which have arisen in diverse eras and places thus providing diverse outlets for the same religious sense.

This is not the place to refute the foundations of this theory— 237
these foundations are philosophical preconceptions which a priori exclude any supernatural intervention of God in the world and reject a priori the notion that any religious doctrine might contain objective truth. But as for the application of this theory to the origin and development of our dogmas, notice the following points: (a) Harnack, not by applying principles of the art of criticism, but on preconceived opinions determines what *must* be the essence of Christianity and then *eliminates* everything else from the teaching of Christ. Do you think a man fills the role of a historian when he measures the essence of the gospel from its adaptability with the genius "of modern culture," or "the clear vision of the living man," or "the high experience of something" noble—when he takes such nonsense for a criterion and then proceeds to set aside "with tranquil mind" the very sources of the gospel and the texts that he finds bothersome? (b) Harnack offers so little explanation of how the most fundamental of all the dogmas—the divinity of Christ the Redeemer—could have arisen that he himself cannot keep quiet over the fact that it is a truly marvelous happening for which the whole of history offers no parallel! (c) Again, he assumes that the dogmas themselves were borrowed from Greek philosophy, whereas actually all that is present is an adaptation of some terminology, or philosophical explanation, or at the most some very feeble analogy to the real doctrine. (d) He takes for an objective increase in dogma what is nothing more than an organic explanation of it, or what we call relative progress. For a fuller elucidation of this point consult the explanations given by the theologians in their proofs of each individual dogma.[32]

3. **Anton Günther's theory.** According to Günther (d. 1863): 238
(a) the deposit of faith as received by the apostles contained only a few historical facts, only a few fundamental doctrines. From these, over the course of the ages, the vast gamut of Catholic doctrine blossomed forth, under the direction of the Holy Spirit, indeed, but by the assistance of philosophy. (b) The definitions of

the Church are not strictly (*simpliciter*) true, but only relatively true; they show a way of conceiving the divine truth which is very apt for a given age, but which, with the progress of philosophy, can be seen to be false so that it will have to be changed again and given a *different* meaning.

This theory: (a) rests upon a false foundation: for the apostolic deposit very definitely contains a large number of dogmas—some more clearly, others more obscurely—and contains them in explicit fashion. (b) In the articulation of the deposit this theory assigns the major part of the work to philosophy and thus makes, not the magisterium of the Church, but the philosophers the real doctors of the faith. (c) This theory looks on the very doctrine of the faith not as a divinely given treasure, but rather as a philosophical discovery which needs to be developed by human genius. Finally, the climax of the whole theory—the assertion about the relativity of truth and the changeableness of dogmas in their very meaning—has been solemnly condemned by the Vatican Council:

> If anyone says that as science progresses it is sometimes possible for dogmas which have been proposed by the Church to receive a different meaning from the one the Church has understood and understands, let him be anathema.—DB 1818; TCT 83.

239   4. **Alfred Loisy's theory.**[33] Loisy wanted to show, against Harnack, that the Catholic Church such as it is found today is not a corruption of the gospel, but its continuation and legitimate evolution, and in perfect conformity with the mind of Christ. Nonetheless, wanting to view the matter exclusively on historical and critical grounds he came to the point of saying that not even the substance of our dogmas, of our sacraments, of our hierarchy were truly and really founded by the historic Christ. Christ, Himself, who showed no consciousness of His own divinity, preached penance and hope in an eschatological kingdom which was just around the corner and over which He himself would preside; there is the essence of Christianity, there the genuine gospel of Christ. Unfortunately Christ was mistaken in this hope and in place of the "heavenly kingdom" (the eschatological kingdom) there appeared the Church, which continues the gospel because it administers penance and prepares men for the transcendental kingdom in a way accommodated to historical circumstances. Indeed the gospel, that is, the

THE OBJECT OF DIVINE FAITH

expectation of the kingdom of heaven, is "the living impulse," which Christ imprinted on the human race and from this "living impulse," from this "living and complex fact" as from a fruitful root or germ, under the stimuli of historical circumstances and the needs of later generations, little by little there grew up and flourished all the dogmas, sacraments, and hierarchy of the Church. Now since all of these things take their root from the gospel, they are not corruptions of it but its genuine evolution. Still, none of these things were strictly contained in the gospel of Christ, not even in that way in which a conclusion is contained in its premises.

Consequently the dogmas of the Church are *not immutable;* they do not express the divine truth itself which is immutable, but which we cannot reach; they express, rather, human conceptions of that truth, conceptions which are necessarily both inadequate and which correspond to the mentality of the era in which they were elaborated and sanctioned. They are subject, therefore, to continuous amelioration and consequently to change. As a matter of fact many of the dogmas (for example, the dogma of three Persons in one Nature, or of one Person in two natures) were defined by the Church under the influence of ancient philosophy in formulae so rigid that they cannot, for the modern mind, be purged of all contradiction. Definitions of this type ought to have been and still ought to be refined so that they may be adapted to progress in the sciences and in the new philosophy—in this way mysteries will grow less enigmatic and faith and science will be reconciled.

Furthermore, one should not conclude that these are novel ideas. Has not the Church always acknowledged that sort of evolution by which from the ancient root of the faith the tree of new professions of faith has blossomed forth? In one thing only have the ancients sinned and, generally speaking, the Catholic theologians still sin, that, namely, they admit an evolution which is not sufficiently "vital." But in our time it has come about that the Church has already begun to acquire a consciousness of this "evolution" which as a matter of fact has always existed!

240 This theory of Loisy's—if you take away all the studied and devious obscurity of the words and phrases—amounts to this: (a) Our *dogmas,* even the most fundamental of them, do *not take their origin* from any supernatural revelation but *from man himself:* they are intellectual interpretations of "faith," of the religious sense, and so forth. (b) The only sort of *truth* which belongs to our dogmas is what is called *vitalizing* truth: in other words, the concepts and dogmatic formulae correspond to our experiences and our aspirations and are very suitable for interpreting and nourishing our religious life—nothing more. For they do not represent objective reality, divine realities such as they are in themselves; they do not represent them only *inadequately* [which would be true] but in *no way* do they represent them, not even by way of analogy! They are rather like purely algebraic symbols: purely arbitrary signs of a quantity which is strictly unknown. (c) The *evolution of dogmas* is a continuous change, not only in the formulae and the philosophical vesture in which the truth is garbed, but even in their very meaning or their intellectual content.

How far apart from Catholic principles all these points are need not be belabored.

Nor does it help any that Loisy ceaselessly insists that in teaching all these points he is playing the part of historian and critic, and therefore that all the dogmas of the Church can be proven by faith, can be legitimated by faith, etc. For that kind of "faith," namely a persuasion which rests on purely subjective motives, as a matter of fact legitimates nothing, and cannot stand up under critical analysis. If history and the critical art as a matter of fact were to lead to Loisyean conclusions, then faith in the Catholic sense would no longer be a rational worship. It can, indeed, happen that we may reach certitude by theological principles about a matter which historical studies, because of a lack of available documents, can either not prove at all or cannot prove sufficiently; but it is strictly absurd to think that something can be true theologically which has been proven to be false historically, or vice versa.

Finally, (a) those points which Loisy asserts about the relativity of our knowledge, he owes, not to history, but to false philosophical principles; (b) when he is actually dealing in historical matters he indulges too much in a priori opinionizing by eliminating sources or texts just at his own whim, or by accommodating facts to fit his own viewpoint and so on.

Notes

1. *Homiliae in Ezechielem,* ii. 4. 12.
2. John 16:12–15.
3. See, for example, Palmieri, *De romano pontifice* (2nd. ed.) p. 191. This opinion is practically abandoned today.

4. S.Th., II–II, q. 1, a. 7, *corpus*.
5. Gal. 4:4 and Eph. 1:10.
6. Acts 2:17; I Peter 1:20.
7. Heb. 9:26; I Cor. 10:11.
8. Heb. 7:11–28; 12:27–28; II Cor. 3:11; Matt. 24:14; 28:18–20; I Cor. 11:26.
9. John 16:12–15; 14:26.
10. I Tim. 6:20; II Tim. 1:13–14; 3:14; Jude 3; Rom. 16:17.
11. See, for example, St. Irenaeus *Adversus haereses* IV. 33:2; Tertullian *De praescriptione* 8:20–22; Vincent of Lérins *Commonitorium* 21.
12. See Franzelin, *Tractatus de traditione et scriptura*, theses 23 and 25; Scheeben, *Handbuch d. kath. Dogm.*, I, no. 63; Heinrich, *Dogm. Theol.*, II, no. 78; Bainvel, *De magisterio vivo*, p. 117; Cardinal Newman, *Essay on the Development of Christian Doctrine* (1845) and the same work vastly improved (1878); Prunier, *Evolution et immutabilité* (Collection, *Science et Religion*) 1898; De la Barre, *La vie du Dogme catholique* (1898).

For more *recent* works consult the following: De Grandmaison, *Le Dogme Chretien: sa nature-ses, formules-son développement* (a collection of various essays published posthumously in 1927); Marín-Sola, *L'Evolution homogène du Dogme Catholique* (1924); H.-D. Simonin, "La théologie Thomiste de la foi et le développement," *Revue Thomiste* (1935) p. 537 ff.; Garrigou-Lagrange, "L'Immutabilité des vérités définies et le surnaturel" *Angelicum* 25 (1948) 285–298; Salaverri, *De ecclesia Christi* (2nd ed. 1952) cap. IV, art. 1, pp. 730–740.

13. *De principiis* Prologue.
14. *Sermo* 294, towards the end.
15. *Contra Julianum* i. 6. 22.
16. *Epistula* 30. 2.
17. *In epistulam ad Romanos*, cap. 14, lectio 3.
18. *Commonitorium*, 6.
19. *Ibid.* 23.
20. For some striking observations of what is meant by the *Catholic sense*, or the collective consciousness of the Church, see De La Barre, *La vie du Dogme*, p. 156. For a more recent treatment of the same theme see Karl Adam, *The Christ of Faith* (New York, 1957) pp. 4–18.
21. *Commonitorium* 23.
22. *De civitate Dei* 16. 2.
23. *Enarratio in psalmos* 54. 22; see also, *De Genesi contra Manichaeos*, 1. 2.
24. *Registrum epistularum* vii. 3; ed. by P. Ewald and L. M. Hartmann, "Monumenta Germaniae historica," *Epistulae*, I. (Berlin, 1891).
25. How great a pall of obscurity may occur in some *section* of the Church is vividly brought out by these words of Vincent of Lérins, treating of the new practice introduced in the African churches of rebaptizing heretics: "Well, then, maybe the new-fangled practice found no supporters?"—"O, quite the contrary. It found such mighty intellectual backing, such rivers of eloquence, so great a crowd of defenders, so plausible a likeness to truth, so many utterances of the Divine Law, but obviously interpreted in a new and evil fashion, that. . . ."—*Commonitorium* 6.

26. See Katschthaler, "Begriff, Nützen und Methode der Dogmengeschichte," *ZkTh* (1882). Denis Petavius (d. 1652) is usually rated as the father of this branch of science because of his *De dogmatibus theologicis*. Actually, though, the tenor of this work is more polemical than historical. The real history of dogmas was begun towards the close of the eighteenth century by Protestants. Among Catholics who have specialized in this field may be mentioned Klee, Ginoulhiac, Bach, Schwane, Tixeront, and many others, especially modern theologians, who have traced out the history of individual dogmas.

27. St. Augustine *Enarratio in Psalmos* 9. 12. We do not deny, of course, that even theologians can be helped and actually are helped by the illumination of the Holy Spirit. But one must beware of conceiving of the interior leadership of the Holy Spirit as something altogether separated from, or even in a sense opposed to, the external leadership of the Church's magisterium. To this matter, also, apply the words of Leo XIII:

> "The admonitions and inspirations of the Holy Spirit are not, most of the time, grasped except with some sort of help and, as it were, preparation on the part of the external magisterium. Augustine himself bears witness in the matter that He gathers fruit from the good trees both by externally watering and cultivating them through some servant and also through Himself by interiorally granting the increase."—*Testem benevolentiae*, January 22, 1899.

28. Vincent of Lérins *Commonitorium* 23.

29. *Essay on the Development of Christian Doctrine*, Part II, chapters 5-12.—This book, even though written with a perfectly Catholic mentality, is not always absolutely accurate and perfectly nuanced in its utterances. No need for raised eyebrows over that: it was a kind of profession of faith by a newly-converted teacher dealing with doctrinal matters of an extremely delicate nature.—Since the preceding observation by Van Noort, much writing about Newman has appeared, clarifying and justifying many of his ideas about the genesis of faith. Apparently some of the clouds that clustered around his name and the epithet of "fideist" were due to misrepresentation of his ideas by the Immanentists in France. Roger Aubert writes:

> "The followers of the method of Immanence invoked with even more insistence the authority of another Cardinal, Newman. In him they were delighted to point out a predecessor of genius and thought that his title as well as his prestige as a convert would throw up a shield against too violent accusations. Unfortunately the interpretation they made of Newman was not very faithful and his ideas, so fruitful, were on the verge of being compromised by the excess of imprudent disciples." (*Le problème de l'acte de foi*, (1950) p. 343). The same author blames Abbè Dimnet and Bremond for introducing Newman to the French theological world under the image of a fideist (see *ibid.* p. 348).

A fine recent work in English presenting a balanced picture of Newman's ideas about faith is: *Newman, Faith and the Believer* by Philip Flanagan, D.D. (Westminster, Md., 1946).

30. See *Dogmengeschichte*, Introduction, and *Das Wesen des Christentums*. For the rest, Harnack in many points follows Ritschl.

31. *Esquisse d'une philosophie de la religion d'après la psychologie et l'histoire*.

THE OBJECT OF DIVINE FAITH

32. See Van Breda, in *De Katholiek*, 125 (1904) 1 ff.; Christian Pesch, in *Stimmen aus Maria-Laach*, 60 (1901) 41, 154, 257.

33. As found in the works: *L'Évangile et l'Église* and *Autour d'un petit livre*, along with some other works of the same author put on the *Index* by a decree of Dec. 16, 1903. Loisy had already earlier voiced similar ideas in different periodicals under the pseudonyms *Després, Jacques Simon*, and especially under the name *A. Firmin*.—A good analysis of the books mentioned above is given in *Revue Thomiste*, 11 (1903) p. 70 and 593; see also the excellent article by Portalié, *Le Dogme et l'Histoire*, in *Bulletin de litt. eccles.* (Toulouse) 1904, p. 62. See also RPA 6 (1908) p. 83 ff.

Article V

THEOLOGICAL TRUTHS

Introduction: Difference Between Truths of Faith and "Theological Truths":
   1. The former are revealed by God Himself and alone command an assent of divine faith.
   2. The latter are not revealed but are intimately connected with revelation and command a fitting assent.

Assertion 1. Some truths are so necessarily intertwined with revelation that to deny or doubt them would cause injury to revelation itself.
   1. Truths which are *necessary presuppositions* to the acceptance of revelation.
   2. Truths which are *necessary consequences* of revelation.
   3. Truths which are connected with revelation *by reason of its goal.*
   4. All these types of truth are directed to the guardianship and practical application of the deposit of the faith.

Corollary: Theological truths must not be confused with "truths accidentally inspired."

Assertion 2. Theological truths which the *magisterium* of the Church teaches infallibility, must be held with an assent of ecclesiastical faith.
   1. The Church's infallible *magisterium* extends not only to revealed truths but to truths intimately bound up with revelation.
   2. The term "Ecclesiastical faith":
      a. meaning of the terminology.
      b. defense of the terminology.

Corollary: Even though the act of ecclesiastical faith differs in species from the act of divine faith, it is properly referred to the habit or virtue of faith.

THE OBJECT OF DIVINE FAITH

Assertion 3. Theological truths which the Church's *magisterium* teaches merely authentically, must be held with a religious assent.
1. Meaning of "merely authentic proposal."
   a. authentic *magisterium* of individual bishops, provincial councils, and Roman congregations.
2. Meaning of "religious assent."
   a. some theologians have thought an authentic proposal required no internal assent but merely respectful silence.
   b. Rebuttal of that opinion based on:
      (1) theological arguments;
      (2) pronouncements of the *magisterium*.
3. Obligation to give internal assent to merely authentic teaching:
   a. Since the very nature of an authentic proposal is necessarily *provisory* in character, so too is the assent that is demanded.
   b. The different problem facing the ordinary run of the faithful and an expert in a given field when confronted with a proposal of the authentic *magisterium*.

Assertion 4. The same religious assent must be given to theological truths which the theologians commonly and constantly propose as certainly to be held.
1. Meaning of the term "theologian" in this connection.
2. The specific conditions which must be met before one can say such a religious assent is required.
3. Ultimately this assent is given, not to the theologians, but to the ordinary *magisterium* of the Church.

Article V

THEOLOGICAL TRUTHS

Nothing can be believed by *divine faith* and nothing can be proposed by the Church as a *dogma of faith* unless it has been revealed by God. Still it would be an extremely serious error to conclude from that fact: "therefore one may reject or call into doubt any non-revealed truth he chooses to without committing sin, or injuring the Catholic profession of faith";[1] or, worse still: "therefore the Church cannot pass judgment on, or cannot define any non-revealed truth."[2]

Quite a few truths, not themselves formally revealed, because of their intimate connection with revelation must be held by all Catholics with a fitting assent. These are called *theological truths,* which must now be discussed.

241 *Assertion 1. Some truths are so necessarily intertwined with revelation that to deny or doubt them would cause injury to revelation itself.*

This assertion may be *proved* by showing the intimate connection between such truths and revealed doctrine itself.

1. Some truths and facts, not in themselves revealed, are bound up with revelation as *necessary presuppositions.* In other words they are so bound up that faith must necessarily take them for granted, because if they were not already antecedently established, faith itself would necessarily totter. If, for example, someone doubted whether human reason could prove with certitude[3] the authenticity of the revelation made by Christ, he ought, as a necessary consequence, to be doubtful about the truthfulness of the entire gamut of Christian doctrine. Similarly, anyone who thought that the gospels were mainly literary creations to express in a colorful way the religious feelings of the authors, ought necessarily to be doubtful about events in the life of Christ narrated in historic fashion. Again, anyone who would doubt whether Pius IX were the legitimate successor of St. Peter should likewise and necessarily doubt the definition of the Immaculate Conception handed down

by that pope. Similarly, if one doubted whether Pius XII were the legitimate successor of St. Peter he should doubt whether the dogma of the Assumption, defined by that pope, were true or not.

2. Other truths are connected with revelation as a *necessary consequence*. These are truths which are deduced with certitude by a genuine discursive syllogism from one premise which is revealed and another which is obvious to reason: *theological conclusions*.[4] Anyone who would sneer at the truth of such a conclusion would himself soon arrive at the point of doubting the truth of the revealed premise itself, or else, at least, would incite such doubts in the minds of others. Briefly, if one premise is lucidly clear to reason, and the syllogism logically flawless, a man who refuses to accept the conclusion can only do so because he suspects there is something wrong with the other premise. But in the case envisaged—a theological conclusion—the other premise is a revealed premise.

3. Finally, some truths are necessarily connected with revelation *by reason of its goal* (finaliter). These are truths which deal with means necessary, or very useful, for achieving the goal of revelation. To this category belong decisions relating to the universal discipline of the Church, or the approval of Religious Orders, or decisions about the canonization of saints, or judgments about the rights of the Church herself. Surely, the goal of revelation as a whole is to increase the glory of God, to establish and widen the kingdom of God upon earth, and to make men holy. This goal of revelation is achieved by the application of revealed truth to the actions of normal life. Consequently, if the very purpose of revelation is not to be frustrated, all men must be certain about the particular ways in which the application of revelation can and should be made to fit diverse situations and circumstances. For example, if it were perfectly licit for any individual to judge that the disciplinary laws sanctioned for the universal Church, or that the various forms of religious life approved by the Church were really an obstacle to eternal salvation; or to call into doubt the holiness of those people the Church herself sets before us as models for imitation and objects of veneration; or to deny to the Church herself the very rights[5] which she needs to carry out her mission, the goal of revelation itself would be vastly hindered, and revelation itself rendered for the most part useless.

Truths not-formally revealed but bound up with revelation in one of the three ways just pointed out look directly to the *guardi-*

anship and *practical application* of the deposit of the faith; thus, indirectly, they belong to the deposit itself and to Catholic faith.

They are called *theological truths* or are dubbed as *theologically certain*. Prescinding for the time being from what obligation there is to accept them *after* a proposal by the Church, we say that those who perceive their necessary connection with revelation ought to hold them with a *theological assent;* for it belongs to theology or the science of the faith to investigate which matters are bound up with revelation and precisely how tightly they are bound up with it.

I say: (a) "prescinding for the time being from the question of what obligation arises *after* a proposal by the Church": for since the guardianship and practical application of revealed truth has been committed to the rulers of the Church, theological truths do not belong merely to the science of theology, but they also constitute the secondary object of the ecclesiastical magisterium.

I say: (b) "by those who *perceive* their necessary connection with revelation"; for antecedent to a judgment by the Church there will at times be doubt whether the matter is so necessarily bound up with revelation that a denial or attack upon it would constitute a real danger to the faith, or, whether the conclusion which *some* theologians deduce from the revealed premise is *correctly deduced* therefrom. This is how there arise theological opinions, disputed questions and the like.

245 Corollary

We must not confuse "theological truths" with *truths accidentally inspired*. The latter are truths which are secular in content but which are, nonetheless, really contained in Sacred Scripture. For example, that the census which brought the Blessed Virgin Mary to Bethlehem was *"ordered by"* or *"took place under the governorship of Cyrinus of Syria."*[6] Both these types of truth are bound up with religion, but one in one way and the other in a different way. Theological truths are bound up with religion by reason of their very content, by reason of the very object with which they deal, whereas "truths accidentally inspired" are bound up with religion only because of their connection with the speaker (ratione dicentis). Again, theological truths are *not* revealed and consequently do not constitute or furnish an object for divine faith; contrariwise, accidentally inspired truths contained in Scripture are the Word of God and consequently do constitute or furnish an *accessory* (i.e., accidental) object for divine faith. The only difficulty which can arise with regard to the latter is this: whether such truths are really or only "apparently" contained in Sacred Scripture: that is, whether the Scriptural loci in which they appear should be interpreted in their obvious sense or in some other fashion.[7]

246 Assertion 2. *Theological truths which the Magisterium of the Church teaches infallibly must be held with an assent of ecclesiastical faith.*

Since it was established in the volume, *Christ's Church*, that the Church's infallible teaching power extends to matters *connected* with revelation[8] and that its infallible authority deserves an *absolutely firm assent*, the only question which remains is what name to give that assent and how to describe its nature. These points will be discussed in just a moment.

Meantime, notice that the Church possesses infallibility not only when she is defining some matter in solemn fashion, but also when she is exercising the full weight of her authority through her ordinary and universal teaching. Consequently, we must hold with an absolute assent, which we call "ecclesiastical faith," the following theological truths: (a) those which the Magisterium has infallibly defined in solemn fashion; (b) those which the ordinary magisterium dispersed throughout the world unmistakably proposes to its members as something to be *held* (tenendas). So, for example, one must give an absolute assent to the proposition: "Pius XII is the legitimate successor of St. Peter"; similarly (and as a matter of fact if this following point is something "formally revealed,"[9] it will undoubtedly be a dogma of faith) one must give an absolute assent to the proposition: "Pius XII possesses the primacy of jurisdiction over the entire Church." For—skipping the question of how it begins to be proven infallibly for the first time that this individual was legitimately elected to take St. Peter's place[10]—when someone has been constantly acting as pope and has theoretically and practically been recognized as such by the bishops and by the universal Church, it is clear that the ordinary and universal magisterium is giving an utterly clear-cut witness to the legitimacy of his succession.

247 The term, *ecclesiastical faith,* and its distinction from divine faith is rather commonly admitted by most recent theologians. Still there are quite a number of theologians who reject that term and that distinction by saying that the assent with which we hold truths not formally contained in revelation but infallibly proposed by the Church is, as a matter of fact, *divine faith*.[11] They defend this viewpoint by a double argument.

They say: 1. Even when it comes to matters only connected with revelation the Church plays the part of God's messenger and does so with divine assistance. Consequently, God speaks through His messenger, the Church: or, the testimony of the Church is the testimony of God; therefore the assent owed to such testimony is an assent of divine faith.

Answer: That the Church in defining truths connected with revelation is playing the part of a divine messenger in such fashion that God *"speaks"* through the Church—I make a distinction. In the *strict* sense of the term, meaning that the Church proposes truths received from God in exactly the same way as did the prophets and the apostles *acting as organs of revelation;* or, in such fashion that when the Church so speaks she is doing so by real *inspiration* and under the impulse of God in exactly the same way as did the sacred writers, who were *not* the "principal" cause of their message but only its *instrumental* cause—this *I deny*.

That the Church plays the part of a divine messenger in a *loose,* broad sense of the term, namely, that in carrying out the general mission entrusted to her by God the Church does herself make judgments, acting as the *principal* cause, about matters necessarily bound up with revelation and does by her own judgment (which God by various means preserves from error, but means which do not include either revelation or genuine inspiration) does issue doctrinal decrees—this *I concede*. Surely the power of jurisdiction (which includes the magisterial office) is not purely instrumental, or ministerial, but is in its own way a principle power.[12] For the Church's rulers by a power which is their very own, or inherent in them (even though bestowed upon them from above), found or establish decrees, whether doctrinal or disciplinary, of which the *principal* cause is *themselves,* not God.

It follows logically that the Church's testimony in matters bound up with revelation can be called "divine" testimony only in a very loose, or improper use of the term. For even though it proceeds from men backed up by divine authority and fortified by divine assistance, it really proceeds from men as from its principal cause

THE OBJECT OF DIVINE FAITH

and thus is and remains *intrinsically human testimony*. Now human testimony can never deserve an assent of divine faith.

Nevertheless, the Church's testimony does differ vastly from every other sort of human testimony both by reason of its *dignity* and, above all, by its *certitude*—both of which factors accrue to it *extrinsically*. First, by its *dignity* because that testimony is given to execute the general duty imposed upon the Church by God; and secondly, by the certitude it brings: for every other sort of human testimony, of whatsoever kind, offers a certitude that is only strictly moral (i.e., having its foundation in the hypothesis of the human-moral order); whereas the testimony of the Church, by reason of the divine assistance guiding it, offers a metaphysical-moral certitude and it is, on this score, equivalent to divine testimony.

Since the Church's testimony differs in *kind* (species) both from divine testimony, by reason of its principle, and from human testimony, by reason of its certitude, it holds a kind of midway position between both types of testimony. There is then, good reason for acknowledging the existence of "ecclesiastical faith" which holds a position midway between divine faith and merely human faith and is specifically different from each of them. That is the reason also why many theologians in order to make a very clear distinction between divine and ecclesiastical faith (and also from a "religious assent," which will be discussed below) reserve the term *"to believe'* for matters of divine faith, whereas for assents of an inferior kind they use the term: *"to hold"* (*tenere* vs. *credere*).

Argument 2: They say: we only know of the Church's infallibility in reference to connected matters, by divine revelation. Consequently when we accept some definition on these matters, we do indeed directly (proximately) give our assent to the Church, but ultimately we give it to God Himself; and thus you have faith only mediately (indirectly) indeed, but a faith which is truly divine.

Answer: This argument presumes that the nature of faith depends not only upon the very motive proper to the assent (in the case at hand, the authority of the Church) *but also upon the means* by which we have *become acquainted with* the existence and value of this motive (in the case at hand: divine revelation). But, that point cannot be granted as will be obvious from the matters discussed when we take up the *analysis of the act of faith* itself (see below nos. 291–304). In the meantime, this point will suffice for a refutation of that argument: if the position of these theologians were valid then divine faith itself ought to be called *mediately human*, for the existence and value of the authority of God revealing, insofar as it is the motive of faith, is not known in any other way than by human means.

250 Corollary

Even though the act of ecclesiastical faith differs from the act of divine faith in kind or species, there is good reason for referring it to the theological habit, or virtue of faith. Habits normally encompass many other activities which bear a relationship to something itself unified. That is why we distinguish between the principal acts of such habits and acts which are merely connected with them.[13] So the act of putting on spiked shoes in a locker room, or of washing golf balls is referred to the golfing habit even though they are not an intrinsic part of the golf-swing. So, too, the one infused habit of faith extends itself to, or encompasses all assents which are connected with divine faith, whether connected by way of safeguarding and defending the faith, or by way of preparing for faith as, for example, the judgment of credibility.

251

Assertion 3. Theological truths which the Church's Magisterium teaches merely authentically, must be held with a religious assent.

1. *A merely authentic proposal.* An authentic teacher, i.e., endowed with real authority in the Church, means a teacher possessing the right and duty to teach doctrines on faith or morals in such fashion that the subjects are for that very reason, namely that it proceeds from such a person or group, bound to accept it.* Those who possess the fullness of the magisterial office (the popes, ecumenical councils, and the catholic episcopate dispersed throughout the world but acting in unison) and exercise it at its maximum power are infallible. It is true: (a) those who possess the fullness of this magisterial power may exercise their teaching office without using its full authority, i.e., without intending to hand down a strictly definitive judgment (as, for example, can very easily occur in encyclical letters of the popes). (b) There are others who possess an authentic teaching office, but do not possess the fullness of the magisterium, or the charism of infallibility. These are: the individual bishops acting as teachers for their own individual

---

* See Pius XII's allocution to bishops in 1956, reminding bishops they are the authentic teachers in their own dioceses.

dioceses; provincial councils etc. acting for their own respective provinces; and some Roman Congregations acting for the entire Church. In all these cases one has a proposal which is merely authentic, "authoritative only."

With regard to the teaching of the *individual bishops,* Cardinal Franzelin has this to say: "Because of their necessary subordination [to the Roman Pontiff] and unity [with him] in doctrine it follows that their authentic teaching refers only to the teaching and safeguarding of such doctrine as has already been proposed either by an explicit definition, or by the consent of the Church, or by decisions of universal providence [that is, utterances of the pope when not speaking ex cathedra, or decisions of the Roman Congregations], but their teaching does not extend to settling questions that are controverted among Catholics."[14]

The authentic teaching of *provincial councils* is indeed wider in scope than that of individual bishops; still, it does not belong to them, either, to pass judgment on doctrinal matters which are genuinely doubtful. "Fagnanus wisely warns (so says Benedict XIV) that questions which are controverted among Catholic theologians and have not yet been defined by the Apostolic See should not be easily settled by provincial synods."[15] Finally, the decrees of such provincial synods must be sent to Rome to the Sacred Congregations of the Council[16] or the Propagation of the Faith for approval before they can be promulgated.

Among the various *Roman Congregations,* doctrinal questions are passed upon by the Congregation of the Holy Office and by the Pontifical Commission on Scriptural Matters.[17] These sacred congregations are tribunals of the supreme pontiff. From him they receive their jurisdiction (ordinary) and in his name and by his authority they edit decrees. With good reason, then, such decrees are said to be decrees of the Holy See. Those decrees are published with the knowledge, approbation, and confirmation of the supreme Pontiff; still, so long as they truly are and remain decrees of the Congregation itself; so long as the Congregation itself is the person teaching and handing down decisions, those decrees are not infallible. A decision issuing from a sacred congregation will only have the force of an ex-cathedra decision at such time as the pope makes it his very own; when, strictly speaking, the pope himself is the person teaching and judging; and, furthermore, when there are not lacking the clear-cut and necessary signs of a definitive judgment binding the universal church. In such a case the sacred Congregation merely acts in the capacity of a consultant or a publisher.[18]

252 2. A *religious* assent means an intellectual assent given out of a religious motive, i.e., out of a motive of obedience to the religious authority established (whether directly or indirectly) by Jesus Christ. It differs, therefore, from a theological assent and an assent of purely human faith. A man gives a theological assent when he perceives with his own mind the connection between some truth and revealed doctrine; he gives an assent of purely human faith if he accepts some truth connected with revelation on the authority of some theologian who attests to the connection.

Now some theologians maintain that all one owes to doctrinal decrees issuing from Roman congregations (for it is about such decrees that most of the dispute centers, though it applies also, in proper proportion, to other authentic decrees enumerated above) is a respectful silence,[19]* or a reverential silence. In other words, all that one is obliged to do is neither to teach orally or in writing the doctrine which has been condemned; nothing further is required.

But the more common teaching—which we think should be subscribed to absolutely—exacts something further: the yielding of the mind through some sort of *internal* assent. Notice, I say: through *some sort* of internal assent. Since we are here dealing with non-infallible authority, quite obviously there cannot be exacted an assent that is utterly firm and strictly irrevocable, such as is the assent of both divine and ecclesiastical faith.

Generally speaking, it is not unreasonable to give an internal assent to a non-infallible authority. Even in our normal daily home and social life we do submit our intelligences a thousand times or more to human experts who are not at all infallible: the family doctor, dentist, garage mechanic etc. We do not do so as though we thought it was impossible for them to err, but because we are either morally certain or, at least, have a reasonable assumption that they are not now *factually* making a mistake. Now, if it be reasonable to believe any expert in his own field, why, speaking in general terms, should it not also be reasonable to assent to the decrees that issue from sacred congregations? For: (a) these con-

---

* This seems to be the position, for example, of Karl Adam in his discussion of the possession of the beatific vision by Christ. See *The Christ of Faith*, pp. 271–272. See note 19 at the end of this article.

gregations are usually made up of men who are themselves well versed in the theological sciences and who receive assistance from other experts; and they are made up of men recognized for their wisdom or prudence. (b) These men exercise their teaching office under the eyes of the Supreme Pontiff and in the center of the Church—a center with which the universal Catholic Episcopate is in constant communication, and thus they are in a position to gauge the mind of the universal magisterium more easily and more deeply than any private theologian. (c) These men are certainly not lacking in a special grace to carry out their extremely serious task.

Furthermore, we have some very explicit statements by the popes on the question at hand. Pius IX, in reference to a Congress of German theologians* at Munich in September, 1863, wrote as follows about the subjection due to the Church's non-infallible teaching authority:

> Since we are dealing with that subjection which obligates in conscience all those Catholics who are engaged in the contemplative sciences for the sake of bringing new advantages to the Church by their writings, for that very reason the very members of that congress ought to realize that it is not enough for learned Catholics to accept and reverence the aforesaid dogmas of the Church. They must also subject themselves *both to decisions pertaining to doctrine which issue from the pontifical Congregations,* and also to those parts of doctrine which are retained by the common and constant consent of all Catholic [theologians] as theological truths and conclusions so certain that opinions contrary to those points, even though they may not be dubbed heretical, do, nonetheless, deserve some theological censure.[20]

St. Pius X expressed himself in no less emphatic terms on the same question:

> We do now declare and expressly prescribe, that all are bound in conscience to submit to the decisions of the *Biblical Commis-*

* The Congress had occasioned some disquiet in ecclesiastical circles due to the presence and utterances of Dollinger. The members of the Congress had asserted that all Catholics in their scholarly writings were obliged in conscience to obey the dogmatic decrees of the infallible Catholic Church. The pope wanted them to acknowledge something further.

sion, which have been given in the past and which shall be given in the future, in the same way as to the Decrees which appertain to doctrine, issued by the Sacred Congregations and approved by the Sovereign Pontiff; nor can they escape the stigma both of disobedience and temerity nor be free from grave guilt as often as they impugn these decisions either in word or writing; and this, over and above the scandal which they give and the sins, of which they may be the cause before God by making other statements on these matters which are very frequently both rash and false. (*Praestantia Sacrae Scripturae,* transl. RSS, p. 41.)

But if an assent of the sort just described is per se reasonable why should not those who possess a legitimate office, and the public authority which goes with it, be able to exact such an assent of their subjects, for the sake of gently and safely protecting matters of faith and religion, *in virtue of this very authority?* If they do exact it, the assent given will be rendered out of a duty of subjection to the authority established by Christ and, consequently, out of a motive of religion. There is good reason, therefore, for describing it as "religious assent."*

253 As a matter of fact the rulers of the Church do demand such a subjection and such an internal assent. It seems obvious that when the authentic teachers propose some doctrine or condemn some error they do so with the intention of having both the faithful and the theologians adhere mentally to those doctrines and reject from their heart those errors.†

Finally, Pius XII, in the closing paragraphs of his encyclical, *Humani Generis,* reminds teachers in seminaries and other ecclesi-

---

* The nature of a "religious assent," then, may be briefly described as follows. It is an assent of *faith* (taken in the generic meaning of the term) and as such is elicited from the intelligence at the order of the will. The will can *prudently* order the assent because there is a legitimate presumption that the authentic teacher is not making a mistake; furthermore, the will is attracted to order the assent by the obligation of subjection towards the magisterium established by Christ and, consequently, from a motive of *religious* obedience.

† When the Holy Office corrected Father Feeney's teaching on *outside the Church no salvation* it did so for the express purpose of having him submit to its decision and to instruct the faithful about his erroneous doctrine. Similarly, when Pius XII issued his encyclical *Humani Generis* and outlined a number of errors, he made unmistakably plain that he wished the theologians to mentally adhere to points laid down and in precisely the way they were laid down.

astical institutions of their serious duty to give religious submission to the ordinary teaching authority of the Church. This directive is surely not restricted to the Pontiff's own teaching but to all the exercises of the authentic magisterium.

> Let teachers in ecclesiastical institutions be aware that they cannot with tranquil conscience exercise the office of teaching entrusted to them, unless in the instruction of their students they religiously accept and exactly observe the norms which we have ordained. That due reverence and submission which in their unceasing labor they must profess towards the teaching Authority of the Church, let them instill also into the minds and hearts of their students. (NCWC transl. #42, p. 19)

254 Granted the need for submission to the authentic magisterium, it still remains true that just as a merely authentic proposal is by its very nature incomplete and provisory, so, too, is the religious assent due it. Quite frequently the decrees of these congregations do not look directly to the truthfulness of a given doctrine, but rather to its *security*. Now the security of a doctrine, i.e., whether it is *safe* to admit or to teach this or that point, or whether religion would thereby suffer some injury, depends somewhat on the circumstances and, above all, on the present state of the question—something which may change with the addition of new evidence or arguments. Illustrative of this point one may consider some of the answers given by the Biblical Commission in 1906, 1908 and 1909 in reference to the Mosaic authorship and use of sources in the composition of the Pentateuch, the authorship of the book of Isaias, and the formation of Eve from Adam, with the response of the Biblical Commission to a letter of Archbishop Suhard on January 16, 1948. While the Commission, in the last named letter, is very careful to assert that if one interprets the earlier answers properly he will "readily grant that these answers are in no way opposed to further and truly scientific examination of these problems in accordance with the results obtained during these last forty years," still it is quite clear that much more liberty of interpretation is afforded the exegete today in regard to these questions than earlier. In June, 1906, the Biblical Commission admitted that it was licit to affirm that Moses "in order to compose his work, made use of written documents or oral traditions." (RSS p. 149, Letter to Cardinal Suhard). On January 16, 1948, the same Biblical

Commission states: "There is no one today who doubts the existence of these sources or refuses to admit a progressive development of the Mosaic laws due to social and religious conditions of later times, a development which is also manifest in the historical narratives." (RSS p. 149). We have moved from the admission of probability to a factual assertion. Similarly, while in June 28, 1908, the Biblical Commission answered "In the negative" to the question of whether there were enough "solid arguments, even when taken cumulatively to prove that the book of Isaias is to be attributed not to Isaias alone, but to two or even more authors" (RSS p. 120)—today Catholic exegetes generally acknowledge multiple authorship. In so doing, they do not feel that they are lacking in due submission to the Biblical Commission; it is simply that the state of the question has changed and better evidence is at hand today to gauge the question. Similarly in June 30, 1909, the Biblical Commission listed as one of the points whose "literal and historical meaning" it was not licit to call into question, "the formation of the first woman from man." Today, the opinion is gaining ever more weight among exegetes that the story of the formation of Eve from Adam is not to be taken in a literal sense but is a symbolic expression by the sacred author of woman's real equality and dignity as a human person with man. While the prior response has not been taken off the books, the *general directives* of the Biblical Commission in regard to the first eleven chapters of Genesis allow such freedom of interpretation to the exegete, provided it be based on solid argumentation.

Experts and Religious Assent

Now if this be the way matters stand, in dealing with a decree which says: "it is not safe," or "it cannot be safely taught that," one would satisfy the obligation of religious assent were he to say to himself: "this opinion, in the way it is explained today and in accord with the present stage of inquiry, is not probable and seems false." Nor, could one always blame an expert in a given field who would not totally abandon all hope of a better explanation and who, furthermore, because of the very opportunity afforded by the decree, might continue to search for new evidence or explanations. Finally, even if a decree looks more directly to the *truthfulness* rather than security of doctrine, the assent given is always founded on the *presumption* that the authentic magisterium, even though it can err, has de facto not erred. But this presumption admits of degrees. When some decree is laid down, the normal condition of the general run of the faithful is as follows: either they will not have any arguments of great importance to the contrary, or if they do have some strong reasons they will rather easily say to themselves: "those reasons are not hidden from the magisterium and, still, it has not refrained from making an apodictical judgment. Consequently, it must have found those arguments superficial and not solidly grounded." Now, people in that condition should unqualifiedly adhere to the magisterium's teaching as at least *practically certain* i.e., uniquely probable. For, in the position described, the presumption in favor of the magisterium sufficiently eliminates purely private arguments. Still, if these arguments are rather serious ones so that, in a sense, they somewhat weaken the aforesaid presumption, an opinionative assent to the decree as to the *more probable* position would suffice. In fact, it can even happen that some *expert* in the field might have reasons so very serious and solid to the contrary that it would be licit for him to *suspend* all assent until infallible authority makes its intervention, meanwhile keeping a reverential silence. But this case, though possible, is certainly extremely rare, and especially at the time at which the decree is edited. Afterwards, given the passage of time and an accession of new arguments, such a position could more easily occur. Consequently, the obligation to give an internal assent must be taken as the *general, normal rule* which admits, however, of an exception, granted the latter be very rare.

Contrariwise, when the point under discussion is something clear-cut and obvious, and the error of a few rash people is quite clear so that the decree is no longer directed to doubtful matter but is simply issued to safeguard already established and certain truth, it is not surprising that the decree should exact an absolutely full and perfect subjection of the intelligence.[21] Good examples of this different aim of a decree are found in the encyclical *Humani Generis*. Besides describing the limits of free discussion in relation to a problem like evolution, the Holy Father scored the direct and obvious errors of some rash Catholics who were calling into question even fundamental truths like the existence of angels, the real presence of Christ in the Eucharist, etc.

The obligation one has to give a religious assent can, perhaps, be illustrated by this example: just as one owes obedience of the *will* to a superior who is legitimately issuing an order, unless there be present a vehement suspicion that he is commanding something dishonest, so, too, one owes to the authentic magisterium when it is teaching an obedience of the *intellect* unless in a given case there should be a mighty suspicion that it is making a mistake.

Corollary

What has been said above in reference to truths "connected" with revelation, also applies to those matters which the merely authentic magisterium proposes as "revealed" truths.

Assertion 4. The same religious assent must be given to theological truths which the theologians commonly and constantly propose as certainly to be held.

By the term *theologians* is meant here not any seminary professor, but those outstanding teachers and schools of theology which the Church herself has approved either explicitly or tacitly. The term refers especially to the great scholastic doctors (Anselm, Albert the Great, Alexander Hales, Bonaventure, Thomas Aquinas, Scotus, etc.), and the schools founded by them which have flourished from the 12th to the 18th century. (Lercher, *Institutiones Theologicae Dogmaticae*, vol. 1, no. 543; Dieckmann, *De Ecclesia*, vol. 2, no. 880). The reason these schools are singled out and enjoy a dignity superior to that of later theologians is that the Church herself either instituted these schools, or approved them and watched over them—they were pontifical institutions. The Church herself called these theologians *magistri*, gave them the mission of teaching, and established them as public masters. (Dieckmann, *op. cit.*, no. 881).

What is required in the assertion above is: (a) the agreement not of any single, particular school of theology (say, the Thomist) but a morally universal agreement of all the schools (Thomist, Scotist, Suaresian, Carmelite, etc.) and indeed an agreement not of simply one or two generations, but one which is constant.*

---

* The *Wirceburg Theologians* give this wise warning: "take care not to assert too confidently or too rashly the unanimous consent of the theologians until, at least, an inspection of the major and most celebrated authors attesting to a point begets trust that the rest do the same." (*Theologia wirceburgensis*, vol. I, no. 237). And it should be noted that later scholastic theologians often call 'común' a doctrine which indeed many authors do hold, but which many others also dispute. (See Pesch, *Praelectiones dogmaticae*, I, no. 599). This is especially true of the moral theologians who use the term "common" (in

THE OBJECT OF DIVINE FAITH

(b) This must be an agreement on the point as *certain;* for an agreement that is merely *opinionative,* however universal it might be, does not bind anyone. Finally, it is required (c) that the theologians teach, at least in equivalent terms, that the matter under scrutiny is so necessarily connected with revelation that it cannot be called into question without danger to faith or religion.

This final statement is proven from the words of Pius IX, cited above, who makes equivalent the truths we have been discussing with those which the authentic magisterium teaches. The reason for this is the intimate bond which unites the theological schools with the Church's magisterium. In virtue of this intimate bond it is altogether to be presumed that the agreement of the theological schools expresses the mind of the ordinary and universal magisterium. Consequently, you can see also that the religious assent in question is strictly given not to the theologians (they do not possess an authentic magisterium) but to the Church's magisterium whose mind is manifested with a kind of moral certitude by the theologians.

Notes

1. The words: "without [committing] sin, or injury to [injuring the] the Catholic profession of faith" are taken from the encyclical, *Quanta cura,* of Pius IX; see DB 1698.

2. See, for example, proposition 22 condemned in the *Syllabus of Errors:* "The obligation which absolutely binds Catholic teachers and writers is restricted to only those matters which are proposed by the infallible judgment of the Church as dogmas of the faith to be believed by all."—DB 1722.

3. See DB 1627.

4. See above no. 194.

5. See, for example, DB 601; 1626–1628; 1775; 1776.

6. Luke 2:2; see the Greek text.

7. See, for example, Ecclesiastes 1:5: "Sun may rise and sun may set, but ever it goes back and is reborn." (Knox translation)

8. See *Christ's Church,* nos. 87–96.

9. See above no. 200.

10. On this point see, for example, Palmieri, *De Romano Pontifice,* 2nd ed., p. 657.

11. See, for example, Schiffini, *De virtutibus,* p. 213 and Tuyaerts,

---

a looser sense) to designate a doctrine held by many reputable authors; as is obvious in this usage, the opposite opinion can also be "common," in fact, it could even be more common. (Lercher, *op. cit.,* vol. I, p. 328, note 6). Here in the assertion the term "common" is equivalent to morally universal.

l'Evolution du Dogme (Louvain 1919) p. 85 ff. This same point has been raised again recently by Garcia (see TD circa 1956) and others. Roger Aubert in his monumental *Le Problème de de l'acte de foi* (2nd ed. 1950) has some beautiful things to say about the Church acting as a sort of luminous medium through which the individual believer, in accepting her infallible teaching, is put into direct contact with God (see *op cit.*, pp. 732–737). He does not, however, directly tackle the problem of "ecclesiastical faith" or articulate in intellectual terms the precise and necessary distinction between the Church acting as God's "spokesman" in a loose sense of the term, and the Church acting strictly as an organ of revelation. Consequently, his treatment of this matter is more edifying than clarifying.

12. See Van Noort, *Christ's Church*, no. 41 (3).
13. S. Th., Ia–IIae, q. 54, a. 4, c.
14. *De Divine Traditione et Scriptura*, 3rd ed., p. 148; see also Van Noort II, *Christ's Church*, no. 198.
15. *De Synodo*, book VII, ch. 1.
16. See CIC, canon 247.
17. That the *Biblical Commission*, even though it is not a Congregation, is, in this matter, on a par with the Sacred Congregations is clear from Pius X's motu proprio, *Praestantia Sacrae Scripturae*, which will be quoted below in no. 253.
18. Examples of a congregation acting simply in the capacity of a consultant or publisher are found in DB 1619 and 1091. No. 1619 refers to the condemnation of the works of George Hermes by Gregory XVI in which the Sacred Congregation of the Index acted in the capacity of a publisher; no. 1091 contains the condemnation of the proposition that Peter and Paul were *equal* heads of the Church. This proposition (which denied the primacy of the Roman Pontiff) was condemned by Innocent X, with the Congregation of the Holy Office acting as publisher of the condemnation.
19. See, for example, Bouix, *De papa*, part II, section 5, no. 5; Vemeulen, *De romano pontificis in ferenda infra haeresim censura infallibili judicio* (Ultraj. 1874) p. 113; N. Peters, *Grundsatzl Stellung*, p. 79. This viewpoint seems to be adopted by Karl Adam in his treatment of Christ's possession of the beatific vision during his earthly life and its reconciliation with his statement about not knowing the day of judgment. Adam, in dealing with this difficult problem comes up with the rather peculiar idea that Jesus' earthly possession of the beatific vision was *potential* rather than actual. He could turn to it for knowledge or refuse to do so; in this matter he refused to turn to the Beatific vision and, hence, could say quite *literally* "of that day or hour no one knows, neither the angels, nor the son of man, but only the Father." Apart from the oddity of this bit of theologizing (which we think is definitely erroneous) Adam has to reconcile his new theory with a decree of the Holy Office June 7, 1918 stating that it was "not safe to teach" the following three points: (1) it is not certain that Christ had the beatific vision while on earth; (2) it is not certain that Christ's human knowledge was relatively omniscient; (3) the opinion of some moderns about a restricted knowledge in Christ is equally acceptable with that of older theologians about the universality of his knowledge. Karl Adam interprets this decree to mean simply that one may not

lecture in public on the opinions reprobated by the Holy Office and cites P. Dieckmann in favor of this viewpoint. Evidently, therefore, he does not accept the position that non-infallible decrees of the congregations require an internal religious assent. For his treatment of the whole problem of the beatific vision in Christ see *The Christ of Faith* (1957) pp. 266–276; for his evaluation of the binding force of the decree of the Holy Office, see *loc..,cit* pp. 271–272.

20. Letter, *Tuas libenter* (Dec. 21, 1863) to the Archbishop of Munich. See DB 1684.

21. This seems to be the case, for example, with the Apostolic Letter, *Eximiam tuam* (June 15, 1857) sent to the archbishop of Cologne in the case of Gunther, and also for the letter sent by Cardinal Patrizi, in the name of the pope, to the bishops of Belgium (August 30, 1866) in the case of Professor Ubaghs. See Granderath, *Die Machtvollkommenheit der romischen Congregationem bei Lehrdecreten*, in ZkTh (1895) p. 623.

More recently we have an example of a Roman Congregation exacting complete and perfect submission of the intelligence in the case of Fr. Feeney on the doctrine, "Outside the Church no Salvation." Here a Roman Congregation was not simply rebuking a doctrine as "unsafe," but censuring a clear-cut error—an error recognized by everyone but the Feeneyites and easily refutable by appeal to definitive papal pronouncements which had settled the same question long before Fr. Feeney even started to ruminate about it. See the letter of the Holy Office, *Haec Suprema* (August 8, 1949) to Archbishop Cushing of Boston. The latin text is given in AER 128 (1952); an English translation of the doctrinal gist of the letter is given in TCT nos. 266–280.

Article VI

THEOLOGICAL CENSURES

I. *Notion and Kinds of Censures:*
   1. Censures are *ecclesiastical* and *theological:*
      a. ecclesiastical are directed against persons;
      b. theological are directed against doctrines.

   Corollary: Theological censures should not be confused with placing books on the *Index.*

II. *The Way in Which Censures Are Inflicted:*
   1. *Categorically*: Each proposition receives its own precise censure.
   2. *In global fashion:* A number of censures, gathered together as a unit, are annexed to a whole series of propositions.
   3. Propositions may be censured "just as they lie," or, "in the author's meaning."
      a. Explanation of the censures, *just as they lie*
      b. Explanation of the censures, *in the author's meaning.*

III. *An Explanation of Some Specific Censures:*
   1. heresy;
   2. erroneous;
   3. rash;
   4. false;
   5. bad sounding;
   6. captious;
   7. offensive to pious ears.

IV. *The Use of Condemned Propositions:*
   1. One must weigh the purpose of the infliction of the censure.
   2. Inferring opposite propositions from those condemned.

V. *Theological Labels:*
   1. Why theologians use these labels.
   2. The value of theological labels.
      a. Normally these labels are fallible.
   3. Why there is no perfect uniformity in the usage of theological labels by various authors.

VI. *A Schema of Theological Labels Commonly Used Today.*

Article VI

THEOLOGICAL CENSURES*

The Church employs a twofold method in teaching us what should be believed with divine faith or held with some other fitting assent. She may *positively affirm* that a given doctrine is contained in revelation, or, at least, inextricably bound up with it; or she may *reject* doctrines as being more or less contrary to revelation. Rejected doctrines are often branded with some sort of *censure*.

256 I. Notion and Kinds of Censures

Censures fall into one of two major categories: *ecclesiastical* and *theological*. Ecclesiastical censures are those inflicted by the Church on persons who are guilty of some crime. These censures are dealt with in Canon Law. Theological censures are directed at doctrines, not persons.

A *theological* censure may be defined as: a qualification which brands some proposition as more or less harmful to faith or religion.

Theological censures are divided into: (a) *merely doctrinal* (or *private*) censures which are inflicted by theological experts who do not possess an authoritative magisterium—such, for example, were the censures inflicted in former ages by the theological faculties of universities: (b) *authoritative* (public, *judicial*) censures. These are inflicted by the Church's infallible magisterium, or, at least, by her authentic magisterium. Here we are solely concerned with the authoritative or judicial censure. Obviously a merely doctrinal or "private" censure has no more weight to it than the intelligence and arguments of the man inflicting it. Finally, it is well to recall

---

* The following works are useful, and fairly modern, studies of "theological notes" and censures: Quilliet, *Censures Doctrinales*, in DTC, vol. 2, sect. II, cols. 2101-2113; Cartechini, *De valore notarum theologicarum* (Rome, 1951); Salaverri, *Sacrae theologiae summa*, vol. I (Madrid, 1952) pp. 781-796; Healy, "Theological Qualifications and the Assent of Faith," found in CTSA (New York, 1954); Kaiser, *Sacred Doctrine* (Westminster, Md., 1958) pp. 311-319.

here the prohibition issued by Innocent XI against the rash use of censures by private theologians:

> Finally, so that doctors whether scholastic or any other people whatsoever may in the future abstain from damaging quarrels and that peace and charity may be safeguarded, the same Holy Pontiff orders them under holy obedience, both in printed books and manuscripts and in theses, disputations and sermons as well, to avoid every censure and note and also all violent outcries against those propositions which are still disputed here or there among Catholics until the matter has been brought to the attention of the Holy See and a judgment passed upon those same propositions. (DB 1216)

Corollary

Theological censures should not be confused with either the mere prohibition of the reading of some book, which occurs by placing it on the *Index*, or with disciplinary decrees which, for the sake of peace and to avoid scandal, forbid for a time the public defense of some doctrine, or order some public controversy to be discontinued.

II. The Way in Which Censures Are Inflicted

1. Censures may be inflicted either categorically, or in global fashion.

a. *Categorically*. A censure is said to be inflicted categorically when each individual proposition deserving condemnation has annexed to it the precise censure which belongs to it. Frequently, several censures may be attached to a given proposition. These should not be taken to be synonymous for they express different degrees of reprobation. The most famous example of categorical censures is found in the bull of Pius VI: *Auctorem fidei*.[1]

b. *In global fashion*. Censures are inflicted globally, or in cumulative fashion, when one finds not individual censures attached to individual propositions, but rather a number of censures gathered together as a unit and annexed to a *whole series* of propositions. Such censures are said to belong to the propositions *respectively*, that is, each individual proposition adduced deserves at least one of the annexed censures, and each of the annexed censures refers to at least one of the series of propositions. An example of this global type censure is found in the condemnation of the propositions of Michael de Molinos and Quesnel.[2]

258   2. Propositions may be censured "just as they lie," or, "in the author's meaning."

a. They are said to be condemned *just as they lie* when the propositions such as they are found in the decree of condemnation, even apart from any inspection of the context from which they were extracted, obviously exhibit a meaning which deserves condemnation. An example of this is found in Denzinger-Bannwart's *Enchiridion Symbolorum,* nos. 1151–1212.

b. They are said to be condemned *"in the author's meaning"* when the propositions taken concretely, i.e., as found in the author's work from which they were extracted, possess a perverse connotation but are expressed in such fashion that gazed at nakedly in themselves (such as they are found in the document condemning them) they could still reasonably be interpreted as having an orthodox sense. Notice very carefully that "the author's meaning" does *not* signify the meaning which the author himself may have in his own mind; it signifies that meaning which the words as found in this author's book and in this context express *objectively.* An example of condemnation "in the author's meaning" is found in Denzinger's *Enchiridion,* nos. 1001–1079.

To this condemnatory category of "the author's meaning" are also referred those cases in which a proposition is censured, not precisely because of the very meaning directly disclosed by the words, but either because of the *manner* of its utterance—which is injurious or scandalous—or because of the *implied* tendency or implied meaning of the author. Examples of this type censure are found in Denzinger-Bannwart, nos. 1441, 1525, 1450; for the implied meaning of the author was this: all these points are verified in us, the Jansenists.

259   **III. An Explanation of Some Specific Censures**

A great number of censures are listed by the theologians. Those most frequently used are found in the Constitution, *Unigenitus,* of Clement XI, and in the Bull, *Auctorem fidei,* of Pius VI.[3] We shall explain the significance of only the major censures and such censures as pose some special difficulty.

1. *Heresy.* A proposition is said to be heretical which is definitely and directly opposed, either in contradictory or contrary

fashion, to a *dogma** in the strict sense. A doctrine is said to be "notoriously" heretical if from the very terms in which it is couched it obviously contradicts a dogma which has been solemnly defined.

Akin to "heresy" are the following censures:

a. *Close to heresy*. This means a proposition which is directly opposed to a doctrine which is close to faith.⁴

b. *Smacking of heresy*. This means a proposition which offers serious grounds for fearing a heresy may be hidden within it. If the grounds for fearing heresy are reasonable indeed, but not so serious, the proposition is said to be *"suspected" of heresy*. Some propositions in themselves smack of heresy. For example: "It is ridiculous to carry the Eucharist about through the public streets"; others smack of heresy only because of the circumstantial background of the people uttering them, or the eras in which they appear. For example, "faith justifies" in the mouth of a Lutheran, or, "Christ is less than the Father"² in the mouth of an Arian; or "Christ is a paragon of behaviour"³ or, "a model of humanity,"⁴ in the mouth of a liberal Protestant. You will find other examples in Denzinger, *Enchiridion*, nos. 1522, 1528.

2. *Erroneous*.† A proposition is described as erroneous if it is directly opposed to a truth which is absolutely certain, and at least inextricably bound up with revealed doctrine.⁵

I say: "*at least* inextricably *bound up* with revealed doctrine," because the censure of "error" is also applied to a proposition opposed to a doctrine that is not only certain but also held by most theologians to be revealed. For a doctrine of this sort will frequently be "close to faith" and hence it follows that every proposition which is "close to heresy" is also "erroneous," but not vice versa. In stating this we are following the opinion of Cardinal

---

* Consequently it is clear that to have a heresy it is required that the doctrine under attack be one which is: (a) revealed; and (b) clearly proposed by the Church for our belief. A doctrine or teaching which attacks a doctrine that is truly revealed but not yet clearly proposed as such by the Church can be called *material* heresy; but it is not strictly (formal) heresy because the notion of heresy includes the idea of opposition to the common profession of faith of the whole Church. It should be clear, too, that "objective" heresy does not necessarily imply *subjective* heresy. For a doctrine which is actually heretical can be innocently proposed by someone who has no heretical intention and consequently does not commit the crime of heresy.

† Here we are discussing the *specific* connotation of this censure; for if one uses the term "error" in a broader sense, it is obvious that the term also embraces outright heresies: as, for example, when one speaks of "the *Syllabus of 80 Errors*."

Franzelin;[5] for theologians disagree somewhat in pinpointing the specific notion of "error."

3. *Rash*[6] means a proposition which, without any sufficient grounds, departs from a theological teaching which is truly common in the Church, or which opposes practices or institutions which have been approved by the Church. Examples of this censure are found in Denzinger, *Enchiridion*, nos. 1540, 1531, 1544. The characteristic note of "rashness" is found in this, that serious authority in matters of faith and morals is brushed aside as of little account. —These three censures, *heretical*, *erroneous*, and *rash* are the main censures.

260   4. *False.* The censure of falseness is divergently explained by different authors. Some say: "falsity" should not be taken as a specific censure but rather as a generic qualification belonging to every injurious proposition in its own fashion. Others consider it a specific censure which is akin to the censure of "error"; for, they say, a proposition is designated as false which is contrary to a truth or a fact which is bound up with revelation as a necessary presupposition.[7]

5. *Bad sounding* means a proposition which expresses a meaning that is in harmony with the faith, but expresses it in incongruous terms. Obviously, in this type of censure much depends upon the native characteristics of various languages. So, for example, the following sounds bad to Latins, but not to the Greeks: "the Father is the *cause* of the Son";[8] likewise it would have a bad ring to a Dutch ear to describe the Blessed Virgin as: "the *divine* Mother" (i.e., a goddess) instead of "the Mother of God."

6. *Captious* is the censure given to a proposition which expresses a perverted meaning in well-sounding terms. See, for example, Denzinger, *Enchiridion*, no. 1368.

7. *Offensive to pious ears* is the censure given to a proposition which offends the reverence due to holy things by its manner of utterance. As, for example, this prayer: "St. Mary Magdalen, prostitute, pray for us." The term "pious ears," referred to, do not mean exclusively elderly ladies in a sodality, but well instructed Catholics anywhere who would be justifiably offended by an irreverent treatment of holy things.

261   **IV. The Use of Condemned Propositions**

A knowledge of the propositions on which the ecclesiastical

magisterium has inflicted some censure is very useful to the theologian. From them he learns not only what to avoid, but also what he ought to hold; for the manifestation of an error by its very nature lays open the opposite truth. However, to have an intelligent* understanding of what precisely the Church means to reject by her censure and precisely what doctrine should as a consequence be retained as sound, we add these further *precisions:*

I. One must weigh the question of whether the censure has been inflicted because of the very meaning of the proposition, or only because of its manner of utterance, or because of the implied intention of the author. It is easy to see that if a proposition has been condemned simply because of its manner of utterance, one cannot therefrom infer the falsehood of the proposition itself, nor come to any conclusion about the truth of an opinion which is contradictorily opposed to it.

The censure, *not safe,* even though it begets a large presumption that the proposition under scrutiny is false does not guarantee that point necessarily.

II. When a proposition has been censured because of its very meaning, the teaching which is *contradictorily* opposed to it should be accepted as the true and sound (or, at least, as "safe" teaching).

I say: *contradictorily* opposed. Since two *contrary* propositions

---

* Quilliet, in his article on doctrinal censures (DTC, vol. 2, part 2, no. VII, cols. 2101–2103) gives the following wise advice about not misusing censured propositions in theological work: "To interpret a theological censure correctly, to gain an exact appreciation of its value, and to make an irreproachable and adequate use of it, it is important before all else to determine precisely its character and its particular bearing. . . . Once that has been done, the *value* of the censure can be measured according to its character and according to the authority which inflicted it. For the censures passed by the supreme authority, it is useful to remember here that to discover the exact thought and teaching of the Church, it *does not always suffice to take the contradictory of condemned propositions.*

Among the censures we have seen, there is one which presents an undeniable character of *relativity*: I mean those propositions which are condemned because of their *form* or their *bad effects.* Without doubt one must always scrupulously admit and hold that such propositions are condemned and forbidden. At the same time it is necessary to be careful not to draw exaggerated conclusions, precipitous or false conclusions, as if one had only to reverse the condemnations and one would have the truth with certainty. We must not forget in such cases that the elision of an unfortunate or wrong-sounding term can render orthodox a bad-sounding proposition. Again, a change in circumstances can modify to the point of making disappear the injurious character of this or that assertion."

DIVINE FAITH

can be simultaneously false, the condemnation of one of them does not allow us to infer the truth of the other. Furthermore:

a. One must accurately determine the exact meaning which has been condemned in the proposition. For this it is often necessary to consult the very documents which contain and can clarify the meaning of the condemned propositions. See, for example, Denzinger, *Enchiridion*, nos. 1762 and 1780. Especially one must notice whether the condemned proposition is condemned in absolute or only in qualified fashion. See, for example, Denzinger, *Enchiridion*, nos. 1093 and 1096 giving the following condemned propositions of Cornelius Jansen: 1093 states: "In the state of fallen nature *no one ever* resists interior grace"; condemnation: "declared and condemned as heretical." 1096 states: "It is Semi-Pelagian to say that Christ died or shed his blood for all men whatsoever." Condemnation: "Declared and condemned as false, rash, scandalous, and *understood in the sense* that Christ died for the predestined alone, wicked, blasphemous, insulting, derogatory to divine piety, and heretical."

b. In *complex* propositions, one must see whether they have been censured in a complex sense or in a distributive sense. To determine this point, in addition to consulting the documents containing the condemnation, one must sometimes also look to the analogy of faith.* See, for example, Denzinger, *Enchiridion*, nos. 1184, 1186, and 1763.

261a V. Theological Labels

As has been seen above, the Church in her official teaching makes use of both positive and negative teaching; affirming what is to be held and rejecting what is to be denied by the faithful in matters of faith and morals. The notes used by the Church are official or authoritative qualifications. They may be infallible or fallible judgments depending upon the intention of the Church's official magisterium. We now wish to consider briefly what were described above as "merely doctrinal" or "private notes and censures." Theologians wishing to expound the Church's official teaching and also theological theories, naturally wish to do so in as scientific a way as possible. It has been customary, therefore, for

---

* The analogy of faith means the necessary interdependence and harmony of all the Christian mysteries.

THE OBJECT OF DIVINE FAITH

theological manuals to formulate precise "theses" or to sum up doctrine in exact and succinct propositions, somewhat the way geometrical theorems are enunciated, and then to go on to explain and prove the contents of the propositions by adducing proofs from the official magisterium, from Scripture, Tradition, and reason. So, we may read in a theological manual a proposition like: "There are seven and only seven sacraments of the New Law," or "The Son proceeds from the Father by way of intellectual generation." These succinct propositions have the advantage of laying before the theological tyro the heart of the matter to be discussed; they sum up much in a few technically exact phrases that destroy all ambiguity, prevent muddled apprehension and so make for easy memory retention. Appended to such propositions or theses, the theologians usually add, wherever possible, a theological note or "label" to indicate to the student the theological "value" or degree of certitude which attaches to the given proposition. It will be labeled as "of faith," or "proximate to faith," or "theologically certain," or, negatively, as "erroneous," "heretical," "rash," etc.

What is the value of these labels? Only a few general points need be made here. First, these labels are, by the very source from which they stem, normally fallible. Theologians do not possess an official magisterium, either infallible or fallible—that office pertains to the pope and bishops. The only exception to this generic principle is the case in which the theologians are morally unanimous (as explained above, see no. 207a) in holding a doctrine to be of faith or morals—in which case they are said to be infallible because their morally unanimous consent throughout long ages and all around the world can only be explained on the basis that their teaching reflects the teaching of the universal Church on this or that point of doctrine. Secondly, if a theologian labels a proposition with a note which the Church herself has already given—a judicial, infallible note—to a specific teaching, the note is infallible because it is simply a presentation in a manual of the Church's own note. In all other cases than those just mentioned, the theological note is taken to be a fallible judgment. It has of course a real authority to it as being the judgment of a theological expert the same as the judgment of any expert in his own field.

Again, it should be noted in general that there is no perfect *uniformity* among theological authors in the usage of various labels. They may express the same theological judgment with a slightly

(289)

DIVINE FAITH

THEOLOGICAL LABELS

Theological label	Requisites	Assent deserved	Opposite Censure
I. Of Faith "Divine & Catholic F." "Dogma of F." "of defined F."	1. A truth *revealed* by God 2. *Proposed* by the Church *as* revealed.	Act of divine and Catholic Faith	HERESY
II. Of Divine Faith	1. A truth *revealed* by God 2. *Not* yet proposed, or not clearly proposed by the Church	Act of divine faith	Error in divine faith
III. Proximate to F.	Intimately bound up with revealed doctrine, if not actually revealed.	Assent of Certitude	Proximate to heresy
IV. Of Ecclesiastical Faith	1. Infallibly proposed by the Church *as true*	Assent of Certitude	Error in Ecclesiastical Faith
V. Theologically Certain	A conclusion strictly deduced from one revealed premise and one rational premise	Assent of Certitude	Error
VI. Catholic Teaching*	Taught everywhere throughout the Catholic world, but not necessarily infallibly.	At minimum: Assent of religious obedience	Rash
VII. Safe Teaching	Does not contradict any known truth	Opinionative assent	Unsafe

* The label "Catholic Teaching" is an elastic one. It may be used to cover a variety of assents all the way from "religious obedience," to an "assent of faith." It is often used by theologians when they are unable or unwilling to make a more precise judgment of the matter. Thus the label "Catholic teaching" can be used to describe the contents of an encyclical, viewed as a whole without descending to particular propositions enunciated within the encyclical.

variant turn of phrase. So, one author may simply dub a proposition as: "of faith," whereas another may spell it out precisely as: "of divine and Catholic faith"; one may simply list a proposition as "certain" where another uses the more precise terms, "theologically certain" or "certain by authority." There is room for some confusion in this, though none for dismay. One should not be surprised that the science of theology, like every other science, tends to grow ever more exact as it reaches maturity. Its methodology while remaining substantially the same tends to become more or less precise in accord with the seriousness or lack of it with which theology is pursued in different eras. Consequently, one cannot expect more ancient theologians to have at their disposal technical vocabulary which was invented only at a later era. Their judgments and their reasonings are more important to us than their critical apparatus. Consequently in inspecting the theological labels given to various propositions by different authors it is often necessary to know the way a particular author is accustomed to use his labels. Without pretending that the preceding schema is necessarily the best delineation of these labels, or one that ought to be adopted, we do prefer it as one that is fairly commonly employed by many modern authors and useful to that extent.

Notes

1. See DB no. 1501 and ff.
2. See DB nos. 1121–1288, and nos. 1351–1451.
3. See DB no. 1451 and 1501–1593.
4. See above margin number 212, no. 4.
5. *De Traditione* (3rd ed.) p. 151.
6. Here, again, we are singling out the *specific* connotation of this censure; it may also occur in looser usage.
7. So, for example, G. M. Jansen, *Prelectiones dogmaticae*, vol. I, p. 871.
8. See S. Th., 1a, q. 33, art. 1.

CHAPTER II

The Act of Divine Faith

PROPOSITION: *The Act of Saving Faith is Elicited by the Intellect, At the Command of the Will, and Under the Help of Divine Grace*

    Explanation of the Proposition:
        1. The intellect's part;
        2. The will's part;
        3. The part of grace.

Proof:
    1. First part: the intellectuality of faith
        a. from Sacred Scripture
        b. from Tradition
    2. Second part: intervention of the will
        a. from Sacred Scripture
        b. from Tradition
    3. Third part: the need for grace
        a. from Sacred Scripture
        b. from Tradition

Corollary: Meaning of: "the beginning of faith" and the "pious will to believe."
    1. In analyzing the supernatural act of faith, theologians usually list an orderly series of steps preceding the act of faith.
        a. a brief discussion of the steps.
    2. An historical error about "the beginning of faith":
        a. the Council of Orange did not use this phrase in the same sense as later theology uses it.

CHAPTER II

The Act of Divine Faith

To present an orderly exposition of the nature, genesis, and properties of divine faith, we shall divide the material as follows. Article I will discuss the subjective principles (intellect, will, grace) which produce the act of faith; Article II will discuss the preparation requisite for arriving at faith; Article III will analyze the act of faith itself; Article IV will discuss the properties of faith (truthfulness, obscurity, freedom, and firmness); Article V will discuss which persons are capable of making an act of faith and the necessity of making that act. Finally, as an Appendix, we shall discuss the relationship between faith and science.

Article I

THE SUBJECTIVE PRINCIPLES WHICH PRODUCE THE ACT OF FAITH

265 PROPOSITION. *The act of saving faith is elicited by the intellect, at the command of the will, and under the help of divine grace.*

The proposition lists the three causes, or subjective principles, which must concur in producing the act of faith: intelligence, will, and grace.

The *intellect* is the immediate center, or faculty, or the *principle which elicits* an act of faith. This point must be maintained contrary to the viewpoint of the original Protestants, most present-day Protestants, and many other modern thinkers. Sixteenth century Protestants (along with many contemporary ones) in asserting that a firm conviction about one's own justification belongs to the very essence of faith itself, taught that "the assent of faith belongs more to the heart than to the brain, and more to the will (or emotions) than the intelligence."[1] Many modern writers reduce faith to a kind of "religious sense" or affection. It is *certain* that the act of faith is an *intellectual* act from the teaching of the Vatican Council which defines faith as the virtue by which "we believe *as true* those matters revealed by God,"[2] etc. The same point is brought out even more vigorously in the oath against Modernism.

The *will* is the principle which *commands* faith. This point is itself *of faith* from the Catholic dogma on the freedom of the act of faith. Faith's freedom will be discussed at length below in Chapter IV which deals with the properties of faith. Notice, also, that the command of the will determining the intelligence to the assent of faith is, insofar as it stems from grace, usually described by theologians as the *pious* will to believe.*

Grace is the principle which *elevates* or *supernaturalizes* the act

---

* The term "pious" will is misleading in English here. The real equivalent for *"pious* will to believe" is: "the *supernatural* will to believe." A fuller discussion of this phrase and its historical significance will be found below in no. 269, corollary.

of faith. Grace is required so that the act of faith may be of such a kind that it is "the beginning of human salvation, the foundation and root of all holiness" (Council of Trent). Divine grace, in other words, is necessary if the act of faith is to be saving or supernatural, for the intellect and will are simply physically incapable of producing a supernatural act unless they are elevated and activated by a supernatural influx from God. The necessity of grace holds for all truly salutary (saving) faith. In other words, it holds not only for "formed" or "living" faith, i.e., the faith of a man living in the state of grace; it holds also for "unformed" or "dead" faith, i.e., the faith of a man who truly believes all the truths of Christianity but nevertheless lives on in a state of mortal sin. This point is of some importance not simply as a protest against the errors of the 16th century reformers who confused faith with hope and charity and thought that a man who did not live a good life showed "ipso facto" that he did not have genuine faith; it is a point about which even contemporary Catholics and others sometimes become confused, v.g., by implying that a Catholic living a bad life must necessarily have lost the faith. This confusion is begotten from a twofold source: (a) forgetting that faith is essentially an *intellectual* act, an acceptance of something as true because God has said so; (b) forgetting that man has a free will, that he may choose to act against what he knows to be right. A doctor knows the rules of health very well, but he may disregard them and become a physical wreck, the while retaining his medical knowledge; so, too, a Christian knows the rules of spiritual good health, but may flaunt those rules and become a spiritual wreck, the while he retains his knowledge. We say this point is of some importance because it helps priests and other apostolic minded people in dealing with hardened sinners. Every priest runs up against Catholics who are ten, twenty, thirty years away from the sacraments; when they turn around suddenly by God's grace and go to confession they do not begin to "believe" the Apostles Creed; they simply begin to *act* upon it. We might compare the state of a man living in mortal sin but who still retains the supernatural equipment of faith to a house in which all the lights are out, because the bulbs have burned out or the fuses, but the wiring remains intact. It is relatively easy to replace light bulbs or fuses, but it is an entirely different story if the wiring has been ripped out and the electrical circuitry destroyed by the denial of the truths of the faith; the job of restoring light and heat and music to such a house is a much more difficult enterprise.

The necessity of grace for making an act of faith is itself a *dogma of faith* as is clear from these words of the Vatican Council:

> No one can consent to the teaching of the gospel in the way that is necessary to obtain salvation without the illumination and inspiration of the Holy Spirit . . . consequently faith itself and in itself, even if it does not work through charity, is a gift of God.[3]

Finally, since the necessity of grace for making any act supernatural (including the act of faith) pertains more to the volume on *Christ's Grace* we omit any fuller explanation of it here. We shall, however, advert to the fact, later on in the analysis of the act of faith itself, that modern theologians have re-emphasized the need of recognizing the role of grace in the act of faith more so than the nineteenth century theologians who were more concerned with defending the reasonableness of faith, against the attacks of rationalists, than its supernatural and mystical aspects.

266 *Proof of the proposition:*

1. First part: the intellectuality of faith

a. From *Sacred Scripture*. Obviously one should not look into the New Testament to find an elaborate, abstract, theological discussion of the nature and properties of faith, replete with definitions and distinctions and arguments; nor even an isolated concentration on this one aspect—the intellectual—of the complex act we call faith. Scripture is not a scientific enterprise that marshals its doctrine in neat thought categories, and logically demonstrates in orderly fashion the truths it contains and the interconnection and over-all harmony of those truths, or even the inner logical coherence of each of those truths considered in themselves. Rather, Scripture is the word of God given to us in simple, concrete, often imagistic fashion: it aims not simply at scientific exposition, but at conviction and persuasion and so is replete with metaphors, irony, rebukes, impassioned pleas, animadvertences to concrete circumstances of time, place, particular communities, individuals and the like. Theology, on the other hand, does proceed in scientific fashion: face to face with the raw data of revelation presented in the word of God it seeks to draw together in logical grouping, to isolate and to compare, to marshal arguments, and to draw conclusions and, finally, to give us a coherent, over-all view of the contents of revelation. In a word, it concentrates on the *intelligible* aspect of revelation, prescinding from what is moving or persuasive, or what is merely circumstantial, as must any science. Consequently only someone extremely naive would expect to find in Scripture a scientific presentation of any doctrine, or, vice versa, would be irritated because theology presents its material in abstract, dry, logical fashion rather than in the living language of God's word.

With all that said, one should still expect to find in Sacred Scripture some clear-cut indications, even though not in a scientific mode of presentation, that faith has an intellectual aspect to it. And so it is. But before listing some of the specific texts establishing this point, it is well to bear in mind that the Scriptural usage of faith is usually a more global, more complex notion than a simple acceptance of truth on God's word. The term *pistis* usually presents the living act of faith in a living person as the response of the whole person to an encounter with God; consequently it shows, one might say, the "normal" condition of faith—that is, faith accompanied by hope and prodding one to charity, rather than in its "abnormal," or merely "abstractive," condition as separated from charity in the case of a sinner, or mentally isolated from its vital effects in the mind of a theologian for purposes of more detailed study. The words of Roger Aubert on this point are appropos and penetrating:

> Let us start by observing that it is necessary to use texts with great care when one runs across the terms *pistis* or *pisteuein*. *Pistis* is actually a complex notion, which greatly surpasses faith in the actual theological use of the term. Already revelation *apokalipsis*, appears in Scripture in a fashion much more expanded and concrete, less notional, than in Scholastic theology: it is the descent upon earth of the Messianic Kingdom and messianic benefits, offered to men of good will. So, too, *pistis*, man's response to this offering of divine goods, is conceived as a vital act, as an attitude taken up by the whole personality which submits to the new economy of salvation and aligns itself with Christ; as an insertion into the divine work to which one abandons oneself

with a complete submission of heart and an absolute confidence in the efficacy of the redemption brought by Christ. This complex character of faith which includes not only confidence in God and hope in the realization of his promises, but even the adoption of a new life, is actually recognized by Catholic authors, even conservative ones. Finally, it is this complex character which explains the unequaled (*hors pair*) importance of *pistis* as a principle of justification: in a word, *pistis* constitutes the fundamental Christian attitude at the conclusion of the total process of conversion.

On the other hand, it is beyond doubt that this total orientation of the person converted, necessarily implies an intellectual element; for to hand oneself over body and soul to God and to His Son, Jesus Christ, it is obviously necessary to have some knowledge of who they are, of what they expect of us and of what they promise us in exchange. And the further away one became from the living impression Christ had made on those who had been conquered among his following the more it became important to define very sharply Jesus' message, to strike down false opinions and deviations of every sort, in a word, to present an orthodox doctrine, a doctrine which would permit the Christian to think correctly about the religious object to which he was orienting himself.

This point is quite clear in the Joanine writings where it is often a question of believing sharply delineated truths concerning Christ and his prerogatives and where faith is presented as a homage to God's truthfulness, something which proves clearly that it is more than a question of simple confidence in God's goodness. But the same holds even for St. Paul, and Protestants themselves are more and more beginning to recognize that the Pauline *pistis* implies along with confidence in Jesus Christ, the knowledge of his work as contained in the gospel preached by the missionaries. Doubtless in St. Paul, who does not exhibit the theory of the Logos, the notion of revelation has not the same importance as in St. John, and for Paul, Christ is rather the Saviour than the Teacher, more the source of divine energy than the principle of Truth. Nonetheless the doctrinal aspect of faith appears in the great epistles and St. Paul, in the Captivity epistles, proves the need of forewarning neo-converts against the peril of false doctrines. He considers as an essential element of spiritual progress true knowledge of the providential plan revealed by God and of the fact that the apostles have received it as their mission to make known that plan.

It is to this aspect of knowledge in the notion of *pistis* that there corresponds the act of faith and virtue of faith described by later theology. (Roger Aubert, *Le Probleme de l'acte du foi*, 2nd ed. 1950, pp. 3–5).

In the *synoptics:* The term *pistis*, in the sense of accepting statements or facts *as true* appears at least thirteen times in the synoptic gospels: five times in Mark, six times in Luke, and twice in Matthew.[4] While it occurs with almost double that frequency in the sense of *trust* in a person[5] these instances suffice to show that the intellectual element in faith was never totally absent from the Christian teaching. For example, Mark 16:9–20 shows faith clearly in the sense of accepting as true the fact of Jesus' Resurrection and also the acceptance of the gospel message as a whole: *"And they hearing that he was alive and had been seen by her, did not believe it"* (Mark 16:11).... *"At length he appeared to the Eleven as they were at table; and he upbraided them for their lack of faith and hardness of heart, in that they had not believed those who had seen him after he had risen. And he said to them: 'Go into the whole world and preach the gospel to every creature. He who believes and is baptized shall be saved, but he who does not believe shall be condemned* (Mark 16:14–17).

In *St. Luke*, Zachary is struck dumb for refusing to believe the angel's message that his barren wife would conceive a son: *"I am Gabriel who stands in the presence of God; and I have been sent to speak to thee and bring thee this good news. And behold thou shalt be dumb and unable to speak until the day when these things come to pass, because thou hast not believed my words, which will be fulfilled in their proper time"* (Luke 1:19–20). The Virgin Mary, on the other hand, is singled out for praise because she believed as true the angel's prediction that she miraculously conceive the Messias: *"And blessed is she who has believed, because the things promised her by the Lord shall be accomplished"* (Luke 1:45). In St. Matthew, too, acceptance of someone's word as true is the meaning of Christ's warning about false Christs who would appear in the last days: *"Then if anyone say to you, 'behold, here is the Christ,' or 'there he is,' do not believe it. For false Christs and false prophets will arise and will show great signs and wonders, so as to lead astray, if possible, even the elect. Behold, I have told it to you beforehand. If therefore they say to you, 'Behold he is in the desert,' do not go forth; 'behold he is in the inner chambers' do not believe it"* (Matthew 24:23–26).

b. The *Joanine* writings are so replete with the notion of faith or belief in the sense of "accepting as true," it seems almost superfluous to cite specific instances. Suffice it then to recall that John's purpose in writing his gospel was to establish as true the divinity of Christ and the specific promise of the Eucharist: *"Many other signs also Jesus worked in the sight of his disciples, which are not written in this book. But these are written that you may believe that Jesus is the Christ, the Son of God, and that believing, you may have life in his name"* (John 20:30–31). After the discourse on "the bread from heaven" when the unbelieving crowd and many of His disciples melted away, Jesus made belief in the truth of His promise a condition for remaining with Him: *"Jesus then said to the twelve: 'are you, too, minded to go away?' Simon Peter spoke up: 'Lord' he said to him, 'to whom shall we go? You have a message of eternal life; we firmly believe and are fully convinced that you are the Holy One of God'"* (John 6:67–70).

c. The *Pauline* writings also unmistakably bear out the intellectual element of faith: *"For if you confess with your lips that Jesus is the Lord, and believe in your heart that God raised him from the dead, you shall be saved. Because with the heart a man believes and attains holiness, and with the lips profession of faith is made and salvation secured"* (Romans 10:9). Again we see described in *Hebrews* explicit acceptance of two doctrines is demanded of the believer as a "sine qua non" of salvation: *"Without faith it is impossible to please God, since whoever comes to God must believe that he exists and rewards those that seek him . . . by faith we understand that the world was fashioned by God's word in such a way that what is visible has an invisible cause"* (Hebrews 11:6 and 3). Again, *Sacred Scripture* clearly distinguishes faith from both hope and charity. It juxtaposes faith as obscure knowledge* to vision and asserts that trust (fiducia) and charity are possessed through faith, that is, that they arise from faith:[6] Illustrative of the point is this famous passage from St. Paul: *"Charity never fails, whereas prophecies will disappear and tongues will cease, and knowledge will be destroyed. For we know in part and we prophesy in part; but when that which is perfect has come, that which is imperfect will be done away with. . . . We see now through a mirror in an obscure manner, but then face to*

---

* See below, Faith's Obscurity, No. 307–312, for detailed consideration of this point.

face. Now I know in part, but then I shall know even as I have been known. So there abide faith, hope and charity, these three: but the greatest of these is charity" (I Corinthians 13:8–13).

d. Finally *St. James,* in the famous passage on "faith without good works is dead" which Luther expurgated, clearly distinguishes faith from virtuous living and indicated that it could exist without bearing any fruit. That he means faith in the sense of acceptance of something as true is quite clear from his ironic reference to the fact that devils also accept truths: "Thou believest that there is one God. Thou dost well. The devils also believe, and tremble." (See the whole passage: James 2:14–26).

Other[3] scriptural texts could be adduced but those already given are more than sufficient to show that the object of faith is truth. That is why St. Thomas is right in concluding that: "to believe is directly an act of the intellect because the object of this act is truth which properly belongs to the intellect."

e. From *Tradition:*

The witness of Tradition to the intellectuality of faith is found in the primordial custom of exacting from catechumens a profession of faith in the main mysteries of the Christian religion, as summed up in the Apostles Creed. That very fact shows unmistakably the constant conviction of the Church that the faith "which is the beginning of justification" is an intellectual assent to revealed mysteries and not at all a firm conviction (fiducia) about one's own personal justification.

2. Second part: intervention of the will*

267

a. *Church's Magisterium.* The fact that the will must intervene in bringing about the assent of faith is clear from the Vatican Council's teaching on the freedom of the act of faith: a man who believes is not necessitated to do so by rational arguments, but he offers to God a free obedience:

> Faith itself and in itself, even if it does not work through charity, is a gift of God, and its act is a work pertaining to salvation; by it a man offers to God Himself a *free* obedience insofar as he consents and cooperates with his grace which he *could* refuse ... if anyone says that the assent of Christian faith

* For a detailed consideration of the work of the will see below, no. 313 ff.

is *not free,* but is necessarily produced by arguments of human reason; or that God's grace is only necessary for that living faith which works through charity, let him be anathema. (Constitution, *De Fide,* ch. 3 and canon 5 [DB 1791 and 1814], itals. ours.)

b. From *Sacred Scripture:* The fact that the intervention of the will is necessary is implied in all those Scriptural loci in which faith is commanded and a reward is promised to those who believe, while punishment is threatened to those who refuse to believe. Obviously, one can deserve a reward or a punishment only if an action is in one's own control, or free; and God does not command one to do what is either mechanistically determined or impossible of doing. A few texts suffice to establish this point: *"His commandment is this, that we should believe in the name of His Son, Jesus Christ, and love one another. . . ."* (1 John 3:32); *"Go into the whole world and preach the gospel to all creation. He that believes and is baptized will be saved; he that does not believe will be condemned"* (Mark 16:15–16).

c. From *Tradition:* As early as the second century we have a statement by St. Irenaeus, indicating that the early Church was fully aware of the act of faith as a free act, even under the influence of grace:

> Not only in works but even in faith the Lord has kept the mind of man free and in his own power. And for this reason he who believes him has eternal life; but he who does not believe the Son does not have eternal life but the wrath of God will remain upon him.[8]

268 3. Third part: the need for grace

a. From the *Church's Magisterium.* The necessity of grace to produce the supernatural act of faith is clear from the statements of the Vatican Council (Constitution, *De Fide,* ch. 3) cited above in no. 267.

---

* Here we have reverted to the Confraternity Translation because KL while readable, somewhat obscures the doctrinal import of these texts by some unhappy stylistic transpositions. An important idea, loosely thrown into subordinate sentence structure or misplaced from the viewpoint of English emphasis, can easily be lost sight of altogether. Compare, for example, KL with the Confrat. ed. on John 6:43.

THE ACT OF DIVINE FAITH

b. From *Sacred Scripture:**

Do not be terrified in any way by the adversaries, for this is to them a reason for destruction, but to you for salvation, and that from God. For you have been given the favor on Christ's behalf —not only to believe in him, but also to suffer for him (Philippians 1:28–30).[9]

Ephesians 2:8: *For by grace you have been saved through faith; and that not from yourselves, for it is the gift of God; not as the outcome of works, lest anyone may boast.*[10]

John 6:43–46: *. . . Jesus said to them, "Do not murmur among yourselves. No one can come to me unless the Father who sent me draw him, and I will raise him up on the last day. It is written in the Prophets, 'And they shall all be taught of God.' Everyone who has listened to the Father, and has learned, comes to me. . . . The words that I have spoken to you are spirit and life. But there are some among you who do not believe."* For Jesus knew from the beginning who they were who did not believe, and who it was who should betray him.
And he said, *"This is why I have said to you, 'No one can come to me unless he is enabled to do so by my Father'"* (John 6:64–67).

The context of the above quotation is, of course, the promise of the Eucharist. While the discourse has as its main theme the nature and effects of this marvelous bread from heaven, there is no doubt[8] that faith is clearly indicated as a necessary means to accept this Eucharistic promise and that the faith needed is a gift of God who works interiorly in the believer's soul. The full meaning, therefore, of verses 44 and 66 is: "No one can come to me (*by faith*) unless my Father draw him."

c. From *Tradition.* St. Augustine, commenting on the text, "no one can come to me (by faith) unless the Father who sent me draw him," states:

And yet no one comes unless he wills to. He is drawn, therefore, in marvelous ways to will by Him who knows how to work interiorly in the very hearts of men; not that men—something which is impossible—should believe unwillingly, but that from being unwilling they should be rendered willing."[11]

And elsewhere Augustine writes:

> God acts with suasions that we may will and believe; what is more, God Himself brings about in a man the very will to believe.[12]

269 Corollary

Meaning of: "Beginning of Faith" and "Pious will to believe."

In analyzing the supernatural act of faith, theologians usually try to give an orderly listing of the series of steps which should, in the case of an adult, normally *precede* the actual act of faith itself. All of these steps are grouped under the label: *preambles to faith.* Without insisting that all of these steps must be present and articulated in the mind of the individual convert in real life, they mean that these are the normal steps which should be taken by a human mind if its approach to faith is to be reasonable and not simply a wild leap into the dark. Since the act of faith is not simply a work of God, but also a work of man's mind the theologians expect the mind to follow its normal methods of rumination, albeit enlightened and strengthened by God's grace. Now if a man is to act rationally in accepting something as true because God has said so, he must:

1. be sure that God is truthful (certitude about God's authority)
2. be sure that God has spoken (certitude about the fact of revelation)
3. see that it is *prudent* and reasonable to accept truths solely on God's authority (judgment of credibility)
4. see that he has an *obligation* to accept what God has revealed (judgment of credentity)
5. *order* his intelligence to accept God's revelation (pious will to believe)
6. *accept* intellectually what God has revealed. (assent of faith, or the act of faith itself.)

These various steps might be listed as a series of mental affirmations, variously enuntiated by individuals, but somewhat along this line: 1. "I know that God is truth itself and cannot lie"; 2. "I am sure that God has spoken through Jesus Christ"; 3. "It certainly seems *reasonable* to accept what Christ has taught"; 4. "I *must* believe Christ's teaching because God obliges me to"; 5. "Go ahead, believe!"; 6. "I do believe, Lord."

Now in referring to these various steps (which will be discussed below—see Section II, article II, nos. 270-287) modern theologians have used the technical phrases "beginning of faith" and "the pious will to believe" to designate the last few steps prior to faith. Since the act of faith is supernatural and needs the help of grace the theologians tried to pinpoint the last point in the whole mental process where grace would have to enter in. In so doing they had recourse to the terminology used by the II Council of Orange (529) in its condemnation of the semi-Pelagian heresy and therein found the terms: "beginning of faith" and "pious will to believe." These terms were then lifted and applied technically to designate several of the steps that are *preliminary* to faith. So, for example, Van Noort in the previous edition of this work stated: "the pious will to believe" plus the speculative—practical judgment upon which it rests—'I have an obligation to believe'—are called *the beginning of faith*. In other words, step no. 5, as we have outlined it above, would be called "the pious will to believe," while step no. 4 together with step no. 5 would be called "the beginning of faith."

An historical error:

While the technical labels listed above, "beginning of faith" and "pious will to believe," are useful theologically in pinpointing the place where grace must meet nature in the process of arriving at faith, modern research seems to show that the later theologians made an historical "faux pas" in attributing to the Council of Orange the same meaning for the terms as their later technical usage. The council in speaking of "beginning of faith" did not mean the steps which are *preliminary* to faith; it meant the first act of supernatural faith itself and the series of acts prior to justification; and the Council, by the phrase, 'pious will to believe,' did not mean the command issued by the will, "go ahead, believe!", but rather the will, as enflamed by charity and leading the new convert toward God, or what later theologians would call "formed faith." Roger Aubert sums up the matter this way in discussing the 5th canon of the II Council of Orange which contains the phrases under discussion:

Theologians have often thought that the *initium fidei* which is mentioned here designated those acts which are preparatory to the act of faith itself; as a matter of fact, we have seen that this term, as employed in the controversies of the age, designates the first act of faith and even the whole ensemble of acts through which the new convert becomes disposed for justification. The *(pius) credulitatis affectus*, consequently, does not designate, as it does in modern theology, that movement of the will which carries along with it (entraine) intellectual assent; rather, it is the intervention of the will which transforms simple belief into a *fides in Deum*—faith moving towards God—a faith which is animated by love and which is the principle of the Christian life. This, finally, is what explains the parallel drawn up between *fides* and *pietas*. (*Le problème de l'acte du foi*, p. 37)

So long as one keeps in mind, however, that the technical phrases "pious will to believe" and "beginning of faith" cannot be appealed to as resting on the authority of the 5th canon of the II Council of Orange, there is nothing to prevent using them as convenient designations for illustrating the point where grace must enter into the process of coming to faith. This delicate problem, not so explicitly posed in earlier analyses of the act of faith, is itself a theological refinement for which one can be grateful to modern theology.

Vocation to faith:

Because the speculative-practical judgment, "I must believe," plus the command of the will, "go ahead believe!" are so inextricably bound up with the actual assent of faith, "I do believe," it is quite clear that God's illuminating and strengthening grace are necessary for the production of these acts. Briefly if the act of faith is truly supernatural, beyond man's native powers, and consequently absolutely needs the help of divine grace, those immediately prior mental acts, so inextricably bound up with the assent of faith itself that the "I-do-believe" issues forth from the command of the will, must themselves be helped by grace. Why? Otherwise one would have a purely natural act (the command of the will) producing an intrinsically supernatural effect—the assent of faith.

The grace of illumination and inspiration which precede the last two steps leading to faith (judgment of credentity and the

THE ACT OF DIVINE FAITH

command of the will) is called "the grace of vocation" or *vocation to the faith*. This vocation is a free gift of God which, just as it is denied to no adult except through his own fault, cannot be merited by any natural work.

Notes

1. Calvin, *Institutes*, III, 2, 8.
2. See above, no. 183, where the full definition of the Council is given and commented on.
3. Constitution, *De fide*, ch. 3; confer canon III, 5.
4. Shearer, "The Concept of 'Faith' in the Synoptic Gospels," in *Expository Times*, vol. 69 (January, 1957) pp. 3–6.
5. *Ibid.*
6. "Now there remain these three: faith, hope, charity" (1 Corinth. 13:13); "For we walk by faith and not by sight" 2 Corinth. 5:7; "In whom [Christ] we have hope and access in confidence through faith in him" (Ephesians 3:12).
7. For a brief presentation of Patristic views on faith, see Roger Aubert, *Le probleme de l'acte du foi, pp. 13–42.*
8. *Adversus haereses*, IV, 37, 5.
9. CCHS comments on this verse that it is: "an important statement that faith itself is not the reward of merit strictly so-called." CCHS, p. 1129, no. 906c.
10. CCHS comments on this verse as follows: "This great privilege issues from a twofold gift: grace on the part of God, faith on the part of man—faith being the instrument for grace to act. This gift is wholly from God, and the Council of Orange (529) used this text to prove that the *beginnings* of faith are a gift of grace." CCHS, p. 1122, no. 900e.—For the exact meaning of the term, "beginning of faith," as employed by the Council of Orange, see Corollary, no. 269 ff.
11. *Contra duas epistulas Pelagianas*, I, 19, 37.
12. *De spiritu et littera*, 34, 60.

Article II

PREPARATION FOR THE ACT OF FAITH

#1. INTELLECTUAL PREPARATION REQUIRED

Introduction: If God spoke to us directly we should need no special investigation before making an act of faith. As matters stand we need the work of inquiry: consequently three things belong to the intellectual preparation for faith:
   a. knowledge of God's authority;
   b. certitude about the fact of revelation;
   c. an acquaintance with the truths which must be believed.

I. *Certitude About the Fact of Revelation Is an Absolute Necessity*

II. *Any Species of Certitude Suffices Provided It Excludes Fear of the Opposite:*
   1. Not necessary to have metaphysical certitude but moral certitude suffices;
   2. One does not have to have "scientific" moral certitude but either of these suffice:
      a. an absolute popular certitude;
      b. respective or relative certitude.
   3. The reason "respective" certitude suffices.
   Corollary: Immanentists are wrong in overstressing what might be called the aesthetic approach to faith.

III. *How Do Uneducated Catholics, and Especially Children Reach Certitude About the Fact of Revelation:*
   1. Normally the ordinary run of the faithful can reach an absolute, popular certitude.
   2. As for some of the faithful, particularly the slow-witted, they have arguments that are sufficient for themselves.
   3. In this whole matter much must be attributed to divine grace.

4. Respective certitude can and should give way to absolute certitude.
5. Some abnormal situations.
   a. Can a man in good faith, through invincible ignorance, leave the Church without formal sin?
      (1) a delicate and disputed question.

IV. *The Judgment of Credibility and Credentity:*
   1. Judgment of credibility: meaning.
   2. Judgment of credentity: meaning.
   Scholion: The way in which revealed truths must be presented to us by the Church before we can elicit an act of faith.
   Corollary: A large share of our preparation of the act of divine faith is due to human faith.

#2. PREPARATION FOR FAITH ON THE PART OF THE WILL

I. *Remote Negative Preparation:*
   1. Removing obstacles to faith:
      a. pride;
      b. lightheadedness;
      c. dissolute living;
      d. prejudices.

II. *Remote Positive Preparation:*
   1. The will applies the intelligence to study the arguments of credibility.
   2. The will gives courage to persevere in this arduous task.
   3. Motives that attract the will during this remote preparation.

III. *Direct and Immediate Cooperation:*
   1. After the judgment of credibility is reached the intervention of the will is still required.
      a. This is a free act of the will, but not motiveless.
   Corollaries:
   1. The best arguments are of little value to the hostile mind.
   2. The major part always depends on God's grace.

Article II

PREPARATION FOR THE ACT OF FAITH

The act of faith is not a blind, obsessive leap in the dark. If a man is to behave reasonably in making that act, much is demanded of both his intellect and will. This article, therefore, falls naturally into two sections: one deals with the intellectual preparation, the other with the voluntary preparation requisite for coming to faith.

270   #1. Intellectual[1] Preparation Required

If a person were to hear God Himself directly making a revelation and were simultaneously aware that it was the First Truth he was listening to, he could elicit an act of faith without making any special investigations. He would be perceiving directly both the material and the formal object of faith. With us, to whom God does not speak directly, the situation is different. Before we can believe it is necessary for both the formal and the material object of faith to be personally applied to us, or rendered present to our understanding. The formal object of faith is applied to our intelligence when we have reached certitude about God's authority and the fact of a revelation; the material object is applied to our intelligence when the truths contained in that revelation become known to us. Consequently, three things belong to the intellectual preparation for faith: (a) knowledge of God's authority; (b) certitude about the fact of a revelation; (c) an acquaintance with the truths which must be believed.

As for knowledge about God's authority (omniscience and veracity) nothing special needs to be said. The existence of God, the supremely perfect Being, is known to everyone who follows the lead of sound reason; from even a dim knowledge of the supremely perfect Being anyone can immediately infer that God can neither make a mistake nor tell a lie.[2]

The question that is most agitated concerns knowledge of the fact of revelation. Since we are here ex professo dealing only with divine-catholic faith, by the term "fact of revelation" we mean the fact of the Christian-Catholic revelation, i.e., the fact, or more correctly, the facts that Christ and his Apostles were heralds of a divine revelation and that the Roman Catholic Church safely preserves and proposes this revelation. As for knowledge of just which truths must be believed, we shall discuss this briefly in a scholion.

I. Certitude About Revelation a Must 271

First of all it must be held that *certitude about the fact of revelation,* in the sense explained above,³* *is required before one can make an act of divine-catholic faith.* Certitude means the firm adherence of the intellect to one side of a contradiction without fear of the opposite side. Consequently certitude is a state or mental attitude of the *knowing* subject: it is a relationship of a man's intellect to some proposition. Consequently it must be sharply distinguished from "evidence" or the luminosity of truth which is sometimes described as "objective" certitude. This assertion is proven from the condemnation made by Innocent XI of the following proposition:

> The assent of faith which is supernatural and useful for salvation can be reconciled with a knowledge of revelation that is only *probable,* in fact even with the fear with which one might fear that God has not spoken.⁴

Clearly, then, "certitude about the fact of revelation" refers to the state of mind of the believing subject or person.

The same point can be *proven* by theological reasoning. The assent of faith must be firm, in fact the very firmest kind. But the will cannot command an assent of this sort unless the fact of divine utterance is established with certitude. Consequently St. Peter exhorted the faithful exposed to persecution to be "always ready to give satisfaction to anyone who asked for an explanation of that hope which is in you."⁵

II. Any Real Certitude Suffices 272

On the other hand it must be noted that *any species* of certitude about the fact of revelation, i.e., every determination of the intellect to one side, so long as it *actually excludes fear of the opposite side,*

---

* So to make an act of merely divine faith what is required and suffices, is certitude about the fact of revelation in a restricted sense, i.e., certitude about a divine utterance regardless of how it may have been made and regardless of the way in which we became aware of it. See above nos. 184 and 189.

suffices. The reason is this: as often as you have present a conviction of this sort, the act of the will commanding faith to be given is always prudent and reasonable. Consequently:

1. It is not necessary to have a metaphysical or physical certitude, but a *moral certitude*[*6] suffices. For moral certitude, i.e., that certitude which rests upon arguments which presuppose the stability of the moral order, is a genuine certitude. Even if the arguments which beget it are not most of the time so compelling as to exclude all possibility of doubt, they do at least exclude the possibility of *reasonable* doubt; so they suffice to beget in any sincere man an adhesion of the mind whose firmness is not weakened by fear of the opposite.

From another point of view, apart from a miraculous intervention by God, the fact of revelation cannot be known by us other than by moral certitude, for both the miracles and prophecies which prove the divine mission of Jesus Christ and then the institution of the Church, together with the promises made to it, are made known to us by human testimony. All the rest of the arguments, too, which normally are adduced, namely moral miracles, moral laws (i.e., constant and uniform fashions of human behavior) suppose that point. Briefly, if one does adduce arguments based upon moral miracles and the like, one obviously supposes that the moral certitude arising therefrom suffices for one to elicit an act of faith prudently. Therefore unless moral certitude about the fact of revelation were sufficient, the faith which God nevertheless exacts of everyone[7] would be rendered impossible for everyone.

273 2. One does not have to have "scientific" moral certitude, but these suffice: both an *absolute popular certitude* and also that certitude which is called *respective* or *relative* certitude.

Absolute certitude means that which rests upon arguments which necessarily demonstrate the objective truth of the matter and which consequently suffice to convince any man, even a very learned man provided he be sincere and of good will. Now if arguments of this sort are perceived less distinctly, less perfectly, and above all less reflexively, you have what is described as a *popular* certitude. If the arguments are known both more distinctly and more reflexively so that they can be clearly marshalled and

---

* Understand here moral certitude in the *strict sense* of the term, not that great probability which, since most of the time it suffices for prudent action, is often described by moral theologians as "moral certitude."

defended you have what is known as a *scientific*, or philosophical certitude, which itself admits of greater or lesser degrees of perfection.

Respective (or relative certitude) prescinds from the *objective* value of the arguments upon which it rests. It rests on arguments or reasons which are either not connected with the truth necessarily, or are known in such a defective fashion that their necessary connection with the truth would be doubtful to sharper minds. Still, they factually suffice to convince minds that are either uncritical, or imbued with certain prejudices. So, for example, the word of parents usually is fully sufficient to persuade a child; similarly, arguments that point out the extreme usefulness or the practical necessity of some point could suffice to persuade some man imbued with neo-Kantian prejudices; the beauty of a doctrine might bowl over an artist, etc.

The real reason we say 'respective" certitude suffices to prepare for faith has been pointed out above: just as often as you have factually present a firm adherence of the mind which *actually* excludes fear of the opposite side, the will to believe is a reasonable will. This point receives indirect confirmation from the fact that otherwise faith would be rendered impossible for many men and particularly for those of weak intelligence and for children. For how could one ever square such an impossibility of reaching "scientific" certitude with the mind and teaching of Christ who wanted above all else to preach his gospel to the poor and ignorant, and who said of little children: "of such is the kingdom of heaven"? In fact the obsolete opinion of a few theologians who attributed to people of the type we are discussing a kind of *experiential perception* in virtue of which they would infallibly discern revealed truth from any error was a purely gratuitous manufacture.[8]

Corollary 274

You can see, therefore, that some moderns (Immanentists) are wrong when they demand that a man should with his soul perceive the beauty, the harmony, and, in fact, the necessity of the Catholic religion; that he should learn by experience that this religion satisfies our deepest aspirations, and, what is more, that it satisfies them so perfectly that without it human life would be deprived of all value and dignity; when they insist that a man driven by divine grace should experience in himself that "human life" postulates an increase of truth and of moral strength such as the Catholic Church alone offers, etc. Here we are not at present concerned with discussing the objective value of arguments and experiences of this sort; we do not deny their very great usefulness, nor do we contest the fact some men may through such arguments alone reach at least a 'respective" certitude about the fact of revelation. But that such arguments are *necessary* if a man is to act reasonably in embracing the faith, or for him to be obliged to embrace it—this is altogether false and contrary to Catholic doctrine. The Vatican Council states:

> If anyone shall say that divine revelation cannot be made credible by miracles and therefore that *only* by the *internal* experience of each one, or by private inspiration ought men to be moved to faith, let him be anathema.—Constitut. *De fide,* canon III,3.

275 III. Uneducated Catholics and Certitude

As for the question: *how do uneducated Catholics and especially children reach certitude about the fact of revelation,* we offer the following points for consideration.

1. In the Catholic Church even the ordinary run of the faithful can easily* reach and normally do reach *absolute certitude, granted it is a popular certitude.* Provided they have not neglected such instruction as is accessible to everyone, (i.e., in Catholic schools, sermons, newspapers) they already know in a fashion proportionate to their intelligence and culture a number of motives of credibility which are absolutely sufficient in themselves. For example, they know some of the miracles of Christ, preserved by unanimous tradition, and along with some knowledge of the apostolicity of the Church they are aware of the Church's marvelous unity, catholicity, indestructibility, etc. It is true that they do not know those arguments fully nor perceive all their force, and that they could not solve all the objections raised against them. Still that is not necessary for them. Since they are either unaware, or outrightly despise such difficulties (which difficulties, as a matter of fact, do not destroy but merely *obscure* the force of those motives of credibility) they remain in tranquil and legitimate possession of the

---

* Roger Aubert is skeptical about this point, but he has misunderstood Van Noort's position. See below, no. 277, for an exposition and refutation of his critique.

truth. On this point it is well worth pondering the comment of the theologians of the Vatican Council:

> For even though the less instructed members of the faithful do not distinctly know all the motives of credibility and could not themselves explain them, they do nonetheless know in a way suited to themselves the one, holy, catholic, and apostolic Church and in this [Church] there always hovers before their eyes a changeless, utterly sufficient and sure motive of credibility, or rather a whole complex of arguments so that it is not now a question of "those believe quickly who are scatterbrained," but resting as they do upon extremely firm foundations which make for the full certitude of credibility, they are "always prepared," insofar as suits their individual condition, "to give satisfaction," namely through the Church and in the Church, "to everyone asking the reason for that hope that is in them." For just as in certain natural truths, God so arranging things by his natural providence, the whole human race reaches full certitude apart from any scientific demonstration—a certitude which can indeed be explained more fully and distinctly by philosophical investigation, but which is not invalidated by any superficial arguments to the contrary, so, too, the divine goodness and wisdom in the sphere of supernatural providence has endowed the Catholic Church with such brilliant characteristics that in her, apart from scientific investigations, for which the great majority of men are not prepared, even the uneducated possess an easily readable handbook of motives of credibility which make for full certitude—motives which can be established in a more distinct and more fully explained way through the apologetic sciences; but no prudent doubt can arise through opposed arguments to undermine that certitude. Certainly God and his Christ did not destine faith for the learned alone or make his revelation knowable with certitude by them alone; rather (sed) the poor [and ignorant] have the gospel preached to them.[9]

276 2. As regards some of the faithful, especially children and extremely dull adults, even though they may be lacking in arguments that are strictly sufficient, they are not lacking in arguments that are sufficient for *themselves*. Such arguments (only accidentally but nonetheless truly) suffice to exclude all prudent doubt for *men of this sort* and to produce *in them* a firm assent. Such arguments are mainly the authority of their parents and of a parish

DIVINE FAITH

priest. "Since," says Cardinal De Lugo, "there do not occur to him [i.e., a child] reasons which might make a learned man hesitate with prudent fear, he cannot prudently fear, and, for his capacity, those motives are extremely strong which for other people would be weak."[10] Let us remember our own childhood years; what persuaded us as children more fully or perfectly about the truthfulness of many things so much as the serious and repeated assertion of our parents: "Do not play with matches!"—"Put on your rubbers or you will catch a cold!" etc. So it comes about that all the faithful, even those of the least intelligence, factually possess, *at least, a respective certitude* about the fact of revelation. And this, since it excludes, at least, *for the time being*, all prudent doubt, suffices to prepare for a reasonable eliciting of the act of faith.[11]

277 Before despising this way of "human authority" by which children and uneducated people come to the faith, one should stop to consider how correct and *prudent* they are in judging that even in religious matters they should follow the lead of those who are wiser than themselves and whom God has provided for them as instructors. They cling to the only means which is directly available to them, and it is a means that is *of itself* good and suitable to their condition; for the fact that parents sometimes make mistakes or deliberately deceive, even if it occurs fairly frequently, happens only *accidentally*.—On this point see the criticism made by Roger Aubert, *Le problème de l'acte du foi* (2nd ed. 1950) pp. 249–251. His criticism of this way of "human authority" or of "respective certitude" amounts to these three points: (1) it destroys the *reasonableness* of the act of faith; (2) it is applicable to the heretic as well as the Catholic; (3) it ends up in pragmatism.

Here are his words:

> Billot and Bainvel are in accord in saying, along with many theologians of earlier ages, that a child often has no other reason for believing than the word of his mother, and the peasant no other reason than the word of his parish priest. Can one still speak of a *reasonable* certitude? And, under such circumstances, are not simple people exposed to taking for revealed doctrine what actually is not? One must grant that point; but since, in the theory of faith of simple authority, the infallibility of divine faith does not depend upon the judgment of credibility, the evil is not serious. But then there is the case of heretics who could apply the same line of reasoning to justify

themselves. Bainvel consoles himself on this point in thinking that they do arrive in this way at the certitude required about the fact of revelation, and that "apart from some exception in details, which have no great consequences for them, it is the true doctrine of the gospel that they hear." Perhaps: but what shall one say about people who are living in a non-Christian milieu? "God will come to their aid!" One would like to know in what precise way. For, we could object with Rousselot, "what if it should suit a child to prefer the pagan to the parish priest?" "What a weak foundation for supernatural faith!" Rousselot goes on to add about this theory of respective or relative certitude. And, as a matter of fact, is it really reasonable to accept as certain arguments which are uncertain? No doubt simple people are excusable for so doing, but one cannot say that they are acting "reasonably" in so doing, let alone that they are *obliged to do so by prudence*. This last element, added by Billot to the classic theory of relative certitude, and considered by Harent as "luminous justification" for such certitude, seems on the contrary to add an element of pragmatism, in allowing one to admit as true, for generic reasons of docility, what one suspects to be perhaps false in itself. (*L'Acte du foi*, p. 250)

In reply to the first criticism that the way of "respective certitude" makes the act of faith unreasonable because it makes one take as "certain" what may really be "uncertain," we think the learned author has fallen into the unhappy trap of belaboring the theory for something it does not hold. He has fallen into the semantic trap of confusing "subjective" certitude (a mental state of a person which excludes prudent fear of error) with what is sometimes dubbed "objective certitude" (a mental state of a person which de facto corresponds to extra-mental truth). In the theory, at least as elaborated by Van Noort (see nos. 271–272 above), what is required for acting reasonably in making the act of faith is simply this subjective attitude of mind which excludes *here and now* prudent fear of making a mistake. It says nothing whatsoever about this subjective certitude's having an objective certitude correspond to it. But Aubert's criticism is precisely this: "things really uncertain may be taken as certain."

Again, the criticism seems to envisage that the state of "relative" certitude must remain static or fixed. Van Noort is careful to delineate that children and simple people may and ordinarily should move from this position of "relative" certitude to one of "absolute" certitude (see nos. 275–279).

The second criticism, that non-Catholic Christians, or even infidels could appeal to the same line of reasoning to justify their position ("my minister told me so") is not perhaps so formidable as it sounds, or, is so only insofar as it introduces the far more complex question of the whole economy of the salvation of infidels —which finds its proper place for treatment in the treatise on Grace. For the present it is enough to advert to these two points: (a) Bainvel's explanation that non-Catholic Christians may by human authority reach certitude about the fact of revelation and the gist of the true doctrine of the gospel and hence would be in a position (with the help of grace) to elicit an act of faith should not be brushed aside as useless. It has some real plausibility to it. (b) More importantly, this does not put the position of non-Catholic Christians and Catholics on an ex-aequo basis for, as the Vatican Council assures us: "the most merciful God strengthens by His grace those whom He has transferred from darkness into His wonderful light so that they may persevere in this light and He does not desert unless deserted." (Vatican Council, Constitutio, *De Fide*, chapter 3). Briefly, God's grace goes in one direction only: to truth and reality. Those who are already in the true faith will be kept in that faith if they are faithful to His grace; contrarywise those who are innocently in error will, if they are faithful to His grace, be led gradually away from their errors and towards the fullness of the truth; but no man can say when or how, for the mechanics of the process are a secret of God's providence. As for infidels and the process by which they may reach justification and ultimately salvation, see the various theological theories given in the treatise on Grace. Roger Aubert would like to know "precisely how" God comes to their aid; so would we all. But the mysteriousness of the process does not perturb our certitude that God does will all men to be saved and consequently that He must make it possible for the infidel to reach faith in those truths which are necessary for salvation by necessity of means. And if God wishes to use a respective certitude, generated by the teaching of a muezzin, or a parent, to help simple people to come to believe in Him as a rewarder and punisher, who is to deny His right to do so, or to scoff at the reasonableness of such people in so acting?

The third criticism, that the theory of respective certitude is really a lapse into "pragmatism" is rather a label than an argument. Actually the theory of respective certitude does not suggest that people *should* "for general reasons of docility accept as true that which they suspect may be false." The people in question (children and simple, uneducated men) have no such suspicion or uneasiness. The charm of their position is precisely that the word of a pastor, or nun, or parent has removed such fears from their mind and given them a subjective certitude that they have the truth.

Actually this theory is built on the same hard fact that the theologians of the Vatican Council observed: "God and His Christ did not destine faith and make His revelation knowable with certitude only for highly educated men, rather the poor [i.e., and ignorant] are to have the gospel preached to them." (*Collectio Lacensis*, Vol. VIII, p. 533.)

Consequently the argument is constructed this way: certitude that God has spoken is a requisite for acting reasonably in accepting what God has said; but children and uneducated people cannot reach certitude of the fact of revelation by a scientific study of apologetics such as would be given in a college; therefore they must reach the required certitude in some other way. This way, in religious matters as well as in others, seems to be simply the way of human authority. It is their only means of reaching such knowledge and is, actually, in proportion to the development of their intelligence and education. The theory is, then, not an appeal to pragmatism but a simple analysis of the facts of the case and the construction of an argument by the exclusion of inadmissible alternatives; v.g., that God does not want simple people to reach faith, or, that certitude is not required for the act of faith, or, that simple people must have some sort of miraculous knowledge bestowed upon them by grace, etc.

3. Finally in this whole matter much must be attributed to divine *grace*, which, granted apart from a miracle, it does not take the place of the motives of credibility, can nonetheless bring it about that: (a) difficulties which obscure the truth be eliminated, and (b) that the arguments of credibility be grasped in such a way as to entice and convince. That is why St. Thomas says: "He who believes is led by the authority of divine teaching as confirmed by miracles and, even more so, by the interior instinct of God calling him"[12]; and the Vatican Council itself states: "So that the assent of

our faith might be in harmony with reason God has willed that there should be conjoined to the *internal helps* of the Holy Spirit the external arguments of his revelation'; and a little bit afterwards the Council states: "to which testimony [namely of the Church] there is added the efficacious aid which comes from supernatural grace."[13]

279   4. We stated above that respective certitude excludes all prudent doubt, *at least for the time being,* for we readily admit that the arguments on which it rests do not sufficiently exclude the possibility of doubt for the future as well. Actually the relative arguments which satisfy—say a 10 year old boy—will usually not satisfy him when he becomes an adult. What follows? Should such a boy on a certain day suspend his faith in order to begin a skeptical inquiry about the fact of revelation and the truth of the Church? Not at all. For unless either the boy himself or his parents have been completely derelict in their duty, such a boy will quite soon have added to his relative arguments, arguments that are strictly valid. The force of these arguments while only dimly grasped at the beginning will, with the passing of boyhood years, be more firmly grasped so that little by little, without even being aware of it, and with no intermediate interval of doubt, his relative certitude will give way to strict, or absolute certitude. Again, in this process divine grace and divine providence plays a part, in fact the major part.

What we have said of a young boy holds true, in proportionate fashion, for every uneducated Catholic when he begins to run into objections against the truth of his religion. Suppose such a simple Catholic man has up to this point only a relative certitude. He would certainly act imprudently and consequently sinfully if at the first difficulty that popped up he were *immediately* to retract his assent; for the force of the dawning objections will not, at least at the beginning, destroy the weight of the arguments of credibility which have rendered him certain up to this time. *Holding on to his assent, therefore,* such a man should, in accord with his ability and circumstances, begin to investigate the foundations of his religion, with the conviction that the more sincerely and diligently he seeks an answer, and the more earnestly he prays for divine light, so much the more profoundly will he be convinced by absolutely valid arguments about the truth of his religion. For it simply cannot happen that a fact (i.e., the fact of revelation) which is demonstrated by many arguments, part of which are very obvious, and a fact the knowledge of which is necessary for salvation should, upon sincere inquiry, not be seen to be clothed with such arguments of truth as to exclude all prudent doubt; particularly since "the most gracious God strengthens by his grace those whom he has brought out of darkness into his wonderful light so that they may persevere in this same light, and does not desert anyone unless He is first deserted."*

5. Thus far we have discussed only normal situations. But if one pushes the inquiry more deeply and wants to know whether *by accident and in exceptional circumstances* one might come across a case in which some naive Catholic might be set in such circumstances that through invincible ignorance and consequently without formal sin he might judge that the Catholic Church is not the true Church and depart from it:—the theologians are not of one mind.

Some[14] deny the possibility in such a way as to assert that the point has been *defined* by the Vatican Council[15] (see quote of canon). This is certainly too rigorous a position as Granderath and Vacant[16] have proved. The intention of the Council was to define against Hermes and others that a Catholic man cannot *objectively* have any just reason for changing or suspending his faith. It was not discussing the subjective attitudes of individual persons.

Setting aside any question of a "definition," most theologians deny the case could happen. They base their position on this axiom: *God does not desert unless He is deserted.* From this axiom some

---

* Vatican Council *Constitution on Faith*, ch. 3.—The contrary will happen to the dissident Christian whose good faith begins to be troubled by difficulties. I do not say that a heretic (material) who clings to his sect with respective certitude, should *immediately* on encountering some difficulty, suspend his assent or that he can do so prudently. Nonetheless by the very fact that objective truth is lacking to that sect and that the grace of God can direct one only on the road to truth, such a heretic will if he sincerely scrutinizes the foundations of his sect *some day finally* discover its falsity. On this point the Vatican Council says (*loc. cit.*): "The most gracious God stirs up and helps with his grace those who are wandering astray so that they can 'come to the knowledge of the truth' . . . and emphasizes the vast difference between the position of the born-Catholic and the born-heretic in *canon 6:* "If anyone says that the position of the faithful and of those who have not yet reached the only true faith is the same, so that Catholics could have good reason for suspending their assent and calling into question the faith that they have already accepted under the teaching authority of the Church, until they have completed a scientific demonstration of the credibility and truth of their faith; let him be anathema." (TCT 74; DB 1815).

draw the conclusion that the very departure from the true Church is always *in itself* a formally sinful act; others, that no one ever departs from the Church without *at least by prior sins* having deprived himself of a special help of grace (i.e., to retain faith.)[17]

The matter can be explained only with utmost caution, and it is dangerous to dispute about it publicly. Still if I may venture to express my own opinion on it, I think that only one point is *certain* in virtue of the previously mentioned axiom. No Catholic who has already made an act of true faith will ever, without blame on his part, come to such a point that he will deny or call into doubt those truths which must be believed by *necessity of means*.[18] The reason is this: anyone who was to lose faith even in these articles would lack a means utterly necessary for salvation: God would truly have deserted him. But God does not desert unless He is deserted.—For the rest we leave the secrets of conscience to God. Our job is to labor with all our strength both in catechising and in advice, and also in writings adapted to the needs of our day, so that the foundations of the faith may be more diligently and fully known. "It is clear," says Cardinal Franzelin, "how grave a necessity there is for a fuller, more distinct instruction of the simple faithful in these anguished times when the attack of the enemies of the faith is sharper and the danger of perversion greater."

281 **IV. The Judgment of Credibility and Credentity**

Once a man reaches a state of certitude about God's authority and the fact of the Christian revelation, the way is prepared for two judgments; one speculative, and the other speculative-practical.

a. The *judgment of credibility*. This means Christian-Catholic doctrine is now viewed as truly believable, or "credible." In other words it can be believed without sinning against prudence. A man might make the judgment of credibility in this or a dozen similar ways: "Well it all makes good sense—I certainly wouldn't be acting rashly or unreasonably if I were to accept this doctrine, seeing that it is backed up by so many proofs of its divine origin." This judgment flows spontaneously from an acknowledgment of God's truthfulness and the fact of revelation. That is why the Vatican Council, after mentioning the brilliant marks with which God has ornamented his Church to show its divine origin, immediately concludes to the "evident credibility of the Christian faith."[19]

b. The *judgment of credentity*. This means Christian-Catholic doctrine clearly *ought* to be believed. In other words it is morally right and obligatory for me to assent to it with divine faith. A man might express that judgment somewhat as follows: "Holy smoke— if God has said all this stuff then I'd better accept it!" This second judgment, presupposing the former, flows spontaneously from a recognition of man's *dependence* on his God in virtue of which he is bound to surrender his intelligence to God when he speaks. That is why the Vatican Council states:

> Since man totally depends on God, his Creator and Lord, and created reason is completely subject to uncreated Truth, we are obliged to offer to God, when he speaks, the complete homage of our intelligence and will by an act of faith—DB 1789*

The judgment of credibility and the judgment of credentity are really two distinct judgments. In fact, they are separable in time, seeing that the former may be elicited without the second following necessarily. Still, since they are intimately bound together and in practice rarely are ever so separated, theologians usually lump them together under the one label of: *judgment of credibility.*

Scholion. The way in which revealed truths must be presented before one can elicit an act of faith.

282

Just as an act of faith is utterly impossible without proof that a revelation has really occurred, so, too, no specific doctrine can be held by faith unless it is certain that that doctrine is truly contained in the deposit of revelation. Now the means Christ himself established to give us certitude on this point is a proposal of revealed truths by the Catholic Church. A brief discussion of this matter will suffice.

1. The Church's public proposal of revealed truth, which we discussed above,[20] offers to all who are convinced of her divine origin and infallibility, full certitude about the revealed character

---

* See also canon 1 of chapter 3 (*Constitution on Catholic Faith*): "If anyone says that human reason is so independent that it cannot be commanded by God to believe: let him be anathema." (DB 1810; TCT 69). The Catholic dogma, therefore, cannot possibly be squared with any viewpoint which maintains that no truth or law may be imposed upon man *from outside*, that nothing can be reasonably accepted by us from outside which is not demanded by our own needs or desires, in brief, which is not demanded by our own "activity."

of the doctrines she teaches. Still, this public proposal does not reach individual Catholics directly. It comes to them only mediately or indirectly, partly through the authoritative proposal of pastors and preachers,[21] and partly through the private proposal of such truths by parents, nuns, brothers, lay teachers, pamphlets and the like. Obviously the testimony of such people does not per se necessarily guarantee that the doctrine taught by them has been revealed and is really contained in the Church's public proposal. Still, the ordinary run of the faithful normally have absolute certitude that the religious truths known to themselves explicitly are truly proposed by the Church for their beliefs. Even the poorly educated know at least a few truths explicitly, for example, the Apostles Creed and a number of major truths about the sacraments, the Eucharist, Penance and Matrimony. In accepting these truths they do not rest solely on the *bare word* of their pastor, but in some fashion, granted only dimly and confusedly, they discern the proposal of the universal Church insofar as they realize that these doctrines are accepted by all Catholics.[22] Those better educated know many truths explicitly and at the same time more easily and more perfectly reach certitude about the public teaching of the Church. Even if a relative handful of Catholics, meaning children and the weak-witted, lack absolute certitude, they do at least possess respective certitude which in this matter, too, must be acknowledged as sufficient.

283 2. Sometimes it happens that a member of the faithful hears some subtler point of doctrine insisted on and proposed to himself as revealed, say for example in a sermon, without immediately being convinced that it is really revealed. In a case of this sort such a proposal will normally "bind a man not to disbelieve it until he investigates further, or, perhaps, it may even oblige him to believe it with some sort of faith, in the loose sense of the term. But it will not bind him to believe it with such faith as admits of no hesitation until he reaches certitude about just what is the Church's teaching."[23] For the rest, as Pesch[24] acutely observes: in such cases the ordinary run of the faithful do not even think of eliciting or not eliciting an act of faith specifically for this or that recondite truth; most of the time they simply persevere in their assent towards all such truths as must be believed, contenting themselves with some such formula as: "I believe whatever the Church has proposed for belief."

Corollary 284

From the matters discussed in this article, it should be clear that a large share in our preparation for the act of divine faith is due to human faith. On this point we might do well to recall the general observation made by Father Pesch: "All men, even the most erudite, have gathered by far the greatest part of their knowledge not by personal investigation of the internal structure of things, but by human faith. For if we were to take away all the knowledge we have acquired in this way, our intellectual riches would not be very great. In this or that field of science we do perhaps penetrate into the intimate explanation of things, but in all other fields we rest on the authority of others. It should, then, occasion no surprise that even in religious matters there is a wide scope left open for the play of human faith."[25]

#2. PREPARATION FOR FAITH ON THE PART OF THE WILL

I. Indirect Cooperation of Will

To get ready for the act of faith and to actually elicit it, our will must cooperate in many ways. First, the will cooperates indirectly by removing obstacles to faith; secondly, it cooperates directly by taking the steps through which faith is finally reached. This direct cooperation, again, may be either *remote* (in producing the judgment of credibility) or *proximate* (in producing the act of faith itself). We make this distinction between remote and proximate cooperation by the will for purposes of clarity; at the same time we warn that in practice they are not usually separated; in fact, they are usually so intimately bound up and blended together that their boundary lines can scarcely be chalked out.

Many obstacles to faith stem either directly or indirectly from 285 the will. Unless they are removed they prevent a man from arriving at the judgment of credibility and from faith itself. These obstacles are above all: *pride, lightheadedness, unmortified passions,* and *prejudices.*

a. *Pride.* Pride is a disordered complacence about one's own excellence. A man who is so puffed up with pride that he is unwilling to acknowledge the possibility of mysteries (i.e., mysteries deflate our intellectual conceit because they are above reason), or to bow to laws or commands imposed on him from outside; who is so self-sufficient that he considers a divine revelation to be useless, or even harmful, or at least an infringement on human dignity, will not even think the arguments of credibility, no matter what kind they be, worth considering, or if he does examine them will do so with the sole intention of weakening and obscuring their probative force. A man of this sort does not want to believe—he wants to be knocked flat on his back by evidence so overwhelming it is impossible for him to refuse his consent. Arrogant men of this sort were rebuked by Christ for "demanding" signs from heaven. "An evil and adulterous generation seeks a sign and a sign shall not be given it. . . ."

b. *Lightheadedness or worldliness.* A mind that is scatterbrained or so wrapped up in temporal affairs that it will never make a serious inquiry about the big things in life, or even thinks of them as stupid in accord with the popular maxim of those who "leave heaven to clergymen and sparrows," while they are content with temporal goods.

c. Another great obstacle is *undisciplined passions* and especially an *impure life*. Anyone addicted to vice has a natural aversion to dogmas and above all to the divine commandments of Christianity and consequently flees away from the obligations they impose. Those whose whole life centers on sexual pleasure are usually enervated and normally have a loathing for spiritual matters.*

d. *Prejudices,* no matter what their origin, often so blind people that they are unwilling to make any inquiry about the fact of revelation or the truth of the Catholic Church. How many highly educated men especially in our day are convinced there can be no certitude in metaphysical matters; how many there are who 'a priori' exclude any hypothesis of revelation, or of miracles as obsolete errors of the dark ages. Many people have a deep conviction that one ought to stick to the religion in which he was born. What many born-Protestants think of the Catholic Church shines out in a proverb popular in some parts of Germany: "that's as stupid as becoming a Catholic!"

---

* On this point G. F. Romanes writes: "Now nothing is so inimical to Christian belief as unchristian conduct. This is especially the case as regards impurity: for whether the fact be explained on religious or non-religious grounds, it has more to do with unbelief than has the speculative reason." (*Thoughts on Religion*, 1895, p. 166).

Obviously the removal of obstacles such as the above depends **286** exclusively on the will, or at least cannot be removed without the will's intervention. Certainly, in real life, prejudices will hardly ever be dispelled unless the Catholic religion starts to seem *attractive* from some angle or other and thus begins to appear worthy of consideration. To making Catholicism appear attractive, the internal criteria* are the most useful. They point up the superb goodness of that religion: its sparkling holiness, its usefulness (suitability for fulfilling our intellectual, moral, and social needs), its beauty, etc. Finally, even other arguments of the most diverse sort can begin to attract a man's will to the Catholic religion. In fact, as Mazzella aptly notes the will often receives its first impulses for inquiring about the faith from motives of an *inferior* order which are accommodated to the person's dispositions.[26] So a man's first attraction to the faith may come from wanting to marry a Catholic girl.

II. Direct Cooperation of Will

Directly, though still remotely, the will cooperates in the pro- **287** duction of the act of faith by applying the intelligence to a consideration of the arguments of credibility, by sustaining and directing its efforts until finally it reaches the judgment of credibility.[27]

Arguments from the moral order, guaranteeing the fact of revelation, are usually such as to make known the truth with sufficient strength, but not with such lucidity as to exclude as well the possibility of imprudent doubt. For the enemies of the faith from a thousand different sources have assembled an enormous rubbish pile of difficulties to obscure the fact of revelation. To mention but a handful: difficulties of textual criticism; historical, philosophical, and psychological difficulties; similarities between Christian liturgical practice and ancient mystery religions, discrepancies in narrations of some event by evangelists, the 'formgeschichte' method of demythologizing the gospels etc. Everything including even Christ's existence has been denied. Some of these arguments have a first-glance plausibility about them; others are backed up by the extrinsic authority of names of men who are very erudite (e.g., Hume, Harnack, Cullman, Bultmann, Wittgenstein, Tillich, Schweitzer, etc.). Finally, some of the arguments are based on materials that are beyond the reach of most laymen and can be investigated only

---

* See vol. I, *The True Religion*, No. 32.

by specialists in the field. So, for example, the extravagant claims about the Dead Sea Scrolls made by Dupont-Sommer and others. Obviously, then, unless a man has a sincere will to apply and continuously keep the mind unruffled in weighing all matters impartially, it can easily happen that the intelligence will get bogged down by difficulties for so long a time as to become captive to them.*

The same thing is true even when it is a question of giving a demonstration of the true religion in scientific fashion. A scientific demonstration (i.e., apologetics) is quite a complex business since it draws its principles of argumentation from many sources and in most of the arguments many different circumstances must be examined and weighed. Think, for example, of the apologetic demonstration of the empty tomb.

III. Direct and Immediate Cooperation

288   The will cooperates in faith *directly* and immediately by the command with which, though under the prior illumination of the judgment of credentity, it applies the intellect to elicit the formal act of faith. Briefly, a man having reached the judgments: "yes, this is believable" and "in fact I *ought* to believe it," says to himself: "Go ahead—stop hesitating—believe!" Thereupon follows the strict act of faith: "I *do* believe this to be true." This command of the will to believe, which is called the "supernatural will to believe" ("pius credulitatis affectus")† even though it follows after the judgment of credibility and credentity is a free act which can be given or withheld, as we shall see later on when discussing the freedom of the act of faith. For the present, notice simply this one point. The will to order the very assent of faith is itself moved by the goodness which the intelligence apprehends in such an assent. That goodness is first of all the rightness and obligation to subject one's created intellect to God, and then the desire of saving one's soul. Nevertheless, along with this main motive—the moral obligation of bowing one's intellect to uncreated truths—(a motive which is in itself sufficient) there can be joined and it is useful to have joined other motives as well which move the will more gently, or in particular

---

* As Pascal shrewdly observes: "there is enough light for those who desire only to see, and enough darkness for those whose disposition is just the reverse." *Pensees, cet. de B. Pascal.* Ed. P. Taugere, II (Paris 1844) p. 151.

† See above, no. 269, *Corollary.*

instances, more forcefully.* Now in a process so complex the first requirement is that the will keep the intellect constantly at its labor. This is sometimes a wearying work. Secondly, given the weakness of our intelligence, a truth that has to be demonstrated by diverse and complicated reasonings will not shine forth with utter lucidity and vividness. As a consequence, given the nature of the truths that are to be accepted and the multitude of the objections raised against them, there almost always remains the possibility of imprudent hesitation—a hesitation that can be overcome only by an order of the will. Briefly, the arguments will never knock one flat on one's face; if they did there would be no room for faith—a free assent.

You can see that in the work of preparing and forming a judgment of credibility the intervention of the will is required not to add weight to the objective criteria (something the will simply cannot do) but that (a) the intelligence may be seriously and constantly applied to the job of weighing fairly the objective value of the criteria; and (b) so that any fear that might possibly remain after an evaluation of the criteria, but whose groundlessness is perceived by the intellect itself, may be expelled.

The motives attracting the will in this whole business can be very varied. It may be simply a sincere desire of finding out the truth; it may be a love for God as known naturally and the obligation of searching for a religion He may have revealed; it may be the clear perception of the falseness of one's own sect, or, at least, serious and prudent doubts; with different temperaments, yet other motives may move men even more effectively to order the assent of faith.[28]

Corollaries

1. Since faith depends in such large measure on the will, you can see that those are not mistaken who say: "the heart too has its reasons for believing," and who therefore insist that in apologetics, whether scientific or popular, one must not neglect the affective preparation of the person. Actually, even the strongest and best laid-out arguments are of little help if the listeners do not care to weigh them sympathetically, or at least with an unhostile mind. That is why the internal criteria of revelation are so useful, in fact for many men downright necessary. They directly display the good-

* See vol. I, *The True Religion*, pp. 172–176.

ness and beauty of the Catholic religion and thus have a great influence in moving the will. All that being said, a man would still be going too far, in fact he would fall into a vicious error, if he concluded from the part played by the will that faith depended exclusively on the will and affections, or that the act of faith was directly an act of the will, and hence that only "reasons of the heart" suffice to make one embrace or hold on to faith. Some apologetes are not sufficiently removed from such an error—such apologetes as put such stress on the internal arguments as to conclude that even if the external arguments do not lack objective value they are for all practical purposes almost useless.

2. Since in this present article we have been considering solely the preparation required on *man's part* for coming to faith, we have said practically nothing at all about the work of God's *grace*. We do not, of course, forget that in this whole business a great deal, in fact, the major part depends on God's help whose task it is to open the hearts of men[29] to pay heed to what is said by preachers and without whose anticipating grace no one comes to faith.[30] It should, then, be clear how important it is for those who hope to win souls to God by their words, both to give themselves earnestly and constantly to prayer, and secondly to live in such holy fashion as to deserve to be chosen as the instruments of grace in making many converts. Surely if the conversion of those in error and of unbelievers depends first of all on grace, holiness counts more than knowledge. That is what accounts for the laconic remark of the erudite Cardinal Dupperon: "If you want them [non-catholics] conquered, send them to me; but if you want them converted, send them to Francis de Sales, the bishop of Geneva."[31]

Notes

1. See Gardeil, *La Crédibilité et l'Apologétique,* 1908; see Bainvel, in RPA (1908) vol. VI, p. 161.

2. This point is established by philosophy and confirmed by revelation in the treatise, *God: Unity and Trinity,* no. 6 ff.

3. Consequently what is required and suffices for an act of *merely* divine faith is certitude about the fact of revelation taken in a restricted sense, i.e. a "divine utterance," regardless of the way in which it takes place or the way in which we become aware of it. So a prophet receiving a purely internal communication from God could make an act of divine faith in it provided he was certain that God was communicating with him. See above nos. 184 and 189.

THE ACT OF DIVINE FAITH

4. DB, 1171; see the theses to which Bautain was obliged to subscribe in the year 1840, listed in DB 1622–1627. Pertinent here, too, is the condemned proposition contained in the decree *Lamentabili*: "The assent of faith rests ultimately upon a collection of probabilities." DB no. 2025.

5. I Peter, 3:15.

6. We mean here "moral certitude" in the *proper sense* of the term, not that "large probability" which is often referred to by Moralists as "moral certitude" simply because it usually suffices for acting prudently.

7. See Hebrews, 11:6; Mark, 16:16.

8. See Schiffini, *De virtutibus*, p. 264; Pesch, *Praelectiones dogmaticae*, vol. VIII, no. 177.

9. *Collectio Lacensis*, vol. VII, p. 533.

10. *De Fide, disputation* 5, no. 36.

11. See below, no. 279.

12. S.Th., IIa–IIae, q. 2, art. 9, ad 3.

13. Constitutio, *De Fide*, ch. 3.

14. So, for example, J. B. Heinrich, *Dogmatica Theologia*, vol. I, no. 62 and vol. II; Scheeben, in *Kirchenlexikon*, under the word, *Glaube*, vol. V., p. 668.

15. Constitutio, *de Fide*, ch. 3 and Canon III, 6.

16. Granderath, *Constit. Dogm. Conc. Vatic. explicatae atque illustratae*, p. 61 ff.; Vacant, *Études théologiques sur les Constit. du Concile du Vatican*, vol. II, p. 165 ff. Dr. N. Paulus holds the same view in *Der Katholik* (1896) vol. II, p. 93.

17. This view is held, for example, by Pesch in *Praelectiones dogmaticae*, vol. VIII, nos. 381–385.—The distinction is of some importance. For if the very *defection* from the Church is always formally sinful, then the defection itself must be retracted if a man is to be saved; but if the defection itself, even if it be indirectly caused by preceding sins and negligence, is not necessarily formally sinful, it can happen that the unfortunate man may be saved without having retracted his defection.

18. This is the view, for example, of Tanner, *de Fide*, q. 2, dubium 5, no. 139.

19. Const., *De Fide*, ch. 3.

20. See above no. 206 and ff.

21. Pastors and preachers by the fact of possessing jurisdiction in the internal forum, can, in some sense, be assimilated to authentic teachers.

22. "The poor woman who believes on the word of her pastor knows quite well that her pastor and her parish are in doctrinal communion with the other pastors and parishes of the dioceses, and the pastors with the bishop, with Rome, with the Church spread out all around the world." *La Foi et l'acte de foi*, p. 108.

23. Suarez, *De Fide*, disputatio 8, sect. 13, no. 9.

24. *Praelectiones dogmaticae*, vol. VII, no. 30.

25. *Ibid.*, no. 298.

26. *Praelectio Scholastico-dogmatica*, vol. III. 3rd ed., p. 618. Semeria observed (*La vie della fede*, 1903, p. 11 ff.) that what first attracted a number of famous converts were such motives of an inferior order. So Brunetière

was first attracted by the principle of social authority which the Church strongly inculcates; Coppée was attracted by the consolation which the Church brings to the sick and afflicted; Huysmans was attracted by the beauty of Catholic worship and symbolism. In *The Road to Damascus* and other convert stories, edited by John C. O'Brien, you will find this same variety of attraction exhibited in the lives of more recent and famous converts like Claire Booth Luce, Karl Stern, Avery Dulles, Evelyn Waugh, etc.—Finally, we cannot overlook the fact that many men first begin to investigate and weigh the truth of the Catholic Church because they have sincerely and deeply fallen in love with a Catholic girl.

27. Bainvel writes: "In the preliminary investigations, the will ordinarily plays a great role. It is the will which gives the force to set the soul on the search, it is the will which directs that search, which sustains it in the midst of difficulties; it is the will which scorns earthly mirages and triumphs over vain fears; it is the will especially—and I cannot insist on this point too much —which establishes between the soul and truth some sort of mysterious harmony analogous to that begotten by love, a kind of *connaturality* (the word is St. Thomas') thanks to which the truth (which without it might perhaps make its appearance, but in a cold light and with an appearance which disturbs as can the undeniable merits of an enemy) appears as a friend whose presence rejoices and delights, and whose charms ravish one, and the thought of whom evokes delightful sympathies." *La Foi et l'acte du foi*, p. 132.

28. Bainvel writes: "If this austere notion of duty and of obligation is always at the bottom of faith, there are mingled with it other viewpoints which attract the will more sweetly, and at times more strongly. There is an alliance with God to be made; there is a loving advance made by the Sovereign Generosity to be received with welcome and love; there is a door opening into the depths of divinity and into the secrets of God in this world, which an infinite condescendence wills to place at my disposal; there is the assured possession (not indeed presently by sight, but by mental union with Him who sees and who knows) of sublime and extremely necessary truths; there is the sure solution of my most agonizing doubts; there is the saving hand which God stretches out to my own insufficiency and feebleness, of which I am keenly aware; there is the sure refuge against error offered to my intelligence and my will. What more shall I say? The motives which attract me to the faith are extremely varied and they make me receive it as a precious gift. In good people these motives easily become aligned with charity; in sinners they normally lead the way to motives of repentence (justice) or hope or to that incipient love of which the Council of Trent speaks and which does not yet imply sanctifying grace." *La Foi et l'acte du foi*, p. 140.

29. See Acts, 16:14.
30. See John, 6:44.
31. Quoted in Hurter, *Theologiae Dogmaticae compendium*, vol. I, no. 102.

Article III

THE ANALYSIS OF THE ACT OF FAITH

Introduction: What is meant by the analysis of faith?

I. *The Formal Motive of Faith Cannot Be Resolved Into the Arguments of Credibility*
   1. Explanation.

II. *Various Theories Explaining Precisely How God's Authority Is Not Only the Proximate but the Complete and Final Motive of Faith:*
   1. Suarez' theory:
      a. Exposition and critique.
   2. De Lugo's theory:
      a. Exposition and critique.
   3. Billot's theory:
      a. Exposition and defense.

   Scholion: The supernaturality of the formal object of faith in Billot's theory.

Article III

THE ANALYSIS OF THE ACT OF FAITH

291   By the analysis of the act of faith we mean breaking it down into its component causes. As by chemical analysis a compound may be resolved into its constitutive elements, so by logical analysis the act of faith may be resolved into its constitutive elements. After what has been previously discussed this analysis would pose no special problem, were it not for the fact there still remains one further question—and an extremely difficult question at that: *how is the "authority of God revealing" not only the proximate motive of faith but even its ultimate motive?*

292 **I. The Point at Issue**

We have previously shown that the authority of God revealing is the real motive of our faith. But since God's authority and the fact of revelation are only known to us through rational arguments, it might seem as though the analysis of the act of faith were not complete unless, after the question: "why do you believe in the Blessed Trinity?", and the reply: "because of the authority of God revealing"—one were to pose the further question: "and how do you know that God is truthful and has really spoken?" If one feels the problem must be posed that way and ought to answer the further question by saying: "I know God's authority and the fact of revelation from the arguments of credibility," then he will not be able to escape the conclusion: therefore our faith is ultimately resolved into the arguments of credibility. In other words, the arguments of credibility are not simply a previous *condition* for *faith,* but actually the final, the ultimate motive for faith.

Now, it is absolutely certain that such a conclusion cannot be admitted. First of all the sources of revelation and the documents of the Church's magisterium always assign the First Truth Revealing (God Himself) and it alone as the motive for faith. Again, if faith were to rest ultimately on the arguments of credibility it

THE ACT OF DIVINE FAITH

would neither be a theological virtue*, nor could it deserve an assent that is firm above all other assents. It could deserve an assent of only such firmness as is found among various men in correspondence with the various arguments of credibility with which they are acquainted. But this firmness is quite diverse among different members of the faithful.

Consequently all theologians hold and absolutely must hold that the act of faith is *not* resolvable into the arguments of credibility, but exclusively into the authority of God revealing. Briefly, the authority of God revealing is the *unique, proximate and simultaneously the ultimate reason* (motive) why, for example, I assent to the mystery of the Blessed Trinity. But the question still remains: *how is the matter to be explained?* And this is the famous dispute over the analysis of the act of faith that has been fiercely controverted since the end of the sixteenth century. In dealing with this dispute we shall give a brief sketch of the three major theories on this point. No one of these theories has been either officially accepted or officially rejected by the Church.

Before analyzing these theories we wish to call the reader's attention to one important fact. The followers of the *first* and *second* theological theories agree on these two points: (a) the assent of the *act of faith itself* is virtually a *double*[1] assent, that is, it is an assent first to the formal object (authority of God revealing), and thence to the material object (the truth to be accepted); and (b) the assent to the material object depends upon our assent, that is, on *our knowledge* of the formal object. With these two points taken for granted these theologians try to solve the problem by showing that a member of the faithful (who prior to faith knew of God's truthfulness and the fact of revelation from the arguments of crediblility) *in the very act of faith itself* knows those same truths in a more excellent way, i.e., he knows them *immediately*. He knows these truths immediately either through faith (the followers of the first opinion) or through a kind of understanding (the followers of the second opinion). The *third* theological theory does not admit the two presuppositions mentioned above, but seeeks an entirely different mode of solution.

---

* A theological virtue (faith, hope, charity) has God for its direct object or goal; contrariwise, moral virtues have for their direct object or goal some created object or activity.

293 II. The First Theory

According to Suarez* and many other[2] theologians, our faith is ultimately resolved into "the authority of God revealing," *as believed by divine faith*. The theory boils down to the following. The assent of faith to the material object (i.e., to the Incarnation, or the Trinity), which all theologians admit must be supernatural and firm above all other assents, is founded upon an assent to the formal object (authority of God revealing). But it is impossible for an assent of a superior order (the supernatural order) to be grounded in an assent of an inferior order (the natural order); neither can a greater certitude be *per se* grounded in a lesser certitude. The necessary consequence is that *in the very act of faith* God's authority and the fact of revelation *should be believed by divine faith*.

Now, if one suggests that in the act of faith itself the formal object is believed because of another revelation priorly believed, the question will rise again: "why is that prior revelation believed?" —and so on to infinity. Consequently, it must be admitted that in the very act of faith the formal object is believed, not because of another and distinct revelation, but because of that very same revelation by which one believes the material object (i.e., the individual truth). In other words it is necessary to grant that in the act of faith the material object is believed because of an act of faith in the formal object: the assent to a particular truth is an assent of *mediate* faith. Briefly, the material object is *co-believed* (concreditur) along with the formal object. But the formal object itself is believed for its own sake: this is an assent of *immediate* faith. And if this be the way matters stand, then indeed our act of faith is supernatural from every viewpoint and is firm above all other assents, and, furthermore, is quite evidently resolved solely into the authority of God revealing.

How the formal object can be believed because of the very same revelation which discloses the material object is explained by these theologians as follows. In the revelation of any truth *three things*, strictly speaking, are revealed. For example when God reveals that He is a trinity, by a *signate* act He reveals the *mystery of the*

---

* This theory is often referred to as the *Thomist* theory, though many who glory in the name of "Thomist" refuse to dignify it with that term because they do not think it represents the mind of St. Thomas.

Blessed Trinity (the material object) and simultaneously by an *exercised act* (*actu exercito*) He reveals that it is *He Himself* speaking (the fact of revelation) and that *He is truthful*[3] (his own authority). Consequently, in every act of faith we really believe three things: when we elicit an act of faith in the mystery of the Blessed Trinity, we do indeed believe in the *Trinity* because of the authority of God revealing—this is a mediate assent; but simultaneously, and with a logical priority we believe the very authority of God revealing (i.e., that *God is saying this,* and *God in saying this is truthful*) and this latter, implicit revelation we believe for its own sake (propter seipsam) and with an assent that is immediate. If, finally, one wants to know how it is *possible* for the authority of God *to be believed because of itself,* Suarez will reply: "this is a great mystery of faith."[4]

Critique. Suarez' theory gives an excellent explanation of how our faith is ultimately resolved solely into the authority of God revealing. But the very theory itself; (a) must appeal to a "mystery"—a mystery which is certainly not a divinely revealed mystery. Furthermore (b) an *immediate* assent of faith and *to believe a proposition for its own sake* seems to be not so much a mystery as a contradiction in terms.[5] An assent of faith is by its very nature an assent given because of testimony; it is an assent because of something else, and consequently a *mediate* assent. Similarly, to believe is to assent to a proposition because of an *extrinsic* reason, because of a reason distinct from the proposition and consequently not because of the proposition itself.

III. The Second Theory

According to *de Lugo,*[6] whose position is also adopted by Cardinal Franzelin,[7] our faith rests ultimately on "the authority of God revealing" *as directly known from intrinsic reasons* (ex rationibus intestinis). The assent of faith, as all agree, is founded upon the authority of God and the fact of revelation. Now, if it can be shown that *in the very act of faith* the faithful are aware of God's truthfulness and the fact of a revelation—not mediately, through arguments, reasonings, human faith and the like—but directly, immediately from the very terms themselves, in almost the same way as one knows first principles, it will be evident that our faith is ultimately resolved not into the arguments of credibility, but exclusively into the authority of God revealing. For if the authority of God revealing in the very act of faith is known from itself, that is, from the mere apprehension of the terms, there is no room for posing the further question: "how do you know that God is truthful and has really spoken?"

But that is how matters stand. In the act of faith both God's truthfulness and the fact of a revelation are known directly and from themselves. Obviously *God's authority* (i.e., his infallibility and truthfulness) is understood from a consideration of the terms themselves, at least if enuntiated as follows: "*If* God speaks, He tells the truth."[8] As for the *fact of revelation* (or, taken concretely, this proposition: "the doctrine of the Catholic Church is a divine revelation") it can be grasped of itself in the following way. Divine revelation viewed concretely consists of a twofold element: words which enuntiate some truth, and facts (miracles and the like) which demonstrate that the words are a divine message. Now these miraculous facts do not merely accompany the formal message, they really are part and parcel of it (eam adintegrant); together with the formal message they make up the integral message from God. Now this integral message, i.e., the Church's doctrine viewed not nakedly as a message but as garmented with the miraculous facts which God has used from the beginning of the world to the present day to accredit[9] that message, stands before the intellect of the believer as the *subject* of a proposition. The intellect, then, from the very nature of that subject viewed in this way (i.e., concretely), and hence not without a consideration of the elements entering into its makeup, yet nonetheless directly and without any discursive reasoning, understands that the only *predicate* suitable to such a subject is: "a divine communication."

Finally, de Lugo himself admits that that immediate knowledge of the fact of revelation is always obscure, whereas the immediate knowledge of God's truthfulness can be either obscure or clear. Finally, he mentions that this knowledge (of God's authority and the fact of revelation) is a supernatural knowledge since it is only produced by the intellect as elevated by grace.

296   *Critique.* In evaluating this theory of de Lugo we can be brief. Passing by all other difficulties which could be raised, we press only this point: no matter how subtly and ingeniously the matter be argued, both by Lugo himself, and then even more so by Cardinal Franzelin, our knowledge of the fact of revelation just simply is not direct knowledge; it is indirect, mediate knowledge carefully as-

THE ACT OF DIVINE FAITH

sembled from the arguments of credibility. The Salmanticenses put their finger on this weakness in the theory as follows:

> If a man does not assent that God has revealed the mystery of the Incarnation unless it be proposed to him by the Church as a fact confirmed by miracles, witnessed to by martyrs etc., he is obviously not assenting to the aforesaid proposition because of the immediate connection of the terms, but because of arguments which demonstrate its credibility.[10]

IV. The Third Theory[11]

The third theory, which seems to us the true one, takes the following tack.

1. The authority of God revealing, insofar as it is the formal object of faith, is not known to us in any other way than by the arguments of credibility.

2. The act of faith itself is not a virtually double assent, that is, an assent first to the formal object, and then secondly an assent to the material object. It is a simple assent to the material object (i.e., to the individual truth: "I believe in the Trinity"; "I believe in the Real Presence"). Consequently there is no room for any such question as: "how is the authority of God *known* or *affirmed* in the very act of faith?"

3. The motive of faith is the "authority of God revealing" (something known to us *prior* to faith); the motive is not "*our knowledge* of the authority of God revealing." God's authority, regardless of how we got acquainted with it, deserves an assent that is firm above all other assents. Consequently:

4. The question: "how did you get to know about the authority of God revealing?" is no longer seeking the motive for the act of faith itself, but rather for its purely previous *condition;* it is, in other words, seeking the *applicatory* cause of the motive, or a necessary prerequisite before the motive itself (God's authority in revealing) can be brought to bear upon the intellect. Consequently, this question simply does not pertain to the analysis of the act of faith itself.

We shall give a brief exposition of each of these four assertions.

Assertion 1, namely, that the authority of God revealing, insofar as it acts as the formal object of faith,* is not known to us in any

---

* I say: insofar as it is the *formal* object of faith. For nobody disputes the

DIVINE FAITH

other way than mediately, through the arguments of credibility, flows spontaneously from the rejection of the preceding theories. For neither the Suarezian "faith," nor the Lugonian "understanding" can withstand critical examination. Furthermore, the matter is corroborated by the experience of individual believers. Who, in looking reflexively upon his own act of faith and its preparation, has ever experienced that he was in that act now being certified in *some different* way than by the arguments of credibility about the motive of faith? It follows that all *our knowledge* about "the authority of God revealing," insofar as it acts as the formal object of faith, is truly resolved into the arguments of credibility as its motive cause. It follows, further, that even our faith is resolved into the arguments of credibility as its previous "sine qua non" condition. For it is impossible for the authority of God revealing to function as a formal object in my intellect unless it first be introduced there; i.e., unless its existence be known to my intelligence.

299 *Assertion 2*, namely that the formal act of faith is not a double assent, at least virtually distinct, but a single and simple assent to the material object alone is proven by the very analysis of this act. Surely some one who believes, say for example in the Blessed Trinity, does not by this very act elicit first of all an assent to the authority of God revealing, and then an assent to the mystery of the Trinity. What he does is simply assent to the mystery of the Trinity because of the authority of God revealing, an authority already known and acknowledged by other acts. In other words in the very act of faith a man says: "O, God, I believe in the Trinity because you have said so." At that precise moment he is no longer scratching around trying to resolve the question of whether God is truthful or to be trusted, or whether, perhaps, someone has gotten mixed up on the facts alleged to be revealed—that perhaps God revealed a quaternity rather than a trinity, etc. Those points are already taken for granted when he launches into the act: "I do believe." If he doubted either of those points he could not make the act of faith; he would not be ready for it. If he thought God could

---

fact that the divine truthfulness and the fact of revelation, since they are also revealed truths, can and should be believed by us with divine faith; but, in that case they take on the aspect of a *material* object. Consequently, in the particular act of faith whereby we acknowledge God's truthfulness and his revelation by faith, we believe in the *revealed* authority of God the revealer, because of the authority of God revealing *as something already known from another source*.

make a mistake, or that He does not always tell the truth, he would not say "yes" with any firmness or finality. Even if he granted that God is necessarily truthful but was not sure whether God had ever made any affirmation about three persons in one nature, he would not feel any definite obligation to submit himself to such a baffling truth.

To put the matter technically but very accurately—the act of faith itself does not reach out to the authority of God as a *quod* but as a *quo;* it does not reach for the authority of God as *subject matter* for the intelligence to feed upon, or affirm, or know, or believe in the very act of faith; but it reaches out to it uniquely as a *means*, as a *quo* or as to that *because of which* something else is affirmed and believed. Thus one eliminates as simply impertinent, as having no bearing on the matter, as something rendering the analysis of faith hopelessly muddled, the question: "in what way *in the very act of faith itself* is the authority of God affirmed."

Assertion 3. The third and major assertion of this theory makes a sharp distinction between our "knowledge" (or certitude about God's authority) and that very authority of God revealing which is known to us. It states that the latter (God's authority) is the real motive of our faith; not our *knowledge* of it.

To grasp this point more clearly we have to realize that the terms "to believe" and "faith" are at times employed in a twofold way. Sometimes they are used in the strict sense of the words, other times only in an analogous way. I may, for example, assent to a proposition whose intrinsic truthfulness I do not perceive solely and precisely *because I am sure* of the veracity of the testimony in a given case; I am sure that the testimony in a given case is genuine or true. This is what we call *scientific,* or "historical" faith. It can also happen that, while sure of the veracity of the testimony, I assent to the matter testified to precisely and formally *because of the dignity possessed by the witness—a dignity that demands that he be trusted.* This sort of belief is called faith of *simple authority.*

It is by faith in the first usage of the term ("scientific faith") that we believe, for example, historical matters (such as that Caesar crossed the Rubicon) which are narrated by many contemporary witnesses who are in agreement, or in the Nile River which we may have never seen. Indeed in this way we can in a particular case believe the assertion of a man whose integrity we count for very little. Think, for example, of the testimony given by a racketeer to

DIVINE FAITH

a Congressional Committee for the sole sake of protecting himself from other gangsters etc. It is by this sort of "faith" that even the devils believe the mysteries of Christian revelation "coerced by the evidence of signs which convince them that something believed by the faithful is true."[12] Now, in this sort of faith *certitude* about the veracity of the testimony is not simply a "condition" previous to assent; it is truly the *ultimate motive* on account of which the assent is given. Consequently, in such faith the firmness of our assent is directly commensurable with our certitude as to the veracity of the testimony. Now, if it were by such faith that we believed the mysteries of revelation, our faith truly would be ultimately resolved into the arguments of credibility. But in such a mode of believing you have only weakly imitated the genuine notion of faith. For faith is so-called because it means *trusting in another* (fides dicitur ... quasi alteri *fidens*); but it is clear that in the assent of "scientific faith" there is little trust and consequently little honor, or reverence shown to the witness. Heaven forbid that we should believe in God with faith of that sort.

301   By faith taken in the *second sense* (faith of simple authority) you alone have verified in the full sense of the term the proper notion of faith. This is the sort of faith, for example, a child puts in his mother, or a student puts in his teacher—someone whose wisdom and perfect sincerity he admires. For faith of simple authority to be possible it is, indeed, antecedently necessary that the truthfulness, or moral integrity* of the witness be established, and likewise the fact of some testimony given; this is a previous *condition*. But when these points are established, the real (formalis) reason for assenting and the measure of the firmness of the assent is uniquely the authority as such, that is the moral dignity of the person speaking, in virtue of which he has a right to receive the docile acquiescence† of the listener. It is quite clear that the moral dignity of the witness, which calls for his being trusted, even

---

* I mean, by the *moral integrity* of the witness, of course, his *habitual* trustworthiness which rules out any *habitual* will to deceive; for in scientific faith it is not at all required that a witness be habitually trustworthy, provided I am certain that he is not deceiving *in this particular case*.

† Who has never heard that final and unassailable argument of a good mother: "What! you don't believe *your own Mother?!*" And her indignation is perfectly proper; for the very relationship of motherhood and maternal love give her a special title so that her child should trust her and believe with the kind of faith of which we are now speaking.

though it cannot move me unless I know about it, takes its force in no way from my knowledge and clearly remains the same regardless of the particular mode, or way in which it became known to me. So, for example, the testimony of an Einstein in mathematics or of a Robert Teller in relation to the hydrogen bomb can suffice for my assenting to something he says in his own field regardless of whether I learned that he was an authority in the matter from reading *Time* magazine, or by being assured by other scientists, or in some other way.

Now we ought to believe God not with the "scientific faith" described above, but with the faith of simple authority:

> Since man entirely depends upon God as upon his creator and Lord, and since created reason is completely subject to uncreated truth, we are bound to offer to God, when he reveals, the full homage of our intelligence and will by faith.[13]

Who would ever think of dignifying by the term a "believer," or "member of the faithful," a man who, having the question put to him: "why do you believe the mystery of the Blessed Trinity?" would reply: "I believe not because I trust God as the First Truth, but purely and simply because I know he has *not told a lie* in this case!" For the authority of God, (i.e., God's moral dignity which demands that He be trusted no matter how it becomes known to us) precisely because it is divine authority, deserves an assent that is firm above all others. Consequently, the very nature of divine faith demands that once it has been proved that God, the Supreme Truth, has spoken, the *will* should determine the intelligence to assent with such firmness as corresponds (*not* to the sureness of our "knowledge" about God's authority, but) to the very weight of divine authority in itself, or to the right which God has that created reason should utterly bow down before Him, that is, should assent with the greatest firmness possible. That helps us to understand why the following proposition was condemned: "The will cannot bring it about that the assent of faith should be any more firm in itself than is deserved by the weight of the arguments which incline (i.e., motives of credibility) one to give assent."[14]

You can see therefore: (a) why it is that the assent of faith can be firm above all other assents, even though our certitude about God's veracity and the fact of revelation is only simply firm; and

(b) why that assent of faith has no other motive cause than the First Truth Itself revealing.

302 *Assertion 4.* The fourth assertion flows spontaneously from the preceding one. It asserts that the question "how did you come to know about the authority of God revealing?" does not actually deal with the real, internal motive of faith, neither its proximate nor its ultimate motive; it deals rather with a mere previous condition, and consequently does not belong to the analysis of the act of faith itself. Billot puts the matter aptly this way: "If I ask a member of the faithful: 'why do you believe in the Trinity?' his reply ought to to be: 'because He who has revealed the Trinity, God, is deserving of belief, and indeed of a belief beyond all else.' The answer is perfectly satisfactory and it is not possible to make any further inquiry along the same line. For if you were to inquire further along the same direct line and in the same chain of causes, you ought to ask: 'why do you believe something which has been said by someone who *deserves* to be believed?' Such a question is stupid and impertinent. But if you should insist on pushing the inquiry by saying: 'how do you know that God is worthy of faith and has revealed the Trinity?' you would no longer be inquiring about the real motive of faith under which, or because of which I assent; you would simply be inquiring as to what way I had presupposed the existence of that authority which I do take as the reason for my assenting; and in so doing you would be seeking no longer the motive of faith itself, considered in itself, but the motive of the knowledge which preceded the act of faith and is related to it as a prerequisite condition. Therefore in a discussion of the objective resolution of the act of faith considered in its intrinsic, constitutive causes, there is nothing else to seek beyond the authority of the speaker, on whom ultimately faith itself rests."[15]

303 Consequences

Therefore the assent of divine faith is not a logical conclusion. Cardinal de Lugo[16] and those who follow his theory on the analysis of faith, state that the assent of faith takes place in syllogistic fashion. It arises through a formal, or at least virtual (implicit), discursive process from two premises, one of which is the authority of God revealing, the other the fact of revelation, somewhat in this fashion: *What God has revealed is true; but God has revealed that He is a Trinity; therefore it is true that God is a Trinity;* or: Whatever Christ said is true; but Christ said that He is God; therefore Christ is God.

Now we do not at all deny the legitimacy of this conclusion; we simply say that a man who would assent to the truth of the Blessed Trinity, or the divinity of Christ, *formally as it is a conclusion* from these premises would not elicit an act of faith in the full sense of the word, but only an act of "scientific" faith. The importance of the point is this: if the assent of faith were merely a logical conclusion, it would rest upon the assent to the premises as on its true motive cause, and consequently could not be any firmer than the assent to the premises. But the arguments of credibility, by which we know the truth of those premises, deserve indeed a firm assent, but not an assent of such firmness as the act of faith demands.

Scholion. The supernaturality of the formal object of faith.

304

We saw earlier[17] that the reason Suarez proposed his theory about the authority of God revealing as something to be "believed" by divine faith, was to safeguard not only the supreme firmness of faith, but also its completely supernatural character. If the act of faith is to be completely supernatural, so maintain the followers of Suarez' theory, it is not sufficient for its principle or efficient cause to be supernatural (the faculty as elevated by grace); the formal object itself must be supernatural;* that is, the formal object of faith should itself be known by faith from revelation. So, unless we are mistaken, do they understand the matter. It remains therefore, for us to see *whether and in what sense the formal object must be supernatural.* Now although the theologians express themselves in different ways in treating this point we think the reply should be as follows. That the act of salutary faith requires a supernatural formal object, i.e., a motive that exceeds the exigencies of created nature and which bears an orientation to our supernatural goal: *I grant* the point. That it requires that the motive must be known through faith; this *I deny.* But the authority of God revealing, even though it become known through rational arguments, is truly something supernatural: for that God should speak to mankind and should interpose His authority, is not at all owed† to our nature;

* According to the scholastic axiom: *acts are specified by their formal object.*

† The essence of the notion of supernatural lies in something being completely unowed, or gratuitous. The notion of the supernatural is treated ex professo in the volume: *God the Creator.*

nor does God do that for any other reason except in relation to our supernatural goal. The conclusion is clear.

Notes

1. By the beginning of the twentieth century, most theologians abandoned this notion of the act of faith being a double assent:
   > "Around the year 1900, contrary to those who made faith a complex act wherein one first affirms the authority of God and the fact of revelation and then, as a consequence, the revealed truth, the vast majority of theologians are in accord in teaching that the act of faith is a simple act." Roger Aubert, *Le probleme de l'acte du foi*, 2nd ed. (1950), pp. 236–237.

2. Suarez, *De fide*, Disputatio III, sect. 6 and 12; Billuart, *De fide*, Diss. 1, art. 1; Heinrich, Dogmatic Theologia, vol. I, no. 58 and vol. II; Scheeben, *Handbuch der Katolischen Dogma*, vol. I, no. 686; G. M. Jansen, *Praelectiones Theologiae dogmaticae*, vol. I, p. 720; Brouwer, *De fide*, p. 169; Wilmers, *De fide divina*, pp. 351–362.—Some theologians think that *Suarez himself* can perhaps be explained in a different fashion (See Franzelin, *De Traditione*, 3rd ed., p. 661; Suarez, *De Incarnatione*, Disputatio 54, sect. 5, no. 111). Consequently the theory we have outlined in the text should perhaps be attributed to Suarezians rather than to Suarez himself. Similarly, some present-day theologians say that Scheeben should not be included in the category of those who accept the Suarezian theory. So Roger Aubert, *Le Probleme de l'acte du foi*, 2nd ed. (1950) p. 235, note 17.

3. For he who makes known some proposition *so that it may be believed*, implicitly affirms that he is neither mistaken nor telling a lie.

4. *De fide, disputatio* III, sect. 6, no. 8; on this point, however, see Wilmers, *De fide divina*, p. 367.

5. The words are those of Father Kleutgen: "It is not so much a mystery as a contradiction." *Theologie der Vorzeit*, IV, no. 265.

6. De Lugo, *De fide*, Disputatio 1, sect. 6 and 7.

7. Franzelin, *De Traditione et Scriptura*, Appendix, ch. 4 and 5.

8. Strictly speaking: God, *if He exists and speaks*, is truthful. God's existence, however, is manifest from the divine locution and therefore from the fact of revelation.

9. Here is Cardinal Franzelin's own description of how God's miracles envelop and garment the formal revelation:
   > "If one considers the accouterments (fastigium) of the divine revelation made in Christ, and particularly the whole life of Christ, his miracles, his death and above all his resurrection (his choice of a few uneducated men for the conversion of the entire human race, the mission of the Holy Spirit viewed in its obvious effects; and then the whole history of the human race and particularly the history of the people of Israel with all its supernatural manifestations as a preparation and education leading to Christ, and the whole of subsequent Christian history as an effect flowing from Christ himself; the apostolic preaching, the miraculous propagation of the Christian religion by means which are altogether contrary to those normally used by men and which, looked at merely humanly, seem suitable not so much for

obtaining as for blocking the effect sought; and yet the effect, which is not explainable by human cause, is mighty and widespread through the human race, and accomplished amid fire and sword and all sorts of tortures during the more than three centuries through which it was savagely persecuted —the change of all ideas of the theological and moral order, and the change of the whole way of life, public and private; and the no less miraculous preservation of the whole institution through all the past centuries, the morally perpetual holiness found in all eras and constant, heroic practice by multitudes of virtues never even known outside of this religion, the esteem it was held in by everyone, the supernatural charisms that manifested themselves even in external effects; and, finally, the fact that this whole complex of divine things had long before been prophesied, both in a general way and in particulars—all this I say, looked at simultaneously are as it were the rays by which the message proposed shines forth as something divine and demonstrates its divine origin." *De Traditione et Scriptura*, p. 672.

10. *De fide*, disputatio no. 189.

11. This third theory was mainly propagated, after the Salmanticenses (*De fide*, Disputatio 1, dubium 5) and others, by the famous Cardinal Billot who was professor at the Gregorian University from 1885–1911. The theory appears in his treatise *De Ecclesia*, vol. I (1898) pp. 29–62 and in his treatise *De virtutibus infusis* (Rome, 1901). Bainvel adopted and popularized Billot's theory, leaving out scholarly apparatus, in his work, *La foi et et l'acte du foi*, (2nd ed. Paris, 1908). The same theory is substantially followed by H. Mazzella, *Praelectiones theologiae dogmaticae*, vol. III, 3rd ed., p. 511; Pesch, *Praelectiones dogmaticae*, no. 320 ff; Schiffini, *De virtutibus infusis*, p. 195; Mannens, *Theologiae dogmatica*, vol. I, p. 443.

12. James 2:19, and St. Thomas, *De veritate*, 14, 19, ad 4, where it is clear that St. Thomas distinguished this twofold type faith of which we are here speaking.

13. Vatican Council, Constitution, *De fide*, ch. 3.

14. See DB, no. 1169. The proposition should be understood as referring to the arguments which *dispose* one towards making an act of faith (i.e., the motives of credibility) and not, of course, as referring to the formal motive of faith itself (i.e., authority of God revealing). For even if the will *could* bring it about that the intellect (not indeed by divine faith but in some other way) would assent to a proposition with a greater firmness than the formal object deserved, an excessive firmness of this sort would not be rational.

15. *De ecclesia*, vol. I, p. 48.—Human faith is resolved in the same fashion, provided it be faith in the full sense of the term. Think, for example, of a theologian who, regardless of how he got that way, was certain that this or that theory was propounded, say by St. Augustine or St. Thomas and who would formally adhere to this theory precisely because of the authority of those great saints. Isn't it obvious that the sole authority of Augustine and Thomas is the motive, and in fact the ultimate motive of his assent, and not at all the testimony of modern theologians through whom perhaps he first learned how much Thomas' authority counts and that Thomas did hold this particular theory?

16. *De fide*, disputatio 7.

17. See above, no. 293.

Article IV

THE PROPERTIES OF FAITH

I. *Faith's Truthfulness:*
   1. Explanation and proof.

II. *Faith's Obscurity:*
   1. Explanation and proof.
      a. Obscurity due to both its formal object and its subject matter;
      b. Can one simultaneously "believe" and "know"—disputed question.

III. *Faith's Freedom:*
   1. Proof from the *magisterium*.
   2. A philosophical discussion of the non-necessary character of the act of faith.
   Corollary: Why it is quite natural for doubts to arise in the mind of even an earnest believer.

IV. *Faith's Firmness:*
   1. The assent of faith is firmer than all other assents;
   Proof: a. from Sacred Scripture;
   b. from theological reasoning.
   Corollary: The firmness of faith does not entail the rejection of any natural truth.
   Scholion: The inequality of faith.

Article IV

THE PROPERTIES OF FAITH

The main properties of salutary faith are four: truthfulness, obscurity, freedom, and firmness.

I. Faith's Truthfulness

Here we are speaking of faith not in its objective sense, the faith *which* we believe (i.e., Apostles' Creed), but of faith in the subjective sense (i.e., as found in a living subject or person); the faith *by* which we assent to revealed truths. We say that *this assent of faith is necessarily and infallibly connected with truth.* Consequently it would be contradictory for a false doctrine, or even a true but non-revealed doctrine, to be embraced by an act of *supernatural* faith. This point is *certain* from the Council of Trent which, in referring to the certitude of faith, describes it as that "which cannot be subject to error" (Trent, Session VI, on Justification, ch. 9, DB 802.)*

If the assent of supernatural faith were subject to error, the error could have only one of two causes: either God would have revealed something false, or else a man by a supernatural act of faith would assent to a doctrine which he himself considered to be revealed even though factually it was not revealed. The prior alternative is patently absurd—God cannot lie; but the second point needs a little elucidation.

A man may, indeed, take for a "revealed" proposition something

---

* The context is concerned with refuting the false confidence of the reformers who thought that a man could be absolutely certain that he was in the state of grace provided he had enough confidence (fiducia). In rebuking this false confidence the Church says that while one has no doubt about Christ's merits or the efficacy of the sacraments, still one can have some apprehensions about his own dispositions and consequently cannot reach the sort of certitude about his own justification which is granted about revealed truths by faith:

"... when a man considers himself and his own weakness and indisposition he can have fear and apprehension about his own [state of] grace, since no one can know with the certitude of faith, which cannot be subject to error, that he has himself received God's grace." (loc. cit.)

actually false, or, even if true, something which has not been revealed; and he may with all his strength *try* to assent to such a proposition with an act of divine faith. Despite that effort, all he will produce will be an assent of natural faith. That point may be established as follows.

A man cannot produce a supernatural assent of faith unless God co-works with him by elevating through His grace both the will commanding the assent and the intelligence eliciting it. But, it is unthinkable that God would use his grace to elevate the intellect to produce an assent to something false or non-revealed. Surely to assent to an error, or to assent to something as revealed which actually is not, goes against the very nature of the intellect whose goal is truth and, consequently, is an evil to the intelligence. It would be repugnant, then, for God to bestow a supernatural help to aid the intellect in working against its very own order.

306 To grasp the previous point more clearly we add these two observations:

a. One should not be surprised at the fact that we do not consciously *experience* any difference between an assent we described as natural and an assent of "supernatural" faith. For the influx of grace surpasses not only all natural sense-experience but even the experience of self-consciousness. Briefly, you cannot smell, touch, or see grace; neither can you intuitively and reflectively perceive its workings in one's consciousness. This point will be taken up 'ex professo' in the volume on grace.

b. Although God cannot bestow his grace to help the intellect to assent to something false, it does not follow that He cannot cooperate supernaturally with a man's *will* which orders such an assent. For *to want* to assent with an act of salutary faith to a proposition which is innocently but ignorantly thought to be revealed, is not an evil but a good act of the will. Consequently even though the assent of the intellect will itself be purely natural, as described above, the command of the will preceding that assent can be both supernatural and meritorious.[1]

307 II. Faith's Obscurity

Christian faith actually implies a knowledge which is obscure, or dim. It is juxtaposed to what is evident, or obvious. This is clear from the statement of the Vatican Council:

THE ACT OF DIVINE FAITH

Divine mysteries of their very nature so excel the created intellect that even when they have been given in revelation and accepted by faith, that very faith still keeps them veiled in a sort of obscurity, as long as "we are exiled from the Lord" in this mortal life: "for we walk by faith and not by sight" (II Cor. 5:6 ff.)—DB 1796; TCT 76.

The same point is alluded to clearly by Benedict XII in his Constitution on the Beatific Vision. The face to face vision of God does away with faith because it clearly shows us what before we had simply taken on God's word:

> We define that this vision of the divine essence and the enjoyment of it do away with acts of faith and hope in those souls, insofar as faith and hope are theological virtues in the proper sense. (Constitution, *Benedictus Deus*, January 29, 1336; TCT 886; DB 530)

Sacred Scripture, too, in many places bears witness to the obscurity of faith:

> *Faith is the substance of things to be hoped for, the evidence of things that are not seen.* (Heb. 11:1)
>
> *We see now through a mirror in an obscure manner, but then face to face. Now I know in part, but then I shall know even as I have been known.* (1 Cor. 13:12-13)
>
> *Always full of courage, then, and knowing that while we are in the body we are exiled from the Lord—for we walk by faith and not by sight.* (2 Cor. 5:6-7)

Finally, Christ himself juxtaposes faith to clear knowledge or evidence: "Because thou hast seen me, Thomas, thou hast believed: blessed are they who have not seen, and yet have believed" (John 20:29). In the context it is clear that Thomas' "seeing" and "believing" are not identical. Thomas saw the man, he saw the glorified wounds, but he believed in the divinity of the risen Christ: "My Lord, and my God" (v. 28). And Christ had rebuked him precisely for being "unbelieving" because he had earlier refused to accept the testimony of the other apostles—a testimony that merited full credence—but insisted, as the skeptic is wont to do, on laying down very specific conditions before he would believe. After Thomas' submission Christ laid down what would be a sort of general, fundamental law for his kingdom on earth: "Blessed are they who have not seen, and yet have believed," i.e., blessed are those who believe without demanding a personal and obvious experience in relation to revealed truths.*

Theological label. That faith, in a general way, is obscure as contrasted with a natural assent to evidence, can, we think, be rated as a *dogma of faith*. If its proposal as such by the solemn magisterium is not absolutely clear-cut, it does seem to be clearly proposed by the ordinary and universal magisterium, and it seems also to be clearly contained in Scripture.†

The cause of faith's obscurity

The obscurity of faith is due both to its formal object (motive) and its material object (subject matter).

a. Faith is obscure because of its *formal object* for that motive is not internal evidence for a truth, but God's authority. Even though God's testimony guarantees *that* (quod) a thing is true, it does not disclose the intrinsic reason for its being so, or *what* (qualis) sort of thing it is. Consequently it is essential to faith that *faith itself should not make one see into the intrinsic truthfulness of the doctrine accepted*. This is the first and major cause of the obscurity.

b. Faith is also obscure because of its *subject matter*. The proper object of faith, both its primary object and, to at least a large extent, even its secondary[2] object, is of such a nature that we can in no way discover its intrinsic truthfulness seeing that it completely surpasses the grasp of created reason. This is the second reason for the obscurity. Think for example of the mystery of the Trinity, or the Real Presence, or the Hypostatic Union, etc.

The previous two points are *certain*. But there is much dispute

---

* This explanation is adapted from Lercher, *Institutiones Theologiae Dog.* I, #658 (rev. ed. Schlagenhauffen) p. 409.

† That faith is obscure at least insofar as we accept divine truths "not because of their intrinsic truthfulness as perceived by the natural light of reason but because of the authority of God revealing," has been solemnly defined by the Vatican Council (DB 1789; 1811; TCT 63;70) Finally, that faith is *essentially* obscure by the fact that in clinging to the authority of God revealing it is shown not to be a *perfectly* evident assent, seems to be a solidly established theological thesis. See Lercher, *op. cit.*, #656 c), p. 408.

as to whether the very nature of faith *necessarily* demands a subject matter that is obscure. Since the Christian revelation contains quite a number of truths which can also be known from intrinsic evidence, for example, the existence of one God, the immortality of the soul, etc., this disputed point is usually formulated as follows:

Can one and the same person, about one and the same object, and under the same aspect, simultaneously produce both an act of faith and an act of knowledge?

Notice the terms. The *same person* because it can happen "that something which is seen or known by one man, may be believed by another man who has not seen it demonstrated."[3] Think, for example, of an automobile accident witnessed by one person and accepted on his word by another. *Simultaneously*, i.e., at roughly the same time. For again it can happen that a man may first believe something and then later on acquire demonstrative knowledge of it. So a high school student might take his teacher's word for some nuclear experiment, and later on as a physics major verify it by using a cyclotron. *Under the same aspect:* someone can, for example, know by a demonstration that God is one in nature and yet believe in the trinity of persons.[4] Finally, note that the question as posed refers only to life on earth: for it is certain from Sacred Scripture itself that the beatific vision excludes faith.[5]

1. St. Thomas and his followers[6] *deny* that the same person can simultaneously "believe" and "know," in the sense just described. Their arguments are based on both authority and experience. (a) The *authority* of Sacred Scripture clearly teaches that faith is "an argument for things that appear not," i.e., a conviction about truths which are not seen; and it draws as a consequence that faith ceases when one shares in the beatific vision in heaven. Many of the fathers seem to be of the same mind. Witness *St. Augustine*: "I do not know whether a man should be said to 'believe' what he sees: for faith itself which is described in the Epistle to the Hebrews is defined as follows: 'now faith is the substance of things hoped for, the conviction about things which are not seen. . . . For even the man to whom it was said: 'because you have seen you have believed,' did not believe the thing he saw, but he saw one thing and believed another: for he saw the man, and believed him to be God. But even if some things are said to be "believed" which are seen, as everybody says he "believes [what he sees with] his own eyes," still that is not the faith which is built up in us; rather, from the

things which are seen we are driven to believe those things which are not seen."⁷ (i.e., the arguments perceived produce a judgment of credibility: the believableness of things not perceived). St. Gregory the Great states: "That is truly said to be believed which cannot be seen, for that simply cannot be believed which is seen."⁸

(b) From one's own *experience*. We all know that "no one assents because of the testimony of a speaker when he is presented with documentary evidence of the matter and sees to be true what is asserted by another. And if he may seem to believe, this is not faith in the strict sense of the term—which reaches out to testimony precisely as a motive and resting upon it believes the object; but it is an act of "evidence" which gazes upon the harmony between the testimony and the object and is terminated to both of them as to an object quod, as standing under that harmony."⁹

According to St. Thomas, then, a Christian philosopher does not, strictly speaking, believe in the existence of God; he produces only an act of knowledge with regard to this truth, but an act of knowledge which is nonetheless "rendered intensively more perfect and more certain because of the presence of divine testimony."¹⁰ It does not follow, however, that the merit of a philosopher's faith is diminished thereby. For "when a man has the will to believe such matters as are of faith, solely because of divine authority, even though he may possess a demonstrative argument for some of those matters, for example, the existence of God, the merit of his faith is not for that reason either taken away or diminished."¹¹ As for the objection raised from the words of Sacred Scripture: "it is necessary for one coming to God to believe *that he is*," these theologians reply: there it is not a question of God's existence purely and simply, but of God insofar as he is the author of the supernatural order.¹²

310 2. Suarez and many other theologians¹³ *affirm* that simultaneous belief and knowledge are possible. There is nothing to prevent the intelligence from assenting to a truth because of a twofold and distinct motive. It can, in other words, assent because of intrinsic evidence for the matter, and simultaneously because of the authority of God. Consequently nothing prevents the same truth from being simultaneously known and believed by divine faith; in fact, not only can such a thing take place it really ought to take place, for the Church commands all her members, including the most learned, to say: "I believe in one God": furthermore, the Vatican

Council clearly teaches: "by divine and Catholic faith must be believed all those matters which are proposed by the Church as divinely revealed." But among such matters are a number of truths which can also be known by demonstration.*

The followers of this opinion reply to the arguments of the Thomists, given above, as follows: (a) Sacred Scripture and the fathers speak in this fashion (i.e., believing is not seeing) because faith is mainly and primarily concerned with "things that appear not," whereas it is concerned with other truths only secondarily; (b) one's own experience proves rather that men quite frequently admit some truth both because of intrinsic evidence and simultaneously because of divine testimony, which yields a far superior certitude.

Critique. The second opinion is the more common among the more recent theologians; but the first seems to be truer, provided it be restricted to such matters as are *perfectly* evident so that there does not remain any obscurity to trouble the perfect acquiescence of the mind. And we do not think that this qualification, which is also admitted by some followers of the second opinion, is very far from the mind of St. Thomas.†

311

Corollary

312

A number of theologians, following de Lugo,[14] maintain that the essential obscurity of faith demands also some *lack of clarity about the origin of the revelation;* i.e., an absence of *perfect* evidence about the fact of a revelation. Briefly, the first recipient of a revelation, say the Blessed Virgin, or the Apostles, or the Prophets would

---

* Thomists reply: what the Church here requires of the faithful is not belief precisely in the existence of one God, but belief in the one God who is Father, Son and Holy Spirit; and the Vatican Council did not intend to teach with what exact assent the individual faithful should hold the individual revealed truths; it simply wished to state the subject matter of Catholic faith in generic terms (in confuso); in fact; "those points which can be demonstratively proven are listed among the matters to be believed not because all men must hold them by faith in the strict sense, but because they are a prerequisite to matters which are of faith and it is necessary for them to be presupposed at least by faith in people who do not have demonstrative knowledge of them." (S.Th. II-IIae, q. 1, a. 5, ad 3.)

† We might add: when Thomas says "to know demonstratively" he means it in a very full sense; and given his intellectual powers one could well see how he would say he could not believe what was clearly evident to him—whereas the same might not be true for others less well-equipped mentally—who often say they "know" something and mean it in a much less technical sense.

not be in the position to elicit an act of faith *freely* because of the overwhelming, first-hand evidence that God was communicating with them. For, they say, if the fact of a revelation shone forth to anyone with such clarity as to exclude even the possibility of imprudent doubt, the assent of faith would not possess that obscurity which is required for its real liberty.

But, it is certain that utterly perfect evidence about the fact of a revelation does not open up, or disclose the intrinsic truth of the matters to be believed; consequently *it* does not remove the obscurity of faith, properly so called. If God tells us He is a trinity, that discloses the fact; it does not show me how such a thing can be.* But why it is that perfect evidence does not destroy faith's freedom we shall now discuss.

313 III. Faith's Freedom

The assent of divine faith is a free act. This is a *dogma of faith* from the *Vatican Council*: "Faith itself and in itself, even if it does not work through charity, is a gift of God, and its act is a work pertaining to salvation; by it a man offers to God Himself a free obedience insofar as he consents and cooperates with His grace which he *could* resist"; and: "if anyone says that the assent of Christian faith is not free, but is necessarily produced by arguments of human reason; or that God's grace is only necessary for that living faith which works through charity, let him be anathema." (Const. *De fide*, ch. 3 and canons on ch. 3 canon 5 [DB 1791 and 1814]). This definition was aimed at George Hermes (d. 1831). Hermes made a distinction between *intellectual faith (fides cognitionis)* by which we assent with our intelligence to a revealed truth, and *voluntary faith (fides cordis)* which operates through

---

* Lercher maintains that this opinion of de Lugo's is "practically abandoned" today. "Cardinal de Lugo thought that the essential obscurity of faith was to be sought uniquely in a lack of clarity about the origin of revelation (inevidentia attestantis), i.e., because of a lack of evidence about the fact of revelation, and that an act of divine faith could not be squared with perfect evidence about the witness. But this opinion is practically abandoned today, mainly, it seems, because of the hard consequences it entails. Surely in this hypothesis only one of two alternatives could follow: either the Blessed Virgin did not make an act of divine faith in the conception divinely brought about in herself, or if she did, she could only do so because it was possible for her, at least imprudently, to be doubtful about the reality of the divine message. The same thing would have to be said about the faith of the Apostles and of Paul's faith." (Lercher-Schlagenhauffen, *Institutiones Theologiae Dogmaticae*, vol. 1, (1951) #657, p. 408.)

THE ACT OF DIVINE FAITH

charity.[15] He maintained that voluntary faith is indeed free and a gift of God, but that "intellectual" faith is the necessary result of rational arguments and needs no grace to produce it.

What we are discussing here is faith's internal freedom. (i.e., its non-necessary character as a psychological act; we are not discussing the *moral* obligation of positing such an act when once one knows God has spoken). So the meaning of the Catholic dogma is this: even after weighing the arguments of credibility, and even after reaching a judgment of credibility, the assent of faith still depends upon a free command from the will. Since we have previously established[16] the fact of faith's freedom in *authoritative* fashion by citing the source of revelation, all that remains to do is to examine the point philosophically and show why it is possible for the act of faith to be free.

The intellect considered in itself is no more determined to adhere to a proposition than not to adhere to it. If then it is to cling to a proposition firmly, it must be determined to do so by something which moves it. Now the intellect can be moved either by its own proper object, i.e., by the intrinsic and luminous truthfulness of the matters presented to it, or it can be moved by the will.

Whenever the intrinsic truthfulness of a matter is directly, or at least indirectly, evident to the intellect, there is no need for the will to intervene. In such a case the assent of the intellect is an act of knowledge and a necessary assent.*

---

* At least where you have *perfectly* verified the notion of knowledge, i.e., where the truth is so perfectly apparent to the intellect that the intellect is completely satisfied. But what often happens is that the truth is apparent to the intellect but not with such perfect clarity; when, for example, you have on the one hand internal arguments which truly establish the matter, but on the other hand there still remain some difficulties not perfectly resolved. In such a case the intellect is not completely quieted, and all possibility of doubting is not excluded, but only the possibility of reasonably doubting; in order to have firm adherence in such a case the will should intervene to remove the hesitation which is unreasonable. In such a case you have an assent of knowledge indeed but an assent that falls a trifle short of the perfection of knowledge in that the truth is not utterly apparent. Nonetheless, the assent remains strictly scientific since the per se cause of the firm adherence is the truth itself as grasped, whereas the will in removing the unreasonable hesitation only concurs in the production of that assent as an *accidental cause*. (causa per accidens).—The case is altogether different in the assent of faith; there the order of the will is a cause per se, the direct cause of the firm adherence, as will be clear in the text. (On this point, see Billot, *De Ecclesia*, I, p. 32.)

DIVINE FAITH

But, if the intrinsic truthfulness of a matter is not apparent, the intellect cannot cling to it firmly unless it be "pushed to do so by the will which chooses to assent because of some motive which is sufficient to move the will, but not to move the intellect, namely that it sees it is "good" or fitting to give assent; and that is the "disposition of the believer."[17] In other words, because in faith the truthfulness of the matter is not apparent to the intellect the intellect cannot assent to it except under an order from the will.

315 At this point recall the difference between scientific faith and the faith of simple authority, which alone deserves the name faith in the full sense of the term. The assent of scientific faith, that is, an assent offered precisely (formaliter) because of certitude about the veracity of testimony in a given case, is indeed always ordered by the will, but it is not always ordered freely. It is always ordered by the will, for whenever the intrinsic truthfulness of a matter is not luminously clear, the intellect cannot assent to it except under a push from the will. It is not, however, always ordered freely, for whenever the veracity of the testimony shines before the mind with complete evidence and the matter testified to poses no special difficulty, the will necessarily moves the intellect to assent, because not-to-want to assent in such a case would argue such an enormous unreasonableness that it would not have even the slightest appearance of something "good." But the will cannot desire anything unless it is at least apparently something good.* And thus the assent of faith of simple authority,—the sort of assent the act of salutary faith should be—always proceeds from a free order of the will.

316 From what has been said two conclusions follow.

1. If anyone has such *perfect* evidence for both God's truthfulness and the fact of revelation that he cannot even foolishly doubt

---

* Briefly, I may want something that is objectively worthless so long as subjectively it seems good to me; if it appears to me as totally worthless I cannot desire it at all. It is undesirable. The will by its nature seeks only what is good—real good or apparent good. That is why, for example, none of us would seriously question the existence of Rome or of Napoleon. But a necessary assent of this sort can take place only in scientific faith in which the genuine notion (ratio propria) of faith is only deficiently verified. For no matter how great the evidence for the fact of the testimony and the veracity of the witness that shines before me, the will is never necessitated to order an assent precisely (formaliter) because of "authority"; i.e., because of the moral dignity which endows the speaker with a right to receive the docile submission of the mind of the listener.

them (imprudenter), his faith will be free, not indeed with the liberty of contrariety (i.e., choose the opposite—evil) but with *liberty of exercise* (act or not act). For he would not be able to either deny or doubt the revealed truth but would assent to it necessarily at least because of his certitude about the veracity of the witness, i.e., by faith analogously so called.* Nonetheless, such a person will truly be free to offer or not to offer his assent precisely (formaliter) because of God's authority as such, i.e., by an assent of theological faith. This explains how it is that the angels, while not yet in possession of the beatific Vision, and why the Prophets, the Blessed Virgin, and the Apostles produced a free and meritorious act of faith about those truths the revelation of which was perfectly evident to them. They are mistaken, therefore, who along with Lugo[18] and others think that a free act of faith cannot be squared with perfect evidence about the origin of a revelation (in attestante).

2. As for those to whom the fact of a revelation is *not perfectly evident*, so that they can still doubt it, even though in so doing they would be acting unreasonably, their faith is free with both *liberty of exercise* and *liberty of contrariety*. Not only can they abstain from giving an assent formally because of God's supreme authority as such, they can even deny or doubt the revealed truths, for example, by either rejecting or doubting the very existence of a divine revelation. And this is normally the situation of those who do not receive a revelation first-hand.

Even though the absence of perfect evidence as to the occurrence of a revelation is not required for the essential freedom of the act of faith, it certainly does increase its freedom and, consequently, increases the merit of our faith. In this sense we understand the words of Christ to Thomas: "Blessed are they who have not seen and yet have believed."

Corollary

From what has been discussed above about faith's obscurity and freedom, we are able to understand easily St. Augustine's statement: "To believe is nothing else than to think (*cogitare*) with assent."[19] "Cogitare" (= coagitare) is used there in the sense of the

---

* It is in this way, as we already said above (no. 300) that "devils believe and tremble" (James 2:19): with a faith that is not only natural faith but faith simply in an analogous sense, i.e., scientific faith, S.Th. IIa—IIae, q. 5, a. 2; *De Veritate*, 14:9, ad 4.

deliberation and inquiry which arise spontaneously in the intellect so long as it is not yet satisfied through the clear-cut vision of truth. As St. Thomas says:

> Because [in the assent of faith] the intellect is not terminated to one thing in such a way as to bring it to its own proper goal, which is the clear-cut grasp of something intelligible, that is why its activity is not satisfied but it still keeps on ruminating and inquiring about those matters which it believes, even though it assents to them most firmly. For in what belongs to it by its own nature it is not satisfied, nor is it terminated to one thing, but it is terminated only extrinsically. And that is why the intellect of the believer is said to *be held captive*, because it is held on strange terms and not its own. That, too, is the reason why in the believer there can arise motions contrary to what it holds must firmly [i.e. indeliberate doubts] whereas that cannot happen in one who understands and knows.[21]

318 IV. Faith's Firmness

In discussing the state of certitude, we must distinguish carefully a twofold element, one negative, the other positive. The negative element means the exclusion of fear of the opposite side being true; the positive element means the firm clinging of the mind to a truth. From the viewpoint of *exclusion of doubt* (or, fear of the opposite) there are no degrees: every genuine certitude equally excludes doubt. Please note, however, we are speaking of the actual, here-and-now exclusion of doubt; we are not speaking of the exclusion of the *possibility* of doubting. Not every type of certitude excludes such possibility, but only that type of certitude which arises from evidence seen with naked clarity, v.g., that a triangle has only three sides, or that a whole is necessarily greater than one of its parts, etc.

As for the *firmness with which the mind clings to a truth*—and in this certitude formally consists—varying degrees can be found in direct correspondence with the motive or evidence for the assent. Briefly, the more the motive is seen to imply necessity for a proposition, the more firmly will the mind cling to it.

Now the *assent of faith is essentially an assent that is the firmest of all* (*firmus super omnia*). This means no one produces an act of salutary faith unless he values the authority of God revealing more than any other motive and, consequently, judges that nothing could be so flagrantly contradictory as to have God's testimony witness to something false. If this be the case, then, the will, moved by grace, can and should make the intellect—despite the fact that it is not satisfied by clear-cut understanding—assent to revealed truths with utter firmness, by valuing more God's judgment (which by believing it adopts as its own) than its own judgment, however clear-cut that may seem to be. That is why St. Thomas says:

> As regards the firmness of adherence, faith is more certain than any understanding or knowledge, because the First Truth, which causes the assent of faith, is a stronger cause than the light of reason which causes the assent of understanding or science (knowledge).[22]

The assertion as to faith's firmness may be *proven* from data given in Sacred Scripture and from theological reasoning.

a. *Sacred Scripture.* Scripture demands an adherence that is *utterly certain:* "*Therefore, let all the house of Israel know most assuredly that God has made both Lord and Christ, this Jesus whom you crucified*" (Acts 2:36). It demands an assent that is *most full:* Abraham "*in view of the promise of God did not waver through unbelief but was strengthened in faith, giving glory to God, being fully aware that whatever God has promised he is able also to perform*" (Romans 4:20-21). Again, Scripture teaches that God's authority is to be preferred to *men's testimony:* "*If we receive the testimony of men, the testimony of God is greater; for this is the testimony of God which is greater, that He has borne witness concerning His Son. He who believes in the Son of God has the testimony of God in himself. He who does not believe the Son, makes him a liar; because he does not believe the witness that God has borne concerning his son*" (1 John 5:9-10). It teaches that God's testimony is preferable even to the testimony of one's own *senses:* "*For we were not following fictitious tales when we made known to you the power and coming of our Lord Jesus Christ, but we had been eyewitnesses of his grandeur . . . and this voice we ourselves heard borne from heaven . . . and we have the word of prophecy,* surer still (firmiorem) to which you do well to attend, as to a lamp shining in a dark place. . . .*" (2 Peter 1:16-19). Finally, Scripture

---

* *Word of prophecy,* i.e., the sum of the messianic prophecies of the Old Testament which declares the glorious reign of the Messias.

exhibits the assent of faith as morally *irrevocable:** so strong that even if an apostle, or an angel were to teach a different gospel than that accepted by faith, they should be rejected by the Christian believer: *"But even if we or an angel from heaven should preach a gospel to you other than that which we have preached to you, let him be anathema! As we have said before, so now I say again: If anyone preach a gospel to you other than that which you have received, let him be anathema!"* (Galatians 1:8–10).

b. *Theological reasoning.* This helps us to understand why the assent of faith should be the firmest of all assents. Salutary faith is a meritorious work which honors God. But anyone who would not prefer God's testimony to any other motive for assenting would certainly not honor God—rather he would insult God. The deepest reason, we might say, why God is so insistent on faith is precisely this point that faith is such a tremendous act of surrender and worship. It is one thing for a man to give up worldly goods for God, quite another to give up that which is dearest—his own judgment and sweet will. This means surrendering all that is deepest and most truly his very own.

319 Corollaries

1. Since the assent of faith must be *firm above all other assents,* it follows that the faithful should always be prepared to reject as an error any opinion which is *unmistakably* opposed to a truth which is *unmistakably* revealed, however strong may *appear* the reasonings backing up such an opinion. But it does *not* follow that they should be prepared to reject more vigorously any naturally evident truth, or demonstrated fact, than a truth of the faith. Such a mental disposition is impossible. Anyone who would demand such a disposition would obviously be resting upon an absurd premise— the premise that God could have revealed some truth that is contradictory to a naturally evident truth. It is, indeed, *more* unthinkable that a truth revealed by God should be false than that a naturally evident truth should be so, and consequently the assent of faith surpasses all evident knowledge in its firmness; nevertheless, it is *also unthinkable* that a naturally evident proposition should be false, v.g., that a triangle is not a square.

2. Faith's firmness should not be confused with its *irrevoca-*

---

* *Morally irrevocable.* See below, margin no. 320.

bility. For the assent of faith is physically revocable, as is obvious from the fact that it is a free assent. But the assent of faith is irrevocable *morally*. That is, one cannot revoke it licitly, or without sin. And this moral irrevocability stems effectively from the unshakeableness of the certitude about the fact of a revelation (as explained above, no. 279-280) and is commensurate with it. Further, the assent of faith is by its nature irrevocable *affectively* (i.e., so far as the will is concerned) insofar as a man cannot adhere to a revealed truth with an assent firm above all others without thereby, at least implicitly, meaning to retain that assent forever.

Scholion. The inequality of faith. 321

No one produces an assent of salutary faith unless he clings to revealed truth with utter firmness, by valuing God's authority above all other motives. From this precisive viewpoint (i.e., from the evaluation of the formal object or motive) faith is equal in all believers. Nonetheless, from other viewpoints faith can be "greater," or, if one prefers the term, "more firm" in one man than in another. This is true from several angles:

a. From the viewpoint of the *intensity of the act* of faith. For the assent (which from the viewpoint of the valuation placed on its motive—God's authority—is firm above all others) can both be commanded with greater or less effort and devotion by the will, and elicited by the intellect with more alacrity, fervor, etc. Think, for example, of a man resisting with all his strength some doubt which is beginning to rise in him, say, against the mystery of Christ's real presence in the Eucharist. That is why St. Thomas says:

> It is of the very nature of faith that the First Truth should be preferred above all else. Still, among all those who do prefer it to all else, some men subject themseves to it more surely, [with more intense application of the intellect] and more devoutly [with greater fervor of will].[23]

b. From the viewpoint of its *practical impact on the moral life*. If you take two Catholics you may find that faith languishes in the one, whereas it is so vivid and alive in the other that it has a tremendous influence upon all his judgments and actions.* So, for

---
* Notice, though, that a "languid" faith is not necessarily to be identified with "dead"—("unformed faith"—faith in man in mortal sin); nor, is an

example, the saints are often described as living by the *spirit* of faith, i.e., viewing all things from the standpoint of revealed truth. This practical influence on the moral life depends both upon the intensity and the frequency with which one elicits acts of faith.

c. From the viewpoint of its *deeprootedness in the soul*. For the roots of faith are deeper and more firm in one man than in another so that if both are exposed to equal, external dangers to faith (v.g., dangerous reading) one man falls away from the faith more easily than the other. On the intellectual side, faith is more deeply rooted in the man who knows more thoroughly both the force of the motives of credibility and the superficiality of the arguments raised against the faith. On the voluntary side, faith is more deeply rooted in the man who has a will that is more tenacious and prompt to believe and who is more immune to desires that militate indirectly against faith (pride, worldliness, carnal vices).[24]

d. Finally, the *virtue* of faith, viewed simply *in itself*, can be more perfect in one man than in another as will be seen in the treatise on *Christ's Grace*. Briefly, God may freely bestow more grace on one person than on another, in accord with His own sweet pleasure—think of the Blessed Virgin, St. Paul and others; and the infused virtues of faith, hope, and charity increase proportionately with the increase of sanctifying grace.

From the above points it should be clear what is meant by saying that some people are "strong in faith," others "weak"*; and in what sense faith can be said to increase or diminish† in individual believers.

"active" faith necessarily identical with "living" faith ("formed" faith—faith in man in state of grace). Nonetheless an active, or alive faith will not remain long "unformed," nor will a languid, or lukewarm faith long remain "formed."

* Consequently, it is completely wrong to conclude from the statement in Matthew 14:31—"O you of little faith, why did you doubt"—that little faith, or small faith means such faith as includes doubt about its *object*. The passage in question deals with faith insofar as it begets confidence (*fiducia*—see above no. 178) and Peter's faith is called "little" insofar as the terror begotten at the sound of the rising wind conquered the confidence begotten by his faith—and this indeed does point to a lack of *intensity* to his faith.

† The formal discussion of the acquisition, loss, increase, or possible dimunition of the infused virtues of faith, hope, and charity appears in the volume, *Christ's Grace*. Here, for practical purposes, it is sufficient to note that the infused virtue of faith can only be lost by a mortal sin directly against the formal object of this virtue; it cannot be whittled away to the vanishing point merely by non-exercise of the infused habit, nor by venial sins of negligence with regard to it. Otherwise, sanctifying grace, and along with it, eternal life, could be lost by venial sins—which is a flagrant contradiction of the very notion of venial sin.

THE ACT OF DIVINE FAITH

It is easy to see that a greater perfection of faith, in the sense explained above, and which admits of many degrees, is of immense importance for the whole business of salvation. But this perfection depends both upon one's own cooperation, and also, ultimately, upon the measure of grace received. That is why we pray daily: "Lord, increase our faith!"

Notes

1. See de Lugo, *De Fide,* disputatio 4, 85 ff.
2. See above, nos. 201 and 202.
3. *S.Th*, IIa–IIae, q. 1, art. 5, corpus.
4. *Ibid.,* ad 4.
5. See I Corinthians 13:9-13; II Corinthians 5:7.
6. S.Th., IIa–IIae, q. 1 art. 4 and 5; *De Veritate,* q. 14, art. 9; Salmanticenses, *De fide,* Disputatio III, dubium II and III; Zigliara, *Summa Philosophiae, Ontologia* vol. III, ch. 2, art. 2, VII; De Groot, *Summa de Eccles.,* q. XX, art. 2, IV and V; Billot, *De virtutibus infusis,* thesis 11.
7. *Tractatus in Joannem* 79, no. 1; see also 40, no. 9.
8. *Dialogus,* bk. IV, ch. 6; see also *Homilia in Evangelium* 26, no. 8.
9. Salmanticenses, *De Fide,* Disp. III, dubium II and III, no. 33–36.
10. *Idem,* no. 86.—We add this passage taken from the same Salmanticenses:

> Granted that it is contradictory for a man to believe a truth which he knows clearly, it is nonetheless not contradictory to believe that that same truth has been revealed by God. As a matter of fact, we who clearly know that God exists, do not believe that truth; yet all the same we do believe that God has revealed his existence . . . and by the very fact that we believe the aforementioned truth has been revealed by God, we do attain a greater certitude about the infallibility of that truth. . . . Therefore, even though the testimony of God, which is faith's proper motive, does not move [the intellect] actually (exercitive) and in the fashion of a motive specifying the evidential assent of this truth: "God exists"; it does concur nonetheless after the fashion of a motive extrinsically regulating the greater certitude of the aforesaid assent. (*Loc. cit.,* no. 85)

11. *S.Th.,* IIa–IIae, q. 2, art. 10, ad 1.
12. Salmanticenses, *loc. cit.,* no. 51.
13. Suarez, *De fide,* Disputatio III, sect. 9; de Lugo, *De fide,* Disputatio II, sect. 2; Franzelin, *De Deo Uno,* sect. I, thesis 9; Jansen, *Praelectiones theologicae,* vol. I, p. 734; Brouwer, *De fide,* p. 244; Pesch, vol. VIII, p. 402; Wilmers, *De fide,* p. 206; Mannens, *Theologia Dogmatica,* vol. I, no. 744; Schiffini, *De virtutibus infusis,* no. 78.
14. De Lugo, *De Fide,* Disputatio, II, sect. 1.
15. *Erkentnissglaube* and *Herzensglaube.* See *Collectio Lacensis,* vol. VII, p. 529.
16. See above, no. 267.
17. St. Thomas, *De Veritate,* q. 14, art. 9.
18. De Lugo, *De Fide,* disputatio II, sect. 1.

19. *De Praedestinatione Sanctorum*, ch. 2, no. 5.
20. 2 Corinthians 10:5: ". . . bringing every mind into captivity to the obedience of Christ. . . "
21. *S.Th.*, IIa–IIae, q. 2, art. 1.
22. *De Veritate*, q. 14, art. 1, ad 7; see also *S.Th.* IIa–IIae, q. 4, art. 8.
23. *S.Th.*, IIa–IIae, q. 5, art. 4, ad 2.
24. See de Lugo, *De Fide*, disputatio 16, no. 66–68.

Article V

WHO HAS FAITH? — AND IS FAITH NECESSARY?

I. *Which Persons Are Capable of an Act of Supernatural Faith?*
   1. Angels and saints do not make acts of faith.
   2. Devils and the damned do not make acts of faith.
   3. Formal heretics do not make acts of faith.
   4. Sincere Protestants and other purely material heretics are capable of making supernatural acts of faith.

II. *The Necessity of Making an Act of Faith:*
   Meaning: Is an act of faith an absolutely and indispensably necessary means for obtaining salvation: A twofold question to be solved:
   1. Is faith necessary by necessity of means for salvation?
   2. What is the bare minimum of revealed truth which must be explicitly believed?
   1. An act of faith is necessary by necessity of means for salvation.
       a. Some outmoded opinions to the contrary.
       b. Virtually unanimous teaching of all theologians today on necessity of faith for salvation.
       Proof:
           (1) from Sacred Scripture.
           (2) from Tradition.
           (3) from intrinsic reasoning on nature of Beatific Vision and process of Justification.
       c. What theological certitude can be granted to this teaching about the absolute necessity of faith?
           (1) No contrary opinion can be given the status even of probability.
   2. What is the bare minimum of revealed truth which must be explicitly believed.

- a. All are agreed that at least these two articles of faith must be explicitly believed: *God exists* and is a *rewarder* to those who seek Him.
- b. Necessity of belief in the mysteries of the Incarnation and the Trinity—a disputed question.
    - (1) Theoretically, the negative opinion seems far more probable.
    - (2) In practice the affirmative opinion must be followed whenever possible because it is the *tutior pars*.

Scholion: The precise meaning of the two articles of faith which must be believed in explicit fashion.

Article V

WHO HAS FAITH? — AND IS FAITH NECESSARY?

I. Persons Capable of Faith 322

Since we are here exclusively concerned with the *act* of faith, not the habit* of faith, we can be brief. Three categories of persons are considered: (1) the angels and saints; (2) the devils and the damned; (3) heretics, formal and material.

1. The *angels and saints* in heaven do not make acts of faith. This point is certain from *Sacred Scripture* which describes faith as giving way to sight; the imperfect yields to the perfect:

> *Charity never fails whereas prophecies will disappear, and tongues will cease, and knowledge will be destroyed. For we know in part and we prophesy in part; but when that which is perfect has come, that which is imperfect will be done away with. When I was a child, I spoke as a child, I thought as a child. Now that I have become a man, I have put away the things of a child. We see now through a mirror,† in an obscure manner, but then face to face. Now I know in part, but then I shall know even as I have been known. So there abide faith, hope and charity, but the greatest of these is charity.* (I Corinthians, 13:8–13)

And again *Sacred Scripture* tells us:

> *Always full of courage, then, and knowing that while we are in the body we are exiled from the Lord—for we walk by faith and not by sight.* (2 Corinthians 5:6–7)

Theological reasoning bears out the same point. St. Thomas writes:

---

* The virtue, or habit, of faith is discussed in volume, *Christ's Grace* (vol. 7 of this series) nos. 165–181: "The infused virtues."

† The mirrors in St. Paul's day were very dim indeed—made of metal, not glass.

> Faith by its very nature presumes an imperfection on the part of the subject, namely that the believer does not see what he believes. Beatitude, on the other hand, by its very nature demands perfection on the part of the subject, namely that the one beatified should see that by which he is beatified . . . consequently it is clear that it is impossible for both faith and beatitude to coexist simultaneously in the same person.[1]

A fuller explanation of this first point can be found in Pesch.[2]

2. *The devils and the damned* do not make acts of faith. The reason for that assertion is that they possess neither the help of grace, nor the good will which is absolutely required for someone to believe with faith of simple authority (see above, no. 316).

3. *Formal heretics* do not make an act of divine faith even in those revealed truths which they accept. Divine faith signifies an utterly firm assent given because of God's authority which is valued above all else. Now someone who refuses to admit even one doctrine, sufficiently proposed to him as revealed, clearly shows that he does not value God's authority above all else, rather he puts it in second place to his own free choice. "Consequently it is evident that such a heretic who does not possess faith in one article (of the creed) does not have faith in the other articles, but simply a kind of opinion which suits his own will."[3] That is why Leo XIII writes:

> Those who select from Christian doctrine only what they prefer, rest on their own judgment and not on faith; for they do not at all 'lead every intellect into captivity in homage to Christ'; for they more truly obey themselves rather than God.[4]

It is true that heretics and unbelievers rarely ever openly question God's authority. Rather they ex professo reject or call into doubt the fact of revelation, either universally or at least for some specific doctrine. Still, they are not thereby excused from the sin of heresy or infidelity. For they have sufficient knowledge that a particular doctrine has been revealed (otherwise they would not be formal heretics, or positive unbelievers, but simply innocently mistaken). Yet despite that fact they are unwilling to accept it. But in order not to evade too openly their obligation to believe they either create difficulties for themselves, or, at least, uniquely confine their attention to the difficulties which obscure the revealed origin of such a doctrine. Thus precisely because of a *defect in the* *will to believe,* they designedly prepare for themselves a kind of voluntary ignorance about the fact of the revelation; which actually is nothing other than to set a trap both for themselves and for others.*

This has been the case with every genuine heresiarch from Pelagius to Luther. They first declare that since a doctrine is unswallowable, it cannot be revealed and hence no one will find that the Church teaches it "as revealed." After the evidence is offered that the Church has indeed always taught the doctrine and taught it as revealed, they demonstrate by stepping out of the Church, that the real, root cause of their objections was the original one of not being willing to submit their minds, not simply unawareness of the fact as revealed. So Pelagius first maintained that he was opposed to the doctrine of original sin not because it was "revealed" but because Augustine had manufactured the dogma. After he was confronted with overwhelming evidence of the revealed character of the doctrine from the Church's unanimous tradition, and Scripture, he tried one dodge after another, but finally left the church for the reason which had been there from the first: unwillingness to bend his mind to so mysterious a truth. Similarly, Luther unable to accept certain Catholic truths, first appealed from an ill-informed pope to a better informed pope. After the better informed pope reiterated the same revealed teaching, he appealed from the pope to Scripture, and finally, from Scripture to his own interpretation of Scripture. The root reason in each instance is unwillingness to buckle the mind down to accept exclusively on God's authority what appears to be totally unreasonable to one's own intelligence. Consequently, one's own intelligence, or preference, or feelings, is always given first place; God's authority if not theoretically, at least practically is subordinated to that intellect, or preference, or prejudice.

Do Honest Protestants Have Supernatural Faith?

One must make, however, an entirely different judgment in regard to men who without any serious fault on their own have left

* In somewhat the same way those who refuse to obey a legitimate superior seldom admit that they are unwilling to obey legitimately constituted authority: rather they seek to obscure the justice of the command given by saying, for example, that the superior is not properly acquainted with the circumstances, or that he has been rendered hostile to them because of the efforts of people who are envious of them and so forth.

the church—purely material heretics. Most non-Catholic Christians today fit into this category. A person validly baptized as a child receives the infused virtue of faith. And he retains that virtue so long as he does not commit some formal sin of infidelity. If such a person, raised among non-Catholics, and blamelessly ignorant of the nature of Christ's church, should cling to some heretical sect, he will still produce an act of supernatural faith in all the revealed doctrines which the sect still professes. As for the non-revealed doctrines which he may admit along with the sect, those remarks hold true which we have made above (see above no. 305). With good reason observes the erudite Brouwer:

> If, after a [serious] doubt has arisen about the truth of his sect, he should neglect to search for the truth, he will sin seriously; still, he will not always lose the habit of faith. Such serious negligence does not always imply deliberate doubt or denial of divine authority, neither does it necessarily expel the sincere will to believe—the will by which he is prepared to give an assent of faith to truth when sufficiently proposed to him. A fortiori, the habit of faith is not expelled if he begins a serious inquiry about the truth, even if in the meantime, while in doubt as to which is Christ's true Church, he suspends the assent of faith, but is ready to believe just as soon as the truth becomes sufficiently known to him.[5]

323 II. The Necessity of Making an Act of Faith

It is customary to distinguish between necessity of means and necessity of precept* in reference to the act of faith. The moral obligation (necessity of precept) of making an assent of faith in different circumstances is treated in Moral theology. Here we are concerned solely with necessity of means, i.e., whether making an act of faith in the strict sense of the term is a necessary means to salvation.

Obviously the necessity of making an act of faith can only refer and factually does refer only to adults; babies (who die before reaching the age of reason) are saved by the *virtue* of faith which they receive in baptism. With these points taken for granted, and skipping also the error of rationalists who in ruling out revelation itself necessarily also reject any act of faith, there remains a two-

---

* See *Christ's Church*, no. 159, for a full explanation of this distinction.

fold question to be treated. One question refers to the absolute necessity of an act of faith in the strict sense of the term; the other refers to the necessary content of that act, i.e., the bare minimum of revealed truth which must be believed if one is to be saved.

1. *Whether an act of faith in the strict sense of the term is absolutely necessary for justification and for salvation.* A few theologians, in order to harmonize more easily God's will to save all men with the impossibility under which many pagans seem to lie of being prevented from knowing about revelation, have stated that the necessity of making an act of faith in the strict sense is not an absolute necessity. They maintained that for men who were in invincible ignorance about a supernatural revelation, an act of faith in a loose sense of the term would suffice. This would mean *a knowledge about God's existence and His role as a rewarder, based upon the testimony of the created universe*—a knowledge which, in a loose and improper use of the term, can be dubbed a "revelation."[6] Other theologians corrected this opinion in such fashion as to say that the type of knowledge just described (i.e., *purely natural from the viewpoint of its formal object*) would suffice *provided it were supernatural from the viewpoint of its principle,* i.e., if elicited under the help of elevating grace. This opinion, which once appeared attractive to Ripalda (d. 1648) even though he did not dare to embrace it as his own,[7] has in modern times been defended by the illustrious Gutberlet[8] and by G. Konings.[9] The arguments backing up this opinion are these: (a) Some texts of *Sacred Scripture* praise a knowledge of God and of the natural law that is based solely on creation; hence they conclude that even this type of knowledge, in default of knowledge of a revelation, could lead a man to his goal.[10] (b) The same point is openly implied, in fact sometimes plainly taught by some of the fathers, especially the earlier ones.[11] (c) There is no intrinsic argument which can demonstrate the absolute necessity of an act of faith in the strict sense.

Nevertheless the *almost unanimous opinion* maintains the absolute necessity of the act of faith for justification. I say: act of faith, or *faith in act,* for the absolute necessity of real faith by at least an implicit *desire* is denied by no one.

324

This doctrine is *proved* as follows:

1. From *Sacred Scripture.* The main text appealed to is: *"Without faith it is impossible to please God; for it is necessary for one*

(375)

coming to God to believe that He is and is a rewarder to those who seek Him."[12] It is quite obvious here that it is a question not of something simply necessary by precept, but of a necessary means. What is required is actual faith, that is, an act by which the two truths clearly mentioned are believed. One cannot understand here faith in a loose sense of the term, since the entire context is dealing with that faith which is "the substance of things hoped for, the conviction about things that appear not." The scriptural loci which praise the natural knowledge of God and of the natural law can be understood as referring to the indirect usefulness of such knowledge for salvation insofar as it either negatively prepares for faith, or insofar as it renders the preservation of primitive revelation more easy.[13]

2. From *Tradition*. Even though the fathers incessantly taught and insisted on the necessity of faith, they did not deal ex professo with the special question we are here discussing. Consequently, it is often not easy to judge whether in every case they demanded precisely an act of faith in the strict sense; in fact it must be admitted that some of their utterances, especially those of the more ancient fathers, favor[14] the milder opinion. But, on Catholic principles, the genuine meaning of tradition, when not too obvious among the ancients, is made known by the clear consent of later doctors. Now the consent of the schools of theology through many centuries is such that for this precise reason Ripalda did not dare to assert that this opinion, which personally attracted him, was even probable.[15] Furthermore, this doctrine of the schools, to put it at a minimum is openly favored by the Council of Trent and the Vatican Council. The *Council of Trent* in its decree on justification first says that men are made ready "for justice itself, while conceiving faith by hearing they are freely moved towards God, believing to be true those matters which have been divinely revealed and promised," and cites the words of Scripture: "It is necessary for one coming to God to believe" (Session 6, ch. 6); then, in enumerating the causes of justification the Council teaches that the instrumental cause is baptism, "which is the sacrament of faith, without which no one ever receives justification" (ch. 7); finally the Council declares that the words of the Apostle that a man is "justified through faith," must be understood "in that sense which the perpetual mind of the Catholic Church has always held and expressed, namely that we are said to be justified by faith because

faith is the beginning, foundation, and root of all justification, without which it is impossible to please God and to come to the fellowship of his sons" (ch. 8). Now does it seem reasonable to maintain that the council in saying that no one ever received justification without faith (chapter 7) and that it is impossible to please God without faith (ch.8) at this point meant a *different* faith than that which it described a little earlier (chapter 6), namely, faith in the strict sense of the term? The *Vatican Council*, after giving the definition of faith and other points which refer unmistakably and exclusively to faith in the strict sense of the term, adds: "But because without faith it is impossible to please God and to come to fellowship with his sons; therefore no one ever received justification without faith nor will anyone unless he perseveres in it to the end, ever reach eternal life."[16]

3. *Internal arguments*. It must be granted, we think, that one cannot rigorously demonstrate by intrinsic reasoning alone the absolute necessity of an act of faith in the strict sense. From the viewpoint of God's absolute power,* it does not seem contradictory that a man possessing a knowledge of God as really existing and rewarding[17]—a knowledge natural from the viewpoint of its formal object, but supernatural by reason of its elicitive principle (i.e., as ennobled by elevating grace)—should, under the illumination of such knowledge, arrive at making an act of perfect love (an act again, supernatural only by reason of its elicitive principle) and thus be sufficiently readied for justification.

Nonetheless, it seems less harmonious for a man, using only his natural reason, to be admitted to a loving union with God (justification) and as a consequence to an eternal and supernatural enjoyment of God, without first being aware that such friendship and enjoyment was being offered to him by God, and hence without being able to desire those gifts in a definite fashion. Indeed, it is incongruous for a rational nature to operate without knowledge of a definite goal, or to be led to a goal whose existence it has not even suspected. But since we cannot have any knowledge

---

* God's absolute power means God's naked omnipotence viewed in itself, abstracting from any definite economy that God has set up. Anything doable, i.e., not self-contradictory, can be wrought by God's power viewed absolutely. God's selected (*potentia ordinata*) power refers to God's power as limited by his free choice of a definite sort of a universe. God by his potentia absoluta could have given man infused knowledge or three eyes; de facto He settled for ratiocination and bifocal vision.

DIVINE FAITH

of such realities, i.e., of a loving union with God through grace and glory, except through faith in the strict sense, God has ordained by positive law indeed, but by a law that is quite congruous, in fact connatural, that no one should ever factually arrive at justification without an act of faith.*

326 **How sure are we about this absolute necessity of faith?** As to the question *with what certitude* one must retain this teaching on the absolute necessity of faith in the strict sense, we add these statements of theologians. Suarez writes:

> I think that the assertion according to which no one in any era, place or circumstances was ever able to be justified without an act of faith, is certain to such a degree that it cannot be denied without an error against faith.[18]

Melchior Cano writes:

> It is an error, and perhaps heretical to assert that any adult is justified without faith and with only natural knowledge.[19]

Having cited these authorities, and also noting that Suarez and Cano were not specifically considering the question of a knowledge drawn from creation *but enobled by elevating grace*, the erudite Schmid has this comment to make:

> We think one should abstain from so rigid a judgment and we recommend prudence; nonetheless Gutberlet's theory, in our judgment, does not deserve to be ranked with opinions which are probable, and consequently Catholic theology cannot grant it any serious consideration.[20]

327 **Which revealed truths must be explicitly believed by necessity of means?** True faith is necessarily *all-embracive* in this sense that

---

* This ordination of God, granted the universality of His salvific will, necessarily implies that God provides every adult with means that are at least remotely sufficient to make an act of faith in the strict sense, so that no one, except through his own fault, will lack through a whole lifetime the knowledge of revealed truth requisite for such an act. But just how this providence is verified, in accord with theologians' explanations, will be discussed in the volume on *Christ's Grace*. Here we might remark in passing that the praise Christ bestows on faith and his rebuke to those who are lacking faith seem necessarily to imply that faith is fairly readily available to any man of good will.

it must *at least* implicitly assent to whatever God has revealed and the Church proposes for belief.* But a genuine act of faith cannot be elicited without having at least some subject matter to reach in *explicit* fashion. If you assent, you have to assent to something. We ask, therefore, which truths that act of faith, which is absolutely necessary for justification and salvation, must attain to *in explicit fashion,* i.e., in its own proper terms.

Now all are agreed (so long as one abstracts from any more specific determination of the exact meaning of the articles—which we will discuss later) that by necessity of means we must explicitly believe those two articles of faith which the *Epistle to the Hebrews* so clearly proposes, namely, that *God exists* and that *He is a rewarder to those who seek Him.*[21] It is disputed however, whether, after the promulgation of the Gospel, it is also necessary by necessity of means to believe explicitly in the mysteries of the *Blessed Trinity* and in *Christ the Redeemer* (under which latter truth some theologians include more, others less). I state: "after the promulgation of the Gospel," because all admit that under the Old Testament economy neither the mystery of the Blessed Trinity, nor the Redemption by God incarnate and dying were so clearly revealed as to be able to be acknowledged by everyone.†

328

The *affirmative* opinion (i.e., that these two truths must also be believed in *explicit* fashion) is based first of all on those utterances of Sacred Scripture[22] which require faith in Christ as necessary for salvation. From this point it is customary also to infer the necessity of explicit belief in the Trinity because "the mystery of the Incarnation of Christ cannot be explicitly believed, without faith in the Trinity, because in the mystery of the Incarnaton this point is contained, that the *Son* of God assumed flesh, that through the grace of the *Holy Spirit* He renewed the world, and again that He was conceived of the Holy Spirit.[23]

The *negative* opinion maintains that belief by necessity of means in these mysteries cannot be demonstrated either by intrinsic reasoning based upon the nature of the fact (for otherwise such a necessity would also have been present prior to Christ), nor by any positive statute made by God in the New Testament.

---

* See above no. 184, c., and no. 211.
† In fact, as is discussed in the Trinity tract, you merely have adumbrations, or loose prefigurings of this mystery; not its actual revelation even in dim terms.

DIVINE FAITH

For the utterances of Scripture which are adduced as proof either simply extol the efficacy of faith in Christ, or they can be understood in the sense of the necessity of *implicit* faith and then, in the supposition of the truth being preached, explicit faith. As regards the mystery of the Blessed Trinity, they add: explicit faith in the mystery of the Redemption, that is of God incarnate and dying for us, can be possessed at least in a blurry way (in confuso) without explicitly knowing the existence of a trinity of persons in God.

329 Speaking purely theoretically the negative opinion appears far more probable, at least if one is talking about an *absolute* or indispensable necessity of means. For the *normal, ordinary procedure* is this: no adult arrives at justification without first explicitly believing in Christ the Redeemer, and thus believing in the Blessed Trinity. For how without this faith would he be willing to enter the Church and to receive the (virtue of) faith?

It is in this way also we think that the distinction is to be explained—the distinction made by some followers of the negative opinion who state that explicit faith in these mysteries under the New Dispensation is a means which is necessary either in fact or in desire (in *re vel in voto*).[25] For anyone who would in extraordinary fashion be justified without actual knowledge of the Trinity and the Redemption, certainly must get to know those articles as soon as possible so that he can either enter the ordinary route to salvation, that is Christ's Church, or remain in it.

In practice, however, so long as it is possible to do so, one must adopt the affirmative opinion because it is the *tutior pars*.*[26]

330 *Scholion. The meaning of the two principle articles of faith.*

It is common teaching that in virtue of the second article we must believe that God is a rewarder, not in any old way, but that He is a *rewarder in the supernatural order*. So this truth, which by necessity of means must be held by an act of faith, differs from the truth that we can know by natural reason alone, i.e., that God rewards good and punishes evil. However, it is not required that

---

* In a conflict of theological opinions one is normally free to follow the opinion he personally prefers. In certain cases, however, involving something as serious as salvation (as here), or the validity of the sacraments, one is obliged in practice to adopt the stricter viewpoint. The stricter viewpoint is called the "safer side" (*tutior pars*).

the believer have a clear and distinct notion of the *supernatural reward*; it suffices that it be grasped in a vague way as a reward *promised by revelation.* So, practically speaking, this point offers no difficulty: whoever believes by an act of faith in the strict sense, i.e., because of the authority of God revealing, that God rewards those who seek Him by that very fact believes that God will reward him *in accord with His promise.*

As for the first article, many theologians take this to refer to the bare existence of the one true God; but it is better to say that this article means belief *in the existence of God, insofar as He is the cause of grace,* or justification; or insofar as He is supernaturally communicating with men; or insofar as He is helping man towards his supernatural goal; or insofar as He exercises providence over mankind beyond the exigencies of nature. All these descriptions amount to the same thing.[27]

Surely one could not assign any intrinsic argument why it would be absolutely necessary for every man to believe with faith in the strict sense this distinct article if it included nothing which surpasses the grasp of unaided reason. If the truths necessary to believe by necessity of means were restricted to the acknowledgment of the bare *existence* of a God who is a supernatural rewarder, why would it not be sufficient for a philosopher to know the existence of God and believe in Him as a supernatural rewarder? That is why St. Thomas in answer to the objection raised: "The act of faith is not required for justification except insofar as through faith a man knows God: but a man can also know God through natural knowledge; therefore an act of faith is not required for justification," replys as follows: "It must be said that by natural knowledge a man is not oriented towards God *insofar as He is the goal of our happiness and the cause of our justification.*"[28] And elsewhere he writes: "It must be said that the bare existence of God (Deum esse simpliciter) is not the article [of faith] but that God is as faith supposes him, that is as *having a care for everyone,* rewarding and punishing, as is clear from the Apostle in Hebrews 11 who thus specifies that 'He is and is a rewarder'."[29]

Finally, even this difference offers no practical difficulty. No Catholic doubts that in virtue of these two articles one must believe that God both provides for or helps us in a supernatural way and also rewards us in a supernatural way. For whoever believes with an act of strict faith that God exists, necessarily believes in God as revealing Himself in a supernatural way, i.e., *as entering into communication with us beyond the exigencies of nature*, and does so (as is clear from the second article annexed to it) in relation to a supernatural reward.

Notes

1. *S.Th.*, IIa–IIae, q. 67, art. 3, corpus.
2. *Praelectiones dogmaticae*, vol. VIII, no. 397 ff.
3. *S.Th.*, Ia–IIae, q. 5, art. 3, corpus.
4. Encyclical, *Satis Cognitum* (June 29, 1896). Latin text is found in *Leonis XIII allocutiones* (Desclee ed.) vol. VI, p. 171.
5. Brouwer, *De fide divina*, p. 197.
6. This view was held by Andrew Vega and Dominic Soto. (Soto, however, later changed his opinion according to Schiffini). *De virtutibus infusis*, p. 291.
7. Ripalda, *De Ente Supernaturali*, disputatio 20, no. 118–123, and *De fide*, Disputatio 17, no. 142–219.
8. Heinrich-Gutberlet, *Dogmatica theologia*, vol. VIII, p. 494 ff. Gutberlet's position, however, was rejected by F. Schmid, *Die ausserordentliche Heilswege für die gefallene Menscheit* (1899, p. 65 ff.) and B. W. Liese, *Der heilsnotwendige Glaube* (1902).
9. G. Konings, *De Gratia actuali* (1907) p. 113.
10. See, for example, *Wisdom*, ch. 13, 1 ff.; *Proverbs* 1:20 ff.; *Acts* 14:16 and 17:26 ff.; *Romans* 1:18 ff.; 2:13–16.
11. For example, Sts. Justin, Clement of Alexandria, Athanasius, Chrysostom, Augustine, and the author of the book, *De vocatione omnium gentium;* on the patristic viewpoint see Schmid, *loc. cit.*, p. 74 ff.
12. *Hebrews* 11:6. Other Scriptural loci cited are: *Romans* 1:17; *Hebrews* 10:38; *Galatians* 2:16.
13. On this point see F. Schmid, *Die ausserordentliche Heilswege für die gefallene Menscheit*, p. 65 ff.
14. W. Liese, *op. cit.*, has made a careful investigation and analysis of the Patristic teaching on this point.
15. Ripalda, *De Ente Supernaturali*, disputatio 20, no. 123; *De fide*, Disputatio 17, no. 213.
16. Constitution, *De fide*, ch. 3: see, however, *Collectio Lacensis*, vol. VII, p. 160 and 178.—Furthermore, Innocent XI in the year 1679 condemned this proposition: *"Faith in the loose sense of the term, as based on the testimony of the created world, or similar motive suffices for justification."* All the same this condemnation does not establish the point completely. The proposition cited, along with many others, was condemned "just as they lie, as at a minimum both scandalous and in practice harmful." But, according to Gutberlet (*loc. cit.* p. 494) the proposition deserved this censure because it is *too universal* in its enuntiation: for, first of all, it makes no distinction between a knowledge which would be natural or supernatural from the viewpoint of its elicitive principle; and, secondly, the proposition does not restrict the sufficiency of

THE ACT OF DIVINE FAITH

knowledge drawn from the created world to such persons as are in ignorance of a supernatural revelation.

17. Such knowledge of God as a rewarder does not positively exclude a *supernatural* reward, it simply prescinds from that point.

18. Suarez, *De Fide*, disputatio 12, s. 2, no. 5.

19. Melchior Cano, *Relect. de Sacr.* p. 2, q. 2 (as cited in Schmid, *loc. cit.*, p. 110).

20. F. Schmid, *Die ausserordentliche Heilswege fur die gefallene Menscheit*, p. 110–112.

21. Simply to refresh the memory we list here the proposition condemned by Innocent XI: "*Only faith in the one God seems necessary by necessity of means, but not explicit faith in God as a remunerator.*" (DB 1172).

22. *John* 3: 14 ff.; 5:24; 8:24; 11:25; 17:3; *Acts* 4:11–12; 26:15–18; *Romans* 3:22–23; *Galatians* 2:16. For the rest, see Billuart, *De Fide*, dissertatio 3, art. 2.

23. *S.Th.*, IIa–IIae, q. 2, art. 8, corpus.

24. See, for example, Suarez, *De Fide*, disputatio 12, s. 4; de Lugo, *De Fide*, disputatio 12, no. 91 ff; Schmid, *loc. cit.*, p. 130 ff.

25. Suarez, *loc. cit.*, no. 19; de Lugo, *loc. cit.*, no. 107.

26. The following proposition was condemned by Innocent XI:
"A man is capable of receiving absolution no matter how ignorant he may be of the mysteries of the faith, and even if through his very own blameworthy negligence he does not know the mystery of the Trinity and of the Incarnation of Our Lord Jesus Christ." (DB 1214). To the question: "Whether before conferring baptism on an adult the minister is bound to explain to him all the mysteries of the faith, especially if he is dying, because such a procedure would agitate his mind. Or whether it would not suffice if the dying man were to promise that when he recovers from his disease he will take care to get himself instructed?"—the *Sacred Congregation of the Inquisition* replied: "Such a promise does not suffice, but a missionary is bound to explain, even to a dying adult, provided he is not utterly incapacitated, the mysteries of the faith which are necessary by necessity of means, as are especially the mysteries of the Trinity and the Incarnation."—This decree was issued on January 25, 1703, and reissued on March 30, 1898; see *Arch. F. K. Kirchenrecht* (1898) p. 797.

27. See, for example, Billuart, *De fide*, dissertatio 3, art. 1, dicotomia 2; Billot, *De virtutibus infusis*, p. 325–326.

28. *S.Th.*, Ia–IIae, q. 113, art. 4, ad. 3.

29. *In III Sententiarum, distinctio* 25, q. 1, art. 2, ad 2.—Scheeben explains these two passages from St. Thomas in a similar vein. See *Handbuch der Katholische Dogma.*, vol. I, p. 305. See also *S.Th.* IIa–IIae, q. 1, art. 7, corpus.

APPENDIX

FAITH AND REASON

I. *The Alleged Conflict between Faith and Reason, or Science and Religion*
:   1. In Anglo-Saxon countries the notion persists that there is a necessary hostility between science and religion.
       (a) evidence from scientists;
       (b) evidence from theologians and philosophers.

II. *From the Catholic Viewpoint this is a Pseudo-Conflict*
:   1. This treatment cannot enter into a detailed examination of many alleged problems; it lays down broad principles to govern the approach to any specific problem.

III. *The Underlying Causes of the Supposed Conflict:*
:   1. Confusion as to fields of knowledge.
    2. Hunger of the human mind for unity.
    3. Ignorance as to the differences between philosophy and theology, theology and faith, biblicism and theology.
    4. Ignorance as to the limitations of both science and theology.
    5. Confusion engendered by divergent spokesmen for "religion" or "the Church."
    6. Psychological factors: fear, pride, and impatience.

IV. *The Positive Teaching of the Church About the Relationship between Faith and Reason:*
:   1. Faith and reason cover a two-fold area of knowledge, that are really distinct from one another.
    2. There can never be any real quarrel between faith and reason.
    3. Faith and reason render mutual assistance to one another.

Appendix

FAITH AND REASON

I. The Alleged Conflict Between Faith and Reason, or Science and Religion

G. K. Chesterton once observed that Victorian churchmen who were ignorant of science and Victorian scientists who were equally ignorant of religion were constantly attacking one another. "This clumsy collision of two forms of impatient ignorance," he remarked, "is what came to be known historically as the conflict between science and religion."

Chesterton's airy dismissal of the problem did not end it. It perdures, unfortunately, to the present day. Some twentieth-century scientists still tend to view religion and science as unalterably opposed. And some churchmen still remain suspicious of the findings of modern science. To give a few illustrations of this fact we may simply recall that in 1925 J. Y. Simpson brought out a book entitled *Landmarks in the Struggle between Science and Religion,* and as recently as 1953 Professor H. H. Price titled his Eddington Memorial Lecture, *Some Aspects of the Conflict between Science and Religion.* "The present-day German, Protestant theologian, Julius Schniewind, has told us that 'the intrinsic incompatibility of Christology with the world view of modern science is a problem which must be taken very seriously,' and the celebrated theoretical physicist, Erwin Schrodinger, has written of the natural enmity between science and religion'!"* The brilliant Cambridge astronomer, Fred Hoyle, as recently as 1955 devoted the last chapter of his excellent little book, *The Nature of the Universe,* to debunking the traditional Christian viewpoint of the survival of the soul after death (pp. 120–128); the eminent biologist, George Gaylord Simpson, in his book, *The Meaning of Evolution* (1951), grew furiously polemical at any attempts to give a theistic explanation of the process of evolution.

* All above citations from E. Mascall, *Christian Theology and Natural Science,* 1956, pp. 1–2.

APPENDIX

On the other side of the ledger, one is dismayed to read in an able theologian like Parente, the following words in an article on evolution:

> Theologically speaking, it is possible to admit hypothetically a kind of partial evolutionism, provided it is subordinated to the influence of the First Cause. Such evolutionism *could embrace the vegetable and the animal kingdom, but could not be inclusive of man,* for, according to divine revelation, man's soul was created by God and placed in *a body which He fashioned.* But such a concession would have to be backed up by probative scientific evidence which, up to now, is lacking. (*Dictionary of Dogmatic Theology,* 1951, p. 95. Italics ours.)

Finally, in a recent article surveying the historical tension which has arisen between science and religion from the days of Galileo to Darwin, Freud and Schrödinger, a philosopher-scientist observes somewhat sadly that because of past conflicts some Catholics, even today, are uneasy about the success of modern science:

> The Catholic Church, after an auspicious start, lost confidence and treated the new science with suspicion as a potential competitor with theology. This led for a time to the eclipse of science within the Church and to a near rupture of the harmonious, but always precarious balance between faith and natural reason which had prevailed since the time of Aquinas. The Anglican churchmen welcomed the new science as a helpmate of theology; but it ultimately proved a Trojan horse to them. Here, then, is the background we must keep in mind when we talk of the "conflict" between science and Christianity. It will be seen that the tension is due to two main factors—the past efforts of theologians to regiment science and to extend their competence considerably beyond its proper limits, and the growing "Caesarism" of science, which seems to explain everything and to make supernatural modes of thought appear hopelessly old-fashioned. The "Catholic" attitude toward science has been strongly affected by these two factors. The peculiar combination of bad conscience and inferiority complex they can give rise to is vividly illustrated, for example, by the statements about science and scientists that one sometimes finds in certain sections of the Catholic press. (Ernan McMullin, "Science and the Catholic Tradition," *America,* Dec. 12, 1959, p. 347.)

APPENDIX

II. From the Catholic Viewpoint, This is a Pseudo-Conflict

Sufficient evidence has been adduced to indicate that—in Anglo-Saxon countries at least—some suspicion still remains that there is a deepseated and necessary hostility between science and Christianity. It will be the purpose of this chapter to point out that from the viewpoint of Catholic principles the conflict is a pseudo-conflict, or at least an unnecessary one. The Church sees no conflict; others do. Obviously it is not possible to examine in detail the alleged specific conflicts that arise from the vast variety of modern sciences all the way from archaeology, to biology, to physics, psychiatry, and sociology. One man thinks that the Dead Sea Scrolls have shown up the purely natural origin of Christianity; another that the biological theory of evolution has proven man to be simply a vertebrate with a highly developed nervous system; another that the indeterminism of modern physics has disproven the possibility of proving miracles; yet another that neurophysiology has proven man has no free will; another that astro-physics, by showing man's puny stature in a gigantic universe, has indicated that man is of no special interest to God or that the Incarnation would be discredited if science should discover other living things in other galaxies, etc.

To deal with these specific points in detail would require a special volume.* Here we can only indicate the broad principles which are applicable in their own way to each of these specific problems.†

Before giving these principles from the Church's official teaching and traditional theology, it will be well to indicate some of the causes underlying the pseudo-conflict. Once these causes are understood, the largest part of the problem disappears.

III. The Underlying Causes of the Supposed Conflict

Dr. McMullin has indicated one major cause of the conflict.

---

* Dr. Mascall's book, *Christian Theology and Natural Science*, considers most of these problems and deals with them sensibly and within the context of Christian revelation, neatly distinguishing between faith and theology and biblicism, and on the other hand, between scientific facts, theories, and guesses.

† Individual problems that touch the field of theology will be dealt with in their own respective places in various volumes of this theological series. Volume five, for instance, *God the Creator*, will deal with some of the problems concerning man's place in the universe, the problem of evolution, and the fall of man, etc.

APPENDIX

This might be put simply by saying: theologians and scientists have both attempted to appropriate the whole field of knowledge. Or, more technically, there exists a horrible confusion about the formal object of each science. Still the problem, it seems to us, is more complicated than McMullin envisages. There are lesser but real and irritating causes that inflame the whole area. We might list these causes as follows:

1. Confusion as to fields of knowledge.
2. Hunger of the human mind for unity.
3. Ignorance as to the difference between philosophy and theology, theology and faith, biblicism and theology.
4. Ignorance as to the limitations of both theology and science.
5. Confusion caused by the fact that many divergent spokesmen all speak for "religion" in general.
6. Psychological factors: fear and pride, impatience.

1. Confusion as to fields of knowledge

It is an old axiom of scholastic philosophy that "nothing is so formal as a formal object" and that a "diversity of formal objects begets distinct sciences." Put into modern terminology we should say: reality is extremely complex and because it is complex it can be viewed from various special slants, each of which develops its own special methodology. Man, for example, may be viewed as a collection of chemicals: studied from the special slant of chemistry he may be said to consist of so many proteins and carbohydrates, worth so many cents. Man may also be viewed as a living rather than as an inanimate thing, and so he falls under the special slant of biology. A man may be studied exclusively or nearly exclusively from the viewpoint of his mental life, and so he falls under the special scrutiny of the psychologist or psychiatrist. Obviously, each of these sciences takes but a *partial* view of man in accord with its own specialized techniques or methodology. Since each special science concentrates on only one aspect of man (the formal object of the science), it necessarily fails to give a total picture. If it tries to answer questions about a man that belong to another viewpoint, it can only give a caricature of the reality because of the limitations of its own methodology. If a physicist views man merely from the viewpoint of motion of electrons, or protons, he will, by his very methodology, have to eschew questions as to a man's health, his

APPENDIX

moral behavior, his philosophical questions, his life as a politician, or artist, or lover. As the late brilliant mathematician, philosopher, and musician J. W. N. Sullivan observed:

> The humanistic importance of this outlook, in the minds of its authors [Eddington and Jeans], seems to be that it leaves us more free to attach the traditional significance to our aesthetic, religious or, compendiously, mystic experiences. It does not actively reinforce any particular religious interpretation of the universe, but it cuts the ground from under those arguments which were held to prove that any such interpretation is necessarily illusory. This it does by showing that *science deals with but a partial aspect of reality,* and that there is no faintest reason for supposing that everything science ignores is less real than what it accepts.
>
> . . . So far we have dealt with the limitations of science as a method of acquiring knowledge about reality. We have seen that the new self-consciousness of science has resulted in the recognition that its claims were greatly exaggerated. The philosophy based on science had made "matter and motion" the sole reality. In doing so it had dismissed other elements of our experience, those that seemed to us to have the greatest significance and which, finally, made life worth living, as illusory. Science, in spite of all its practical benefits, had seemed to many thoughtful men, perhaps to the majority, to have darkened life. That the new attitude of science, as explained by such men as Eddington and Jeans, has obtained such widespread attention is not, therefore, surprising. It was the metaphysical doctrines that accompanied science that were found so depressing. (*The Limitations of Science,* Mentor ed., 1949, pp. 147–149.)

2. Hunger of the human mind for unity

This fact of the restricted aspect of reality presented by any specialized methodology is complicated still more by the fact that the whole man has a constant hunger to acquire a unified view of himself and the universe. The human mind ceaselessly struggles to reduce all knowledge to relatively simple formulae. The temptation therefore for any investigator is to simplify a complex phenomenon by reducing it to his own methodology. This results in the statements about man being only a chance collection of atoms, or a set of chemicals worth ninety cents. Such statements startle simple

APPENDIX

people. The theologian, however, who looks at man only *sub specie aeternitatis* is also giving a false picture of man. It is not enough simply to see man from the supernatural point of view: man must also grow, eat, enter business, study sciences, etc.

3. Ignorance of the distinction between faith and Scripture and theology

A third and even more treacherous cause of the conflict between science and religion—especially in English-speaking countries—is an almost total ignorance of any distinction between philosophy and theology, between faith and theology, between biblical studies and theology. This is the result of our multi-headed religious inheritance and the colossal neglect of the field of philosophy.

(a) For the sake of the general reader, therefore, we simply call to mind that philosophy is a purely rational discipline, whereas theology, while using reason, takes as its first principles God's revelation. The human soul may hence be scrutinized simply as an object of philosophy, or as an object of psychology, or as an object in theology. Each science will have a different aspect of the human soul to study and will do so in the light of its own methodology. The philosopher will be interested in the soul as a principle of organization, or as a form united with matter, or as being indestructible; the theologian will be interested in the soul from the viewpoint of salvation, of sin and of grace; the psychologist will be interested in behavior patterns and emotional traumas of the human psyche.

(b) Again, theology, while closely bound up with faith, is something truly distinct from faith. Faith gives data revealed by God—that and nothing more. Theology—sometimes defined as the science of faith—will ruminate about the data of faith, correlate the data, seek a deeper understanding of it, attempt to correlate the data with data from natural science, etc.

(c) Biblical studies again are something distinct from both faith and from theology.* Here is the greatest pitfall of all. Many a man refers airily to the conflict between science and faith, or science and religion, when he really means: I cannot see how one can square the problem of the talking snake in Genesis, or the six-day creation, or the tower of Babel with what modern science

* Although there is a "biblical" theology—again a limited field!

teaches. The fundamentalist Bible reader who sees the Bible as God's word—meaning interpreted as he himself reads it literally—is of course in a difficult position. His trouble is not due to the Bible, nor to science, but to his ignorance of biblical studies. Again, Scripture scholars, particularly non-Catholic ones, often fail to see the distinction between Scripture as a science and Theology as a science. Textual criticism, exegis, Oriental linguistics, archaeological data, literary genres, etc.—all these are strictly biblical studies. The theologian begins where the scripture scholar leaves off. To ask: does Genesis really mean six twenty-four-hour days when it uses the word *yom* is a biblical question; to ask: does creation mean making something out of nothing is both a philosophical and a theological question. To ask: does the text, John 20:23, "Receive the Holy Spirit; whose sins you shall forgive they are forgiven," really mean sins are forgiven, is a biblical question. To ask: does forgiveness of sins mean that sanctifying grace enters the soul, or does forgiveness of sins mean a priest is an instrument in the hands of Christ, or does priestly forgiveness fulfill the requirements of a sacrament—these are theological questions. To ask: does Genesis show that mankind fell away from God is a biblical question. To ask: is this fall a fall from a supernatural level to a natural level, or, how does man's fall affect possible living creatures on other planets—these are all theological questions.

To summarize: not to know the difference between faith and theology, between theology and philosophy, between biblicism and scriptural studies—this is hopelessly to muddle any questions which may be posed from the data of science. Not even to know where to start looking for an answer, but merely to lump all these matters together under the vague title, "conflict of science and religion," is to indicate the real origin of the conflict—the confused mind of the person supposing it.

4. Theology and science both progress

Another fertile field of confusion is the failure to understand that both science and theology are *progressive* sciences. Many of the answers given by nineteenth-century science are today as outmoded as phlogiston and the ether. There is good reason to think that some of today's hypotheses will, after sufficient revision, gradually fall into desuetude like their forbears. As Alfred North White-

APPENDIX

head observes acutely in his discussion of "Science and Religion": "Science is even more changeable than theology. No man of science could subscribe without qualification to Galileo's beliefs, or to Newton's beliefs, or to all his own scientific beliefs of ten years ago." (*Science and the Modern World*, Mentor ed., 1948, p. 182.) Some students of science seem to feel that science does not aim at formulating final answers to questions, but simply "hypotheses which are fruitful of further experimentation."* Unfortunately, the man in the street with his present awe for science is apt to take as final any hypothesis proposed by a scientist, whereas the scientist himself would be far more critical. To attempt, then, to wed theology exclusively to the science of any age would of course be futile. Science is so changeable that theology would always be in the position of a recently bereaved widow. Many of the mistakes of earlier theologies are often simply the reflection of an immature science of an earlier era utilized in theology as an analogue to help further some theological problem. Again, too, theology itself —while far more conservative than science—does nonetheless exhibit change.

Theology, too, changes

It is one thing to say that revealed dogmas are immutable, that faith is ever the same; quite another to say that theology is immutable. Dogmas are facts or truths made known by God; theology is the science which seeks, with the aid of reason, to plumb the depths of dogmas, to relate individual dogmas to others, to educe from implicit premises explicit conclusions, to show the marvelous, overall harmony of the revealed deposit, to answer objections against the mysteries of faith, to show the harmony of revealed truth with natural truth, to excogitate theological theories and penetrate more deeply the facts of the faith, and to gather all this vast work of theologizing into one harmonious whole. Obviously, in this wedding of revelation with reason, the latter is at some periods more and at others less successful, sometimes more illuminating, sometimes more obfuscating. That is why we have epochs in which theology as a science rises to brilliant heights and in others where it can grow feeble or descend even to quibbling.

The point to be remembered here is that just as there are scien-

* James B. Conant, *On Understanding Science*, Mentor ed., 1951, p. 32; see also J. W. N. Sullivan, *The Limitations of Science*, 1949, p. 158.

tific facts, theories, hypotheses, and guesses, so, too, there are theological facts, theological theories, hypotheses, and guesses. Dogmatic progress, i.e., progress in faith, can go in only one direction: a deeper, fuller explanation of one and the same revealed truth, without any change in the essential meaning of a dogma. That Christ is both God and man and one person is a dogmatic truth held by Catholic Christians of the first, fifth, fifteenth, and twentieth centuries. But theological theories attempting to penetrate, as far as humanly possible, the mystery of the hypostatic union have not always been identical, or equally successful in grappling with the mystery. That man's will is free and that God's grace is necessary for man freely to work supernatural actions have been truths always accepted by all Catholic Christians; but theological theories explaining the interworkings of grace and free will have not always been the same. There is, within the framework of the same facts of faith, freedom for theological speculation attempting to understand more deeply, more harmoniously the same revealed mysteries. Thus in the mystery of original sin, the facts of the faith taught by the Church have remained ever the same; but one can peruse early scholastic theologians of the twelfth century and find as many as six different theories as to the essence of original sin. Again, one can pick up any theological manual today, read the same revealed facts about the sacraments, yet find at least three theological systems explaining "sacramental causality." The same holds true for the mystery of the Mass: the same revealed truths are held by all about the Mass, but theologians differ in their subtler exposition of precisely how the Mass and the sacrifice of Calvary are identical. The same can be said for theological expositions of the way God knows "free futures" or a dozen other matters. There are the facts; and then there are theological explanations which attempt to penetrate more deeply into the recesses of the mystery. So long as a theological theory does not distort any fact of the faith, the Church more or less leaves her children free to go along with any accepted theological theory about the facts. As one can accept the facts known about light and subscribe either to a wave or corpuscular theory, or hold both as true while not understanding their exact complementariness, so, too, as long as the faithful accept the facts about freedom of the will and the necessity of grace, the Church does not mind particularly whether her children are Suárezians or Thomists.

APPENDIX

What is true of the field of dogmatic theology is even truer of moral theology. Opinions which were once regarded as "probable" are no longer considered so. Some opinions remain on the books simply as an indication of the theological thinking of a given era, rather than as a discovery of theological importance. Again, with the advent of modern medicine, moral theology has had to grapple with new problems never envisaged by older moral theologians: to apply the same unchanging principles to new types of medical operations, techniques, and the like.

The point that remains is this: granted that theology is far more conservative than science, it does nonetheless admit of change. Old solutions gradually wither away and are not abruptly torn up. New solutions are offered, the science prunes itself of relics and attacks new problems.* Frequently, too, theological science, precisely as a scientific correlation and exploration of the data of revelation, finds its own thinking honed and its own speculation elaborated by the discoveries in other fields of learning. Many pseudo-problems in Scripture, for example, have simply melted away in the face of data provided by sciences allied to biblical studies.

5. Divergent spokesmen for "the Church"

Perhaps the bitterest pill for the Catholic theologian to swallow in this whole area is the democratizing of the whole theological process. Here in America anyone may speak up in the name of "religion" or "the Church" . . . and often does. The utterances of some snake-cultist about the conflict of science and religion may be given equal democratic space coverage with the utterances of a Reinhold Niebuhr, or a theologian from an outstanding Catholic university. If Niebuhr disagrees with Karl Barth and Barth with Tillich, Tillich with Bultmann and all four of them with John Courtney Murray, who is speaking for "the Church"?—that nebulous word in the Protestant world, and even more nebulous word in the world of the secular press. All the Catholic theologian can

---

* None of this animadversion, of course, means that one should be reckless about theological discoveries and elaborations of the past. Pius XII warned impatient people about that in his encyclical *Humani Generis*. What it does mean is that the general reader who has a clear-cut notion of the difference between a dogmatic truth and a theological theory will not be dismayed if he finds that theology, too, changes, whereas revealed truths remain unchanged.

do is practice patience and say: when I speak of the "Church's" teaching I mean the teaching of the Roman Catholic Church. And I mean the teaching which all Roman Catholics subscribe to. I can neither be responsible for, nor complimented for the brilliant thinking or the erratic thinking of any individual who labels himself a theologian. Catholic theology is a staple brand served up everywhere around the world.

And only the *bishops* of the Catholic Church have the right to speak authoritatively in the Church's name. Contrariwise, Protestant theology may vary from thinker to thinker.

6. Fear, Pride, Impatience

Finally, there remain the human factors of fear, pride, and impatience which exacerbate feelings in this area and prevent a cool, intellectual appraisal of common problems. It is easy to be dispassionate about an electron; not so easy to be dispassionate about divorce. The Galileo incident may be a relatively rare incident in the annals of Church history, but it has produced a veritable trauma in the minds of many non-Catholic thinkers. They elevate it from the position of an historic mistake into a dogmatic principle. Failing to discriminate between the various levels at which the Church teaches and to see this incident as an example of a mistake on the part of a fallible tribunal of the Church, they feel that it is simply an excellent exemplification of the Church's real attitude toward science. One can only be patient and tactful in trying to place the unfortunate incident in its proper perspective in order to make it intelligible. But until this is done, the unwarranted fears generated by the incident may well serve to build a mentality of hostility toward the Church as simply an anachronism which is opposed, on principle, to human progress. On the other hand, the metaphysical *obiter dicta* of a Freud or Darwin, when homogenized with a scientific theory, tend to make churchmen suspicious of the theories themselves until they learn to discriminate between what is scientific in the theory and what is merely the "off-the-cuff" philosophizing of men with no formal training in philosophy.

Pride, too, enters the picture. It does not matter whether a man is a theologian or a chemist, a philosopher or a physicist, he still remains a man. If he becomes so enthusiastic about his own special branch of learning as to forget that there are other fields

APPENDIX

of knowledge, he will attempt to appropriate the whole field of human learning and reduce all problems to his own methodology. In such a case, every other branch of learning which exhibits independence from his own becomes to him an affront. He will belittle other sciences rather than acknowledge that his is not the only field of learning that really counts.

Finally, there is the factor of impatience. Each man has so short a time to live, life is so complex, and the mind has such a hunger to reduce all things to unity that some people are incapable of leaving some problems unresolved. The problems must be solved immediately. Unfortunately not all problems can be resolved now. Impatience for quick answers often leads to *simpliste* solutions that eventually do harm to all fields of learning. If there is a population explosion and one happens to be a demographer, one may become very impatient with the principles of an ethician or moral theologian and wish to "solve" a complicated problem by a quick resort to birth control. It was along these lines that Chesterton once facetiously remarked: "If you present some people with the problem of ten boys and nine hats, they think the answer is to cut off one boy's head."

IV. The Positive Teaching of the Church About the Relationship Between Faith and Reason

Now we must turn to the Church's official teaching to see what is her viewpoint on the proper relationship between faith and reason, or any product of reason such as the sciences. Her official teaching may be reduced to these three assertions: (1) Faith and reason cover areas of knowledge that are really distinct from one another; (2) There can never be any real quarrel between faith and reason; (3) Faith and reason give mutual assistance to one another.

Assertion 1. Faith and reason cover areas of knowledge really distinct from one another.

Faith and natural knowledge *differ* from one another:

(a) In their principles. The principle for knowing in natural science is the intellect alone; in faith it is the intellect as illumined by supernatural light.

(b) In their *subject matter*. Natural knowledge (*scientia*) embraces only such truths as do not exceed the grasp of reason; but

APPENDIX

faith in addition, and primarily, is concerned with matters which exceed the grasp of unaided intelligence: mysteries.

(c) In their *formal object* or motive. In science (natural knowledge) the motive is either evidence for the matter, or human authority; in faith the motive is the authority of God revealing.

332   Faith, then, *surpasses* natural knowledge in a threefold way: it has a nobler principle, a more sublime subject matter, and a far more powerful motive. It follows that in matters of religion reason should assist, not dominate, faith; similarly philosophy should give assistance to, not dominate, theology. Leo XIII says:

> As it is evident that very many truths of the supernatural order which are far beyond the reach of the keenest intellect must be accepted, human reason, conscious of its own infirmity, dare not affect to itself too great powers, nor deny those truths, nor measure them by its own standard, nor interpret them at will; but receive them, rather, with a full and humble faith, and esteem it the highest honor to be allowed to wait upon heavenly doctrines like a handmaid and attendant, and by God's goodness attain to them in any way whatsoever. But in the case of such doctrines as the human intelligence may perceive, it is equally just that philosophy should make use of its own method, principles, and arguments . . . (*The Church Speaks to the Modern World*, par. no. 8, p. 37).

333   *Assertion 2. There can never be any real quarrel between faith and reason.* The Vatican Council states:

> Even though faith is above reason, there cannot ever be any real quarrel between faith and reason since the same God who reveals mysteries and infuses faith has equipped the human soul with the light of reason. Now God cannot deny Himself and neither can truth ever contradict the truth. The superficial appearance of such a contradiction, however, finds its deepest source in this that either the dogmas of faith have not been understood or explained according to the mind of the Church, or that guesses of men have been accepted as axioms of reason. (DB 1797).

334   *Assertion 3. Faith and reason "mutually assist one another"*

1. *Reason* assists faith because:

(a) "Right reason demonstrates the foundations" on which faith builds. By proving the existence of God and His main attributes, by proving the freedom and immortality of the human soul, the existence of a revelation, and the divine origin of the Catholic Church, reason opens the door to the possibility of faith: *apologetics*.

(b) Reason "illumined by the light of faith, pursues the knowledge of divine realities" (sacred theology). It searches out and demonstrates the existence of revealed truths from the sources of revelation: *positive theology*. It strives to penetrate those revealed truths more deeply; it borrows analogies from the created universe to illustrate and render more plausible those truths; it brings out the harmonious interconnection among the revealed truths themselves and their connection with rational truths; finally it assembles all sacred doctrine into one unified system: *scholastic* (systematic) *theology*. Similarly reason defends the truths of faith, by showing that they cannot be accused of involving contradictions, or (against heretics) by showing that those truths really are contained in the sources of revelation: *polemical theology*. **335**

Faith enriches reason, for: **336**

(a) "It sets reason free from errors." To the Christian philosopher faith is a kind of "guiding star" whose light preserves it from many errors, particularly in matters of religion and natural ethics, as is easily apparent if anyone compares Christian philosophy with the lucubrations of ancient and modern philosophers who were either ignorant of or neglected revelation.

(b) Faith "furnishes reason with extensive knowledge." In other words, it supplies a knowledge of many truths which, even though they are *per se* discoverable by reason itself, are known through faith more swiftly, more surely, and more universally. Think of such basic things as man's personal dignity, the freedom of his will, the ability of the mind to know truth, the immortality of the soul, the authority and yet limitations of state authority— all of which truths are a veritable morass for present-day philosophers. It also supplies reason with a knowledge of mysteries which exceed reason's natural capacity. It is true, indeed, that revealed mysteries (the Trinity, real Presence of Christ in the Eucharist, the Mystical Body, resurrection of the body, etc.) are not known by us scientifically, i.e., in such fashion that they can be fully comprehended by us, or demonstrated on rational grounds, or fitted into the system of any branch of science. Nonetheless the mysteries of faith truly increase the sum of human knowledge and do so in the noblest subject matter of all and with resultant, great practical utility. Indeed it is not true that revealed mysteries bring no positive meaning to the mind.

Scholion. From what has been said it should be easy to reply to those who keep insisting that faith and the Church are opposed to progress in the sciences.

337

1. The Church herself has the profoundest sort of conviction that no discovery of real science can ever contradict the truths of faith; consequently there is no reason for her fearing men of science or their research. What is true is true. And since she is neither unaware nor scornful of the many benefits which accrue to human living from the progress of arts and science; and since she knows furthermore that there is hardly any branch of learning which, sometimes remotely, sometimes proximately, cannot contribute to a defense of faith and to progress in theology, the Church has a high regard for secular learning, recommends it, and to the best of her ability strives to promote it. Certainly the Church does value religion and sound morality more than she does science or culture because while they are good things they are goods of a lesser order and of less use to peoples. And if in matters which somewhat touch on religion and its foundations she does sometimes counsel prudence, or does not immediately clap her hands over every new theory—some of which are at times rashly advanced, and others winded about with a scarcely veiled hostility to religion—she is both using her own right and also having a care for the dignity of true science itself. In fact an unthinking itch for mere novelty is at times no less harmful to the sciences than a too rigid conservatism.

338

2. It is simply not true that the Church takes away the just freedom of science. She does not forbid the individual branches of learning from following their own principles, and their own methods in their enterprises; she does not demand that anything be accepted as a fact of science which actually is not; nor does she forbid anything from being accepted which factually is established by evident reason. One thing alone does she guard against: that an opinion be accepted as a legitimate conclusion of science which is directly and definitely opposed to a revealed dogma, for such an opinion is false. But this manner of acting no more defrauds scientific men of legitimate freedom than a lighthouse or buoy

APPENDIX

deprives a sailor of freedom by warning him of some hidden reef. Do sciences make progress by falling into error, or are the learned in some way ennobled by falling into errors? Is not all science by its very nature bound by truth?

We do, however, concede this one point. When some theory which is regarded as a conclusion or postulate of science is judged by the authentic and non-infallible magisterium, mistakes can happen. Witness the case of Galileo. Speaking strictly, therefore, it can happen that in a decision by this sort of magisterium the freedom of some learned men may be unfairly restricted and the progress of science may be retarded some little bit. But such a case is an exception which happens only by accident and, on history's own witness, only very rarely. The damage therefore that science may perhaps undergo in some particular instance (and a damage owing its origin not to faith, nor even, strictly speaking, to the Church itself, but to some fallible ecclesiastical tribunal)—that loss is compensated for and far surpassed by the many benefits which faith and the Church have brought to mankind in other matters.

Scriptural Index

Genesis
1–11   92, n. 70
1:3–18   73
1:6   90, n. 56
1:16   90, n. 54
7:11   90, n. 56
8:2   90, n. 56

Exodus
12:46   127, n. 15

Leviticus
11:6   90, n. 56

Numbers
9:12   127, n. 15

Deuteronomy
14:7   90, n. 56
24:14–15   35
25:4   35

Josue
10:12–13   90, n. 52

II Kings
7:3   89, n. 39
24:9   90, n. 63

I Paralipomenon
21:5   90, n. 63

Judith
16:8   89, n. 49

Job
3:8   89, n. 49
37:18   90, n. 56

Psalms
2:7   127, n. 11
18:6–7   90, n. 52
18:8–9   107
40:10   127, n. 15
50   88, n. 33
68:26   127, n. 14
77:2   127, n. 15
92:2   90, n. 53
103:2   90, n. 55
103:5   90, n. 53
108.8   127, n. 14
118:105, 130   107
148:4   90, n. 56

Proverbs
1:20 ff.   382, n. 10
6:23   107

Ecclesiastes
1:4   90, n. 53
1:5   277, n. 7
1:5–6   90, n. 52

Wisdom
2:6 ff.   88, n. 33
7:1 ff.   95, n. 88
9:8 ff.   95, n. 88
13:1 ff.   382, n. 10

Isaias
13:21   89, n. 49
40–66   95, n. 89
40:3   127, n. 14
40:22   90, n. 55

Jeremias
5:39   89, n. 49
31:31–34   127, n. 16
31:15   127, n. 14
32   127, n. 14

Daniel
5:25   126, n. 7
3:24–90; 13; 14   16

Osee
11:1   127, n. 15

Zacharias
11:12–13   127, n. 14

I Maccabees
6   90, n. 61
8:23 ff.   88, n. 33

II Maccabees
1:1–2, 19   88, n. 33
1:10   90, n. 62
2:20–33   65
2:24–27   57, 88, n. 29
2:29–31   91, n. 67
9   90, n. 61
12:46   89, n. 40
15:39–40   65
15:39   57, 88, n. 29

Matthew
2:15   127, n. 15
2:17   127, n. 14
3:3   127, n. 14
4:14   36
5:18   48, n. 11
5:33–37   114
13:35   127, n. 15
14:9   94, n. 80
14:31   366, 191, n. 4
15:28   48, n. 15
22:43   48, n. 13
24:14   257, n. 8
24:23–26   301
27:9   127, n. 14
28:18–20   257, n. 8

(403)

SCRIPTURAL INDEX

28:19-20   3, 155, n. 2
28:20   140

Mark
10:3-5   96, n. 90
16:9-20   16, 301
16:11   301
16:14-17   301
16:15-16   304
16:16   333, n. 7

Luke
1:1   38
1:1-3   57, 65
1:3   87, n. 23
1:19-20, 45   301
3:36   90, n. 63
10:7   35
16:15-16   155, n. 2
22:43-44   16
24:44   96, n. 90
24:44-45   32
24:45   127, n. 24

John
3:10   198
3:14 ff.   383, n. 22
3:31-34   198
5:24   383, n. 22
5:39   115
5:39-47   96, n. 90
6:43-46, 64-67   305
6:44   334, n. 30
6:67-70   302
7:53-8:11   16
8:12-19   199
8:24   383, n. 22
8:46-47   199
10:34   32
11:25   383, n. 22
11:50-53   127, n. 12
12:38   84
13:7   126, n. 6
13:18   48, n. 15, 127, n. 15
14:16   140

14:26   140, 257 n. 9
16:12-15   256, n. 2, 257, n. 9
16:13-14   139
17:3   383, n. 22
19:36   127, n. 15
19:36-37   48, n. 15
20:23   392
20:28-29   353
20:30-31   302

Acts
1:8   155, n. 2
1:16   32, 48, n. 14, 48, n. 15
1:16-20   127, n. 14
2:5   90, n. 50
2:17   257, n. 6
2:36   363
4:11-12   383, n. 22
4:25   48, n. 14
7:16   89, n. 42
8:30-31   127, n. 24
8:35   48, n. 15
9:15   155, n. 2
13:33   127, n. 12
14:16   382, n. 10
16:14   334, n. 29
17:26 ff.   382, n. 10
20:25   88, n. 33
26:15-18   383, n. 22

Romans
1:2   33
1:17   382, n. 12
1:18 ff.   382, n. 10
2:13-16   382, n. 10
3:3   191, n. 2
3:22-23   383, n. 22
4:20-21   363
5:14   127, n. 13
10:9   302
10:16, 20   84
14:23   191, n. 6
15:4   50, n. 68
16:17   155, n. 3, 257, n. 10

I Corinthians
1:16   89, n. 37
5:7   127, n. 13
7:12   89, n. 38
10:6, 11   127, n. 13
10:11   257, n. 7
11:2   146
11:26   257, n. 8
13:8-13   303, 371
13:9-13   367, n. 5
13:12-13   353

II Corinthians
3:11   257, n. 8
5:6-7   353, 371
5:7   367, n. 5
10:5   268, n. 20

Galatians
1:8-10   364
2:16   382, n. 12, 383, n. 22
3:8   33
3:16   48, n. 12
4:4   257, n. 5
4:24   127, n. 13
5:6   192, n. 18

Ephesians
1:10   257, n. 5
2:8   305
2:20   49, n. 61

Philippians
1:28-30   305
4:9   155, n. 3

Colossians
2:7   155, n. 3

I Thessalonians
2:13   199
4:1-2   155, n. 3

II Thessalonians
2   156, n. 24
2:15   155, n. 3

SCRIPTURAL INDEX

I Timothy

1:15	88, n. 33
2:2	37
5:12	191, n. 3
5:18	35
5:23	51, n. 70, 89, n. 38
6:20	146, 257, n. 10

II Timothy

1:13–14	146, 257, n. 10
3:14	257, n. 10
3:15–16	28, 33
3:15–17	50, n. 68
3:16	115
4:6	146
4:13	51, n. 70

Titus

1:12	90, n. 59

Philemon

22	51, n. 70

Hebrews

1:5	127, n. 12
4:12	6, n.
5:5	127, n. 12
7:3	127, n. 13
7:11–28	257, n. 8
9:9	127, n. 13
9:26	257, n. 7
10:38	382, n. 12
11:1	192, n. 14, 353
11:3, 6	302
11:6	333, n. 7, 382, n. 12
12:27–28	257, n. 8

James

2:14–26	303
2:19	349, n. 12, 361
5:14	127, n. 19

I Peter

1:20	257, n. 6
3:15	333, n. 5
3:21	127, n. 13

II Peter

1:16–19	363
1:19–21	28, 34
3:15–16	28, 42, 48, n. 20
3:16	26, 107

I John

2:20, 27	108, 127, n. 16
2:21–24	155, n. 3
3:32	304
5:9–10	363
5:9–11	199

Jude

3	257, n. 10
14–15	73

Index of Proper Names

Adam, xvii, 257, n. 20, 270, 278, n. 19
Albert the Great, St., 172
Aldama, xvii, 216, n. 4
Altaner, 178, n. 16
Ambrose, St., 24, 38, 168, 171
Anselm, St., 172
Anthony of Padua, St., 172
Antoine, xviii
Appel, xviii
Arbez-Weisengoff, xv, 51
Aristotle, 9
Arius, 108
Arnobius, 172
Athanasius, St., 20, 23, 26, 38, 172, 382, n. 11
Athenagoras, 36, 172
Aubert, xviii, 258, n. 29, 278, n. 11, 299, 301, 307, 309, n. 7, 316, n., 318, 319, 320, 348, n. 1
Augustine, St., 20, 24, 39, 40, 45, 46, 49, nn. 56 and 60, 58, 70, 89, n. 47, 102, 115, 125, 153, 154, 171, 173, 178, n. 20, 179, n. 22, 201, 215, 239, 240, 245, 258, n. 27, 305, 306, 349, n. 15, 355, 361, 382, n. 11
Auvray, 95, n. 89
Auzou, xv, 97

Bach, 258, n. 26
Bainvel, xv, xvi, xviii, 51, 92, n. 73, 126, n. 6, 143, 155, n. 4, 257, n. 12, 318, 319, 320, 332, n. 1, 334, nn. 27 and 28, 349, n. 11
Balestri, xv, 24, n. 1, 25, n. 4, 26, 50, nn. 62 and 67, 51, 132, n. 68, 134
Bañez, 202, n. 2
Bardenhewer, 178, nn. 1 and 16
Barry, 25, n. 6
Barth, 395

Barton, xv, 47, n. 5, 50, nn. 62 and 67, 51
Basil, St., 38, 152, 172
Batiffol, 25, n. 6, 178, n. 16
Bavinck, 108, 127, n. 17, 128, n. 40, 143, n. 3, 155, n. 18
Bea, xv, 51
Bede, Ven., 172
Beelen, 127, n. 11
Bellamy, 230, nn. 4 and 8
Bellarmine, St. Robert, xvi, 10, 131, n. 63, 132, n. 66, 172
Belser, 25, n. 6
Benedict XII, 353
Benedict XIII, 230, n. 2
Benedict XIV, 170, 218, n. 18, 269
Benedict XV, xv, 51, 93, n. 79, 129, n. 50
Benoît, xv, 97
Beraza, xviii, 216, n. 6
Bernard, St., 171, 172
Berthier, 9
Beysens, 191, n. 7, 192, n. 9
Billot, xv, xvii, xviii, 51, 96, n. 95, 143, 216, n. 4, 318, 319, 335, 346, 349, n. 11, 359, n., 367, n. 6, 383, n. 27
Billuart, 348, n. 2, 383, n. 27
Blanche, 126, n. 7
Bleek-Wellhausen, 130, n. 62
Bonaccorsi, 216, n. 2
Bonaventure, St., 172
Bonfrère, 55
Boniface VIII, 178, n. 15
Bouix, 278, n. 19
Bouyer, xvii, 9, 144
Brémond, 258, n. 29
Brouwer, xviii, 348, n. 2, 367, n. 13, 382, n. 5
Brown, xv, 134
Brunetière, 333, n. 26

INDEX OF PROPER NAMES

Brunsmann-Preuss, 195, n.
Bultmann, 143, n. 4, 329, 395
Burke, xvii, 144, 230, n. 4
Butler, 87, n. 16

Caesarius of Arles, 169
Cajetan, 202, n. 2
Calvin, 46, n. 2, 309, n. 1
Canisius, St. Peter, 172
Cano, xvii, 9, 176, 216, n. 5, 378, 383, n. 19
Carafa, 131, n. 63
Cartechini, xviii, 282, n.
Cathrein, xviii
Cayré, 178, n. 16
Celestine I, 175
Cellerier, 42
Charlier, 129, n. 52
Charue, 90, n. 57
Chauvin, xv, 25, n. 6, 51
Chenu, xviii
Chesterton, 386
Chrismann, 50, n. 63
Clement of Alexandria, St., 23, 36, 172, 382, n. 11
Clement of Rome, St., 22, 35, 148
Clement VIII, 131, n. 63
Clement XI, 284
Conant, 393, n.
Coppée, 334, n. 26
Coppens, xv, 92, n. 74, 111, n., 113, 134
Corluy, 50, n. 67
Cornely, 25, n. 6, 130, n. 62, 132, n. 66
Cotter, 9, 127, n. 18, 128, n. 44
Coventry, xviii
Crehan, xv, 51
Crets, xv, 52
Cristiani, xviii
Cullmann, 143, n. 4, 329
Cyprian, St., 37, 240
Cyril of Alexandria, St., 25, n. 7, 26, 172
Cyril of Jerusalem, St., 20, 38, 172

Damasus, 24
Damian, St. Peter, 172

Daniélou, xvii, 143, n. 4, 144, 156, n. 26
D'Arcy, xviii
Darwin, 396
Dausch, xv, 52, 86, nn. 5 and 7
De Grandmaison, 216, n. 6, 257, n. 12
De Groot, 367, n. 6
De Guglielmo, 126, n. 7
Dejaifve, xvii, 144
De la Barre, 257, nn. 12 and 20
Delattre, 94, n. 81
De Lugo, xviii, 216, n. 6, 217, n. 11, 318, 335, 339, 340, 346, 357, 358, n., 367, nn. 1, 13, 14, and 18, 368, n. 24, 383, n. 24
De Molinos, 284
De San, xvii, 9, 89, n. 44, 156, n. 26, 178, n. 19
Desprès, 259, n. 33
De Vaux, 96, n. 91
De Wette-Schräder, 130, n. 62
D'Hulst, 50, nn. 64 and 65
Di Bartolo, xvii, 10, 50, nn. 64 and 65
Dieckmann, xvii, 10, 144, 276, 279, n. 19
Diekamp, xvii, 10, 144, 217, n. 8
Dimnet, 258, n. 29
Dionysius of Alexandria, St., 23
Dionysius the Areopagite, 172
Döllinger, 271
Donatus, 108
Duesberg, 129, n. 52
Duhamel, 55, 86, n. 5
Duihle de Saint-Projet, 90, n. 56
Dulles, 334, n. 26
Dupont, 79
Dupont-Sommer, 330
Dupperon, 332

Eddington, 390
Einstein, 345
Ephraem, St., 26, 171, 172
Epiphanius, St., 153, 178, n. 12
Eusebius, xi, 23, 37, 49, n. 62, 148-149, 155, n. 10, 172
Ewald-Hartmann, 257, n. 24

INDEX OF PROPER NAMES

Fagnanus, 269
Falk, 129, n. 56
Feeney, 279
Fei, xv, 52
Fessler-Jungman, 178, n. 16
Firmin, 259, n. 33
Flanagan, 258, n. 29
Fonck, 50, n. 67, 132, n. 70
Forestell, xv, 97, 127, n. 18
Francis de Sales, St., 172
Franzelin, xvii, 10, 130, n. 57, 132, nn. 71 and 72, 156, n. 26, 216, 217, n. 13, 257, n. 12, 269, 286, 324, 339, 340, 348, nn. 2, 7, and 9, 367, n. 13
Freud, 369, 387
Friedrich, xviii
Fuller, xv, 134
Funk, 155, n. 8

Galileo, 387, 393, 396, 401
Garcia, 278, n. 11
Gardeil, 216, n. 6, 332, n. 1
Garrigou-Lagrange, 257, n. 12
Gaudeau, 191, n. 1
Geiselmann, xvii, 144
Gelasius, St., 20, 24
Gelin, xviii
Gietmann, 126, n. 7
Gigot, 25, n. 6
Ginoulhiac, 258, n. 26
Girard, 88, n. 35
Gore, 24
Grail, xviii
Granderath, 114, 279, n. 21, 333, n. 16
Gregory Nazianzen, St., 172
Gregory of Nyssa, St., 151
Gregory the Great, St., 39, 171, 233, 246, 356
Gregory VII, 129, n. 46
Gregory XIII, 170
Gregory XVI, 278, n. 18
Guardini, xviii
Gunther, 232, 253, 279, n. 21
Gutberlet, 378, 382, n. 8

Haneberg, 55, 86, n. 4

Happel, 95, n. 87
Harent, xviii, 319
Harnack, 155, n. 5, 165, n. 5, 232, 251, 253, 254, 258, n. 30, 329
Hartmann, 257, n. 24
Hauret, 230, n. 5
Healy, xviii, 282, n.
Hefele, 178, n. 10
Hegesippus, 149
Heinrich, 218, n. 16, 257, n. 12, 333, n. 14, 348, n. 2
Heinrich-Gutberlet, 382, n. 8
Hermes, 278, n. 18, 358
Hettinger, 129, n. 55
Hilary, St., 20, 172
Hippolytus, St., 22, 23, 37
Holden, 50, n. 63
Holzhey, xv, 52
Hopfl-Gut, xv, 25, n. 4, 26, 52, 88, n. 27, 134
Hoyle, 386
Hugon, xv, 52, 88, n. 27, 216, n. 4
Hume, 329
Hurter, 131, n. 64, 334, n. 31
Huysmans, 334, n. 26

Ignatius, St., 149
Innocent I, 20, 24, 96, n. 91
Innocent X, 278, n. 18
Innocent XI, 283, 313
Irenaeus, St., 22, 23, 36, 58, 110, 149–50, 159, 160, 161, 165, n. 1, 235, 257, n. 11, 304
Isidore of Seville, St., 120, 171, 172

Jacquier, 25, n. 6
Jahn, 55
Jansen, 288, 291, n. 7, 348, n. 2, 367, n. 13
Jeans, 390
Jerome, St., 20, 24, 26, 39, 40, 49, n. 62, 57, 70, 81, 87, n. 23, 94, n. 79, 99, 118, 120, 130, n. 59, 168, 171, 216, n. 3
Jocy, xviii
John Chrysostom, St., 38, 58, 67, 127, n. 25, 153, 172, 199, 382, n. 11
John Damascene, St., 171, 172

INDEX OF PROPER NAMES

John of the Cross, St., 172
Johnston, xvi, 89, n. 41, 97
Jones, 129, n. 52
Josephus, 32
Joüon, 42
Jungman, 178, n. 16
Jurieu, 229
Justin, St., 23, 36, 49, n. 25, 171, 174, 382, n. 11

Kaiser, xviii, 282, n.
Kant, 186
Katschthaler, 258, n. 26
Kaulen, 90, nn. 56 and 60
Keil, 130, n. 62
Kihn, 178, n. 16
Kilber, 216, n. 4
Klee, 258, n. 26
Kleinhans, 79, 93, n. 76
Kleist, 155, n. 8
Kleist-Lilly, xi, 118, 185
Kleutgen, 348, n. 5
Knox, 118
Konings, 382, n. 9
Künstle, 178, n. 13

Laberthonnière, 192, nn. 13 and 19
Labeyrie, 237, n.
Lacome, 51, n. 69
Lactantius, 172
Lagrange, 25, n. 6, 50, n. 62, 51, n. 69, 76, 90, n. 65
Lambrecht, 10
Lamy, 42
Lattey, 88, n. 27
Lebreton-Zeiller, xi
Leconte, 90, n. 57
Lederer, 197
Lennerz, 216, n. 4
Lenormant, 50, n. 64
Leo the Great, St., 49, n. 56, 168, 172, 199, 240
Leo XIII, xvi, 43, 52, 54, 60, 61, 62, 67, 70, 80, 93, n. 79, 112, 113, 114, 128, nn. 30 and 38, 225, 241, 258, n. 27, 372, 398
Leonard, 129, n. 53

Lercher, xvii, 10, 144, 156, n. 26, 276, 354, nn., 358, n.
Lercher-Schlagenhauffen, 358, n.
Le Roy, 230, n. 10
Lesêtre, 92, n. 73
Lessius, 55, 86, n. 5
Levie, 52
Liese, 382, nn. 8 and 14
Liguori, St. Alphonsus, 172
Littledale, 9
Loisy, 76, 232, 254, 255, 256, 259, n. 32
Luce, 334, n. 26
Lucian, St., 23
Lusseau-Collomb, xvi, 26, 52
Luther, 105, 303

MacKenzie, xvi, 92, n. 70, 97, 126, n. 18
McCool, 87, n. 16
McDonald, 88, n. 35
McKenzie, xvi, 51, 52, 92, n. 70, 129, n. 52
McMullin, 387, 388, 389
Maisonneuve, 90, n. 56
Mangenot, 127, n. 23
Mannens, 349, n. 11, 367, n. 13
Marin-Sola, 216, n. 5, 257, n. 12
Maritain, 195, n.
Mascall, 386, n.
Mazzella, 329, 349, n. 11
Merit, xviii
Merk, xvi, 52
Meschler, 218, n. 18
Miller, 79, 93, n. 76
Minges, 216, n. 6
Minucius Felix, 172
Mollat-Braun, 128, n. 29
Muratori, 26
Murphy, xvi, 97
Murray, 395

Nestorius, 108
Newman, xviii, 50, n. 64, 186, 232, 250, 257, n. 12, 258, n. 29
Newton, 393
Nicolau, xvi, 25, n. 6, 26, 103, n., 132, n. 68

INDEX OF PROPER NAMES

Niebuhr, 395
Novatian, 108
Nützen, 258, n. 26

O'Brien, 334, n. 26
Orchard, 129, n. 53
Origen, 22, 23, 25, n. 8, 37, 120, 130, n. 57, 151, 172, 239

Pagano, 86, n. 5
Pallavicini, 131, n. 66
Palmieri, 256, n. 3, 277, n. 10
Papias, 149, 155, n. 8
Parente, xvii, xviii, 10, 144, 387
Pascal, 330
Paulus, 333, n. 16
Pautrel, 90, n. 60
Pegis, 189
Perthes, 129, n. 55
Pesch, xvi, xviii, 50, n. 67, 52, 86, n. 5, 88, nn. 27, 31, and 34, 92, n. 72, 178, n. 16, 216, n. 4, 259, n. 32, 326, 327, 333, nn. 8 and 17, 349, n. 11, 367, n. 13, 372
Petavius, 258, n. 26
Peter Chrysologus, St., 172
Peters, 94, n. 82, 132, n. 69, 278, n. 19
Phillips, 192, n. 9, 202, n. 6
Philo, 32
Pirot-Robert, xi
Pius IV, 116, 170
Pius VI, 283, 284
Pius IX, 170, 177, 222, 227, 262, 271, 277
Pius X, St., 117, 170, 271, 278, n. 17
Pius XII, xvi, 52, 78, 91, nn. 68 and 70, 117–118, 126, n. 6, 133, n. 76, 212, 225, 226, 227, 242, 263, 265, 268, n., 272, 395, n.
Polycarp, St., 35
Pope, xvi, 52, 130, n. 56
Portalié, 259, n. 33
Price, 386
Prunier, 257, n. 12
Pseudo-Augustine, 178, nn. 7 and 8

Quasten, 178 nn. 1 and 16

Quesnel, 284
Quilliet, xviii, 282, n., 287, n.

Rahner, xvi, 97
Rauschen, 178, n. 16
Reid, 186
Reilly, 166, n. 10
Reithmayr, 42
Renouvier, 186
Ricciotti, 87, n. 16
Ripalda, 202, n. 2, 376, 382, nn. 7 and 15
Ritschl, 258, n. 30
Robert-Feuillet, 25, n. 6, 26, 52
Robert-Pirot, xi
Robert-Tricot, xvi, 25, n. 2, 26, 52, 134
Rohling, 50, n. 64
Romanes, 328, n.
Rousselot, xix, 319
Rufinus, St., 20, 168, 172
Ruwet, xvi, 27
Ryan 92 n. 74

Sabatier 252
Sabellius, 108
Salaverri, xvii, 9, n. 1, 10, 144, 257, n. 12, 282, n.
Salmanticenses, xix, 367, nn. 6, 9, and 12
Schanz, 42, 129, n. 56, 130, n. 62
Scheeben, 257, n. 12, 333, n. 14, 348, n. 2, 383, n. 29
Schiffini, xix, 216, n. 6, 277, n. 11, 333, n. 8, 349, n. 11, 367, n. 13, 382, n. 6
Schmid, xvi, 52, 88, n. 34, 378, 382, nn. 8, 11, and 13, 383, nn. 20 and 24
Schniewind, 386
Schrader, xvii, 144
Schrödinger, 386, 387
Schroeder, xvi, 50, n. 62, 51, 52, 89, n. 41
Schultes, 216, n. 4
Schwane, 258, n. 26
Schweitzer, 329
Semeria, 50, n. 64

INDEX OF PROPER NAMES

Shearer, 309, n. 4
Siegman, 78, 92, n. 74, 93, n. 76, 111, n.
Simon, 259, n. 33
Simon-Prado, xvi, 27, 52
Simonin, 257, n. 12
Simpson, G. G., 386
Simpson, J. Y., 386
Sixtus V, 130, n. 63
Sixtus of Sienna, 16
Smith, xvii, 9, n. 1, 10, 144
Soanen, 230, n. 2
Sophronius, 173
Soto, 382, n. 6
Stanley, 50, n. 62, 52, 55, n., 96, n. 94
Steinmann, 95, n. 89
Stern, 334, n. 26
Stuhlmueller, 95, n. 87
Suarez, xix, 216, n. 6, 333, n. 23, 335, 338, 339, 347, 348, n. 2, 356, 367, n. 13, 378, 383, nn. 18, 24, and 25
Sullivan, 390, 393, n.
Sylvester Maurus, 202, n. 2
Székely, 42

Tanner, 333, n. 18
Tanquerey, xvii, 9, n. 1, 10, 144
Tatian, 172
Taugere, 330, n.
Teller, 345
Tertullian, 37, 49, nn. 56 and 62, 110, 149, 150–151, 152, 159, 161, 165, n. 1, 172, 235, 257, n. 11
Teuffel, 130, n. 62
Theiner, 131, n. 66, 132, n. 68
Theodoretus, 39, 172
Theophilus of Antioch, St., 36
Thomas Aquinas, St., xi, xviii, 54, 55, 56, 57, 59, 86, n. 10, 87, n. 22, 89, nn. 36 and 46, 102, 113, 126, nn. 2, 3, 4, and 10, 172, 178, n. 8, 179, n. 22, 181, 187, 188, 189, 192, nn. 10, 12, and 15, 197, 199, 202, n. 6, 215, 217, n. 11, 218, nn. 16 and 17, 228, 240, 278, n. 13, 291, n. 8, 303, 321, 333, n. 12, 334, n. 27, 349, nn. 12 and 15, 355, 356, 357, 361, n., 362, 363, 365, 367, nn. 3, 6, 11, and 17, 371, 381
Tillich, 329, 395
Tixeront, xix, 258, n. 26
Toletus, 131, n. 63
Trethowan, xix
Tribbe, 92, n. 74
Tromp, xvi, 50, n. 62, 52
Turinazz, xix

Ubaghs, 279, n. 21
Ubaldi, 42
Urban VIII, 170

Vacandard, 178, n. 1
Vacant, 230, n. 4, 333, n. 16
Vacant-Mangenot, 25, n. 2
Van Breda, 259, n. 32
Van Hoonacker, 92, n. 73
Van Kasteren, 17
Van Noort, 278, nn. 12 and 14, 307, 319
Van Zeller, 129, n. 52
Vasquez, 216, n. 5
Vawter, xvi, 51, 52, 92, n. 70, 129, n. 52, 230, n. 5
Vega, 382, n. 6
Vemeulen, 278, n. 19
Vercellone, 130, n. 57
Vetters, 94, n. 84
Vigouroux, xi
Vincent Lerins, St., 108, 110, 154, n., 157, 163, 164, 166, n. 13, 236, 240, 243, 244, 257, nn. 11 and 25, 258, n. 28
Von Hummelauer, 96, n. 95
Von Scholz, 132, n. 69
Voste, xvi, 50, n. 62, 52, 130, n. 57, 131, n. 63, 132–3, n. 73

Waugh, 334, n. 26
Weisengoff, 89, n. 41
Werenfels, 108
Whitehead, 392
Wikenhauser, xvi, 25, n. 6, 26, 27
William of Paris, 202, n. 2

INDEX OF PROPER NAMES

Wilmers, xix, 202, n. 2, 217, n. 7, 348, nn. 2 and 4, 367, n. 13
Winkler, xvii, 144
Wittgenstein, 329
Wycliffe, 129, n. 56

Zahn, 25, n. 6, 26
Zanecchia, xvi, 52
Zarb, xvi, 27
Zigliara, 367, n. 6
Zizzamia, 87, n. 16

General Index

A

Agreement of Fathers, value of, for interpretation of Scripture, 112, 113; criterion of Tradition, 162

Analogy of faith, 336; theories of, by Suarez, 338, by De Lugo, 339, and by Billot, 331. See Faith

Apocryphal, meaning of, 15, 18

Apostles, incomparability of knowledge of religion of, 237, n.

Apostles' Creed, 168

Apostolic Origin, as criterion of inspiration, 41; of a canonical book or canonical fragment, possible after the death of the Apostles, 85

Apostolicity, as criterion for inspiration, 41

Approbation, of God for matters mentioned in Bible, 68, 74; of the Church regarding private revelations, 215; of doctrine by provincial councils, 221

Article of faith, meaning of, 228; distinction of, between fundamental and non-fundamental, 229

Assent of faith, whether virtually a double assent, 337, 342; whether a logical conclusion, 346

Athanasian Creed, 170

Augustine, St., admitted plurality of literal senses, 102; says St. Jerome wrote under "assistance of the Holy Spirit," 40; does not restrict inspiration to religious matters, 45, 46

Author of Scripture, God as, 29; principal and instrumental, 54; relationship of principal and instrumental to one another, 56, 57, and to the combined product, 59; secondary, *see* Hagiographer, Sacred writer

Authority, of God revealing, the formal object of faith, 197; of the Fathers in interpreting Scripture, 112, 113; in matters of tradition, 172; of Theologians, 176, 222

Autopistia of Scripture, 18

B

"Beginning of faith," notion of, 306; historical error about the phrase, 307

Belief, full meaning of term versus merely analogous meaning, 343

Biblical Commission, Response of, on implicit citations of Scripture, 74; on merely historical appearance of certain books, 81; on historical character of first three chapters of Genesis, 83; on plural authorship of book of Isaias, 95, 96, 274; on the Mosaic authorship of Pentateuch, 96, 273, 274

Blessed in heaven, do not make acts of faith, 371

Bonfrère, taught concomitant theory of inspiration, 55

C

Calvinists, on the *autopistia* of Scripture, 29

Canon of Scripture, meaning of, 15; Alexandrine, 16; Palestinian, 17; Tridentine, 18; Protestant, 9; proto and deutero-canonical books, 16; justification of Tridentine canon, 19

Canonical books, 15; proto and deutero-canonical books, 16

(413)

GENERAL INDEX

Canonicity, meaning of, 15; proof of, of sacred books, 19; doubts of the Fathers about, of certain books, 20, 23

Canon of Vincent of Lerins, 164

"Captivity of intellect," meaning of, according to St. Thomas, 362

Cause, efficient, of dogmatic progress, 248; principal, and relationship to instrumental, 55, 56

Catholics, acknowledge two sources of revelation, 5, 142; admit a twofold rule of faith, 7

Censure, theological, meaning of, 282; doctrinal versus authoritative, 282; various ways of inflicting, 283; explanation of various, 284; proper usage of condemned propositions, 286 ff.; schema of theological labels and opposed censures, 290

Certitude, about fact of revelation, requisite for faith, 313; popular or moral, suffices, 314; respective, in some cases suffices, 314; of the uneducated and of children, 316; respective, criticized as a notion, 318; whether a Catholic can be guiltless in leaving the Church, 323

Charity, why it is termed the "Form" of faith, 190

Chiliasm, as found in the ancient Fathers, 174

Church, the authoritative interpreter of Scripture, 105, 106, 109; not independent of Scripture, 110; no obstacle to biblical studies, 110; proposes revealed truths for belief in various ways, 221 ff.; not opposed to scientific progress, 400

Citations, in Scripture, explicit, 74; and implicit, 74

Close ties of early Christian churches, 161

Commission, Biblical. *See* Biblical Commission

Conclusion, logical, act of faith differs from, 346

Confessions of faith, value for Protestants, 6

Congregations, Roman, possess authentic magisterium, 269; deserve assent of religious obedience, 270

Consent of Fathers. *See* Agreement of Fathers

Conservation of divine Tradition, 158 ff.

Controversies, occasional cause of progress in faith, 245

Council of Trent, on the Canon of Scripture, 18, 19; on secondary authors of books of Scripture, 96, n. 91; on the interpretation of Scripture, 106; on the authority of the Vulgate, 120; on the force of divine Tradition, 138; on the necessity of faith for justification, 376, 377

——Vatican, on twofold source of revelation, 5; on the inspiration of Scripture, 29; original formula presented on inspiration of Scripture and amendment, 96; on interpretation of Scripture, 106; on the material object of Catholic faith, 221; on the immutability of dogmas, 254; on the necessity of faith for justification, 377

Credere Deum, Deo, in Deum, meaning of syntactical changes in formula, 214

Credibility. *See* Judgment of credibility

Creeds, various, 168 ff.

Criteria, of inspiration, 29, 41; of valid tradition, 158

D

Damned, do not make acts of faith, 372

Daniel, book of, considered by some Scripture scholars to belong to the apocalyptic genre, 90, n. 65

Defection from the Church, sinfulness of the act, 323

Definition, by solemn decree, 221;

through the ordinary and universal magisterium, 222
Doctors of the Church, meaning of the term, 171; a list of, 171, 172
Documents, used by sacred writers. See Citations, explicit and implicit
Dogma of faith, meaning of, 227; necessary and useful, 228; material and formal, 229; possibility of the increase in the number of, 233 ff.; which must be known by necessity of means?, 378 ff.
Dogmatic progress. See Progress in Faith
Doubts about the fact of revelation, and the uneducated Catholic, 322

E

Ecclesiastes, book of, does not have Solomon as author, 74
Ecclesiastical Faith. See Faith, ecclesiastical
Error, meaning of, in strict sense, 71; exclusion of, from the Bible, 69 ff.; the theological censure of, 285
Evidence, does perfect, for the fact of revelation remove the obscurity of faith?, 357; is liberty compatible with perfect, for the fact of revelation?, 361
Evolution of dogma. See Progress in Faith
Existence of God, belief of the philosopher in, 356; as the principal article of faith, 381
Extension, of inspiration, to all parts of Scripture, 43; to the words and phrases of Scripture, etc., 66

F

Faith, divine, definition of, 188; division of, 189; formal object of, 196 ff.; material object of, 205 ff.; increase of, 233 ff.; subjective principles producing act of, 296 ff.; intellectual preparation required for, 312 ff.; voluntary preparation required for, 327 ff.; ultimate analysis of, 336 ff.; properties of, 351 ff.; truthfulness of, 351; obscurity of, 352; freedom of, 358; firmness of, 362; the inequality of, 365; persons who possess, 371; necessity of, 374; relationship between faith and reason, 386 ff.
————ecclesiastical, meaning of, 188; differs from divine faith, 265 ff.; referred to virtue of divine faith, 268; truths to be held by, 265
————human, related to human knowledge, 327
————improper and false notions of, 185; genuine notion of, 186; dependence of, on will, 187; division into human, divine and ecclesiastical, 188; ancient Protestant division, into historical, of miracles, and in promises, 191, n. 5; scientific, vs. simple authority, 343; in loose sense and justification, 375
"*Filioque*" in the Nicene-Constantinople Creed, 170
Firmness, of faith, 362
"First Truth," name for God, 202, n. 5
Formal object, of faith, 196 ff.
Formally revealed, meaning of, 206; distinction of formal explicit and formal implicit revelation, 206; varied ways truth is contained formally but implicitly, 206 ff.
Franzelin, on significance of approbation of private revelations by the Church, 216; on the ultimate analysis of faith, 339

G

Grace, the supernaturalizing principle of faith, 296, 297, 304; and the judgment of credibility, 321, 332
Granderath, views of, on the obvious sense of Scripture, 114
Gunther, theory of, on evolution of dogma, 253

GENERAL INDEX

Gutberlet, and opinion that faith, in loose sense of term, sometimes suffices for justification, 375

H

Hagiographer, instrumental author of Scripture, 54; action of, real human activity under God's assistance, 56; action of, truly personal, 57; meaning of term "the pen of God" as applied to, 58; obscurities of Scripture, due to, 59; action of God affects the intellect of, 61 ff., and the will of, 64, and the executive faculties of, 65; awareness of own inspiration in, 65; meaning of, is God's meaning, 68, 71; the approval of God recorded by, 68; God's approval of the sentiments of, as a man, 69; uses any legitimate literary genre, 71, 72; describes scientific phenomena in accord with external appearances, 72; writes under pseudonym, etc., 73; does not guarantee every document cited, 74; use of implicit citations, 74; intention of, not strictly historical always, 75 ff.

Harnack, theory of origin and evolution of dogmas, 251 ff.; on the intercommunication of the primitive Churches, 165, n. 5

"Heart has reasons for believing," meaning of, 331

Henoch, book of, probable use of, in the Epistle of Jude, 73, 90, n. 57

Heresy, notion of, 284; occasion for progress in faith, 245

Heretics, formal, do not make act of faith, 372; material, can make acts of faith, 373

Hermes, juxtaposed faith "of heart" to faith "of head," 358

Historical writing, recent opinions of Catholic scripture scholars on Old Testament, 80 ff.

Host, view on belief in real presence of Christ in an individual with divine faith, 212, 217, n. 11

I

Illumination, of intelligence of sacred writer, 62 ff.

Imperfections, of style, *etc.*, belong to the sacred writer, 59 ff.; are not errors, 71

Impurity, as an obstacle to faith, 328

Inequality of faith, 365

Inerrancy of Scripture, 69 ff.

Infallibility of Scripture, 69 ff.

Inspiration, notion of, 29; criterion of, 29, 41; proof of existence of, 31 ff.; extension of, to all parts of Scripture, 43; description of its nature, 54 ff.; knowledge of, by the sacred writers, 65; the question of verbal, 66; first effect of: all Scripture is God's word, 68; second effect of: truthfulness of all Scripture, 69 ff.; the critical authenticity of, 84; theories limiting the notion of, 43 ff.; distinction of "subsequent," "negative," and "concomitant," 55; differs from revelation, 72

Instrument, has two distinct actions, 56. See Hagiographer

Intellect, of sacred writer, is illuminated, 61 ff.; elicits the act of faith, 296, 298 ff.

Interpretation, of Scripture, authentic, 105, 109; dogmatic rules governing, 112 ff.; and the writings of the Fathers, 175 ff.

Irrevocability of faith, 364, 365

J

Jerome, St., and "The Law of History," 80, 81

Josephus, on the inspiration of the Old Testament, 32

Jude, Apostle, and the book of *Henoch*, 73

Judgment, solemn, in proposing revealed doctrine, 221; reason why

GENERAL INDEX

the Church makes, 227, 245 ff.; of credibility and credentity, 324; influenced by the will, 330

L

Lagrange, views on the book of *Daniel,* 90, 65
Lamentabile, the decree, 75, 77, 85
Legates, papal, at Council of Trent and discussion of the authenticity of the Vulgate, 131, n. 66
Leo XIII, on inspiration, 43; on description of inspiration, 60 ff.; on infallibility of Scripture, 70; on biblical description of scientific and historical matters, 80; on the proper interpretation of Scripture, 113; on consulting the original text, 125; on the influence of the Holy Spirit and the influence of the visible magisterium, 258, n. 27; on the faith of heretics, 372
Liberty of faith, 358; and perfect evidence of fact of revelation, 361
Literary genres, not to be rejected because they do not always conform to our notions, 71, 72
Loisy, theory of, on origin and evolution of dogmas, 254 ff.

M

Magisterium, authentic, 268; assent due to, 270; living, of the Church, for the preservation of tradition, 158; as a natural force for the preservation of tradition, 160; efficient cause of dogmatic progress, 248; not omniscient in the realm of faith, 249; ordinary and universal, proposes revealed truth, 222
Material object of faith, 205 ff. *See* Object of faith
"Matters of faith and morals," 106
Modernism and Scripture. *See* "*Lamentabile*"
Monuments of tradition, 162; theological value of, 163; viewed individually, 168 ff.

"Motive of faith," diverse connotations of term, 196; attracts will to faith, 331
Mythological beings in Scripture, 72

N

Necessity of faith, 374; which truths must be believed by necessity of means, 378
Newman, criteria of, for distinguishing legitimate, religious progress from corruption, 250

O

Object, formal, of divine faith; notion of, 196 ff.; "the authority of God revealing," and its role in, 199; proposal by the Church as part of, 200; habitual knowledge of, is sufficient, 201; in the act of faith, not *quod* but *quo,* 343; whether supernatural, 347
———, material, of divine faith, 205 ff.; the primary, secondary, and the purely accidental, 213–214; private revelations, part of, 215; of divine-catholic faith, 220 ff.; absolute increase of, in the Old Testament and up to the death of the apostles, 233–34; after the death of the apostles, only a relative increase, 234; and the substance of the faith, 234
Obscurity of Scripture, 110; of faith, 352; can the same truth be both known and believed, 355; does perfect evidence for fact of revelation remove the obscurity of faith, 357
Obstacles to faith, 327 ff.
Occasions for progress in faith, 245
Origin, apostolic. *See* Apostolic origin

P

Part, meaning of, in the decree on authority of the Vulgate, 124
Paul, St., on the inspiration of the

(417)

GENERAL INDEX

Old Testament, 33; his definition of faith, 189

Peter, St., on the inspiration of the letters of St. Paul, 34

Phenomena of nature, described in Scripture, 72

Philo, on the inspiration of the Old Testament, 32

"Pius will to believe," 306–307

Pius IX, on the authority of Roman congregations and the agreement of theologians, 271

Pius X, on the reading of the gospel, 117; on authority of Biblical Commission, 271

Pius XII, on reading Scripture, 117–118; on Religious Assent, 272

Preparation for faith, intellectual, 312 ff.; voluntary, 327 ff.

Pride, as an obstacle to faith, 327

Principles, subjective, which produce act of faith, 296 ff.

Professions of faith. See Creeds

Progress in faith, objective or absolute, 233; occurred in Old Testament, 233; occurred at time of Christ and the apostles, 234; no longer possible, 235

———, subjective or relative, 236; nature of subjective, 242; subjective differs from theological progress, 245; occasions of, 245; usual stages of, 246; the efficient cause of, 248; does not imply corruption, 249; Newman's criteria for genuine, 250; false theories of, 251; Harnack on, 251; Sabatier on, 252; Gunther on, 253; Loisy on, 254

Properties of faith, 351 ff.

Proposal of truth by Church, infallible, requires that matter be object of divine-catholic faith, 220; through a solemn decree, 221; through the universal and ordinary magisterium, 222; understanding and acceptance of, by ordinary faithful, 326; not constituting part of the formal object of faith, 200; notion of a merely authentic, 268; assent due to merely authentic, 270

Protestants, consider Scripture the only source of revelation, 6, 137; and the rule of faith, 6; views on the canon of Scripture, 18; on the clarity of Scripture, 105; on the sufficiency of Scripture, 137, 142; and tradition, 138; notion of faith, 185, 296

Q

"Quicumque." See Athanasian Creed, 170

R

Reading of Scripture, 115 ff.

Reason and Faith, 386 ff.

Redemption, and belief by necessity of means, 238

Revealed data, notion, 205; ways contained in sources of Revelation, 206 ff.; can or should private revelation be believed with divine faith?, 215; meaning of approval of private revelations by the Church, 216

Revelation, differs from inspiration, 72; whether part of the motive of faith, 199

Rewarder, God as, in what way must this truth be believed?, 379

Romanes, on impurity as obstacle to faith, 328, n.

Rule of faith, according to Protestants, 6; according to Catholics, 7

S

Sabatier, on the evolution of dogma, 252

Sacred Writer. See Hagiographer

Scripture, notion of, 13; proof of canon of, in Council of Trent, 19; proof of inspiration of, 31, even for non-religious matters, 43; as the Word of God, 68; infallibly true,

GENERAL INDEX

69; various senses of, 100; "literal" and "typical" sense of, 100; "consequent" and "accommodated" sense of, 101; can literal sense of be multiple?, 101, 102; proof for the existence of "typical" sense of, 103 ff.; authentic interpretation of, 112 ff.; dogmatic rules for interpretation of, 112 ff.; principles for private reading of, 115; legislation of the Church on reading of, 117; various Catholic versions of, 119; pre-Reformation versions of, 119; Vulgate version of, and authenticity of, 120; Council of Trent and the Vulgate version of, 120 ff.; substantial fidelity of Vulgate version of, 123 ff.; sufficiency of, for salvation according to Protestants, 137, 140; sufficiency of, in the writings of the Fathers, 153, 154

Senses of Scripture, 100; "literal" and "typical," 100; "consequent" and "accommodated," 101

Silence, reverential, is more than this required by the teaching of the merely "authentic" magisterium?, 270 ff.

Stages in the development of dogmas, 246

Subject of faith, 371

Subordinationism of ancient Fathers, 174

Substance of faith, always the same, 234

Succession, apostolic, the major means for preserving tradition, 158; value as purely natural factor, 160

Symbol of faith. Notion of, 168; Apostles', 168; *Nicene-Constantinople,* 169; *Athanasian,* 170

T

Theologians, as causes of dogmatic progress, 248; the authority of, 176; agreement of and religious assent, 276

Theological censures. *See* censure
——progress differs from progress in faith, 244–45, 393 ff.
——truths, 262–276

Thomas, St., opinion on plurality of literal senses, 102; on whether a truth may be simultaneously known and believed, 355

Tradition, oral, notion of, 137–38; divine and ecclesiastical, 137; inherent, declarative, and constitutive, 138, 141; is it source distinct from and exceeding Scripture?, 142; proof of the existence of, 146 ff.; principle means of preservation of, 158; auxiliary means of preservation of, 162; monuments of, in general, 162; monuments of, in particular, 168 ff.; and creeds of the faith, 168; and the writings of the Fathers, 170; notion of, in the broad sense, 4–5

Trinity, whether the mystery must be believed by necessity of means?, 379

Truthfulness, of Scripture, 69 ff.; of faith, 351 ff.

Typology in Scripture, 103 ff.

V

Value, theological, of monuments of Tradition, 162; of particular monuments, 168 ff.

Verbal inspiration, 66 ff.

Versions, Catholic, of Scripture printed in the vernacular prior to the Reformation, 119. *See* Scripture

Vincent of Lerins, his canon, 164

Virtually revealed, notion of, 208; whether an object of divine faith, 209

Vocation to faith, 308

Vulgate, origin of, 120; value of, 120; authenticity of, 122; degree of faithfulness of, 123 ff.

W

Will of sacred writer, moved by God, 64; as the principle which orders the act of faith, 296; various ways in which —— cooperates in bringing a person to faith, 327 ff.

Word of God, all genuine Scripture is the ——, 68; distinction between Word of God intrinsically and extrinsically, 68, some criteria for judging between the two, 68 ff.

Writers, Ecclesiastical, 172

www.ingramcontent.com/pod-product-compliance
Lightning Source LLC
Chambersburg PA
CBHW071948070526
44583CB00015B/1110